Java Design Patterns

A Hands-On Experience with Real-World Examples

Third Edition

Vaskaran Sarcar

Apress®

Java Design Patterns: A Hands-On Experience with Real-World Examples

Vaskaran Sarcar
Garia, Kolkata, India

ISBN-13 (pbk): 978-1-4842-7970-0   ISBN-13 (electronic): 978-1-4842-7971-7
https://doi.org/10.1007/978-1-4842-7971-7

Managing Director, Apress Media LLC: Welmoed Spahr
Acquisitions Editor: Celestin Suresh John
Development Editor: Laura Berendson
Coordinating Editor: Aditee Mirashi
Copy Editor: Mary Behr

Cover designed by eStudioCalamar

Cover image designed by Freepik (www.freepik.com)

Distributed to the book trade worldwide by Springer Science+Business Media New York, 1 New York Plaza, Suite 4600, New York, NY 10004-1562, USA. Phone 1-800-SPRINGER, fax (201) 348-4505, e-mail orders-ny@ springer-sbm.com, or visit www.springeronline.com. Apress Media, LLC is a California LLC and the sole member (owner) is Springer Science + Business Media Finance Inc (SSBM Finance Inc). SSBM Finance Inc is a **Delaware** corporation.

For information on translations, please e-mail booktranslations@springernature.com; for reprint, paperback, or audio rights, please e-mail bookpermissions@springernature.com.

Apress titles may be purchased in bulk for academic, corporate, or promotional use. eBook versions and licenses are also available for most titles. For more information, reference our Print and eBook Bulk Sales web page at www.apress.com/bulk-sales.

Any source code or other supplementary material referenced by the author in this book is available to readers on GitHub via the book's product page, located at www.apress.com/978-1-4842-7970-0. For more detailed information, please visit www.apress.com/source-code.

Printed on acid-free paper

First, I dedicate this book to Almighty GOD and the Gang of Four. Then I dedicate this work to all who have great potential to produce top-quality software but could not flourish for to various reasons. My message for them: "Dear reader, I want to hold your hands and help you express your hidden talents to the outside world."

Table of Contents

About the Author

Vaskaran Sarcar obtained his Master of Engineering in software engineering from Jadavpur University, Kolkata (India) and an MCA from Vidyasagar University, Midnapore (India). He was a National Gate Scholar from 2007-2009 and has more than 12 years of experience in education and the IT industry. Vaskaran devoted his early years (2005-2007) to the teaching profession at various engineering colleges. Later he joined HP India PPS R&D Hub Bangalore. He worked there until August 2019. At the time of his retirement from HP, he was a Senior Software Engineer and Team Lead. To follow his dream and passion, Vaskaran is now an independent full-time author. Other Apress books by him include

- *Simple and Efficient Programming in C# (Apress, 2021)*
- *Design Patterns in C# Second Edition (Apress, 2020)*
- *Getting Started with Advanced C# (Apress, 2020)*
- *Interactive Object-Oriented Programming in Java Second Edition (Apress, 2019)*
- *Java Design Patterns Second Edition (Apress, 2019)*
- *Design Patterns in C# (Apress, 2018)*
- *Interactive C# (Apress, 2017)*
- *Interactive Object-Oriented Programming in Java(Apress, 2016)*
- *Java Design Patterns (Apress, 2016)*

The following list is of his non-Apress books:

- *Python Bookcamp (Amazon, 2021)*
- *Operating System: Computer Science Interview Series (Createspace, 2014)*

About the Technical Reviewers

Abhimanyu is a self-motivated technological enthusiast with over 13 years of experience in software development. He is an expert in building big data solutions and large-scale machine learning applications, especially in the retail domain. Currently, Abhimanyu is building data-aware apps and solutions for the world's largest retailer.

Along with his work, he also likes astrophotography, speed-cubing, and playing his acoustic guitar in his free time.

Carsten Thomsen is a back-end developer primarily working with smaller front-end bits as well. He has authored and reviewed a number of books and created numerous Microsoft Learning courses, all to do with software development. He works as freelancer/contractor in various countries in Europe, using Azure, Visual Studio, Azure DevOps, and GitHub. Being an exceptional troubleshooter by asking the right questions, including the less logical ones, in a most-logical-to-least-logical fashion, he also enjoys working with architecture, research, analysis, development, testing, and bug fixing. Carsten is a very good communicator with great mentoring and team-lead skills, and great skills researching and presenting new material.

Harsha Jayamanna has more than seven years of software engineering experience. Java, Spring, JakartaEE, Microservices, and Cloud are several of his expertise areas. He started his career in Sri Lanka and then, after several years, moved to Singapore. Currently, he is working as a software consultant in Sydney, Australia. Writing blog articles, reading technical books, and learning new technologies are his other areas of interest.He can be reached via `https://www.harshajayamanna.com/`.

Shekhar Kumar Maravi is a Lead Engineer in Design and Development whose main interests are programming languages, algorithms, and data structures. He obtained his Master's degree in Computer Science and Engineering from Indian Institute of Technology Bombay. After graduation, he joined Hewlett-Packard's R&D Hub in India to work on printer firmware. Currently he is a technical lead engineer for automated pathology lab diagnostic devices at Siemens Healthcare R&D division. He can be reached by email at `shekhar.maravi@gmail.com` or via LinkedIn at `www.linkedin.com/in/shekharmaravi`.

Acknowledgments

At first, I thank the Almighty. I sincerely believe that with HIS blessings only, I could complete this book. I extend my deepest gratitude and thanks to the following people.

Ratanlal Sarkar and Manikuntala Sarkar: My dear parents, with your blessings only, I could complete the work.

Indrani, my wife; **Ambika**, my daughter; **Aryaman**, my son: Sweethearts, I love you all.

Sambaran, my brother: Thank you for your constant encouragement.

Sekhar, Harsha, Abhimanyu, Carsten: As technical advisors, whenever I was in need, your support was there. Thank you one more time.

Sunil Sati, Anupam, Ritesh, Ankit: Sunil is ex-colleague cum senior who wrote the foreword for the second edition of this book. The others are my friends and technical advisors. Although this time you were not involved directly, still I acknowledge your support and help in the development of *Java Design Patterns* first edition and second edition.

Celestin, Laura, Aditee: Thanks for giving me another opportunity to work with you and Apress.

Sherly, Vinoth, Siva Chandran: Thank you for your exceptional support to beautify my work. Thank you all. Your efforts are extraordinary.

Introduction

It is my absolute pleasure to write the third edition of *Java Design Patterns* for you. You can surely guess that I got this opportunity because you liked the previous edition of the book and shared your nice reviews from across the globe. So, once again I'm excited to join your design patterns journey. This time I present a further simplified, better organized, and content-rich edition to you.

You probably know that the concept of design patterns became extremely popular with the Gang of Four's famous book *Design Patterns: Elements of Reusable Object-Oriented Software* (Addison-Wesley, 1994). The book came out at the end of 1994, and it primarily focused on C++. But it is useful to know that these concepts still apply in today's programming world. Sun Microsystem released its first public implementation of Java 1.0 in 1995. So, in 1995, Java was new to the programming world. Since then, it has become rich with new features and is now a popular programming language. On the other hand, the concepts of design patterns are universal. So, when you exercise these fundamental concepts of design patterns with Java, you open new opportunities for yourself.

My end goal is simple: I want you to develop your programming skills to the next level using design patterns in your code. Unfortunately, this skill set cannot be acquired simply by reading. This is why I made this guide to the design patterns that you want to use in Java.

I have been writing books on design patterns since 2015 in different languages such as Java and C#. These books were further enhanced, and multiple editions of them were published and well received. In the initial version, my core intention was to implement each of the 23 Gang of Four (GoF) design patterns using simple examples. One thing was always in my mind when writing: I wanted to use the most basic constructs of Java so that the code would be compatible with both the upcoming version and the legacy version of Java. I have found this method helpful in the world of programming.

In the last few years, I have received many constructive suggestions from my readers. The second edition of this book was created with that feedback in mind. I also updated the formatting and corrected some typos from the previous version of the book and added new content to this edition. In the second edition of the book, I focused on another important area. I call it the "doubt-clearing sessions." I knew that if I could add some more information such as alternative ways to write these implementations, the pros and cons of these patterns, and when to choose one approach over another, readers would find this book even more helpful. So, in the second edition of the book, "Q&A Session" sections were added in each chapter to help you learn each pattern in more depth. I know you liked it very much.

So, what is new in the third edition? Well, the first thing I want to tell you is that since the second edition of the book is already big, this time I made the examples shorter and simpler. Also, I place the related chapters close to each other. This is why you'll see the Chain of Responsibility pattern after the Observer pattern. The same is true for Simple Factory and Factory Method patterns, Strategy and State patterns, and Command and Memento patterns. In addition, at the beginning of the book, you'll read a detailed discussion on SOLID design principles, which are used heavily across these patterns. Apart from these changes, I add more code explanations for your easy understanding.

Malcolm Gladwell in his book *Outliers* (Little, Brown and Company, 2008) talked about the 10,000-hour rule. This rule says that the key to achieve world-class expertise in any skill is, to a large extent, a matter of practicing the correct way for a total of around 10,000 hours. I acknowledge the fact that it is impossible to consider all experiences before you write a program. Sometimes, it is also ok to bend the rules if the return on investment (ROI) is nice. So, I remind you about the ***Pareto*** principle or the ***80-20 rule***. This rule simply states that 80% of outcomes come from 20% of all causes. This is useful in programming, too. When you identify the most important and commonly used design patterns and use them in your applications properly, you can make top-quality programs. In this book, I discuss the programming patterns that can help you write better programs. You may know some of them already, but when you see them in action and go through the Q&A sessions, you'll understand their importance.

How the Book Is Organized

The book has four major parts:

- Part 1 consists of the first two chapters, in which you will explore the SOLID principles and learn to use the Simple Factory pattern.
- Part 2 consists of the next 23 chapters, in which you learn and implement all of the Gang of Four design patterns.

- In the world of programming, there is no shortage of patterns, and each has its own significance. So, in addition to the SOLID principles and design patterns covered in Part 1 and Part 2, I discuss two additional design patterns (Null Object and MVC) in Part 3. They are equally important, commonly used, and well-known patterns in today's world of programming.

- Finally, in Part 4 of the book, I discuss the criticism of design patterns and give you an overview of anti-patterns, which are also important when you implement the concepts of design patterns in your applications. I also include a FAQ on design patterns.

- Starting from Chapter 2, each chapter is divided into six major parts: a definition (which is termed as "intent" in the GoF book), a core concept, a real-life example, a computer/coding world example, at least one sample program with various outputs, and the "Q&A Session" section. These "Q&A Session" sections can help you learn about each pattern in more depth.

- You can download the source code of the book from the publisher's website. I have a plan to maintain the errata and, if required, I can also make updates/announcements there. So, I suggest that you visit those pages to receive any important corrections or updates.

Prerequisite Knowledge

The target readers for this book are those who are familiar with the basic language constructs in Java and have an idea about the pure object-oriented concepts like polymorphism, inheritance, abstraction, encapsulation, and most importantly, how to compile or run a Java application in the Eclipse IDE. This book does not invest time in easily available topics, such as how to install Eclipse on your system, how to write a "Hello World" program in Java, or how to use an if-else statement or a while loop. I mentioned that this book was written using the most basic features so that for most of the programs in this book, you do not need to be familiar with advanced topics in Java. These examples are simple and straightforward. I believe that these examples are written in such a way that even if you are familiar with another popular language such as C# or C++, you can still easily grasp the concepts in this book.

Who Is This Book For?

In short, you should read this book if the answer is "yes" to the following questions:

- Are you familiar with basic constructs in Java and object-oriented concepts like polymorphism, inheritance, abstraction, and encapsulation?

- Do you know how to set up your coding environment?

- Do you want to explore the design patterns in Java step by step?

- Do you want to explore the GoF design patterns? Are you further interested in learning about Simple Factory, Null Object, and MVC patterns?

- Do you want to examine how the core constructs of Java work behind these patterns?

Probably you shouldn't read this book if the answer is "yes" to any of the following questions:

- Are you absolutely new to Java?

- Are you looking for advanced concepts in Java excluding the topics mentioned previously?

- Do you dislike a book that has an emphasis on Q&A sessions?

- "I do not like the Windows operating system and Eclipse. I want to learn and use Java without them." Is this statement true for you?

- "I am already confident about GoF design patterns and other patterns that you mentioned earlier. I am searching for other patterns." Is this statement true for you?

Useful Software

These are the important software/tools I used for this book:

- I executed and started testing my programs using Java version 16.0.1 and the Eclipse IDE (version 2021-03 (4.19.0)) in a Windows 10 environment. When I started writing this book, they were the latest versions. It is a big book and when I finished the initial draft, Eclipse 2021-09 was the latest edition and I kept updating the software. Before I submitted the final version of the book, I tested the code in Java 17 (version 17.0.1). We can surely predict that version updates will come continuously, but these version details should not matter much to you because I have used the fundamental constructs of Java. So, I believe that this code should execute smoothly in the upcoming versions of Java/Eclipse as well.

- Anything that is the latest today will be old (or outdated) tomorrow. But the core constructs (or features) are evergreen. All new features are built on top of these universal features. So, I like to write code that is compatible with a wide range of versions using the basic language constructs. I understand that you may have a different thought, but I like this approach for various reasons. If you know the latest features, changing the code to them is easy. But the reverse is not necessarily true. Take another common example: when you provide support to your clients and fix code defects in an application, you cannot use the latest language constructs in almost every case, because the original product was created with a software version that is old now.

- You can download the Eclipse IDE from `www.eclipse.org/downloads/`. You'll see the page shown in Figure FM-1.

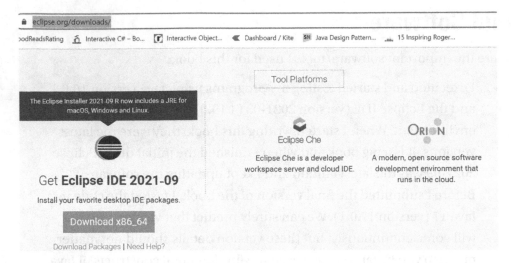

Figure FM-1. *Download link for Eclipse*

- Before I start coding, I use pen/pencils and paper. Sometimes, I use markers and a whiteboard. But when I show my programs in a book, I understand that I need to present these diagrams in a better shape. So, I use some tools to draw the class diagrams from my code. In the second edition of the book, I used ObjectAid Uml Explorer in the Eclipse editor. It is a lightweight tool for Eclipse. But it did not work for me with the updated versions of Eclipse. So, this time I used another nice tool, Papyrus. It is an open-source UML 2 tool based on Eclipse and licensed under the EPL. I was able to generate class diagrams easily using this tool. In some cases, to make them better, I added notes or edited a few things in the diagram so that you can understand it easily. For example, consider Figure FM-2 (taken from Chapter 14, when I discuss the Bridge pattern). You can understand easily that the Papyrus tool will not show you the markers for Hierarchy-1, Hierarchy-2, or BRIDGE inside the dashed rectangle. I edited the original diagram to help you understand the components better.

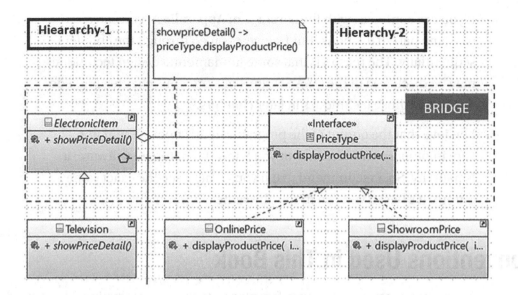

Figure FM-2. *A class diagram that is taken from Chapter 14*

- In short, these diagrams help you understand the code, but to learn design patterns, neither Papyrus nor Eclipse are mandatory. If you want to learn more about this reverse engineering process, you can refer to the following link: https://wiki.eclipse.org/Java_ reverse_engineering.

Note At the time of writing, all links in this book work and the information is correct. But these links and policies may change in the future.

Guidelines for Using This Book

Here are some suggestions so you can use the book more effectively:

- I assume that you have some idea about the GoF design patterns. If you are absolutely new to design patterns, I suggest you quickly go through Appendix A. This appendix will help you to become familiar with the basic concepts of design patterns.

- If you are confident with the coverage of Appendix A, you can start with any part of the book. But I suggest you go through the chapters sequentially. The reason is that some fundamental design techniques may be discussed in the Q&A Sessions of a previous chapter, and I do not repeat those techniques in later chapters.

- I believe that the output of the programs in this book should not vary in other environments, but you know the nature of software: it is naughty. So, I recommend that if you want to see the exact same output, it's best if you can mimic the same environment.

Conventions Used in This Book

Here I mention only two points. In a very few places, to avoid more typing, I have used the word "he" only. Please treat it as "he" or "she", whichever applies to you.

To execute a program, I put all parts in the same folder/package. So, in most cases, I chose the package-private visibility. But if you want, you can increase the respective visibilities to public to reuse those parts. I used separate packages for separate programs to help you find all parts of a program at the same place.

Finally, all the output and code of the book follow the same font and structure. To draw your attention, in some places, I have made them bold. For example, consider the following output fragment (taken from Chapter 15, when I discuss the Template Method pattern) and the line in bold:

Template Method Pattern with a hook method.

Computer Science course structure:

1. Mathematics

2. Soft skills

3. Object-Oriented Programming

4. **Compiler construction.**

Electronics course structure:

1. Mathematics

2. Soft skills

3. Digital Logic and Circuit Theory

Final Words

I must say that you are an intelligent person. You have chosen a subject that can assist you throughout your career. If you are a developer/programmer, you need these concepts. If you are an architect of a software organization, you need these concepts. If you are a college student, you need these concepts, not only to score high on exams but to enter the corporate world. Even if you are a tester who needs to take care of white-box testing or simply needs to know about the code paths of a product, these concepts will help you a lot.

This book is designed for you in such a way that upon its completion, you will have developed an adequate knowledge of the topic, and most importantly, you'll know how to proceed further. Remember that this is just the beginning. As you learn about these concepts, I suggest you write your own code; only then will you master this area. There is no shortcut for this. Do you remember Euclid's reply to the ruler? If not, let me remind you of his reply: **There is no royal road to geometry.** So, study and code. Understand a new concept and code again. Do not give up when you face challenges. These are the indicators that you are growing better.

Lastly, I hope that this book can help you and you will value the effort.

PART I

Foundation

Part I consists of two chapters. In this part, you'll see the usage of

- SOLID principles. They are a combination of five design guidelines.

- The Simple Factory pattern

In an object-oriented programming world, there is no shortage of principles, but these are the fundamental design guidelines for making a better application. This part shows you the case studies using (and without using) these principles and helps you think about their importance. A detailed study of them can help you make efficient and flexible applications.

CHAPTER 1

Understanding SOLID Principles

Java is a powerful object-oriented programming language, and it has many features. If we compare it with the old days, we must say that coding has become easier with the support of these powerful features. But the hard truth is that simply using these features in an application does not guarantee that you have used them in the right way. In any given requirement, it is vital to identify classes, objects, and how they communicate with each other. In addition, your application must be flexible and extendable to fulfill future enhancements. This is one of the primary aims of learning design patterns. This is often termed *experience reuse* because you earn benefits from other people's experiences as you go through their struggles and see how they solved those problems and adopted new behaviors in their systems. A pattern may not perfectly fit into your target application, but if you know the best practices in advance, you are more likely to make a better application.

Hopefully, you can guess that understanding different design patterns may not be very easy at the beginning. You need to know certain principles or guidelines before you implement a pattern in your code. These fundamental guidelines are not only common to all patterns, they are also useful to produce good-quality software.

In the previous editions of this book, I needed to assume that you knew at least some of them. Whenever I referred to these principles, either I explained them briefly or I gave you pointers to where you could learn more. This strategy was helpful to make the book slim.

Now you are holding the third edition of *Java Design Patterns*. Since you liked the previous edition of this book, I wanted to start with materials that can make your learning experience easier. So, I start with some fundamental guidelines that every developer should know before implementing a design pattern. Yes, I sincerely believe the previous line. Let's learn some of these guidelines.

© Vaskaran Sarcar 2022
V. Sarcar, *Java Design Patterns*, https://doi.org/10.1007/978-1-4842-7971-7_1

Robert Cecil Martin is a famous name in the programming world. He is an American software engineer and best-selling author and is also known as "Uncle Bob." He promoted many principles. The following is a subset of them:

- **S**ingle Responsibility Principle (SRP)

- **O**pen/Closed Principle (OCP)

- **L**iskov Substitution Principle (LSP)

- **I**nterface Segregation Principle (ISP)

- **D**ependency Inversion Principle (DIP)

Taking the first letter of each principle, Michael Feathers introduced the SOLID acronym to remember these names easily.

Design principles are high-level guidelines that you can use to make better software. They are not bound to any particular computer language. So, if you understand these concepts using Java, you can use them with similar languages like C# or C++. To understand the thoughts of Robert C Martin about this, go to `https://sites.google.com/site/unclebobconsultingllc/getting-a-solid-start`, which says

> *The SOLID principles are not rules. They are not laws. They are not perfect truths. They are statements on the order of "An apple a day keeps the doctor away." This is a good principle, it is good advice, but it's not a pure truth, nor is it a rule.*

> Uncle Bob

In this chapter, you'll explore these principles in detail. In each case, I start with a program that compiles and runs successfully, but does not follow any specific design guidelines. In the analysis section, I'll discuss the possible drawbacks and try to find a better solution using these principles. This process can help you understand the importance of these design guidelines. I remind you again: examining these case studies will help you think better and make better applications, but they are not rules that you must follow in every context.

Single Responsibility Principle

A class acts like a container that can hold many things such as data, properties, or methods. If you put in too much data or methods that are not related to each other, you end up with a bulky class that can create problems in the future. Let's consider an example. Suppose you create a class with multiple methods that do different things. In such a case, even if you make a small change in one method, you need to retest the whole class again to ensure the workflow is correct. Thus, changes in one method can impact the other related method(s) in the class. This is why the single responsibility principle opposes this idea of putting multiple responsibilities in a class. It says that *a class should have only one reason to change.*

So, before you make a class, identify the responsibility or purpose of the class. If multiple members help you achieve a single purpose, it is ok to place all the members inside the class.

POINT TO REMEMBER

When you follow the SRP, your code is smaller, cleaner, and less fragile. So how do you follow this principle? A simple answer is you can divide a big problem into smaller chunks based on different responsibilities and put each of these small parts into separate classes. The next question is, what do we mean by responsibility? In simple words, *responsibility is a reason for a change*. In his best-selling book *Clean Architecture* (Pearson, 2017), Robert C. Martin warns us not to confuse this principle with the principle that says a function should do one, and only one, thing. He also says that perhaps the best way to understand this principle is when you look at the symptoms of violating it.

I also believe the same, not only for this principle but for other principles as well. This is why in the upcoming discussion you'll see me first write a program without following these principles. Then I'll show you a better program following these principles.

Initial Program

Demonstration 1 has an Employee class with three different methods. Here are the details:

- The displayEmpDetail() shows the employee's name and their working experience in years.

- The generateEmpId() method generates an employee id using string concatenation. The logic is simple: I concatenate the first word of the first name with a random number to form an employee ID. In the following demonstration, inside the main() method (the client code) I create two Employee instances and use these methods to display the relevant details.

- The checkSeniority() method evaluates whether an employee is a senior person. I assume that if the employee has 5+ years of experience, he is a senior employee; otherwise, he is a junior employee.

Demonstration 1

Here is the complete demonstration. When you download the source code from the Apress website, refer to package jdp3e.solid_principles.without_srp to get all parts of this program.

```java
// Employee.java
import java.util.Random;

class Employee {
    public String firstName, lastName, empId;
    public double experienceInYears;
    public Employee(String firstName, String lastName,
                    double experience) {
        this.firstName = firstName;
        this.lastName = lastName;
        this.experienceInYears = experience;
    }

    public void displayEmpDetail(){
            System.out.println("The employee name: " +
                    lastName+","+firstName);
            System.out.println("This employee has " +
                    experienceInYears +"
                    years of experience.");
    }
```

```java
    public String checkSeniority(double experienceInYears){
        return  experienceInYears > 5 ?"senior":"junior";
    }
    public String generateEmpId(String empFirstName){
        int random = new Random().nextInt(1000);
        empId = empFirstName.substring(0,1)+random;
        return empId;
    }
}

// Client.java
class Client {
    public static void main(String[] args) {
        System.out.println("*** A demo without SRP.***");

            Employee robin = new Employee("Robin", "Smith", 7.5);
            showEmpDetail(robin);

            System.out.println("\n*******\n");

            Employee kevin = new Employee("Kevin", "Proctor", 3.2);
            showEmpDetail(kevin);
    }

  private static void showEmpDetail(Employee emp) {
        emp.displayEmpDetail();
        System.out.println("The employee id: "+
                emp.generateEmpId(emp.firstName));
        System.out.println("This employee is a " +
                emp.checkSeniority(emp.experienceInYears)+
                  " employee.");
    }

}
```

Note   For brevity, I do not include the common package name before each segment of the code. The same comment applies to all demonstrations in this book.

Output

Here is a sample output. Note that the employee ID can vary in your case because it generates a random number to get the employee ID.

```
*** A demo without SRP.***
The employee name: Smith,Robin
This employee has 7.5 years of experience.
The employee id: R446
This employee is a senior employee.

*******

The employee name: Proctor,Kevin
This employee has 3.2 years of experience.
The employee id: K822
This employee is a junior employee.
```

Analysis

What is the problem with this design? This answer is that I violate the SRP here. You can see that displaying an employee detail, generating an employee id, or checking a seniority level are all different activities. Since I put everything in a single class, I may face problems adopting new changes in the future. Here are some possible reasons:

- The top management can set a different criterion to decide a seniority level.

- They can also use a complex algorithm to generate the employee id.

In each case, I'll need to modify the Employee class. Now you understand that it is better to follow the SRP and separate these activities.

Better Program

In the following demonstration, I introduce two more classes. The SeniorityChecker class now contains the checkSeniority() method and the EmployeeIdGenerator class contains the generateEmpId(...) method to generate the employee id. As a result, in the future, if I need to change the program logic to determine the seniority level or use a new algorithm to generate an employee id, I can make the changes in the respective classes. Other classes are untouched, so I do not need to retest those classes.

To improve the code readability and avoid clumsiness inside the main() method, I use the static method showEmpDetail(...). This method calls the displayEmpDetail() method from Employee, the generateEmpId() method from EmployeeIdGenerator, and the checkSeniority() method from SeniorityChecker. You understand that this method was not necessary, but it makes the client code simple and easily understandable.

Demonstration 2

Here is the complete demonstration that follows SRP. When you download the source code from the Apress website, refer to package jdp3e.solid_principles.srp to get all parts of this program.

```java
// Employee.java
class Employee {
    public String firstName, lastName, empId;
            public double experienceInYears;
            public Employee(String firstName, String lastName,
                    double experience) {
                this.firstName = firstName;
                this.lastName = lastName;
                this.experienceInYears = experience;
        }

            public void displayEmpDetail(){
                System.out.println("The employee name:
                        "+lastName+","+firstName);
                    System.out.println("This employee has "+
```

```java
                experienceInYears+" years of experience.");
            }
}

// EmployeeIdGenerator.java
import java.util.Random;

class EmployeeIdGenerator {
    String empId;
        public String generateEmpId(String empFirstName) {
            int random = new Random().nextInt(1000);
                        empId = empFirstName.substring(0, 1) + random;
                        return empId;
            }
}

// SeniorityChecker.java
class SeniorityChecker {
    public String checkSeniority(double experienceInYears){
            return  experienceInYears > 5 ?"senior":"junior";
    }
}
// Client.java
class Client {
  public static void main(String[] args) {

    System.out.println("*** A demo that follows the SRP.***");

    Employee robin = new Employee("Robin", "Smith", 7.5);
    showEmpDetail(robin);

    System.out.println("\n*******\n");
    Employee kevin = new Employee("Kevin", "Proctor", 3.2);
    showEmpDetail(kevin);
  }
```

```
private static void showEmpDetail(Employee emp) {
  // Display employee detail
  emp.displayEmpDetail();

  // Generate the ID
  EmployeeIdGenerator idGenerator = new
                          EmployeeIdGenerator();
  String empId = idGenerator.generateEmpId(emp.firstName);
  System.out.println("The employee id: " + empId);

  // Check the seniority level
  SeniorityChecker seniorityChecker = new
                          SeniorityChecker();
  System.out.println("This employee is a " +
  seniorityChecker.checkSeniority(emp.experienceInYears)
                          + " employee.");
  }
}
```

Output

Here is the output. Notice that it is similar to the previous output, except the first line that says this program follows the SRP now. (As I said before, the employee ID can vary in your case).

```
*** A demo that follows the SRP ***
The employee name: Smith,Robin
This employee has 7.5 years of experience.
The employee id: R168
This employee is a senior employee.

*******

The employee name: Proctor,Kevin
This employee has 3.2 years of experience.
The employee id: K258
This employee is a junior employee.
```

POINT TO NOTE

Note that the SRP does not say that a class should have at most one method. Here the emphasis is on the single responsibility. There may be closely related methods that can help you to implement a responsibility. For example, if you have different methods to display the first name, the last name, and a full name, you can put these methods in the same class. These methods are closely related, and it makes sense to place all these display methods inside the same class.

In addition, you should not conclude that you should always separate responsibilities in every application that you make. You need to analyze the change's nature. It is because too many classes can make your application complex and thus difficult to maintain. But if you know this principle and think carefully before you implement a design, you are likely to avoid the mistakes discussed earlier.

Open/Closed Principle

According to Robert C. Martin, the Open/Closed Principle is the most important principle among all the principles of object-oriented design. In the book *Clean Architecture*, he says the following:

> *The Open-Closed Principle (OCP) was coined in 1988 by* Bertrand Meyer. *It says:* **A software artifact should be open for extension but closed for modification.**

In this section, I'll examine the OCP principle in detail using Java classes. Reading *Object-Oriented Software Construction (Second Edition)* by Bertrand Meyer, I found some important thoughts behind this principle. Here are some of them:

- Any modular decomposition technique must satisfy the Open-Closed Principle. Modules should be both open and closed.

- The contradiction between the two terms is only apparent as they correspond to goals of a different nature.

    - A module is said to be open if it is still available for extension. For example, it should be possible to expand its set of operations or add fields to its data structures.

- A module is said to be closed if it is available for use by other modules. This assumes that the module has been given a well-defined, stable description (its interface in the sense of information hiding). At the implementation level, closure for a module also implies that you may compile it, perhaps store it in a library, and make it available for others (its clients) to use.

- The need for modules to be closed and the need for them to remain open arise for different reasons.

- He explains that openness is useful for software developers because they can't foresee all the elements that a module may need in the future. But the "closed" modules will satisfy project managers because they want to complete the project instead of waiting for everyone to complete their parts.

The previous points are self-explanatory. You understand that the idea behind this design philosophy is that in a stable and working application, once you create a class and other parts of your application start using it, any further change in the class can cause the working application to break. If you require new features (or functionalities), instead of changing the existing class, you can extend it to adopt the new requirements. What is the benefit? Since you do not change the old code, your existing functionalities continue to work without any problems, and you can avoid testing them again. Instead, you test the "extended" part (or functionalities) only.

In 1988, Bertrand Meyer suggested the use of inheritance in this context. Wikipedia (`https://en.wikipedia.org/wiki/Open%E2%80%93closed_principle`) mentions his quote as follows:

> *"A class is closed, since it may be compiled, stored in a library, baselined, and used by client classes. But it is also open, since any new class may use it as a parent, adding new features. When a descendant class is defined, there is no need to change the original or to disturb its clients.*

But inheritance promotes tight coupling. In programming, we like to remove these tight couplings. Robert C. Martin improved the definition and made it polymorphic OCP. The new proposal uses abstract base classes that use the protocols instead of a superclass to allow different implementations. These protocols are closed for modification, and they provide another level of abstraction that enables loose coupling. In this chapter, we follow Robert C. Martin's idea that promotes polymorphic OCP.

Initial Program

Assume that there is a small group of students who take a semester examination. (To demonstrate this, I choose a small number of participants to help you focus on the principle, not unnecessary details.) Sam, Bob, John, and Kate are the four students in this example. They all belong to the Student class. To make a Student class instance, you supply a name, registration number, and the marks obtained in the examination. You also mention whether a student belongs to the Science department or the Arts department.

For simplicity, let's assume a particular college has the following four departments:

- Computer Science

- Physics

- History

- English

So, you see the following lines of code in the upcoming example:

```
Student sam = new Student("Sam", "R1", 81.5, "Comp.Sc.");
Student bob = new Student("Bob", "R2", 72, "Physics");
Student john = new Student("John", "R3", 71, "History");
Student kate = new Student("Kate", "R4", 66.5, "English");
```

When a student opts for computer science or physics, we say that they opt for the science stream. Similarly, when a student belongs to the History or English department, they are an arts student.

Start with two instance methods in this example. The displayResult() displays the result with all necessary details of a student and the evaluateDistinction() method evaluates whether a student is eligible for a distinction certificate. If a science student scores above 80 in this examination, they get the certificate with distinction. But the criterion for an arts student is slightly relaxed. An arts student gets the distinction if their score is above 70.

I hope you understand the SRP that I discussed earlier. If it is the case, you won't want to place displayResult() and evaluateDistinction() in the same class, like the following:

```
class Student {
  // Some fields, if any
  public void displayResult() {
    // some code
  }

  public void evaluateDistinction() {
    // some code
  }
 // Some other code, if any
}
```

What are the problems in this code segment?

- First, it violates the SRP because both the displayResult() and the evaluateDistinction() methods are inside the Student class. These two methods are unrelated.

- In the future, the examining authority can change the distinction criteria. In this case, you'll need to change the evaluateDistinction() method. Does it solve the problem? In the current situation, the answer is yes. But a college authority can change the distinction criteria again. How many times will you retest the Student class due to the modification of the evaluateDistinction() method?

- Remember that each time you modify the method, you change the containing class and you need to modify the existing test cases too.

You can see that every time the distinction criteria changes, you need to modify the evaluateDistinction() method in the Student class. *So, this class does not follow the SRP and it is also not closed for modification.*

Once you understand these problems, you can start with a better design that follows the SRP. Here are the main characteristics of the design:

- In the following program, Student and DistinctionDecider are two different classes.

- The DistinctionDecider class contains the evaluateDistinction() method in this example.

- To show the details of a student you can override the toString() method, instead of using the separate method displayResult(). So, inside the Student class, you see the toString() method now.

- Inside main(), you see the following line:

  List<Student> enrolledStudents = enrollStudents();

- The enrollStudents() method creates a list of students. You use this list to print student details one by one. You also use the same list before you invoke evaluateDistinction() to identify the students who received the distinction.

Demonstration 3

Here is the complete demonstration. All parts of the program are inside the package jdp3e.solid_principles.without_ocp. Refer to this package when you download the source code from the Apress website.

```java
// Student.java
class Student {
    String name;
    String regNumber;
    String department;
    double score;

    public Student(String name, String regNumber,
                    double score, String dept) {
        this.name = name;
        this.regNumber = regNumber;
        this.score = score;
        this.department = dept;
    }
}
```

```java
    @Override
    public String toString() {
        return ("Name: " + name +
                "\nReg Number: " + regNumber +
                "\nDept:" + department +
                "\nMarks:" + score +
                "\n*******");
    }

}

// DistinctionDecider.java
import java.util.Arrays;
import java.util.List;

class DistinctionDecider {

List<String> science = Arrays.asList("Comp.Sc.","Physics");
List<String> arts = Arrays.asList("History","English");

 public void evaluateDistinction(Student student) {

   if (science.contains(student.department)) {
    if (student.score > 80) {
     System.out.println(student.regNumber+" has received
                        a distinction in science.");
    }
   }

   if (arts.contains(student.department)) {
    if (student.score > 70) {
     System.out.println(student.regNumber+" has received a
                        distinction in arts.");
        }
      }
    }
}
```

// Client.java

```java
import java.util.ArrayList;
import java.util.List;

class Client {
    public static void main(String[] args) {
        System.out.println("*** A demo without OCP.***");
        List<Student> enrolledStudents = enrollStudents();

        // Display all results.
        System.out.println("===Results:===");
        for(Student student:enrolledStudents){
            System.out.println(student);
        }

        System.out.println("===Distinctions:===");
        DistinctionDecider distinctionDecider = new
                                        DistinctionDecider();
        // Evaluate distinctions.
        for(Student student:enrolledStudents){
            distinctionDecider.evaluateDistinction(student);
        }
    }

    private static List<Student> enrollStudents() {
        Student sam = new Student("Sam", "R1", 81.5, "Comp.Sc.");
        Student bob = new Student("Bob", "R2", 72, "Physics");
        Student john = new Student("John", "R3", 71, "History");
        Student kate = new Student("Kate", "R4", 66.5, "English");

        List<Student> students = new ArrayList<Student>();
        students.add(sam);
        students.add(bob);
        students.add(john);
        students.add(kate);
        return students;
    }
}
```

Output

When you run this program, you'll see the following output:

```
*** A demo without OCP.***
===Results:===
Name: Sam
Reg Number: R1
Dept:Comp.Sc.
Marks:81.5
******
Name: Bob
Reg Number: R2
Dept:Physics
Marks:72.0
******
Name: John
Reg Number: R3
Dept:History
Marks:71.0
******
Name: Kate
Reg Number: R4
Dept:English
Marks:66.5
******
===Distinctions:===
R1 has received a distinction in science.
R3 has received a distinction in arts.
```

Analysis

Now you are following the SRP. If in the future the examining authority changes the distinction criteria, you do not touch the Student class. So, this part is closed for modification. This solves one part of the problem. Now think about another future possibility:

- The college authority can introduce a new stream such as commerce and set a new distinction criterion for this stream.

You need to make some obvious changes again. For example, you need to modify the evaluateDistinction() method and add another if statement to consider commerce students. Now the question is, is it ok to modify the evaluateDistinction() method in this manner? Remember that each time you modify the method, you need to test the entire code workflow again.

You understand the problem now. In this demonstration, every time the distinction criteria changes, you need to modify the evaluateDistinction() method in the DistinctionDecider class. *So, this class is not closed for modification.*

Better Program

To tackle this problem, you can write a better program. The following program shows such an example. It's written following the OCP principle that suggests we *write code segments (such as classes, or methods) that are open for extension but closed for modification.*

The OCP can be achieved in different ways, but abstraction is the heart of this principle. If you can design your application following the OCP, your application is flexible and extensible. It is not always easy to fully implement this principle, but partial OCP compliance can generate greater benefit to you. Also notice that you started demonstration 3 following the SRP. If you do not follow the OCP, you may end up with a class that performs multiple tasks, which means the SRP is broken.

For the current situation, you could leave the Student class as it is. But you want to improve the code. You understand that in the future you may need to consider a different stream, such as commerce. How do you choose a stream? It is based on the subject chosen by a student, right? So, in the upcoming example, you make the Student class abstract. ArtsStudent and ScienceStudent are the concrete classes that extend the Subject class and are used to provide the "department" information (in other words, the subject taken by a student). The following code shows a sample implementation for your ready reference:

```
abstract class Student {
    String name;
    String regNumber;
    double score;
    String department;

    public Student(String name,
                   String regNumber,
                   double score) {
        this.name = name;
        this.regNumber = regNumber;
        this.score = score;
    }

    public String toString() {
        return ("Name: " + name +
                "\nReg Number: " + regNumber +
                "\nDept:" + department +
                "\nMarks:" + score +
                "\n*******");
    }
}

public class ArtsStudent extends Student{
    public ArtsStudent(String name,
                       String regNumber,
                       double score,
                       String dept) {
        super(name, regNumber, score);
        this.department = dept;
    }
}

// The ScienceStudent class is not shown here
```

The previous construct helps you enroll science students and arts students separately inside the client code as follows:

```
private static List<Student> enrollScienceStudents() {
 Student sam = new ScienceStudent("Sam","R1",81.5,"Comp.Sc.");
 Student bob = new ScienceStudent("Bob","R2",72,"Physics");
 List<Student> scienceStudents = new ArrayList<Student>();
 scienceStudents.add(sam);
 scienceStudents.add(bob);
 return scienceStudents;
}

private static List<Student> enrollArtsStudents() {
 Student john = new ArtsStudent("John", "R3", 71,"History");
 Student kate = new ArtsStudent("Kate", "R4", 66.5,"English");
 List<Student> artsStudents = new ArrayList<Student>();
 artsStudents.add(john);
 artsStudents.add(kate);
 return artsStudents;
}
```

Now let's focus on the most important changes. You need to tackle the evaluation method for distinction in a better way. So, you create the interface DistinctionDecider that contains a method called evaluateDistinction. Here is the interface:

```
interface DistinctionDecider {
    void evaluateDistinction(Student student);
}
```

ArtsDistinctionDecider and ScienceDistinctionDecider implement this interface and override the evaluateDistinction(...) method to specify the evaluation criteria as per their need. In this way, the stream-specific distinction criteria is wrapped in an independent unit. Here is the code segment for you. The different criteria for each class are shown in bold.

```
// ScienceDistinctionDecider.java
class ScienceDistinctionDecider implements DistinctionDecider{
    @Override
    public void evaluateDistinction(Student student) {
        if (student.score > 80) {
            System.out.println(student.regNumber+" has
                    received a distinction in science.");
        }
    }
}

// ArtsDistinctionDecider.java
class ArtsDistinctionDecider implements DistinctionDecider{
    @Override
    public void evaluateDistinction(Student student) {
        if (student.score > 70) {
            System.out.println(student.regNumber+" has
                    received a distinction in arts.");
        }
    }
}
```

Note   The evaluateDistinction(...) method accepts a Student parameter. It means now you can also pass an ArtsStudent object or a ScienceStudent object to this method.

The remaining code is easy, and you should not have any trouble understanding the following demonstration now.

Demonstration 4

Here is the modified program. All parts of the program are inside the package jdp3e. solid_principles.ocp.

```java
// Student.java
abstract class Student {
    String name;
    String regNumber;
    double score;
    String department;

    public Student(String name,
                   String regNumber,
                   double score) {
        this.name = name;
        this.regNumber = regNumber;
        this.score = score;
    }

    @Override

    public String toString() {
        return ("Name: " + name +
                "\nReg Number: " + regNumber +
                "\nDept:" + department +
                "\nMarks:"+ score +
                "\n*******");
    }
}
// ArtsStudent.java
public class ArtsStudent extends Student{
    public ArtsStudent(String name,
                       String regNumber,
                       double score,
                       String dept) {
        super(name, regNumber, score);
        this.department = dept;
    }
}

// ScienceStudent.java
class ScienceStudent extends Student{
```

```java
    public ScienceStudent(String name,
                          String regNumber,
                          double score,
                          String dept) {
        super(name, regNumber, score);
        this.department = dept;
    }
}
```

```java
// DistinctionDecider.java
interface DistinctionDecider {
    void evaluateDistinction(Student student);
}
```

```java
// ScienceDistinctionDecider.java
class ScienceDistinctionDecider implements DistinctionDecider{
    @Override
    public void evaluateDistinction(Student student) {
        if (student.score > 80) {
            System.out.println(student.regNumber+" has
                    received a distinction in science.");
        }
    }
}
```

```java
// ArtsDistinctionDecider.java
class ArtsDistinctionDecider implements DistinctionDecider{

    @Override
    public void evaluateDistinction(Student student) {
        if (student.score > 70) {
            System.out.println(student.regNumber+" has
                    received a distinction in arts.");
        }
    }
}
```

```java
// Client.java
import java.util.ArrayList;
import java.util.List;

class Client {
public static void main(String[] args) {
  System.out.println("*** A demo that follows
                               the OCP.***");
   List<Student> scienceStudents = enrollScienceStudents();
   List<Student> artsStudents = enrollArtsStudents();

     // Display all results.
    System.out.println("===Results:===");

    for (Student student : scienceStudents) {
        System.out.println(student);
    }
    for (Student student : artsStudents) {
        System.out.println(student);
    }

    // Evaluate distinctions.

    DistinctionDecider scienceDistinctionDecider =
                    new ScienceDistinctionDecider();
    DistinctionDecider artsDistinctionDecider =
                    new ArtsDistinctionDecider();
    System.out.println("===Distinctions:===");
    for (Student student : scienceStudents) {
     scienceDistinctionDecider.evaluateDistinction(student);
    }
    for (Student student : artsStudents) {
     artsDistinctionDecider.evaluateDistinction(student);
    }
  }
```

```
private static List<Student> enrollScienceStudents() {
 Student sam = new ScienceStudent("Sam","R1",81.5,"Comp.Sc.");
 Student bob = new ScienceStudent("Bob","R2",72,"Physics");
 List<Student> scienceStudents = new ArrayList<Student>();
 scienceStudents.add(sam);
 scienceStudents.add(bob);
 return scienceStudents;
}

private static List<Student> enrollArtsStudents() {
 Student john = new ArtsStudent("John", "R3", 71,"History");
 Student kate = new ArtsStudent("Kate", "R4", 66.5,"English");
 List<Student> artsStudents = new ArrayList<Student>();
 artsStudents.add(john);
 artsStudents.add(kate);
 return artsStudents;
 }
}
```

Output

Notice that the output is the same except for the first line that says this program follows the OCP.

```
*** A demo that follows the OCP.***
===Results:===
Name: Sam
Reg Number: R1
Dept:Comp.Sc.
Marks:81.5
*******
Name: Bob
Reg Number: R2
Dept:Physics
Marks:72.0
```

```
******
Name: John
Reg Number: R3
Dept:History
Marks:71.0
******
Name: Kate
Reg Number: R4
Dept:English
Marks:66.5
******
===Distinctions:===
R1 has received a distinction in science.
R3 has received a distinction in arts.
```

Analysis

What are the key advantages now? The following points tell you the answers:

- The Student class and DistinctionDecider are both unchanged for any future changes in the distinction criteria. They are closed for modification.

- Notice that every participant follows the SRP.

- Suppose you need to consider a new stream, say commerce. Then you can create a new class such as CommerceStudent. Notice that in a case like this, you do not need to touch the ArtsStudent or ScienceStudent classes.

- Similarly, when you consider different evaluation criteria for a different stream such as commerce, you can add a new derived class such as CommerceDistinctionDecider that implements the DistinctionDecider interface and you can set new distinction criteria for commerce students. In this case, you do not need to alter any existing class in the DistinctionDecider hierarchy. Obviously, the client code needs to adopt this change.

- Using this approach, you avoid an `if-else` chain (shown in demonstration 3). This chain could grow if you consider new streams such as commerce following the approach that is shown in demonstration 3. Remember that avoiding a big `if-else` chain is always considered a better practice. It is because avoiding the `if-else` chains lowers the cyclomatic complexity of a program and produces better code. (Cyclomatic complexity is a software metric to indicate the complexity of a program. It indicates the number of paths through a particular piece of code. So, in simple terms, by lowering the cyclomatic complexity you make your code easily readable and testable.)

I'll finish this section with Robert C. Martin's suggestion. In his book *Clean Architecture*, he gave us a simple formula: if you want component A to protect from component B, component B should depend on component A. But why do we give component A such importance? It is because we may want to put the most important rules in it.

It is time to study the next principle.

Liskov Substitution Principle

The Liskov Substitution Principle was initially introduced from the work of Barbara Liskov in 1988. ***The LSP says that you should be able to substitute a parent (or base) type with a subtype.*** It means that in a program segment, you can use a derived class instead of its base class without altering the correctness of the program.

How do you use inheritance? There is a base class and you create one (or more) derived classes from it. Then you can add new methods in the derived classes. As long as you directly use the derived class method with a derived class object, everything is fine. A problem may occur if you try to get the polymorphic behavior without following the LSP. How? You'll see a detailed discussion with examples in this chapter.

Let me give you a brief idea. Assume that there are two classes in which B is the base class and D is the subclass (of B). Furthermore, assume that there is a method that accepts a reference of B as an argument, something like the following:

```
public void someMethod(B b){
    // Some code
}
```

This method works fine until you pass a B instance to it. But what happens if you pass a D instance instead of a B instance? Ideally, the program should not fail. It is because you use the concept of polymorphism and you say D is basically a B type since class D inherits from class B. You can relate this scenario with a common example when we say a soccer player is also a player, where we consider the "player" class is a supertype of "soccer player."

Now see what the LSP suggests to us? It says that someMethod() should not misbehave/fail if you pass a D instance instead of a B instance to it. But it may happen if you do not write your code following the LSP. The concept will be clearer to you when you go through the upcoming example.

POINT TO NOTE

In design patterns, you often see polymorphic code. Here is a common example. Suppose you have the following code segment:

```
class B{}
class D extends B{}
```

Now you can write B obB=new B(); for sure. But notice that in this case, you can also write

```
B obB=new D(); // Also Ok
```

Similarly, you can use the interfaces as the supertype. For example, if you have

```
interface B{}
class D implements B{}
```

you can write

```
B obB=new D(); // Also Ok
```

Polymorphic code shows your expertise but remember that it's your responsibility to implement polymorphic behavior properly and avoid unwanted outcomes.

Initial Program

Consider an example I see every month. I use an online payment portal to pay my electricity bill. Since I am a registered user, when I raise a payment request in this portal, it shows my previous payments too. Let's consider a simplified example based on this real-life scenario.

Assume that you also have a payment portal where a registered user can raise a payment request. You use method newPayment() for this. In this portal, you can also show the user's last payment details using a method called previousPaymentInfo(). Here is a sample code segment for this:

```java
interface Payment {

    void previousPaymentInfo();

    void newPayment();
}

class RegisteredUserPayment implements Payment {
    String name;
    public RegisteredUserPayment(String userName) {
        this.name = userName;
    }
    @Override
    public void previousPaymentInfo(){
        System.out.println("Retrieving "+ name+"'s last
                            payment details.");
        // Some other code,if any
    }

    @Override
    public void newPayment(){
        System.out.println("Processing "+name+"'s current payment
                            request.");
        // Some other code, if any
    }
}
```

Furthermore, you create the helper class PaymentHelper to display all the previous payments and the new payment requests of these users. You use showPreviousPayments() and processNewPayments() for these activities. These methods call previousPaymentInfo() and newPayment() on the respective Payment instances. You use an enhanced for statement (it's often referred to as an enhanced for loop) to serve these purposes. Here is the PaymentHelper class for your instant reference:

```java
import java.util.ArrayList;
import java.util.List;

public class PaymentHelper {

    List<Payment> payments = new ArrayList<Payment>();

    public void addUser(Payment user){
        payments.add(user);
    }

    public void showPreviousPayments() {
        for (Payment payment: payments) {
            payment.previousPaymentInfo();
            System.out.println("------");
        }
    }
    public void processNewPayments()  {
            for (Payment payment: payments) {
            payment.newPayment();
            System.out.println("------");
        }
    }
}
```

Inside the client code, you create two users and show their current payment requests along with previous payments. Everything is ok so far.

Demonstration 5

Here is the complete demonstration. All parts of the program are inside the package jdp3e.solid_principles.without_lsp. Refer to this package when you download the source code from the Apress website.

```java
// Payment.java
interface Payment {
    void previousPaymentInfo();

    void newPayment();
}
```

```java
// RegisteredUserPayment.java
class RegisteredUserPayment implements Payment {
    String name;
    public RegisteredUserPayment(String userName) {
      this.name = userName;
    }
    @Override
    public void previousPaymentInfo(){
      System.out.println("Retrieving "+ name+"'s last payment details.");
        // Some other code, if any
    }

    @Override
    public void newPayment(){
        System.out.println("Processing "+name+"'s current payment
                        request.");
        // Some other code, if any
    }
}
```

```java
// PaymentHelper.java
import java.util.ArrayList;
import java.util.List;
```

```java
public class PaymentHelper {

    List<Payment> payments = new ArrayList<Payment>();

    public void addUser(Payment user){
         payments.add(user);
    }

    public void showPreviousPayments() {
        for (Payment payment: payments) {
             payment.previousPaymentInfo();
             System.out.println("------");
        }
    }
    public void processNewPayments()  {
            for (Payment payment: payments) {
               payment.newPayment();
               System.out.println("------");
        }
    }
}

// Client.java
class Client {

    public static void main(String[] args) {
      System.out.println("***A demo without LSP.***\n");
      PaymentHelper helper = new PaymentHelper();

      // Instantiating two registered users
      RegisteredUserPayment robinPayment = new
                        RegisteredUserPayment("Robin");
      RegisteredUserPayment jackPayment = new
                        RegisteredUserPayment("Jack");

      // Adding the users to the helper
      helper.addUser(robinPayment);
      helper.addUser(jackPayment);
```

```
    // Processing the payments using
    // the helper class.
    helper.showPreviousPayments();
    helper.processNewPayments();

    }
}
```

Output

When you run this program, you'll see the following output:

```
***A demo without LSP.***

Retrieving Robin's last payment details.
------
Retrieving Jack's last payment details.
------
Processing Robin's current payment request.
------
Processing Jack's current payment request.
------
```

This program seems to be fine. ***Now assume that you have a new requirement that says you need to support guest users in the future.*** You can process a guest user's payment request, but you do not show their last payment detail. So, you create the following class that implements the Payment interface as follows:

```
class GuestUserPayment implements Payment {
    String name;
    public GuestUserPayment() {
        this.name = "guest";
    }
    @Override
    public void previousPaymentInfo(){
        throw new UnsupportedOperationException();
    }
}
```

```
    @Override
    public void newPayment(){
        System.out.println("Processing "+name+"'s current payment
                            request.");
        // Some other code, if any
    }
}
```

Inside the main() method you create a guest user instance now and try to use your helper class in the same manner. Here is the new client code (notice the changes in bold). For your easy understanding, I added some comments to draw your attention to the code that causes the problem now.

```
class Client {
    public static void main(String[] args) {
        System.out.println("***A demo without LSP.***\n");
        PaymentHelper helper = new PaymentHelper();

        // Instantiating two registered users
        RegisteredUserPayment robinPayment = new
                            RegisteredUserPayment("Robin");
        RegisteredUserPayment jackPayment = new
                            RegisteredUserPayment("Jack");

        // Adding the users to the helper
        helper.addUser(robinPayment);
        helper.addUser(jackPayment);

        GuestUserPayment guestUser = new GuestUserPayment();
        helper.addUser(guestUser);

        // Processing the payments using
        // the helper class.
        // You can see the problem now.
        helper.showPreviousPayments();
        helper.processNewPayments();
    }
}
```

This time you get a surprise and encounter an exception that may look like the following:

```
***A demo without LSP.***

Retrieving Robin's last payment details.
------
Retrieving Jack's last payment details.
------
Exception in thread "main" java.lang.UnsupportedOperationException
    at jdp3e.solid_principles.without_lsp.GuestUserPayment.previousPayment
    Info(GuestUserPayment.java:10)
    at jdp3e.solid_principles.without_lsp.PaymentHelper.showPrevious
    Payments(PaymentHelper.java:13)
    at jdp3e.solid_principles.without_lsp.Client.main(Client.java:23)
```

You can see that although the GuestUserPayment class implements the Payment interface, it causes PaymentHelper to break. You can understand that the loop

```java
public void showPreviousPayments() {
        for (Payment payment: payments) {
            payment.previousPaymentInfo();
            System.out.println("------");
        }
    }
```

causes this trouble. In every iteration, you call the method previousPaymentInfo() on the respective Payment object and the exception is raised for the GuestUserPayment instance. So, you now know how a working solution can fail when you add a new code segment. What is the solution? You will find it in the next section.

Better Program

The first obvious solution that may come into your mind is to introduce an if-else chain to verify whether the Payment instance is a GuestUserPayment or a RegisteredUserPayment. However, this is not the best possible solution in the sense that if you have another special type of user, you again verify it inside this if-else chain. *Most importantly, you violate the OCP each time you modify an existing class that uses this if-else chain.* So, let's search for a better solution.

In the upcoming program, you remove the newPayment() method from the Payment interface. You place this method into another interface called NewPayment. As a result, now you have two interfaces with the specific operations. Since all types of users can raise a new payment request, the concrete classes of RegisteredUserPayment and GuestUserPayment both implement the NewPayment interface. But you show the last payment detail for the registered users only. So, the RegisteredUser class implements the Payment interface. I always advocate for a proper name. Since Payment contains the previousPaymentInfo() method, it makes sense to choose a better name, such as PreviousPayment instead of Payment. So, now you see the following interfaces:

```java
interface PreviousPayment {

    void previousPaymentInfo();

}

interface NewPayment {

    void newPayment();

}
```

Adjust these new names in the helper class too. Let's look at the updated program which is shown in the following section.

Demonstration 6

Here is the complete demonstration:

```java
// PreviousPayment.java
interface PreviousPayment {

    void previousPaymentInfo();

}
// NewPayment.java
interface NewPayment {

    void newPayment();

}
```

```java
// RegisteredUserPayment.java
class RegisteredUserPayment implements NewPayment,PreviousPayment {
    String name;
    public RegisteredUserPayment(String userName) {
        this.name = userName;
    }
    @Override
    public void previousPaymentInfo(){
        System.out.println("Retrieving "+ name+"'s last
                        payment details.");
        // Some code,if any
    }

    @Override
    public void newPayment(){
        System.out.println("Processing "+name+"'s current payment
                        request.");
        // Some code, if any
    }
}

// GuestUserPayment.java
class GuestUserPayment implements NewPayment {
    String name;
    public GuestUserPayment() {
        this.name = "guest";
    }

    @Override
    public void newPayment(){
        System.out.println("Processing "+name+"'s current payment
                        request.");
        //Some code, if any
    }
}
```

// PaymentHelper.java

```java
import java.util.ArrayList;
import java.util.List;

class PaymentHelper {

List<PreviousPayment> previousPayments = new
                              ArrayList<PreviousPayment>();

List<NewPayment> newPayments = new ArrayList<NewPayment>();
    public void addPreviousPayment(PreviousPayment
                                        previousPayment){
        previousPayments.add(previousPayment);
    }

    public void addNewPayment(NewPayment newPaymentRequest){
        newPayments.add(newPaymentRequest);
    }
    public void showPreviousPayments() {
        for (PreviousPayment payment: previousPayments) {
            payment.previousPaymentInfo();
            System.out.println("------");
        }
    }
    public void processNewPayments() {
        for (NewPayment payment: newPayments) {
            payment.newPayment();
            System.out.println("**********");
        }
    }
}
```

```java
// Client.java

class Client {

    public static void main(String[] args) {
        System.out.println("***A demo that follows the
                            LSP.***\n");
        PaymentHelper helper = new PaymentHelper();

        // Instantiating two registered users.
        RegisteredUserPayment robin = new
                        RegisteredUserPayment("Robin");
        RegisteredUserPayment jack = new
                        RegisteredUserPayment("Jack");
        // Instantiating a guest user's payment.
        GuestUserPayment guestUser1 = new GuestUserPayment();

        // Consolidating the previous payment's info to
        // the helper.
        helper.addPreviousPayment(robin);
        helper.addPreviousPayment(jack);

        // Consolidating new payment requests to
        // the helper
        helper.addNewPayment(robin);
        helper.addNewPayment(jack);
        helper.addNewPayment(guestUser1);

        // Retrieve all the previous payments
        // of registered users.
        helper.showPreviousPayments();

        // Process all new payment requests
        // from all users.
        helper.processNewPayments();
    }
}
```

```
***A demo that follows the LSP.***

Retrieving Robin's last payment details.
------
Retrieving Jack's last payment details.
------
Processing Robin's current payment request.
**********
Processing Jack's current payment request.
**********
Processing guest's current payment request.
**********
```

Analysis

What are the key changes? Notice that in demonstration 5, `showPreviousPayments()` and `processNewPayments()` both process `Payment` instances inside the enhanced for loop. But in demonstration 6, inside the `showPreviousPayments()` method, you process `PreviousPayment` instances and inside the `NewPayments()` method, you process `NewPayment` instances. This new structure solves the problem you faced in demonstration 5. You can see that this modified design conforms to the LSP because objects are clearly substitutable and the program works properly.

Note   I want you to note a minor point. Here the key focus was on the LSP principle, not anything else. You could easily refactor the client code using some static method. For example, you could introduce a static method to display all the payment requests and use this method whenever you need it. But the participant list is very small in this example. So, I have ignored this activity. The same comment applies to similar code segments in this book.

Interface Segregation Principle

You often see a fat interface that contains many methods. A class that implements the interface may not need all these methods. So why does the interface contain all these methods? One possible answer is to support some of the implementing classes of this interface. This is the area the Interface Segregation Principle focuses on. It suggests that you don't pollute an interface with these unnecessary methods only to support one (or some) of the implementing classes of this interface. The idea is that ***a client should not depend on a method that it does not use***. Once you understand this principle, you'll see that you used ISP in the better design following the LSP in demonstration 6. For now, let's consider an example with a full focus on the ISP.

POINTS TO REMEMBER

Note the following points before you proceed further:

- A client means any class that uses another class (or interface).

- The word "Interface" of the Interface Segregation Principle is not limited to a Java interface. The same concept applies to any supertype, such as an abstract class or a simple parent class.

- Many examples across different sources explain the violation of the ISP with an emphasis on throwing an exception such as UnsupportedOperationException() in Java. Demonstration 7 also demonstrate such an example. It shows the disadvantages of an approach that does not follow the ISP (and the LSP). You saw earlier that the LSP can deal with this kind of problem. I mentioned this in the code analysis too.

- The ISP suggests that your class should not depend on interface methods that it does not use. This statement will make sense to you when you go through the following example and remember the previous points.

Initial Program

Assume that you have the interface `Printer` with two methods, `printDocument()` and `sendFax()`. There are several users of this class. For simplicity, let's consider two of them only: `BasicPrinter` and `AdvancedPrinter`. Figure 1-1 shows a simple class diagram for this.

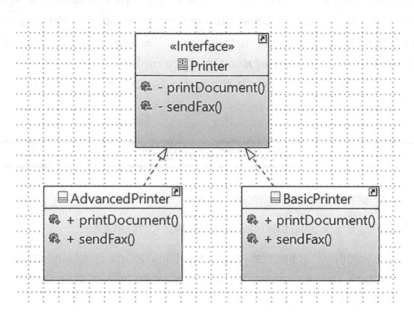

Figure 1-1. *The Printer class hierarchy*

A basic printer can print documents. It does not support any other functionality. So, `BasicPrinter` needs the `printDocument()` method only. An advanced printer can print documents as well as send faxes. So, the `AdvancedPrinter` needs both methods.

In this case, a change to the `sendFax()` method in `AdvancedPrinter` can force the interface `Printer` to change, which in turn, forces the `BasicPrinter` code to recompile. This situation is unwanted and it can cause potential problems for you in the future.

You saw a problematic situation in Demonstration 5. Later, you saw a solution in demonstration 6 when you segregated the interface `IUser` into `IPreviousPayment` and `INewPayment`. In this case, you followed the ISP too. The ISP suggests you design your interface with the proper methods that a particular client may need.

But *why does a user invite the problem in the first place? Or why does a user need to change a base class (or, an interface)?* To answer this, assume that you want to show which type of fax you are using in a later development phase. You know that there are different variations of fax methods, such as LanFax, InternetFax (or EFax), and AnalogFax. So, earlier, the SendFax() method did not use any parameters, but now it needs to accept a parameter to show the type of fax it uses.

To demonstrate this further, suppose you have a fax hierarchy that may look like the following:

```
interface Fax {
    void faxType();
}

class LanFax implements Fax {
    @Override
    public void faxType() {
        System.out.println("Using lan fax to send the
                            fax.");

    }
}

class EFax implements Fax {
    @Override
    public void faxType() {
        System.out.println("Using internet fax(efax) to
                            send the fax.");
    }
}
```

To use this inheritance hierarchy, once you modify the sendFax() method to sendFax(Fax faxType) in the AdvancedPrinter class, it demands you change the interface Printer (yes, you break the OCP here too). But it is not over yet! When you update Printer, you need to update the BasicPrinter class too to accommodate this change. **Now you see the problem!**

Note   You saw that a change in AdvancedPrinter causes changes in the interface Printer, which in turn causes BasicPrinter to update its fax method. So, you can see that though the BasicPrinter does not need this fax method at all, still a change in AdvancedPrinter causes it to change and recompile. The ISP suggests you take care of this kind of scenario.

This is why when you see a fat interface, ask yourself if these methods are required for a client. If not, split it into smaller interfaces that are relevant to clients.

If you understand the previous discussion, you may not start with the following code where you assume that you may need to support different devices/printers in the future:

```
interface Printer {

    void printDocument();

    void sendFax();
}
```

If you start your coding considering the advanced printers that can print as well as send a fax, it is fine. But in a later stage, if your program needs to support basic printers too, you may write something like

```
class BasicPrinter implements Printer {
    @Override
    public void printDocument() {
        System.out.println("The basic printer prints a document.");
    }

    @Override
    public void sendFax() {
        throw new UnsupportedOperationException();
    }

}
```

You have already seen that this code can cause a potential problem for you! It is pretty clear that a basic printer does not need to send a fax. But since BasicPrinter implements Printer, it needs to provide a sendFax() implementation. As a result, when sendFax() changes in the Printer interface, BasicPrinter needs to accommodate the change. **The ISP suggests you avoid this kind of situation.**

In this context, can you remember the issue in demonstration 5? When you throw the exception and try to use polymorphic code in an incorrect way, you see the impact of violating the LSP. Once you modify Printer, you violate the OCP too.

So, in this case, inside main(), you cannot write polymorphic code like the following (because the last line of this code segment will throw the runtime error):

```
Printer printer = new AdvancedPrinter();
printer.printDocument();
printer.sendFax();

printer = new BasicPrinter();
printer.printDocument();
// printer.sendFax(); // Will throw error
```

Also, you cannot write something like

```
List<Printer> printers = new ArrayList<Printer>();
printers.add(new AdvancedPrinter());
printers.add(new BasicPrinter());

for (Printer device : printers) {
  device.printDocument();
  // device.sendFax(); // Will throw error
}
```

In both cases, you will see runtime exceptions.

```
┌─────────────────────────────────────────────────────────────────┐
│                         POINT TO NOTE                             │
└─────────────────────────────────────────────────────────────────┘
```

I want you to note two points, which you probably know. But it is worth mentioning them to avoid any confusion.

First, in this book, I use enhanced for loops a lot. But lambda lovers can replace a code segment like

```
for (Printer device : printers) {
    device.printDocument();
}
```

with

```
printers.forEach(Printer::printDocument);
```

You choose which one you want to use.

Second, I showed a small code segment using List and ArrayList. When you use them in your program, do not forget to import the following import statements:

```
import java.util.List;
import java.util.ArrayList;
```

Demonstration 7

In previous sections, you started with a program that does not follow a specific principle. Let's repeat the same. Here is the complete demonstration that does not follow the ISP. All parts of the program are inside the package jdp3e.solid_principles.without_isp. Refer to this package when you download the source code from the Apress website.

```
// Printer.java
interface Printer {
    void printDocument();

    void sendFax();
}
```

// BasicPrinter.java

```java
class BasicPrinter implements Printer {
    @Override
    public void printDocument() {
        System.out.println("The basic printer prints a document.");
    }

    @Override
    public void sendFax() {
        throw new UnsupportedOperationException();
    }

}
```

// AdvancedPrinter.java

```java
class AdvancedPrinter implements Printer {
    @Override
    public void printDocument() {
        System.out.println("The advanced printer prints a document.");
    }

    @Override
    public void sendFax() {
      System.out.println("The advanced printer sends a fax.");
    }
}
```

// Client.java

```java
class Client {
    public static void main(String[] args) {
        System.out.println("***A demo without ISP.***");
        Printer printer = new AdvancedPrinter();
        printer.printDocument();
        printer.sendFax();
```

```
        printer = new BasicPrinter();
        printer.printDocument();
        // printer.sendFax(); // Will throw error
    }

}
```

Output

When you run this program, you will see the following output:

```
***A demo without ISP.***
The advanced printer prints a document.
The advanced printer sends a fax.
The basic printer prints a document.
```

Analysis

You can see that to prevent the runtime exceptions, I needed to comment out a line of code. I kept this dead code for this discussion. You know that you should avoid this kind of commented code because it can cause potential problems in the long run. Since no one touches the commented code, there is a possibility that in the future lots of changes will occur in the codebase and then this code will become irrelevant. So, when a new developer reads the code, they will be clueless about it.

Most importantly, as said before, in this design, if you change the sendFax() method signature in AdvancedPrinter, you need to adjust the change in Printer, which causes BasicPrinter to change and recompile. I discussed this in detail.

Think about the problem from another angle. Assume that you need to support another printer that can print, fax, and photocopy. In this case, if you add a photocopying method in the Printer interface, both the existing clients, BasicPrinter and AdvancedPrinter, need to accommodate the change.

Better Program

Let's find a better solution. You understand that there are two different activities: one is to print some documents and the other is to send a fax. So, in the upcoming example, you create two interfaces named `Printer` and `FaxDevice`. `Printer` contains the `printDocument()` method and `FaxDevice` contains the `SendFax()` method. The idea is simple:

- The class that wants print functionality implements the `Printer` interface, and the class that wants fax functionality implements the `FaxDevice` interface.

- If a class wants both functionalities, it implements both interfaces.

You should not assume that the ISP says an interface should have only one method. In this example, there are two methods in the `Printer` interface and the `BasicPrinter` class needs only one of them. This is why you see the segregated interfaces with a single method only.

Demonstration 8

Here is the complete implementation. All parts of the program are inside the package `jdp3e.solid_principles.isp`. Refer to this package when you download the source code from the Apress website.

// Printer.java
```
interface Printer {

    void printDocument();
}
```

// FaxDevice.java
```
interface FaxDevice {

    void sendFax();
}
```

// BasicPrinter.java

```java
class BasicPrinter implements Printer {
    @Override
    public void printDocument() {
        System.out.println("The basic printer prints a document.");
    }
}
```

// AdvancedPrinter.java

```java
class AdvancedPrinter implements Printer,FaxDevice {
    @Override
    public void printDocument() {
        System.out.println("The advanced printer prints a document.");
    }

    @Override
    public void sendFax() {
        System.out.println("The advanced printer sends a fax.");
    }
}
```

// Client.java

```java
class Client {

    public static void main(String[] args) {
        System.out.println("***A demo that follows ISP.***");

        Printer printer = new BasicPrinter();
        printer.printDocument();
        printer = new AdvancedPrinter();
        printer.printDocument();
```

```
    FaxDevice faxDevice = new AdvancedPrinter();
    faxDevice.sendFax();
  }
}
```

Output

Run this program. You will see the following output:

```
***A demo that follows ISP.***
The basic printer prints a document.
The advanced printer prints a document.
The advanced printer sends a fax.
```

Analysis

What happens if you use a default method inside the interface? Let me tell you.

- The foremost point is, prior to Java 8, interfaces couldn't have default methods. All those methods were abstract by default.

- Secondly, if you use a default method inside the interface or an abstract class, I remind you that each time you add a method in the base class (or interface), the method is available for use in the derived classes. This kind of practice can violate the OCP and the LSP, which in turn causes difficult maintenance and reusability issues. For example, if you provide a default fax method in an interface (or an abstract class), the `BasicPrinter` must override it, saying something similar to the following:

```
@Override
public void sendFax() {
    throw new UnsupportedOperationException();
}
```

and you saw the potential problem with this!

- But what happens if you use an empty method, instead of throwing the exception? Yeah, the code will work, but for me, providing an empty method for a feature that is not supported at all is not a good solution in a case like this. From my point of view, it is misleading because the clients see no change in output when they invoke a valid method.

There is an alternative technique to implementing the ISP. This can be done using the "delegation" technique. The discussion of this is beyond the scope of this book. But remember the following point: delegations increase the runtime (it can be small, but it is nonzero for sure) of an application, which can affect the performance of the application. Also, based on a particular design, a delegated call can create some additional objects. Unnecessary creation of objects can cause trouble for you because they occupy memory blocks. So, to make an application that should work properly using a very small amount of memory (such as a real-time embedded system), you need to be careful before you create an object.

Dependency Inversion Principle

The DIP covers two important things:

- A high-level concrete class should not depend on a low-level concrete class. Instead, both should depend on abstractions.

- Abstractions should not depend upon details. Instead, the details should depend upon abstractions.

You'll examine both points.

The reason for the first point is simple. If the low-level class changes, the high-level class needs to adjust to the change; otherwise, the application breaks. What does this mean? It means you should avoid creating a concrete low-level class inside a high-level class. Instead, you should use abstract classes or interfaces. As a result, you remove the tight coupling between the classes.

The second point is also easy to understand when you analyze the case study discussed in the ISP section. You saw that if an interface needs to change to support one of its clients, other clients can be impacted due to the change. No client likes to see such an application.

So, in your application, if your high-level modules are independent of low-level modules, you can reuse them easily. This idea also helps you design nice frameworks.

In his book *Agile Principles, Patterns and Practices in C#*, Robert C. Martin explains that a traditional software development model in those days (such as structured analysis and design) tends to create software where high-level modules used to depend on low-level modules. But in OOP, a well-designed program opposes this idea. It inverts the dependency structure that often results from a traditional procedural method. This is the reason he used the word "inversion" in this principle.

Initial Program

Assume that you have a two-layer application. Using this application, a user can save an employee ID in a database. To demonstrate this, let's use a console application instead of a GUI application. You have two classes, UserInterface and OracleDatabase. As per its name, UserInterface represents a user interface such as a form where a user can type an employee ID and click the Save button to save the ID in a database. OracleDatabase is used to mimic an Oracle database. Again, for simplicity, there is no actual database in this application and there is no code to validate an employee ID. Here your focus is on the DIP only, so those discussions are not important.

By using the saveEmployeeId() method of UserInterface, you can save an employee id to a database. Notice the code for the UserInterface class:

```
class UserInterface {
    private OracleDatabase oracleDatabase;

    public UserInterface() {
        this.oracleDatabase = new OracleDatabase();
    }
```

```
    public void saveEmployeeId(String empId) {
        // Assuming that this is a valid data.
        // So, storing it in the database.
        oracleDatabase.saveEmpIdInDatabase(empId);
    }
}
```

You instantiate an OracleDatabase object inside the UserInterface constructor. Later you use this object to invoke the saveEmpIdInDatabase() method, which does the actual saving inside the Oracle database. This style of coding is very common. But there are some problems. I'll discuss them in the analysis section before we look at a better approach. For now, see the complete program, which does not follow the DIP.

Demonstration 9

Here is the complete demonstration. All parts of the program are inside the package jdp3e.solid_principles.without_dip. Refer to this package when you download the source code from the Apress website.

```
// UserInterface.java
class UserInterface {
    private OracleDatabase oracleDatabase;

    public UserInterface() {
        this.oracleDatabase = new OracleDatabase();
    }

    public void saveEmployeeId(String empId) {
        // Assuming that this is a valid data.
        // So, storing it in the database.
        oracleDatabase.saveEmpIdInDatabase(empId);
    }
}

// OracleDatabase.java
class OracleDatabase {
    public void saveEmpIdInDatabase(String empId){
```

```java
        System.out.println("The id: "+empId+" is saved in the
                        Oracle database.");
    }
}

// Client.java
class Client {

    public static void main(String[] args) {
        System.out.println("***A demo without DIP.***");
        UserInterface userInterface = new UserInterface();
        userInterface.saveEmployeeId("E001");
    }
}
```

Output

Here is the output:

```
***A demo without DIP.***
The id: E001 is saved in the Oracle database.
```

Analysis

The program is simple, but it suffers from the following issues:

- The top-level class (UserInterface) has too much dependency on the bottom-level class (OracleDatabase). These two classes are tightly coupled. So, in the future, if the OracleDatabase class changes (for example, when you change the signature of the saveEmpIdInDatabase(...) method), you need to adjust the UserInterface class.

- The low-level class should be available before you write the top-level class. So, you are forced to complete the low-level class before you write or test the high-level class.

- What if you use a different database? For example, you may want to switch from the Oracle database to a MySQL database or you may need to support both.

Better Program

In this program, you see the following hierarchy:

```
// Database.java
interface Database {
    void saveEmpIdInDatabase(String empId);
}
```

```
// OracleDatabase.java
class OracleDatabase implements Database {
    @Override
    public void saveEmpIdInDatabase(String empId) {
        System.out.println("The id: " + empId + " is saved
                            in the Oracle database.");
    }
}
```

The first part of the DIP suggests that we focus on abstraction. This makes the program efficient. So, this time the UserInterface class targets the abstraction Database, instead of a concrete implementation such as OracleDatabase. Here is the new construct of UserInterface :

```
class UserInterface {
  Database database;

  public UserInterface(Database database) {
   this.database = database;
  }

  public void saveEmployeeId(String empId) {
   database.saveEmpIdInDatabase(empId);
  }
}
```

This gives you the flexibility to consider a new database, such as MYSQLDatabase as well. Figure 1-2 describes the scenario.

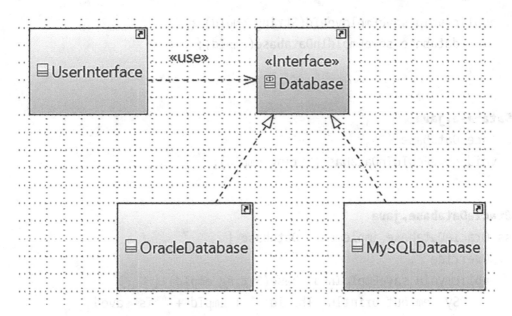

Figure 1-2. *The high-level class UserInterface depends on the abstraction Database. The concrete classes OracleDatabase and MySQLDatabase also depend on Database*

The second part of the DIP suggests making the Database interface considering the need for the UserInterface class. It is important because if an interface needs to change to support one of its clients, other clients can be impacted due to the change.

Demonstration 10

All parts of the program are inside the package jdp3e.solid_principles.dip. Refer to this package when you download the source code from the Apress website. Here is the complete program for you:

```
// UserInterface.java
class UserInterface {
    Database database;

    public UserInterface(Database database) {
        this.database = database;
    }
```

```java
        public void saveEmployeeId(String empId) {
            database.saveEmpIdInDatabase(empId);
        }
}
```

// Database.java
```java
interface Database {
    void saveEmpIdInDatabase(String empId);
}
```

// OracleDatabase.java
```java
class OracleDatabase implements Database {
    @Override
    public void saveEmpIdInDatabase(String empId) {
        System.out.println("The id: " + empId + " is saved
                            in the Oracle database.");
    }
}
```

// MySQLDatabase.java
```java
class MySQLDatabase implements Database {
    @Override
    public void saveEmpIdInDatabase(String empId) {
        System.out.println("The id: " + empId + " is saved
                            in the MySQL database.");
    }
}
```

// Client.java
```java
class Client {
    public static void main(String[] args) {
        System.out.println("***A demo that follows the DIP.***");
```

```
    // Using Oracle now
    Database database = new OracleDatabase();
    UserInterface userInterface = new
                            UserInterface(database);
    userInterface.saveEmployeeId("E001");

    // Using MySQL now
    database = new MySQLDatabase();
    userInterface = new UserInterface(database);
    userInterface.saveEmployeeId("E002");
  }
}
```

Output

Here is the output that you'll see when you run this program:

```
***A demo that follows the DIP.***
The id: E001 is saved in the Oracle database.
The id: E002 is saved in the MySQL database.
```

Analysis

You can see that this program resolves all the potential issues of the program in demonstration 9. In short, in OOP, I suggest following the Robert C. Martin quote:

> *High-level modules simply should not depend on low-level modules in any way.*

So, when you have a base class and a derived class, your base class should not know about any of its derived classes. But there are few exceptions to this suggestion. For example, consider the case when your base class needs to restrict the count of the derived class instances at a certain point.

One last point. You can see that in demonstration 10, the UserInterface class constructor accepts a database parameter. You can provide an additional facility to a user when you use both the constructor and the setter method (setDatabase) inside this class. Here is sample code for you. Notice the additional code in bold.

```
class UserInterface {
    Database database;

    public UserInterface(Database database) {
        this.database = database;
    }

    public void setDatabase(Database database) {
        this.database = database;
    }

    public void saveEmployeeId(String empId) {
        database.saveEmpIdInDatabase(empId);
    }
}
```

What is the benefit? Now you can instantiate a database while instantiating the UserInterface class and change the target database later using the setter method. Here is sample code. You can append the last part of this segment at the end of main() to see new output.

```
// Using MySQL now
database = new MySQLDatabase();
userInterface = new UserInterface(database);
userInterface.saveEmployeeId("E002");

// Changing the target database
userInterface.setDatabase(new OracleDatabase());
userInterface.saveEmployeeId("E002");
```

The previous segment can produce the following output:

```
The id: E002 is saved in the MySQL database.
The id: E002 is saved in the Oracle database.
```

You can follow the same technique for similar examples that are used in this book.

Summary

The SOLID principles are the fundamental guidelines in object-oriented design. They are high-level concepts that help you develop better software. They are neither rules nor laws, but they help you think of possible scenarios/outcomes in advance. I recommend that you understand these principles well before you start reading the design patterns in the following chapters.

In this chapter, I showed you applications that follow (and do not follow) these principles and discussed the pros and cons. Let's have a quick review.

The SRP says that *a class should have only one reason to change.* Using the SRP means you can write cleaner and less fragile code. You identify the responsibilities and make classes based on each responsibility. What is a responsibility? It is a reason for a change. But you should not assume that a class should have a single method only. If multiple methods help you achieve a single responsibility, your class can contain all of these methods. It's ok to bend this rule based on the nature of possible changes. The reason for this is if you have too many classes in an application, it is difficult to maintain. The idea is when you know this principle and think carefully before you implement a design, you can avoid the typical mistakes discussed earlier.

Robert C. Martin mentioned the OCP as the most important object-oriented design principle. The OCP suggests that *software entities (a class, module, method, etc.) should be open for extension, but closed for modification.* The idea is if you do not touch running code, you do not break it. For the new features, you add new code but do not disturb the existing code. It helps you save time on retesting the entire workflow again; instead, you focus on the newly added code and test that part. This principle is often hard to achieve, but partial OCP compliance can provide a bigger benefit to you in the long term. In many cases, when you violate the OCP, you break the SRP too.

The idea of the LSP is *you should be able to substitute a parent (or base) type with a subtype*. It is your responsibility to write true polymorphic code using the LSP. This principle is very important. We discussed it with a typical case study. Using this principle, you can avoid the long tail of `if-else` chains and make your code OCP compliant too.

The idea behind the ISP is that *a client should not depend on a method that it does not use*. This is why you may need to split a fat interface into multiple interfaces to make a better solution. I showed you a simple technique to implement the idea. When you do not modify an existing interface (or an abstract class or a simple base class), you follow the OCP. You have seen that throwing an exception, such as

UnsupportedOperationException(), can break the LSP. This is why an ISP-compliant application can help you to make OCP- and LSP-compliant applications too. You can make an ISP-compliant application using the delegation technique, which I did not discuss in this book. But the important point is when you use the delegation, you increase the runtime (you may say it is negligible, but it is non-zero for sure), which can affect a time-sensitive application. Using delegation, you may create a new object when a client uses the application. This may cause memory issues in certain scenarios.

The DIP suggests two important points. ***First, a high-level concrete class should not depend on a low-level concrete class. Instead, both should depend on abstractions. Second, the abstractions should not depend upon details. Instead, the details should depend upon abstractions***. When you follow the first part of the suggestion, your application is efficient and flexible; you can consider new concrete implementations in your application. When you analyze the second part of this principle, you see that you should not change an existing base class or interface to support one of its clients. This can cause another client to break, and you violate the OCP in such a case. You explored the importance of all these points with examples.

CHAPTER 2

Simple Factory Pattern

This chapter covers the Simple Factory pattern.

Definition

It creates an object without exposing the instantiation logic to the client.

Concept

In object-oriented programming, a factory is an object that can create other objects. A factory can be invoked in many different ways, but most often it uses a method that can return objects with varying prototypes. Any subroutine that can help you create these new objects can be considered as a factory. Most importantly, it helps you abstract the process of object creation from the consumers of the application.

Real-Life Example

Consider a car manufacturing company that manufactures different models of a car. It must have a factory with different production units. Different models of cars are available so some parts are common across these models, such as company logo, name, etc. Some factory units produce common parts for all models. Other factory units produce model-specific parts. When they make the final product, they assemble the model-specific parts with the common parts. So, the goal of using a factory is to have a single production unit for similar parts. This ensures consistent product quality and functionality. As a result, when a part gets to the assembly line, it is certain that it will always behave the same way.

© Vaskaran Sarcar 2022
V. Sarcar, *Java Design Patterns*, https://doi.org/10.1007/978-1-4842-7971-7_2

The Simple Factory pattern is the basis of the Factory Method and Abstract Factory patterns you'll learn in the next two chapters. So, you'll see a fine-tuned version of this example in the next chapter.

Let's consider a simpler example. When a kid demands a toy from their parents, the kid does not know how the parents will fulfill the demand. The parents in this case can be considered as a factory for this small kid. Think from the parents' point of view now. They can make the toy themselves or purchase the toy from a shop.

Computer World Example

This pattern is common to software applications, but before proceeding, note the following:

- The Simple Factory pattern is not treated as a standard design pattern in the GoF's famous book, but the approach is common to any application you write where you want to separate the code that varies a lot from the code that does not vary. It is assumed that you follow this approach in all applications you write.

- The Simple Factory pattern is considered the simplest form of the Factory Method pattern (and Abstract Factory pattern). So, you can assume that any application that follows either the Factory Method pattern or the Abstract Factory pattern also follows the concept of the Simple Factory pattern's design goals.

- You can consider the static method `getInstance()` of the `java.text.NumberFormat` class is an example of this category.

In the following implementation, I discuss this pattern with a common use case. Let's go through the implementation.

Implementation

These are the important characteristics of the following implementation:

- In this example, you are dealing with two different types of animals: dogs and tigers. You can assume that each type of animal can tell something about it, so you have two concrete classes called `Dog.java` and `Tiger.java`. Each implements the `Animal` interface. Here is a sample for your reference:

```java
interface Animal{
    void displayBehavior();
}
class Dog implements Animal{
        public Dog() {
            System.out.println("\nA dog is created.");
        }
        public void displayBehavior(){
        System.out.println("It says: Bow-Wow.");
        System.out.println ("It prefers barking.");
        }
    }
```

- The code for creating objects is in a different place (specifically, in a factory class). Using this approach, when you create either a dog or a tiger, you do not use the new operator in the client code (Q&A 2.2 discusses the reason for this in detail). So, in the client code, you see lines something like

```java
Animal animal = factory.createAnimal("dog");
```

- In the same way, you can create a tiger.

- It means that to get an animal, the client invokes the `createAnimal()` method of the `AnimalFactory` object. Notice that you do not use the new operator in client code to create an object.

- You will further notice that the code that can vary is separated from the code that is least likely to vary. This approach can help you to remove tight coupling in the system. (How? Follow the Q&A Session.)

Note   To make the example meaningful, I introduce method displayBehavior() in this demonstration. This method is not needed to demonstrate the Simple Factory pattern in this chapter or the Factory Method pattern in the next chapter. I use a console message in the constructor of the animal classes. These statements are sufficient to demonstrate these patterns. But as said, the use of the displayBehavior() method can make the example more meaningful. Invoking this method falls in the code region that does not vary in client code.

Class Diagram

Figure 2-1 shows the class diagram.

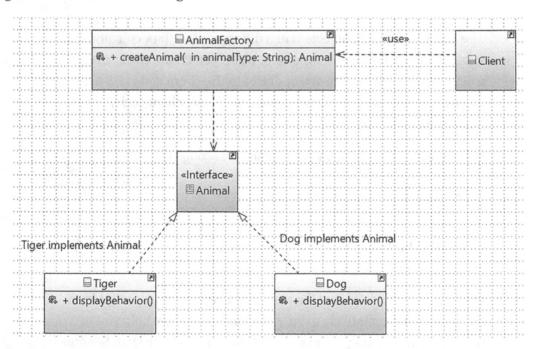

Figure 2-1. *Class diagram*

> **Note**   I mention the usage and realization edges (or links) in this diagram. Next
> time onwards, I won't explicitly mention them because mentioning them repeatedly
> in the upcoming diagrams can make the overall structure clumsy.

Package Explorer View

Figure 2-2 shows the high-level structure of the program.

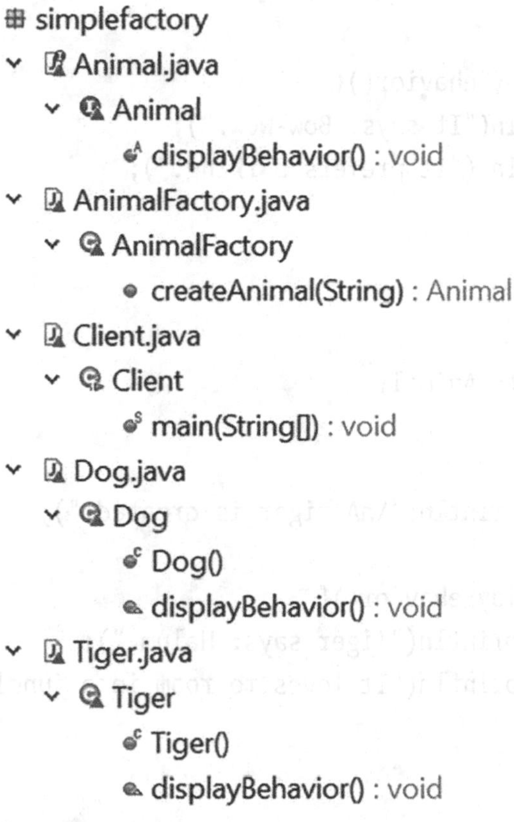

simplefactory
- ∨ Animal.java
  - ∨ Animal
    - displayBehavior() : void
- ∨ AnimalFactory.java
  - ∨ AnimalFactory
    - createAnimal(String) : Animal
- ∨ Client.java
  - ∨ Client
    - main(String[]) : void
- ∨ Dog.java
  - ∨ Dog
    - Dog()
    - displayBehavior() : void
- ∨ Tiger.java
  - ∨ Tiger
    - Tiger()
    - displayBehavior() : void

Figure 2-2. Package Explorer view

Demonstration

Here's the complete implementation. When you download the code, you will see that all
parts of the program are separated and placed in the package jdp3e.simplefactory.
Here's the implementation:

// Animal.java

```java
interface Animal{
    void displayBehavior();
}
```

// Dog.java

```java
class Dog implements Animal{
    public Dog(){
     System.out.println("\nA dog is created.");
    }

    public void displayBehavior(){
     System.out.println("It says: Bow-Wow.");
     System.out.println ("It prefers barking.");
    }
}
```

// Tiger.java

```java
class Tiger implements Animal{
    public Tiger()
    {
        System.out.println("\nA tiger is created.");
    }
    public void displayBehavior(){
        System.out.println("Tiger says: Halum.");
        System.out.println("It loves to roam in a jungle.");
    }
}
```

// AnimalFactory.java

```java
package jdp3e.simplefactory;

class AnimalFactory {
 public Animal createAnimal(String animalType){
   Animal animal;
```

```java
if (animalType.equals("dog")){
 animal = new Dog();
}
else if (animalType.equals("tiger")){
 animal = new Tiger();
}
else{
 System.out.println("You can create either a 'dog' or a 'tiger'. ");
 throw new IllegalArgumentException("Unknown animal cannot be
 instantiated.");
 }
 return animal;
 }
}
```

// Client.java

```java
class Client {

    public static void main(String[] args) {

        System.out.println("*** Simple Factory
                          Demonstration.***");
        AnimalFactory factory = new AnimalFactory();

        Animal animal = factory.createAnimal("dog");
        animal.displayBehavior();

        animal = factory.createAnimal("tiger");
        animal.displayBehavior();
    }
}
```

Output

You will see the following output when you run the program:

```
*** Simple Factory Demonstration.***

A dog is created.
It says: Bow-Wow.
It prefers barking.

A tiger is created.
Tiger says: Halum.
It loves to roam in a jungle.
```

Analysis

Inside the createAnimal() method, you can pass either 'tiger' or 'dog'. Otherwise, you'll see a runtime exception. For example, if you append the following lines in the client code

```
animal = factory.createAnimal("cat"); //Exception
animal.displayBehavior();
```

you'll see an error like the following:

```
You can create either a 'dog' or a 'tiger'.
Exception in thread "main" java.lang.IllegalArgumentException: Unknown
animal cannot be instantiated.
    at jdp3e.simplefactory.AnimalFactory.createAnimal(AnimalFactory.java:12)
    at jdp3e.simplefactory.Client.main(Client.java:16)
```

Q&A Session

2.1 The analysis section shows that you are passing String parameters and you do not ensure the type safety in this application. Is this correct?

Good catch. You are correct. But remember that in each chapter, the key focus is on a particular design pattern, not on these corner cases. You can always employ your preferred mechanism to ensure the type safety. For example, it is ok to use enums to guard this situation. Here is an alternative version of AnimalFactory that shows usage of an enum with the important changes in bold:

```
class AnimalFactory2 {
    public enum Type {DOG, TIGER};
    public Animal createAnimal(Type animalType){
        Animal animal;
        if (animalType.equals(Type.DOG))
        {
            animal = new Dog();
        }
        else if (animalType.equals(Type.TIGER))
        {
            animal = new Tiger();
        }
        // Remaining code is skipped
}
```

To accommodate this change, here is an alternative version of the client code:

```
class Client2 {
    public static void main(String[] args) {

        System.out.println("*** Simple Factory Demonstration-2.***");
        AnimalFactory2 factory = new AnimalFactory2();

        Animal animal =
         factory.createAnimal(AnimalFactory2.Type.DOG);
        animal.displayBehavior();
```

```
animal =
 factory.createAnimal(AnimalFactory2.Type.TIGER);
animal.displayBehavior();

// Compile-time error now
// animal = factory.createAnimal("cat");
// animal.displayBehavior();

    }
}
```

As a result, this time if you pass an incompatible animal such as `'cat'` inside the `createAnimal()` method, you receive a compile-time error instead of a runtime error. We all know that compile-time errors are always better compared to last-minute surprises such as runtime errors.

2.2 In this example, I see that the clients are delegating the object's creation through the Simple Factory pattern. But instead of this, they could directly create the objects with the new operator. Is this correct?

No. In this context, you need to remember the key reasons for using the Simple Factory pattern:

- One of the key object-oriented design principles is to separate the parts of your code that are most likely to change from the rest.

- In this case, only the creation process for objects changes. You can assume that these animals must tell something about themselves, and that part of the code does not need to vary inside the client code. So, in the future, if there is any change required in the creation process, you need to change only the `createAnimal()` method of the `AnimalFactory` class. The client code will not be affected because of those changes.

- You do not want to put lots of `if-else` blocks (or `switch` statements) inside the client code. This makes your client code clumsy.

- How you are creating the objects is hidden inside the client code. This kind of abstraction promotes security.

In short, sometimes the life-cycle management of the created objects must be centralized to ensure consistent behavior within the application. This cannot be done if the client is free to create a concrete object the way they wish.

2.3 What are the challenges associated with this pattern?

If you want to add a new animal or delete an existing animal, you need to modify the createAnimal() method. This process violates the Open/Closed Principle (which basically says that a code module should be open for extension but closed for modification) of the SOLID principles. (Refer to Chapter 1 if you need to recall the concept.)

2.4 Can you make the factory class static?

It depends on the programming language you use. In Java, you are not allowed to tag the word static with a top-level class. In other words, by design, the compiler will always complain about the top-level static classes in Java.

For example, in C#, you can have a static class, but you have to remember the restrictions associated with a static class. For example, you cannot inherit them, and so on. It can make sense when you deal with value objects that do not have an implementation class or a separate interface. It is also useful when you work with immutable classes and your factory class doesn't need to return a brand-new object each time you use it.

In short, a value object is an object whose equality is based on the values rather than the identity. The most important characteristic of a value object is that it is immutable without an identity.

A simple real-life example can be given using five-rupee currency notes and five-rupee coins in India. Their money values are the same, but they are different instances.

In general, I do NOT vote for static factory class because they are basically promoters for global states, which are not ideal for object-oriented programming.

2.5 You could make the createAnimal() method static. Is this correct?

Yes. In fact, this is a common technique and is often termed as a static factory. The only advantage of this approach is that you can avoid instantiating objects from a class to use a method. But if you need to consider subclassing, you face troubles. In Chapter 3, you'll learn about the Factory Method pattern, and you'll see that you need to improve this program where a subclass needs to change the behavior of this method.

Final Comment

I told you earlier that you can consider the static method getInstance() of java.text. NumberFormat class as an example of this category. Now you understand the Simple Factory pattern. You can verify this easily in the Eclipse IDE. For example, right-click the NumberFormat class and then click Open Declaration. Scroll down to find the definition of the overloaded version of getInstance(...) method (see Figure 2-3).

```
private static NumberFormat getInstance(LocaleProviderAdapter adapter,
                                        Locale locale, Style formatStyle,
                                        int choice) {
    NumberFormatProvider provider = adapter.getNumberFormatProvider();
    return switch (choice) {
        case NUMBERSTYLE     -> provider.getNumberInstance(locale);
        case PERCENTSTYLE    -> provider.getPercentInstance(locale);
        case CURRENCYSTYLE   -> provider.getCurrencyInstance(locale);
        case INTEGERSTYLE    -> provider.getIntegerInstance(locale);
        case COMPACTSTYLE    -> provider.getCompactNumberInstance(locale, formatStyle);
        default              -> null;
    };
}
```

Figure 2-3. *An overloaded version of the getInstance(...) method inside the NumberFormat class*

Don't be surprised! It is a new kind of case level in switch statements where you can use "arrow case" labels instead of "colon case" labels (it is available in JDK13 onwards). In the same way, you can verify other examples in this book.

PART II

The Gang of Four (GoF) Design Patterns

The software industry is full of patterns and design guidelines. As you continue coding and making different applications, you will learn their importance and know when to choose one technique over another technique. In the preface of the book, I told you about the *Pareto* principle or the *80-20 rule*, which states that 80% of outcomes come from 20% of all causes.

So what are the fundamental design patterns? If you search the Internet, books, tutorials, or similar places, you'll find that most sources talk about the GoF patterns. The field of design patterns has grown a lot in the past few years, but the GoF patterns are still considered fundamental design patterns. So, once you learn the fundamentals in-depth, your programming life will become easy. In this context, I found an interesting quote from the book *The Almanack of Naval Ravikant* (ISBN-13: 978-1544514222):

> *The really smart thinkers are clear thinkers. They understand*
> *the basics at a very, very fundamental level. I would rather*
> *understand the basics really well than memorize all kinds of*
> *complicated concepts I can't stitch together and can't rederive*
> *from the basics. If you can't rederive concepts from the basics*
> *as you need them, you're lost. You're just memorizing.*

This is why Part II covers the 23 GoF patterns in detail.

CHAPTER 3

Factory Method Pattern

This chapter covers the Factory Method pattern. The Factory Method pattern will make more sense to you if you understand the pros and cons of the Simple Factory pattern, which is covered in Chapter 2.

GoF Definition

It defines an interface for creating an object, but lets subclasses decide which class to instantiate. The Factory Method pattern lets a class defer instantiation to subclasses.

Concept

Here you start with an abstract creator class (often called a creator) that defines the basic structure of an application, and the subclasses (that derive from this abstract class) take the responsibility of doing the actual instantiation process. The concept will make sense to you when you analyze the following examples.

Real-Life Example

The example from the Simple Factory pattern also applies here. Let's revisit it with a different perspective: you know that a car manufacturing company produces different models of a car every year. Depending on a market survey, it decides on a model and starts manufacturing. Based on the model of the car, different parts are built and assembled. This company should always be prepared for customers opting for better models in the near future. If the company needs to do a whole new setup for a new model with only a few new features, that can hugely impact the company's profit margin.

© Vaskaran Sarcar 2022
V. Sarcar, *Java Design Patterns*, https://doi.org/10.1007/978-1-4842-7971-7_3

So, the company should set up the factory in such a way that it can produce parts for the upcoming models easily.

Computer World Example

In database programming, you may need to support different database users. For example, one user may use SQL Server and the other may opt for Oracle. So, when you need to insert data into your database, first you need to create a connection object, such as `SqlServerConnection` or `OracleConnection,` and only then can you proceed. If you put the code into an `if-else` block (or `switch` statements), you may need to repeat lots of similar code, which isn't easily maintainable. Also, whenever you start supporting a new type of connection, you need to reopen your code and make modifications. This type of problem can be resolved using the Factory Method pattern.

- Since the Simple Factory pattern is the simplest form of the Factory Method pattern, let's consider the same examples here. You can say that the static method `getInstance()` of the `java.text.NumberFormat` class is an example of this category. But the following one is a better example.

- The `iterator()` method of the `AbstractCollection<E>` (or `Collection<E>`) is an example of a factory method in Java.

Implementation

In the upcoming example, an abstract creator class called `AnimalFactory` defines the basic structure of the program. As per the definition, the instantiation process is carried out through the subclasses that derive from this abstract class.

I use the same inheritance hierarchy as the Simple Factory pattern in Chapter 2, so this time also you'll see that both the `Dog` and `Tiger` classes implement the `Animal` interface.

The Animal hierarchy is the same: there is no change in the Animal.java, Dog.java, and Tiger.java. So, you'll see the following inheritance hierarchy:

```java
interface Animal{
    void displayBehavior();
}

class Dog implements Animal
{
    public Dog(){
        System.out.println("\nA dog is created.");
    }
    public void displayBehavior(){
        System.out.println("It says: Bow-Wow.");
        System.out.println ("It prefers barking.");
    }
}

class Tiger implements Animal
{
    public Tiger(){
        System.out.println("\nA tiger is created.");
    }
    public void displayBehavior(){
        System.out.println("It says: Halum.");
        System.out.println("It loves to roam in a jungle.");
    }
}
```

You'll see another inheritance hierarchy where two concrete classes called DogFactory and TigerFactory are used to create dog and tiger objects. Each inherits from an abstract class called AnimalFactory. These two concrete classes are used to defer the instantiation process. I've attached supportive comments for your easy understanding of this hierarchy.

```java
abstract class AnimalFactory{

    // This is the "factory method"
    // Notice that I defer the instantiation process
    // to the subclasses.
    protected abstract Animal createAnimal();
}

// The DogFactory class is used to create dogs

class DogFactory extends AnimalFactory
{
    // Creating and returning a 'Dog' instance

    @Override
    protected Animal createAnimal() {
        return new Dog();
    }
}
// The TigerFactory class is used to create tigers

class TigerFactory extends AnimalFactory
{
    // Creating and returning a 'Tiger' instance

    @Override
    protected Animal createAnimal() {
        return new Tiger();
    }
}
```

The remaining code is easy to understand. Let's go to the next section.

Class Diagram

The class diagram in Figure 3-1 shows the key participants of the program.

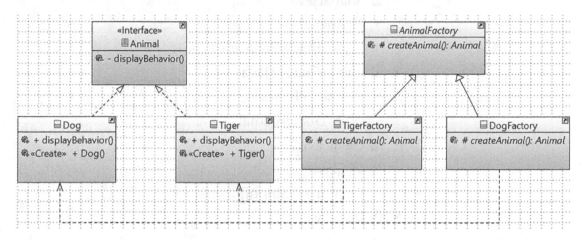

Figure 3-1. *Class diagram*

Package Explorer View

Figure 3-2 shows the high-level structure of the program. Since this figure cannot be accommodated on the remaining page, let us move to the next page.

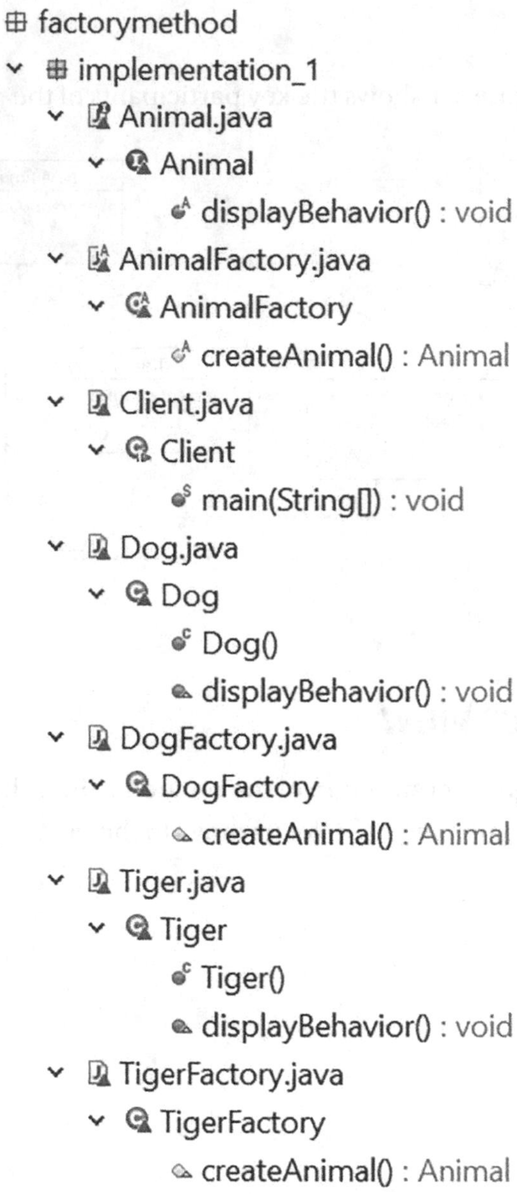

⊞ factorymethod
  ⌄ ⊞ implementation_1
     ⌄ 🗏 Animal.java
       ⌄ ⓐ Animal
          ⚬ᴬ displayBehavior() : void
     ⌄ 🗏 AnimalFactory.java
       ⌄ ⓐ AnimalFactory
          ⚬ᴬ createAnimal() : Animal
     ⌄ 🗏 Client.java
       ⌄ ⓒ Client
          ⚬ˢ main(String[]) : void
     ⌄ 🗏 Dog.java
       ⌄ ⓒ Dog
         ⚬ᶜ Dog()
         ⚬ₐ displayBehavior() : void
     ⌄ 🗏 DogFactory.java
       ⌄ ⓒ DogFactory
         ⚬ createAnimal() : Animal
     ⌄ 🗏 Tiger.java
       ⌄ ⓒ Tiger
         ⚬ᶜ Tiger()
         ⚬ₐ displayBehavior() : void
     ⌄ 🗏 TigerFactory.java
       ⌄ ⓒ TigerFactory
         ⚬ createAnimal() : Animal

Figure 3-2. *Package Explorer view*

Demonstration 1

Here is the complete demonstration. You can see the complete code inside the package `jdp3e.factorymethod.implementation_1`.

// Animal.java

```java
interface Animal{
    void displayBehavior();
}
```

// Dog.java

```java
class Dog implements Animal{

 public Dog(){
   System.out.println("\nA dog is created.");
  }

 public void displayBehavior(){
   System.out.println("It says: Bow-Wow.");
   System.out.println ("It prefers barking.");
  }
}
```

// Tiger.java

```java
class Tiger implements Animal{
    public Tiger() {
        System.out.println("\nA tiger is created.");
    }

    public void displayBehavior(){
        System.out.println("Tiger says: Halum.");
        System.out.println("It loves to roam in a jungle.");
    }
}
```

// AnimalFactory.java

```java
abstract class AnimalFactory{

  // This is the "factory method"
  // Notice that I defer the instantiation
  // process to the subclasses.
```

```java
    protected abstract Animal createAnimal();
}
```

// DogFactory.java

```java
class DogFactory extends AnimalFactory
{
    // Creating and returning a 'Dog' instance

    @Override
    protected Animal createAnimal() {
        return new Dog();
    }
}
```

// TigerFactory.java

```java
class TigerFactory extends AnimalFactory
{
    // Creating and returning a 'Tiger' instance

    @Override
    protected Animal createAnimal() {
        return new Tiger();
    }
}
```

// Client.java

```java
class Client {

 public static void main(String[] args) {
   System.out.println("***Factory Method Pattern Demo.***");
   AnimalFactory factory;
   Animal animal;

  // Create a tiger and display its behavior
  // using TigerFactory.
  factory =new TigerFactory();
  animal = factory.createAnimal();
```

```
    animal.displayBehavior();
    // Create a dog and display its behavior
    // using DogFactory.

    factory =new DogFactory();
    animal = factory.createAnimal();
    animal.displayBehavior();
  }
}
```

Output

Here's the output:

```
***Factory Method Pattern Demo.***

A tiger is created.
It says: Halum.
It loves to roam in a jungle.

A dog is created.
It says: Bow-Wow.
It prefers barking.
```

Modified Implementation

You just saw the simplest form of the Factory Method pattern. In demonstration 1, each factory can produce only one type of object, either a dog or a tiger, but there is no variation. For example, it makes sense if a dog factory makes dogs with different colors. Similarly, a tiger factory can produce tigers with different colors. If you receive such a requirement, how can you proceed? The answer is simple: you pass a color parameter to the factory method. When you do this, it's called a parameterized factory method.

In addition, notice that the AnimalFactory class is an abstract class. ***It means that you can take advantage of using an abstract class. How? Ok, let's suppose you want all the subclasses to follow a common rule that is imposed from the parent (or base) class. It simply means that you need to put the common behaviors/codes inside the parent class.*** In demonstration 1, you called the createAnimal() method for the factory object. This time you do not call this method directly. Instead, you use another method named createAndDisplayAnimal() inside AnimalFactory to invoke createAnimal(). This new method looks like the following (note the changes in bold):

```
abstract class AnimalFactory {

public void createAndDisplayAnimal(String color){
 Animal animal;
 animal=createAnimal(color);
 animal.displayBehavior();
}

// This is the "factory method"
// Notice that I defer the instantiation
// process to the subclasses.
 protected abstract Animal createAnimal(String color);
}
```

You can see that when you invoke the createAndDisplayAnimal() method, this method invokes the factory method. Once it receives the object from the factory method, you can place the common activities right below this line of code.

Demonstration 2

Now the other parts of the program need to adopt the change. You can see all parts of the program inside the jdp3e.factorymethod.implementation_2 package on the Apress website. Here is the complete program with important changes in bold:

```
// Animal.java

interface Animal{
    void displayBehavior();
}
```

```
// Dog.java

class Dog implements Animal{
    public Dog(String color){
        System.out.println("\nA dog with " + color+ " color is created.");
    }
    public void displayBehavior(){
        System.out.println("It says: Bow-Wow.");
        System.out.println ("It prefers barking.");
    }
}
```

```
// Tiger.java

class Tiger implements Animal {
    public Tiger(String color){
        System.out.println("\nA tiger with " + color+ " color is created.");
    }
    public void displayBehavior(){
        System.out.println("It says: Halum.");
        System.out.println("It loves to roam in a jungle.");
    }
}
```

```
// AnimalFactory.java

abstract class AnimalFactory {

public void createAndDisplayAnimal(String color){
 Animal animal;
 animal=createAnimal(color);
 animal.displayBehavior();
}

// This is the "factory method"
// Notice that I defer the instantiation
// process to the subclasses.
 protected abstract Animal createAnimal(String color);
}
```

// DogFactory.java

```java
class DogFactory extends AnimalFactory {
    // Creating and returning a 'Dog' instance

    @Override
    protected Animal createAnimal(String color) {

        return new Dog(color);
    }
}
```

// TigerFactory.java

```java
class TigerFactory extends AnimalFactory {
    // Creating and returning a 'Tiger' instance

    @Override
    protected Animal createAnimal(String color) {
        return new Tiger(color);
    }
}
```

// Client.java

```java
class Client {
public static void main(String[] args) {
    System.out.println("***Factory Method pattern modified demonstration.***");
    AnimalFactory factory;
    // Create a tiger and display its behavior
    // using TigerFactory.
    factory =new TigerFactory();
    factory.createAndDisplayAnimal("yellow");

    // Create a dog and display its behavior
    // using DogFactory.
    factory = new DogFactory();
    factory.createAndDisplayAnimal("white");
 }
}
```

Output

Here is the modified output:

Factory Method pattern modified demonstration.

A tiger **with yellow color** is created.
It says: Halum.
It loves to roam in a jungle.

A dog **with white color** is created.
It says: Bow-Wow.
It prefers barking.

Analysis

In this example, `animal.displayBehavior()` is the common code that all subclasses use. So, you need to get an animal object before you invoke the `displayBehavior()` method. If you do not depend on this animal instance, you can place any other common code before you invoke the `createAnimal()` method from the `createAndDisplayAnimal()` method. Here is a sample:

```
public void createAndDisplayAnimal(String color){
  System.out.println("Showing common behaviors of an animal.");
  Animal animal;
  animal=createAnimal(color);
  animal.displayBehavior();
}
```

Q&A Session

3.1 Why have you separated the `createAnimal()` method from the client code?

If you read the GoF definition, you understand that this is the main purpose: for the subclasses to create specialized objects. If you look carefully, you will also find that only this "creational part" varies across the products. I discussed this in the Q&A Session of Chapter 2.

3.2 What are the advantages of using a factory like this?

Here are some key advantages:

- You are separating the code that varies from the code that does not vary (in other words, the advantages of using the Simple Factory pattern are still present). This helps you maintain the code easily.

- The code is not tightly coupled, so you can add new classes such as Lion and Bear at any time in the system without modifying the existing architecture. In other words, you have followed the Open/Closed Principle.

- A client can use a factory method without knowing how the actual type of object is created.

3.3 What are the challenges of using a factory like this?

Here are some pitfalls:

- When you use the non-parameterized factory method, you introduce more classes (compared to Simple Factory) in the application. It also indicates that you need to put more effort into unit testing. In addition, notice that each particular instance is associated with a subclass. It means that even if you need only one particular instance, you are forced to create a new subclass. Obviously, the use of a parameterized factory method does not increase the total number of classes and can help you overcome this kind of difficulty.

- If you do not start with a factory method, it can be a challenging task to refactor existing code. You need to understand the dependencies clearly before you refactor the existing code into the factory method pattern.

3.4 I see that the Factory Method pattern is supporting two parallel hierarchies. Is this understanding correct?

Good catch. Yes, from the class diagram, it is evident that this pattern supports parallel class hierarchies; I've marked them in Figure 3-3.

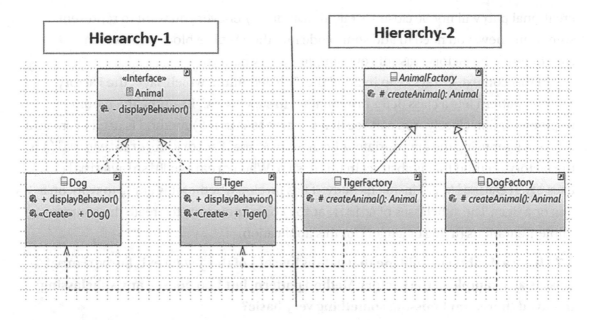

Figure 3-3. *The different inheritance hierarchies in this example*

In short, `AnimalFactory`, `DogFactory`, and `TigerFactory` are placed in one hierarchy, and `Animal`, `Dog`, and `Tiger` are placed in another hierarchy. Note that the creators and their creations/products form separate hierarchies that run in parallel.

3.5 You should always mark the factory method with an **abstract** keyword so that subclasses can complete them. Is this correct?

No. Sometimes you may be interested in a default factory method if the creator has no subclasses. In that case, you cannot mark the factory method with an `abstract` keyword.

However, to see the real power of the Factory Method pattern, you may need to follow the design that is implemented here in most of the cases.

3.6 It still appears to me that the Factory Method pattern is not that much different from the Simple Factory pattern. Am I correct?

If you look at the subclasses in the examples in both chapters, you may find some similarities. But you should not forget the key aim of the Factory Method pattern; it supplies the framework through which different subclasses can make different products. In the case of the Simple Factory pattern, you cannot similarly vary the products. You can think of the Simple Factory pattern as a one-time deal, but most importantly, your creational part will not be closed for modification. Whenever you want to represent something new, you need to add some code into the `if-else` block or a `switch` statement in the factory class of your Simple Factory pattern.

In this context, always keep in mind the GoF definition, which says "the Factory Method pattern lets a class defer instantiation to subclasses." Examine the modified implementation closely. You can see that the `createAnimal()` method is used to create a dog or a tiger using the appropriate subclasses of `AnimalFactory`. So, `createAnimal()` is the factory method that is abstract in this design. When `createAndDisplayAnimal(...)` uses `createAnimal(...)` inside its body, it has no clue whether it is going to work on a dog or a tiger. The subclasses of `AnimalFactory` only know how to create the concrete implementations (a dog or a tiger) for this application.

3.7 I have a doubt: you told me that `getInstance()` **of the** `java.text.NumberFormat` **class is an example of the Factory Method pattern, but I do not see any subclassing involved there. Am I missing something very basic?**

Nice observation. You are making good progress. At the end of Chapter 2, you saw that it is a static method that returns the objects. So, technically it is not a perfect example of a Factory Method pattern. Notice that the GoF uses the words "defer instantiation to subclasses," which tells us that the subclasses should return the actual instances only.

This is why I mention that the `iterator()` method of `AbstractCollection<E>` (or `Collection<E>`) is a better example of the factory method in Java. Let's retrieve its definition in the Eclipse IDE:

```
public abstract class AbstractCollection<E> implements Collection<E> {

    // Previous code skipped
      public abstract Iterator<E> iterator();

    // Remaining code skipped
}
```

What does it mean? You understand that subclasses of this class need to provide the concrete implementation for the `iterator()` method. Here is such an implementation from the `ArrayList<E>` class:

```
public class ArrayList<E> extends AbstractList<E>
    implements List<E>, RandomAccess, Cloneable,
    java.io.Serializable {

    // Previous code skipped

    public Iterator<E> iterator() {
        return new Itr();
    }

 // Remaining code skipped
}
```

Similarly, `AbstractList<E>` that extends `AbstractCollection<E>` has the following method:

```
public Iterator<E> iterator() {
        return new Itr();
    }
```

Now analyze the in-built inheritance hierarchy, which is shown in Figure 3-4.

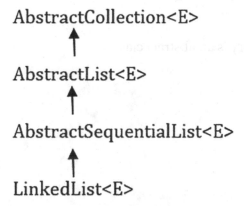

Figure 3-4. *Inheritance hierarchy from abstractCollection<E> to LinkedList<E>*

In short, you can see that the subclasses of `AbstractCollection<E>` such as `ArrayList` and `LinkedList` use the `iterator()` method as per their needs.

You'll learn more about the Iterator pattern in Chapter 18.

3.8 I can say that in the case of the Factory Method pattern, I use a subclassing mechanism (i.e., inheritance) and then implement the factory method that is defined in the parent class. Am I correct?

The answer to this question is yes if you want to strictly follow the GoF definitions. But at the same time, in this context, it is important to note that in many applications/implementations, you may not see the use of an abstract class or interface. For example, in Java, if you can create an XML reader object like this:

```
// Some code before...
XMLReader xmlReader1 = XMLReaderFactory.createXMLReader();
// Some code after
```

This `XMLReaderFactory` is a final class in Java (`XMLReaderFactory` is deprecated since version 9). So, you cannot inherit from it. But see the recommended `SAXParserFactory` class that can be used like the following:

```
// Some code before.
SAXParserFactory factory = SAXParserFactory.newInstance();
SAXParser parser = factory.newSAXParser();
XMLReader xmlReader2 = parser.getXMLReader();
// Some code after.
```

This `SAXParserFactory` is an abstract class.

CHAPTER 4

Abstract Factory Pattern

This chapter covers the Abstract Factory pattern.

GoF Definition

It provides an interface for creating families of related or dependent objects without specifying their concrete classes.

Note The Abstract Factory pattern will make more sense to you if you understand both the Simple Factory pattern (Chapter 2) and the Factory Method pattern (Chapter 3). The Simple Factory pattern does not fall directly into the Gang of Four design patterns, so the discussion of that pattern appears in Part I of the book. I suggest you read those two chapters before you jump into this one.

Concept

An abstract factory is often referred to as a *factory of factories*. In this pattern, you provide a way to encapsulate a group of individual factories that have a common theme. In this process, you do not instantiate a class directly; instead, you instantiate a concrete factory and thereafter create products using the factory.

Note I suggest you read Q&A 4.3 to understand the differences between the Simple Factory, Factory Method, and Abstract Factory patterns.

© Vaskaran Sarcar 2022
V. Sarcar, *Java Design Patterns*, https://doi.org/10.1007/978-1-4842-7971-7_4

You may see variations of client code when you see an implementation of this pattern. For example, you may see an optional factory provider that supplies the required factory to proceed further. Sometimes this provider is composed inside client code. I'll show you some of these variations.

In the upcoming example, you see that, inside the client code, you create a factory instance, and using this instance you create an animal:

```
// Making a wild dog and wild tiger through WildAnimalFactory
AnimalFactory animalFactory;
animalFactory = new WildAnimalFactory();
Dog dog = animalFactory.createDog("white");
Tiger tiger = animalFactory.createTiger("golden and cinnamon");
dog.displayMe();
tiger.aboutMe();
tiger.inviteDog(dog);
```

The previous code segment produces the following output:

```
You opt for a wild animal factory.
A wild dog with white color is created.
A wild tiger with golden and cinnamon color is created.
The wild dog says: I prefer to roam freely in jungles.Bow-Wow.
The wild tiger says: I prefer hunting in jungles.Halum.
The wild tiger says: I saw a wild dog in the jungle.
```

This pattern suits best when products are similar but the product families are different (for example, a domestic dog is quite different from a wild dog). This pattern helps you interchange specific implementations without changing the code that uses them, even at runtime. However, it may result in unnecessary complexity and extra work. Even debugging can become tough in some cases.

Real-Life Example

So what do I mean by the words "product families are similar (or different)?" Take the example of pet dogs and wild dogs. Similarly, you can see tigers in a zoo (or circus) and a jungle. Let's call them pet tigers and wild tigers, respectively. Do you see anything in common? The first obvious thing is both pet dogs and wild dogs are dogs. Similarly, both pet tigers and wild tigers are tigers. But notice that there is another thing in common among them: both wild dogs and wild tigers love to roam in a jungle. Similarly, both pet tigers and pet dogs love to stay in a secure place where the food supply is guaranteed. So, we can say that the pet animals form one set and the wild animals form another set. The abstract factory pattern suits best when you deal with a similar scenario. In the upcoming demonstration, you will see such an implementation.

Consider another example. Suppose you are decorating your room with two different types of tables; one is made of wood and the other one of steel. For the wooden type, you need to visit a carpenter, and for the steel type, you may need to go to a metal shop. Both are table factories. So, based on demand, you decide what kind of factory you need.

Computer World Example

Here are some examples:

- The newInstance() method of javax.xml.parsers. DocumentBuilderFactory is an example of an Abstract Factory pattern in JDK. The newInstance() method is static, but it returns the factory class considering other things, such as classpath scanning, external property, and so on. You can also change the factory class even though it is a static method. When you see the client code variation 2 in this chapter and analyze its uses, you'll find the similarity.

- If you are familiar with the C# programming language, you may notice that ADO.NET has already implemented similar concepts to establish a connection to a database.

Implementation

Wikipedia describes a typical structure of this pattern, which is similar to Figure 4-1 (https://en.wikipedia.org/wiki/Abstract_factory_pattern).

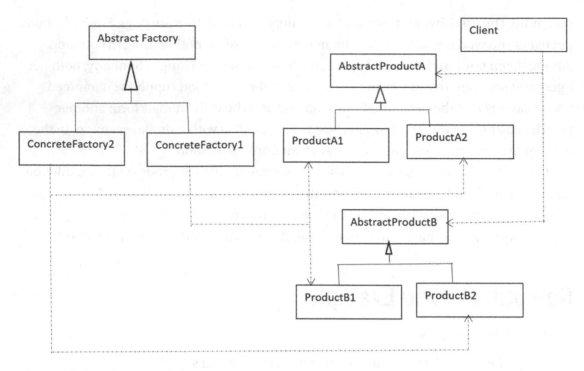

Figure 4-1. *Abstract Factory pattern*

You will follow a similar structure in the implementation in this chapter. In this example, there are two types of animals: pet animals and wild animals. Client.java is the client that is looking for some animals (they are wild dogs, pet dogs, wild tigers, and pet tigers). You'll explore the construction processes of both pet and wild animals in this implementation.

In this implementation, AnimalFactory is an abstract factory. Two concrete factories called WildAnimalFactory and PetAnimalFactory inherit from this abstract factory. These concrete factories are responsible for creating concrete products for dogs and tigers. As per their names, WildAnimalFactory creates wild animals (wild dogs and wild tigers) and PetAnimalFactory creates pet animals (pet dogs and pet tigers). For your reference, the participants and their roles are summarized here:

- AnimalFactory: Abstract factory. It is an abstract class in this implementation.

- WildAnimalFactory: It is a concrete factory and extends AnimalFactory. It creates wild dogs and wild tigers.

- PetAnimalFactory: Another concrete factory that also extends AnimalFactory, but this factory creates pet dogs and pet tigers.

- Tiger and Dog: Abstract products in this case. They are represented using two different Java interfaces.

- PetTiger, PetDog, WildTiger, and WildDog: They are the concrete products in this example. Both PetTiger and WildTiger implement the Tiger interface. Similarly, PetDog and WildDog implement the Dog interface. The Dog and Tiger interfaces have a different number of methods.

- I want you to note one interesting point. In many implementations, you may see that each concrete product has an equal number of methods. But you should not assume that this is mandatory. This is why, in the implementation, you see that tigers have an additional method called inviteDog(). This method represents a relationship between a tiger and a dog. To make this simple, you just use a simple message such as "The wild tiger says: I saw a wild dog in the jungle."

- You'll see variations of client code in this chapter. In variation 2, you'll see the FactoryProvider inside the client code as follows:

```
animalFactory = FactoryProvider.getFactory("wild");
Dog dog = animalFactory.createDog("white");
Tiger tiger = animalFactory.createTiger("golden and cinnamon");
dog.displayMe();
tiger.aboutMe();
tiger.inviteDog(dog);
```

- From the bold formatted line in the previous code segment, you can see that you're NOT directly instantiating the factory instance; instead, you're using the static method getFactory(...) of the FactoryProvider class to get the factory instance.

- Finally, there's another variation of client code where you use object composition.

For now, let's concentrate on the first implementation. It is because, apart from the client code, the remaining parts will be common for the rest of the chapter.

Class Diagram

Figure 4-2 shows the class diagram.

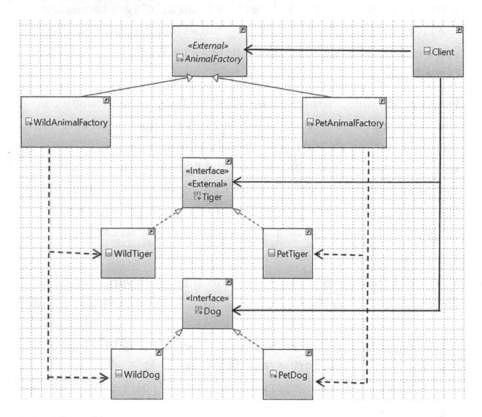

Figure 4-2. *Class diagram*

Package Explorer View

Figure 4-3 shows the high-level structure of the program. This program consists of many parts. I expand the important parts in this diagram.

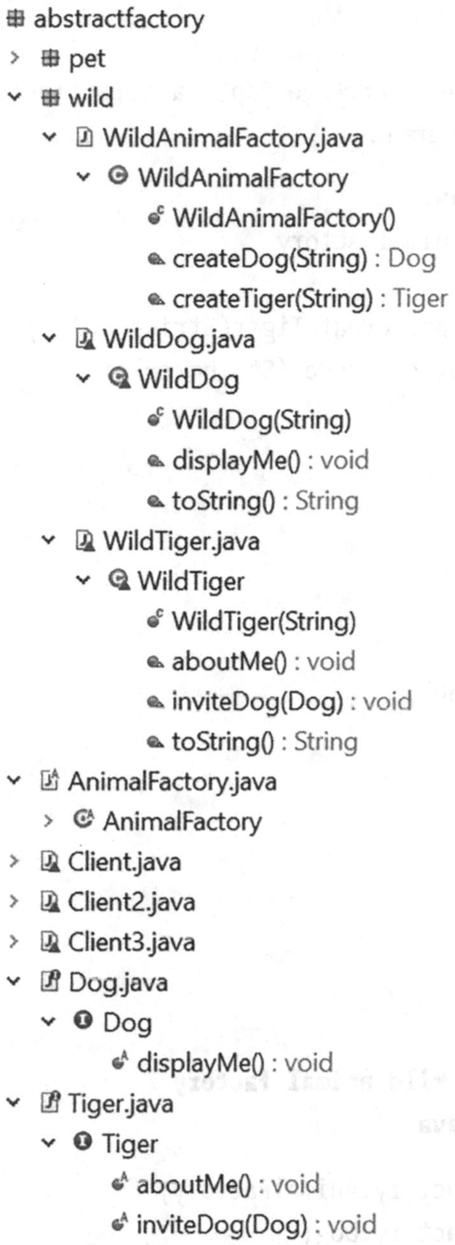

```
⊞ abstractfactory
> ⊞ pet
∨ ⊞ wild
    ∨ ⊡ WildAnimalFactory.java
        ∨ ⊙ WildAnimalFactory
            ✱ WildAnimalFactory()
            ● createDog(String) : Dog
            ● createTiger(String) : Tiger
    ∨ ⊡ WildDog.java
        ∨ ⊙ WildDog
            ✱ WildDog(String)
            ● displayMe() : void
            ● toString() : String
    ∨ ⊡ WildTiger.java
        ∨ ⊙ WildTiger
            ✱ WildTiger(String)
            ● aboutMe() : void
            ● inviteDog(Dog) : void
            ● toString() : String
∨ ⊡ AnimalFactory.java
    > ⊙ AnimalFactory
> ⊡ Client.java
> ⊡ Client2.java
> ⊡ Client3.java
∨ ⊡ Dog.java
    ∨ ❶ Dog
        ⬦ displayMe() : void
∨ ⊡ Tiger.java
    ∨ ❶ Tiger
        ⬦ aboutMe() : void
        ⬦ inviteDog(Dog) : void
```

Figure 4-3. *Package Explorer view*

Demonstration 1

The complete code is inside the package: jdp3e.abstractfactory.

Here's the complete program:

// Abstract Factory.java

```
public abstract class AnimalFactory
{
  protected abstract Tiger createTiger(String color);
  protected abstract Dog createDog(String color);
}
```

// Abstract Product-1
// Tiger.java

```
public interface Tiger
{
  void aboutMe();
  void inviteDog(Dog dog);
}
```

// Abstract Product-2
// Dog.java

```
public interface Dog
{
 void displayMe();
}
```

// Concrete Factory 1: Wild animal factory
// WildAnimalFactory.java

```
import jdp3e.abstractfactory.AnimalFactory;
import jdp3e.abstractfactory.Dog;
import jdp3e.abstractfactory.Tiger;

public class WildAnimalFactory extends AnimalFactory {
    public WildAnimalFactory() {
        System.out.println("You opt for a wild animal factory.\n");
    }
```

```java
    @Override
    public Tiger createTiger(String color) {
        return new WildTiger(color);
    }

    @Override
    public Dog createDog(String color) {
        return new WildDog(color);
    }
}
```

```java
// Concrete product-A1
// WildTiger.java

import jdp3e.abstractfactory.Dog;
import jdp3e.abstractfactory.Tiger;

class WildTiger implements Tiger {
    public WildTiger(String color) {
        System.out.println("A wild tiger with " + color + "
                            color is created.");
    }

    @Override
    public void aboutMe() {
        System.out.println("The " + this + " says: I prefer
                            hunting in jungles.Halum.");
    }

    @Override
    public void inviteDog(Dog dog) {
        System.out.println("The " + this + " says: I saw a
                            " + dog + " in the jungle.");
    }
```

```java
    @Override
    public String toString() {
        return "wild tiger";
    }

}
```

// Concrete product-B1
// WildDog.java

```java
import jdp3e.abstractfactory.Dog;

class WildDog implements Dog {
    public WildDog(String color) {
        System.out.println("A wild dog with " + color + "
                            color is created.");
    }

    @Override
    public void displayMe() {
        System.out.println("The " + this + " says: I prefer
                            to roam freely in jungles. Bow-Wow.");

    }

    @Override
    public String toString() {
        return "wild dog";
    }
}
```

// Concrete Factory2: Pet animal factory
// PetAnimalFactory.java

```java
import jdp3e.abstractfactory.AnimalFactory;
import jdp3e.abstractfactory.Dog;
import jdp3e.abstractfactory.Tiger;
```

```java
public class PetAnimalFactory extends AnimalFactory {
    public PetAnimalFactory() {
        System.out.println("You opt for a pet animal factory.\n");
    }

    @Override
    public Tiger createTiger(String color) {
        return new PetTiger(color);
    }

    @Override
    public Dog createDog(String color) {
        return new PetDog(color);
    }
}
```

// Concrete product-A2
// PetTiger.java

```java
import jdp3e.abstractfactory.Dog;
import jdp3e.abstractfactory.Tiger;

class PetTiger implements Tiger {
    public PetTiger(String color) {
        System.out.println("A pet tiger with " + color + "
                            color is created.");
    }

    public void aboutMe() {
        System.out.println("The " + this + " says: Halum. I
                            play in an animal circus.");
    }

    public void inviteDog(Dog dog) {
        System.out.println("The " + this + " says: I saw a
                            " + dog + " in my town.");
    }
```

```java
    @Override
    public String toString() {
        return "pet tiger";
    }
}
```

// Concrete product-B2
// PetDog.java

```java
import jdp3e.abstractfactory.Dog;

class PetDog implements Dog {
    public PetDog(String color) {
        System.out.println("A pet dog with " + color + "
                                color is created.");
    }

    @Override
    public void displayMe() {
        System.out.println("The " + this + " says:
                                Bow-Wow. I prefer to stay at home.");
    }

    @Override
    public String toString() {
        return "pet dog";
    }
}
```

```java
// Client.java

import jdp3e.abstractfactory.pet.PetAnimalFactory;
import jdp3e.abstractfactory.wild.WildAnimalFactory;

class Client {
    public static void main(String[] args) {

        System.out.println("***Abstract Factory Pattern Demo.***\n");
        AnimalFactory animalFactory;
```

```
    // Making a wild dog and wild tiger through
     // WildAnimalFactory
    animalFactory = new WildAnimalFactory();
    Dog dog = animalFactory.createDog("white");
    Tiger tiger = animalFactory.createTiger("golden and cinnamon");
    dog.displayMe();
    tiger.aboutMe();
    tiger.inviteDog(dog);

    System.out.println("\n***********\n");

    // Making a pet dog and pet tiger through
    // PetAnimalFactory now.
     animalFactory = new PetAnimalFactory();
    dog = animalFactory.createDog("black");
    tiger = animalFactory.createTiger("yellow");
    dog.displayMe();
    tiger.aboutMe();
    tiger.inviteDog(dog);
  }
}
```

Output

Here's the output:

Abstract Factory Pattern Demo.

You opt for a wild animal factory.

A wild dog with white color is created.
A wild tiger with golden and cinnamon color is created.
The wild dog says: I prefer to roam freely in jungles.Bow-Wow.
The wild tiger says: I prefer hunting in jungles.Halum.
The wild tiger says: I saw a wild dog in the jungle.

****

You opt for a pet animal factory.

A pet dog with black color is created.
A pet tiger with yellow color is created.
The pet dog says: Bow-Wow. I prefer to stay at home.
The pet tiger says: Halum. I play in an animal circus.
The pet tiger says: I saw a pet dog in my town.

Analysis

You may notice that you cannot access the PetDog or WildDog classes inside the client code. This is because they are not public and imported.

The Client Code Variations

I told you that you will see variations in client code in different implementations of this pattern. In demonstration 1, you saw such a variation. Next I present two more.

Demonstration 2

Here you see the usage of an optional factory provider. It is used to avoid a dependency between the client code and the factories. This factory provider has a static method to provide the desired factory object to the client. Here is a sample implementation:

```
package jdp3e.abstractfactory;

import jdp3e.abstractfactory.pet.PetAnimalFactory;
import jdp3e.abstractfactory.wild.WildAnimalFactory;

// Factory provider
// (It is optional for you)
class FactoryProvider {
    public static AnimalFactory getFactory(String
                                    factoryType) {
        if (factoryType.contains("wild")) {
            return new WildAnimalFactory();
        } else if (factoryType.contains("pet")) {
            return new PetAnimalFactory();
```

```
        } else {
            throw new IllegalArgumentException("You need
                    to pass either wild or pet as argument.");
        }
    }
}
class Client2 {

    public static void main(String[] args) {
        System.out.println("***Abstract Factory Pattern
                        Demo.Variation-2.***\n");
        AnimalFactory animalFactory;

        // Making a wild dog and wild tiger through
         // WildAnimalFactory
        animalFactory = FactoryProvider.getFactory("wild");
        Dog dog = animalFactory.createDog("white");
        Tiger tiger = animalFactory.createTiger("golden and cinnamon");
        dog.displayMe();
        tiger.aboutMe();
        tiger.inviteDog(dog);

        System.out.println("\n***********\n");

        // Making a pet dog and pet tiger through
        // PetAnimalFactory
        animalFactory = FactoryProvider.getFactory("pet");
        dog = animalFactory.createDog("black");
        tiger = animalFactory.createTiger("yellow");
        dog.displayMe();
        tiger.aboutMe();
        tiger.inviteDog(dog);
    }
}
```

Demonstration 3

Sometimes you see the use of composition in the client code. The following code segment shows such an implementation:

```
package jdp3e.abstractfactory;

import jdp3e.abstractfactory.pet.PetAnimalFactory;
import jdp3e.abstractfactory.wild.WildAnimalFactory;

class Client3 {

    AnimalFactory factory;

    public Client3(AnimalFactory factory) {
        this.factory = factory;
    }

    public AnimalFactory getFactory() {
        return factory;
    }

    public static void main(String[] args) {
        System.out.println("***Abstract Factory Pattern
                        Demo.Variation-3.***\n");
        AnimalFactory animalFactory;
        // Making a wild dog and wild tiger through
        // WildAnimalFactory
        Client3 client = new Client3(new
                        WildAnimalFactory());
        animalFactory = client.getFactory();
        Dog dog = animalFactory.createDog("white");
        Tiger tiger = animalFactory.createTiger("golden and cinnamon");
        dog.displayMe();
        tiger.aboutMe();
        tiger.inviteDog(dog);

        System.out.println("\n***********\n");
```

```
        // Making a pet dog and pet tiger through
        // PetAnimalFactory now.
        client = new Client3(new PetAnimalFactory());
        animalFactory = client.getFactory();
        dog = animalFactory.createDog("black");
        tiger = animalFactory.createTiger("yellow");
        dog.displayMe();
        tiger.aboutMe();
        tiger.inviteDog(dog);
    }
}
```

Q&A Session

4.1 I see that both the Dog and Tiger interfaces contain different number of methods. Is that intentional?

Yes. I used a different number of methods with different names so that you do not assume that these interfaces should have a same number of methods with similar names. This is a change in this third edition of this book.

The inviteDog() method inside the Tiger hierarchy is optional. But I use it to show you the relationship between wild animals and pet animals. This is why, in the output, you see the following lines:

```
The wild tiger says: I saw a wild dog in the jungle.
```

and

```
The pet tiger says: I saw a pet dog in my town.
```

This kind of relationship is important when you create a group of objects that work together to form a kit (or set). This is why this pattern is also known as "Kit."

4.2 What are the challenges of using an abstract factory like this?

Any change in the abstract factory will force you to propagate the modification to the concrete factories. If you follow the design philosophy that says *program to an interface, not to an implementation*, you need to prepare for this. This is one of the key principles that developers should always keep in mind. In most scenarios, developers do not want to change their abstract factories.

113

In addition, the overall architecture is complex, and this is why debugging can become very challenging in some cases.

4.3 How can you distinguish a Simple Factory pattern from a Factory Method pattern or an Abstract Factory pattern?

I discuss the differences between a Simple Factory pattern and a Factory Method pattern in Chapter 3 (See Q&A 3.6).

Let's revisit how client code uses these factories as shown in the following diagrams.

Here's the code snippet from Simple Factory pattern:

```
AnimalFactory factory = new AnimalFactory();
Animal animal = factory.createAnimal("dog");
animal.displayBehavior();

animal = factory.createAnimal("tiger");
animal.displayBehavior();
```

Figure 4-4 shows the Simple Factory pattern.

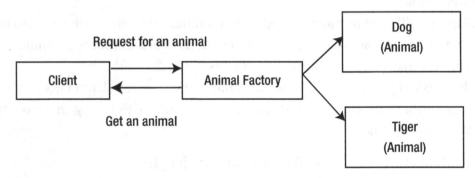

Figure 4-4. *Simple Factory pattern*

Here's the code snippet from the Factory Method pattern (taken from Demonstration 2):

```
AnimalFactory factory;
// Create a tiger and display its behavior
// using TigerFactory.
factory =new TigerFactory();
factory.createAndDisplayAnimal("yellow");

// Create a dog and display its behavior
```

```
// using DogFactory.
factory = new DogFactory();
factory.createAndDisplayAnimal("white");
```

Figure 4-5 shows the Factory Method pattern.

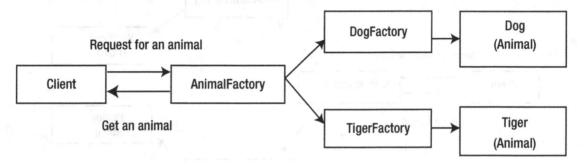

Figure 4-5. *Factory Method pattern*

Here's the code snippet from the Abstract Factory pattern (taken from client code variation 2):

```
AnimalFactory animalFactory;

AnimalFactory animalFactory;

// Making a wild dog and wild tiger through WildAnimalFactory
animalFactory = FactoryProvider.getFactory("wild");
Dog dog = animalFactory.createDog("white");
Tiger tiger = animalFactory.createTiger("golden and cinnamon");
dog.displayMe();
tiger.aboutMe();
tiger.inviteDog(dog);

System.out.println("\n***********\n");

// Making a wild dog and wild tiger through PetAnimalFactory
animalFactory = FactoryProvider.getFactory("pet");
dog = animalFactory.createDog("black");
tiger = animalFactory.createTiger("yellow");
dog.displayMe();
tiger.aboutMe();
tiger.inviteDog(dog);
```

115

Figure 4-6 shows the Abstract Factory pattern.

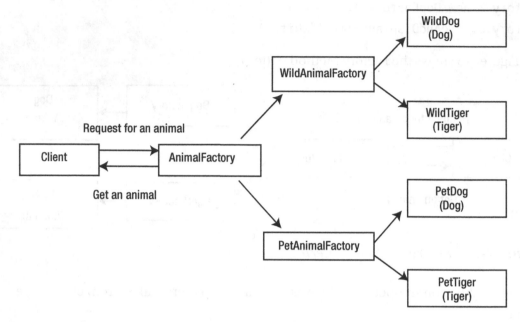

Figure 4-6. *Abstract Factory pattern*

In short, with the Simple Factory pattern, you can separate the code that will vary from the rest of the code (basically, you decouple the client code). This approach helps you to manage the code more easily. Another key advantage of this approach is that the client is unaware of how the objects are created. So, it promotes both security and abstraction.

However, this approach can violate the Open/Closed Principle (you saw this in Chapter 1). You can overcome this drawback using the Factory Method pattern, which allows subclasses to decide how the instantiation process will be completed. Put simply, you delegate the object creation to the subclasses that implement the factory method to create objects.

The abstract factory is basically a factory of factories. It creates a family of related objects, but it does not depend on the concrete classes. In this pattern, you encapsulate a group of individual factories that have a common theme. In this process, you do not instantiate a class directly; instead, you get a concrete factory (you use a provider for this in client code variation 2 and variation 3) and thereafter create products using the factory.

Lastly, I try to keep the examples simple. A factory method promotes inheritance, and its subclasses need to implement the factory method to create objects. The Abstract Factory pattern can promote object composition by creating the related objects using the methods that are exposed in a factory interface. In the end, all of these factories promote loose coupling by reducing the dependencies on concrete classes.

4.4 It would be helpful if you explain how the `newInstance()` method of `javax.xml.parsers.DocumentBuilderFactory` supports the concept of the Abstract Factory pattern.

Notice code segment 1. It is a code snippet to use the newInstance() method of javax.xml.parsers.DocumentBuilderFactory.

Code segment 1:
```
DocumentBuilderFactory factory;
// Get the factory
factory= DocumentBuilderFactory.newInstance();
// Get the builder
DocumentBuilder builder=factory.newDocumentBuilder();
// Making a use of the builder
Document doc=builder.newDocument();
// Some other code skipped
```

Now compare it with the following code (code segment 2). In the client code variation 2, you saw the following lines:

Code segment 2:
```
AnimalFactory animalFactory;
animalFactory = FactoryProvider.getFactory("wild");
Dog dog = animalFactory.createDog("white");
dog.displayMe();
```

If you carefully examine code segment 2, you will see the following steps:

- Get a factory.

- Make a product (Dog, in this case).

- Use the product.

These steps are similar to code segment 1. You may also notice the following:

- Both `AnimalFactory` and `DocumentBuilderFactory` are abstract classes.

- The `DocumentBuilder` is an abstract class and `Dog` is an interface [It means that you can use `Dog` as an abstract class too].

- The `getFactory()` and `newInstance()` methods are static.

I hope you see the similarities now.

CHAPTER 5

Prototype Pattern

This chapter covers the Prototype pattern.

GoF Definition

It specifies the kinds of objects to create using a prototypical instance and creates new objects by copying this prototype.

Concept

This pattern provides an alternative method for instantiating new objects by copying or cloning an instance of an existing object. Thus, you can avoid the expense of creating a new instance using this concept. Why is this important? There are various reasons. Here are some examples:

- You may need some resources to make an instance, but these resources may not be easily available to you.

- The construction of a new instance from scratch is a time-consuming operation.

If you examine the intent of the pattern (the GoF definition) closely, you'll see that the core idea of this pattern is to create an object that is based on another object. This existing object acts as a template for the new object.

When you examine the code for this pattern, in general, you'll see that there is an abstract class or interface that plays the role of an abstract prototype. This abstract prototype contains a cloning method that is implemented by the concrete prototype(s). A client can create a new object by asking a prototype to clone itself. You'll see that the upcoming program (Demonstration 1) follows the same approach.

119

© Vaskaran Sarcar 2022
V. Sarcar, *Java Design Patterns*, https://doi.org/10.1007/978-1-4842-7971-7_5

Real-Life Example

Suppose you have a master copy of a valuable document. You need to incorporate some changes to it in order to analyze the effect of the changes. In this case, you can make a photocopy of the original document and make the changes on the photocopied document.

Computer World Example

Let's assume that you already have a stable application. In the future, you may want to modify the application with some small changes. You must start with a copy of your original application, make the changes, and then analyze further. Surely you do not want to start coding from scratch to merely make a change; this would cost you time and money.

In Java programming, the `clone()` method of the `Object` class is an example of the Prototype pattern. This method can create and return a copy of an existing object. In this context, your class needs to be `Cloneable`. Let's see what Javadoc says about the `clone()` method. Here are some important points for your immediate reference:

- It creates and returns a copy of this object. The precise meaning of "copy" may depend on the class of the object.

- By convention, the returned object should be obtained by calling `super.clone`.

- By convention, the object returned by this method should be independent of this object (which is being cloned). To achieve this independence, it may be necessary to modify one or more fields of the object returned by `super.clone` before returning it.

- The method `clone` for class `Object` performs a specific cloning operation. First, if the class of this object does not implement the interface `Cloneable`, then a `CloneNotSupportedException` is thrown.

Implementation

This example follows the structure shown in Figure 5-1.

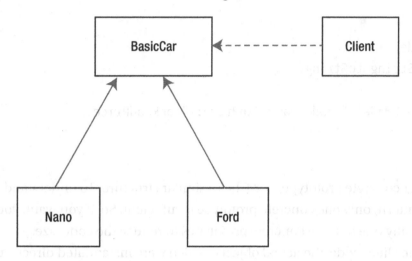

Figure 5-1. *Prototype example*

Here BasicCar is the prototype. It is an abstract class that has an abstract method called clone(). Nano and Ford are the concrete classes (i.e., concrete prototypes) that inherit from BasicCar. Both concrete classes implement the clone() method. Initially, you create a BasicCar object with a default price. Later you modify that price as per the model. The Cient.java file represents the client in this implementation.

Inside the Nano class constructor and the Ford class constructor, you add a random price to the basic price to generate the on-road price of a car. Here is the Nano class:

```
import java.util.Random;

class Nano extends BasicCar {
    public Nano(String modelName) {
        this.modelName = modelName;
        // The base price for a Nano car
        basePrice = 5000;
        // Set the on-Road price
        onRoadPrice = basePrice + (new Random()).nextInt(1000);
    }
```

```
@Override
public BasicCar clone() throws CloneNotSupportedException {
  return (Nano) super.clone();
}

@Override
public String toString()
{
  return "Model:"+modelName+"\nPrice: "+onRoadPrice;
}
}
```

The other concrete prototype, Ford, has a similar structure. To understand the prototype pattern, only one concrete prototype is sufficient. So, if you want, you can drop/ignore any one of these concrete prototypes to reduce the code size.

Inside the client code, the actual objects (which were instantiated directly using the new operator) use the toString() method to show the model and price of the car. There's also an optional method printCarDetail() inside the client code; it's used to increase the on-road price of a cloned car. This may give you an idea of how to edit a cloned object. Here is the method description:

```
private static void printCarDetail(BasicCar car) {
 System.out.println("Editing a cloned model:");
 System.out.println("Model: " + car.modelName);
 // Editing the on-Road price of a car
 // This is an optional step
 car.onRoadPrice += 100;
 System.out.println("It's on-road price:$" + car.onRoadPrice);
}
```

Lastly and most importantly, you'll see the use of the clone() method in the upcoming examples. It is defined in the Object class. You know that the Object class is the root of the class hierarchy. Every class has Object as a superclass in Java.

Class Diagram

Figure 5-2 shows the class diagram. In the upcoming demonstration, you'll see that
BasicCar is an abstract class that implements the java.lang.Cloneable interface.

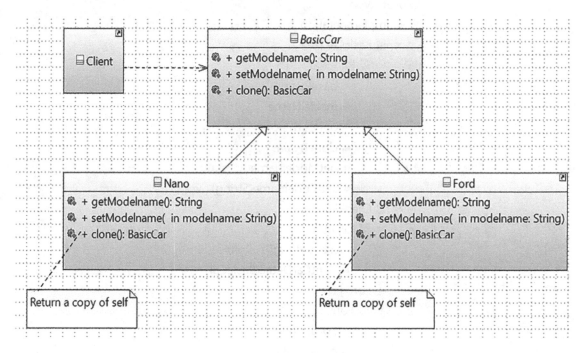

Figure 5-2. *Class diagram*

Package Explorer View

Figure 5-3 shows the high-level structure of the program.

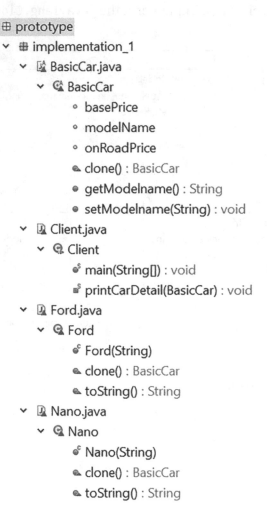

Figure 5-3. *Package Explorer view*

Demonstration 1

Here's the implementation. All classes are stored inside the package `jdp3e.prototype.implementation_1`.

// BasicCar.java

```java
abstract class BasicCar implements Cloneable {
    public String modelName;
    public int basePrice=0,onRoadPrice=0;

    public String getModelname() {
      return modelName;
     }

    public void setModelname(String modelname) {
      this.modelName = modelname;
    }

    public BasicCar clone() throws CloneNotSupportedException {
            return  (BasicCar)super.clone();
    }
}
```

// Nano.java

```java
import java.util.Random;

class Nano extends BasicCar {

    public Nano(String modelName) {
        this.modelName = modelName;
        // The base price for a Nano car
        basePrice = 5000;
        // Set the on-road price
        onRoadPrice = basePrice + (new
                    Random()).nextInt(1000);
    }

    @Override
    public BasicCar clone() throws CloneNotSupportedException {
       return (Nano) super.clone();
    }
```

```java
  @Override
   public String toString()
    {
     return "Model: "+modelName+"\nPrice: "+onRoadPrice;
    }
}
```

// Ford.java

```java
import java.util.Random;

class Ford extends BasicCar {

    public Ford(String modelName) {
        this.modelName = modelName;
        // The base price for a Ford car
        basePrice = 40000;
        // Set the on-road price
        onRoadPrice=basePrice+ (new Random()).nextInt(1000);
    }

   @Override
   public BasicCar clone() throws CloneNotSupportedException {
     return (Ford) super.clone();
   }

   @Override
   public String toString() {
     return "Model: "+modelName+"\nPrice: "+onRoadPrice;
   }
}
```

// Client.java

```java
class Client {
    public static void main(String[] args) throws
                        CloneNotSupportedException {

     System.out.println("***Prototype Pattern Demo***\n");
```

```
    // Working with a Nano car
    BasicCar nano = new Nano("Nano XM624 cc");
    System.out.println(nano);
    System.out.println("-------");

    // Getting a cloned version of Nano
    BasicCar clonedCar;
    clonedCar = nano.clone();
    // Working with the cloned Nano
    printCarDetail(clonedCar);

    System.out.println("-------\n");

    // Working with a Ford car copy
    BasicCar ford = new Ford("Ford Aspire");
    System.out.println(ford);
    System.out.println("-------");

    // Getting a cloned version of Ford
    clonedCar = ford.clone();
    // Working with the cloned Ford
    printCarDetail(clonedCar);
    System.out.println("-------\n");
  }
  private static void printCarDetail(BasicCar car) {
    System.out.println("Editing a cloned model:");
    System.out.println("Model: " + car.modelName);
    // Editing the on-Road price of a car
    // This is an optional step
    car.onRoadPrice += 100;
    System.out.println("It's on-road price: $" + car.onRoadPrice);
  }

}
```

Output

Here is a possible output:

```
***Prototype Pattern Demo***

Model: Nano XM624 cc
Price: 5003
-------
Editing a cloned model:
Model: Nano XM624 cc
Its on-road price: $5103
-------

Model: Ford Aspire
Price: 40020
-------
Editing a cloned model:
Model: Ford Aspire
Its on-road price: $40120
-------
```

Note   You may see a different price in your system because the code generates a random price in the constructors of the Nano and Ford classes. This example also ensures that the price of a Ford is greater than a Nano.

Modified Implementation

Notice that in demonstration 1, before making a clone, the client instantiated the objects as follows:

```
BasicCar nano = new Nano("Nano XM624 cc");
BasicCar ford = new Ford("Ford Aspire");
```

This is fine, but in some examples of the Prototype pattern, you may notice an additional participant that creates the prototypes and supplies them to a client. Experts often like this approach because it hides the complexity of creating new instances inside the client. So let's introduce a CarMaker class and modify the implementation.

Class Diagram

Figure 5-4 shows some important changes in this modified class diagram. This time there is a new class called CarMaker that is used to get a new car or a cloned car. Notice that this class contains two BasicCar references inside it, nano and ford.

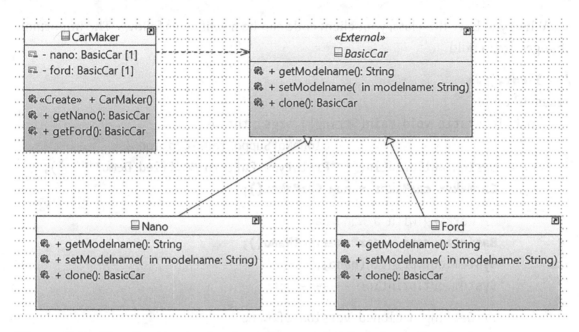

Figure 5-4. *Key changes in the class diagram for demonstration 2*

Demonstration 2

To demonstrate the modified implementation, add the following class called CarMaker:

```
// CarMaker.java
class CarMaker {
    BasicCar nano, ford;

    public CarMaker() {
        nano = new Nano("Nano XM624 cc");
        ford = new Ford("Ford Aspire");
    }

    public BasicCar getNano() throws
            CloneNotSupportedException {
        return nano.clone();
    }
}
```

```
    public BasicCar getFord() throws
            CloneNotSupportedException {
        return ford.clone();
    }
}
```

When you have this class, your client code can be modified as follows. The important changes are in bold.

```
// Client.java
class Client {
    public static void main(String[] args) throws
                                  CloneNotSupportedException {
        System.out.println("***Prototype Pattern Modified Demo***\n");
        CarMaker carMaker = new CarMaker();

        // Working with a Nano car
        BasicCar nano = carMaker.getNano();
        System.out.println(nano);
        System.out.println("-------");

        // Getting a cloned version of Nano
        BasicCar clonedCar;
        clonedCar = nano.clone();
        // Working with the cloned Nano
        printCarDetail(clonedCar);

        System.out.println("-------\n");

        // Working with a Ford car copy
        BasicCar ford = carMaker.getFord();
        System.out.println(ford);
        System.out.println("-------");

        // Getting a cloned version of Ford
        clonedCar = ford.clone();
```

```
        // Working with the cloned Ford
        printCarDetail(clonedCar);
        System.out.println("-------\n");
    }

    private static void printCarDetail(BasicCar car) {
        System.out.println("Editing a cloned model:");
        System.out.println("Model: " + car.modelName);
        // Editing the on-Road price of a car
        // This is an optional step
        car.onRoadPrice += 100;
        System.out.println("It's on-road price: $" + car.onRoadPrice);
    }
}
```

To avoid repetition, I did not show the other participants, which were already shown in demonstration 1. When you download the source code from the Apress website, refer to the `implementation_2` folder inside the `prototype` folder to get the complete program.

Output

Here is a possible output:

```
***Prototype Pattern Modified Demo***

Model: Nano XM624 cc
Price: 5356
-------
Editing a cloned model:
Model: Nano XM624 cc
Its on-road price: $5456
-------
```

```
Model: Ford Aspire
Price: 40501
-------
Editing a cloned model:
Model: Ford Aspire
Its on-road price: $40601
```

Analysis

This output is similar to the previous output and there is no magic. The CarMaker class serves your needs, but there is a potential drawback to it. Notice that you initialize the cars inside the constructor of CarMaker. As a result, it always creates instances of both car types when this class is initialized. If you want to implement a lazy initialization, you can modify the CarMaker class as follows:

```
/**
 * @author Vaskaran Sarcar
 * Alternative version of the CarMaker class.
 */
class CarMaker {
    BasicCar nano, ford;

    public CarMaker() {

    }

    public BasicCar getNano() throws
                    CloneNotSupportedException {

      if (nano!=null) {
          // A Nano instance was created earlier.
          // Returning a clone of it.
          return nano.clone();
        } else {
```

```
        /*
          Create a nano for the first time and return it.
        */
        nano = new Nano("Nano XM624 cc");
        return nano;
      }
    }

public BasicCar getFord() throws
                CloneNotSupportedException {
    if (ford!=null){
        // A Ford instance was created earlier.
        // Returning a clone of it.
        return ford.clone();
    } else {
        /*
          Create a Ford for the first
          time and return it.
        */
        nano = new Ford("Ford Aspire");
        return nano;
      }
    }
}
```

Further Improvements

These are not the ultimate modifications. Why? Let's go through the following points:

- In Chapter 7, when I discuss the Singleton pattern, you'll learn that in a multithreading environment you can produce additional objects when you check the if condition(s). Since you'll get the idea about the possible solutions also in Chapter 7, I won't repeat the same discussion here.

- In Chapter 8, when I discuss the Proxy pattern, I show you the usefulness of the package-private visibility. There you'll see that a client cannot directly make an instance of `ConcreteSubject` so it is forced to use the `ProxySubject` class. You can apply the same concept to prevent direct instantiation of a `Nano` or a `Ford` inside client code and force your client to use the `CarMaker` class only.

I believe that you now have a clear idea about the intent of this pattern.

Q&A Session

5.1 What are the advantages of using the Prototype design pattern?

Here are some important usages:

- You do not want to modify the existing object and experiment on it.

- You can include or discard products at runtime.

- In some contexts, you can create new instances at a cheaper cost.

- You can focus on the key activities rather than focusing on complicated instance creation processes. For example, once you ignore the complex object creation processes, you can simply start with cloning or copying objects and implementing the remaining parts.

- You want to examine a proposed behavior and its impact before you fully implement it in your application.

5.2 What are the challenges associated with using the Prototype design pattern?

Here are some challenges:

- Each subclass needs to implement the cloning or coping mechanism.

- Implementing the cloning mechanism can be challenging if the objects under consideration do not support copying or if there are circular references. For example, in Java, a class with `clone()` method needs to implement the Cloneable marker interface; otherwise, it will throw a `CloneNotSupportedException`.

- In this example, you use super.clone(). This clone() method performs a shallow copy, not a deep copy. (If you want to learn more, put your cursor on the eclipse editor and go through the detailed description). If you need a deep copy for your application, that can be expensive.

Note   The class Object does not itself implement the interface Cloneable. So, if you call the clone method on an Object type, you will receive an exception at runtime.

5.3 Can you elaborate on the difference between a shallow copy and a deep copy?
  The following discussion explains the difference between these two techniques.

Note   The following discussion is added for the readers who are not aware of this difference. I assume that expert programmers are familiar with it. If you know the difference, you can skip the following discussion and continue reading the next Q&A.

Shallow Copy vs. Deep Copy

A shallow copy creates a new object and then copies the non-static fields from the original object to the new object. If there is a value type field in the original object, a bit-by-bit copy is performed. But if the field is a reference type, this method will copy the reference, not the actual object. Let's try to understand the mechanism with a simple diagram; see Figure 5-5. Suppose you have object X1 and it has a reference to another object, Y1. Again, object Y1 has a reference to object Z1.

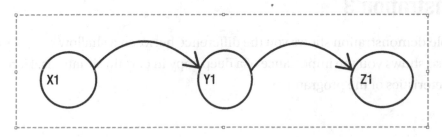

Figure 5-5. *Before the shallow copy of the references*

Now, with a shallow copy of X1, a new object (say, X2) will be created that will also have a reference to Y1 (see Figure 5-6).

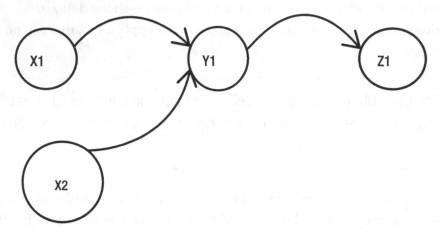

Figure 5-6.   *After a shallow copy of the reference*

You use clone() in the previous implementation. It performs a shallow copy.

But for a deep copy of X1, a new object (say, X3) will be created, and X3 will have a reference to the new object Y3 that is a copy of Y1. Also, Y3, in turn, will have a reference to another new object, Z3, that is a copy of Z1 (see Figure 5-7).

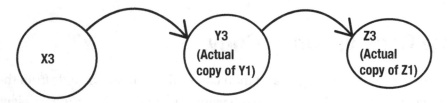

Figure 5-7.   *After a deep copy of the reference*

Now consider the following demonstration for a better understanding.

Demonstration 3

This simple demonstration shows you the difference between a shallow copy and a deep copy. It also shows you the importance of a deep copy in certain situations. Here are the key characteristics of the program:

- This example has two classes, Employee and EmpAddress.

- EmpAddress has a single field called Address. It is used to set the address of an employee. The Employee class has three fields: id, name, and empAddress of types int, String, and EmpAdress, respectively.

- To create an Employee object, you need to pass an id of the employee and their name. At the same time, you need to pass the address.

```
EmpAddress initialAddress = new EmpAddress("21, abc Road,USA");
Employee emp = new Employee(1, "John", initialAddress);
```

- In the client code, first you create an Employee object emp and then you create another object empClone through cloning:

```
System.out.println("\nMaking a clone of emp now.");
Employee empClone = (Employee) emp.cloneEmployee();
```

- Later you change the values inside empClone.

- When you use a shallow copy, you'll see that as a side effect of this change, the address of the emp object also changes, but this is unwanted. (Remember that the basic idea of the Prototype pattern is straightforward: you should not change the original object when you work on a cloned copy of the object).

- In this upcoming example, initially the code for the deep copy is commented out so that you can see the effect of shallow copy only.

Now go through the demonstration. You'll find this program inside the package jdp3e.prototype.shallow_vs_deep_copy.

// EmpAddress.java

```
class EmpAddress implements Cloneable {
    String address;

    public EmpAddress(String address) {
        this.address = address;
    }
```

```java
    @Override
    public String toString() {
        return this.address;
    }

    public EmpAddress cloneAddress() throws
            CloneNotSupportedException {
    // Shallow Copy
    return (EmpAddress) this.clone();
    }
}
// Employee.java

class Employee implements Cloneable {
    int id;
    String name;
    EmpAddress empAddress;

    public Employee(int id, String name, EmpAddress empAddress) {
        this.id = id;
        this.name = name;
        this.empAddress = empAddress;
    }

    @Override
    public String toString() {
        String empDetail = null;
        empDetail = "Employee detail: Id: " + id + " Name:
                    " + name + " Address: " + empAddress;
        return empDetail;
    }

    public Employee cloneEmployee() throws
                        CloneNotSupportedException {
        // For the shallow Copy
        return (Employee) this.clone();
```

```
        // For the deep copy
        // Employee employee = (Employee) this.clone();
        // employee.empAddress = (EmpAddress) this.empAddress.
        // cloneAddress();
        // return employee;

    }
}
```

// Client.java

```
class Client {

 public static void main(String[] args) throws
                        CloneNotSupportedException {
  System.out.println("***Shallow vs Deep Copy Demo.***\n");
  EmpAddress initialAddress = new EmpAddress("21, abc Road, USA");
  Employee emp = new Employee(1, "John", initialAddress);

  System.out.println("The original object is emp which is as follows:");
  System.out.println(emp);

  System.out.println("\nMaking a clone of emp now.");
  Employee empClone = (Employee) emp.cloneEmployee();
  System.out.println("The empClone object is as follows:");
  System.out.println(empClone);

  System.out.println("\n--Changing the detail of the cloned object now.--");
  empClone.id = 10;
  empClone.name = "Sam";
  empClone.empAddress.address = "123, xyz Road, Canada";
  System.out.println("\nNow the emp object is as follows:");
  System.out.println(emp);
  System.out.println("\nAnd the emp1Clone object is as follows:");
  System.out.println(empClone);

 }
}
```

Output From Shallow Copy Implementation

Here is the output of the program:

```
***Shallow vs Deep Copy Demo.***

The original object is emp which is as follows:
Employee detail: Id: 1 Name: John Address: 21, abc Road, USA

Making a clone of emp now.
The empClone object is as follows:
Employee detail: Id: 1 Name: John Address: 21, abc Road, USA

--Changing the detail of the cloned object now.--

Now the emp object is as follows:
Employee detail: Id: 1 Name: John Address: 123, xyz Road, Canada

And the emp1Clone object is as follows:
Employee detail: Id: 10 Name: Sam Address: 123, xyz Road, Canada
```

Analysis

You can see an unwanted side effect. In the previous output, you can see that the address of the original object (emp) is modified due to the modification to the cloned object (empClone). This happened because the original object and the cloned object both point to the same address and are not 100% disjointed. Figure 5-8 depicts the scenario better.

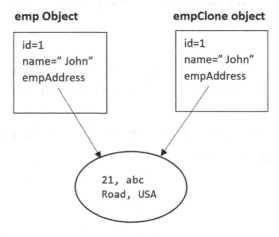

Figure 5-8. _Shallow copy_

Now let's experiment with a deep copy implementation. Let's modify the clone cloneEmployee()of the Employee class as follows. Uncomment the code for the deep copy and comment out the code for the shallow copy here. Notice the changes in bold.

```
public Employee cloneEmployee() throws CloneNotSupportedException {
    // For the shallow Copy
    // return (Employee) this.clone();

    // For the deep copy
    Employee employee = (Employee) this.clone();
    employee.empAddress = (EmpAddress) this.empAddress.cloneAddress();
    return employee;

}
```

Output From Deep Copy Implementation

Here is the modified output:

```
***Shallow vs Deep Copy Demo.***

The original object is emp which is as follows:
Employee detail: Id: 1 Name: John Address: 21, abc Road, USA

Making a clone of emp now.
The empClone object is as follows:
Employee detail: Id: 1 Name: John Address: 21, abc Road, USA

--Changing the detail of the cloned object now.--

Now the emp object is as follows:
Employee detail: Id: 1 Name: John Address: 21, abc Road, USA

And the emp1Clone object is as follows:
Employee detail: Id: 10 Name: Sam Address: 123, xyz Road, Canada
```

Analysis

Notice that this time you don't see the unwanted side effect due to the modification to the empClone object. It is because the original object and the cloned object are totally different and independent of each other. Figure 5-9 depicts the scenario.

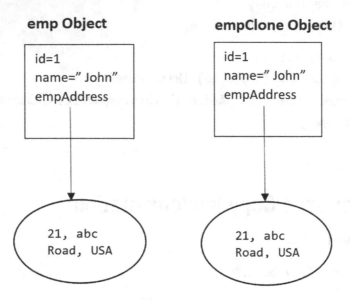

Figure 5-9. *Deep copy*

Q&A Session Continued

5.4 When should I choose a shallow copy over a deep copy (and vice versa)?
   Here are the key differences:

- A shallow copy is faster and less expensive. It is always better if your target object has the primitive fields only.

- A deep copy is expensive and slow. But it is useful if your target object contains many fields that have references to other objects.

5.5 If I need to copy an object, I need to use the clone() method. Is the understanding correct?
   No, there are alternatives available. For example, you can opt for a serialization mechanism when you implement a deep copy, or you can write your own copy constructor, etc. Each approach has its pros and cons. So, in the end, it is the developer's

choice as to which approach fulfills their need. Many objects are really simple, and they do not contain references to other objects. So, to copy those objects, a simple shallow copy mechanism is sufficient.

5.6 In the Javadoc, the return type of the clone() method is protected. But in demonstration 1, it's made public. Is there any specific reason for this?

Yes. When you do this, you enhance its visibility to the maximum, which allows you to access the method from outside the package too. But your observation is correct. Since all parts of demonstration 1 are inside the same package, it was not absolutely necessary.

5.7 Can you show me an example that demonstrates the use of a copy constructor?

Since Java does not support a default copy constructor, you may need to write your own copy constructor. You can consider the following program (Demonstration 4) for your immediate reference.

Demonstration 4

In this example, the Employee and EmpAddress classes both have almost the same description as in the previous demonstration (Demonstration 3). The only difference is that this time, instead of the clone() method in the Employee class, you'll notice the presence of a copy constructor inside it. Let's proceed.

This time you are also using the same instance constructor:

```
public Employee(int id, String name, EmpAddress empAddress) {
    this.id = id;
    this.name = name;
    this.empAddress = empAddress;
}
```

It allows you to create an object of Employee as follows:

```
EmpAddress initialAddress = new EmpAddress("21, abc Road, USA");
Employee emp = new Employee(1, "John",initialAddress);
```

As said before, in this Employee class, there is also a user-defined copy constructor, which is as follows:

```java
// Copy Constructor
public Employee(Employee originalEmployee) throws
                            CloneNotSupportedException {
 this.id = originalEmployee.id;
 this.name = originalEmployee.name;
 this.empAddress = originalEmployee.empAddress.cloneAddress();
}
```

You can see that using the copy constructor, you're copying both the simple type (Id, Name) and the reference type (EmpAddress). So, once an Employee object, say emp, is created, you can create another object named empClone from it using the following code:

```java
Employee empClone= new Employee(emp);
```

As in the previous demonstration, once you create a copy (empClone) from the existing object (emp), you can make changes to the copied object for verification purposes, which is easy to understand. Here is the complete code, which is inside the package jdp3e.prototype.implementation_4:

```java
// EmpAddress.java
class EmpAddress implements Cloneable {
    String address;

    public EmpAddress(String address) {
        this.address = address;
    }

    @Override
    public String toString() {
        return this.address;
    }

    public EmpAddress cloneAddress() throws
                CloneNotSupportedException {
```

```java
        // Shallow Copy
        return (EmpAddress) this.clone();
    }
}

// Employee.java

class Employee implements Cloneable {
    int id;
    String name;
    EmpAddress empAddress;

    public Employee(int id, String name, EmpAddress
                    empAddress) {
        this.id = id;
        this.name = name;
        this.empAddress = empAddress;
    }

    @Override
    public String toString() {
        String empDetail = null;
        empDetail = "Employee detail: Id: " + id + " Name:
                    " + name + " Address: " + empAddress;
        return empDetail;
    }

    // Copy Constructor
    public Employee(Employee originalEmployee) throws
                    CloneNotSupportedException {
        this.id = originalEmployee.id;
        this.name = originalEmployee.name;
        this.empAddress =
            originalEmployee.empAddress.cloneAddress();
    }
}
```

// CopyConstructorDemo.java

```
class CopyConstructorDemo {
 public static void main(String[] args) throws CloneNotSupportedException {
  System.out.println("***A simple copy constructor demo***\n");
  EmpAddress initialAddress = new EmpAddress("21, abc Road, USA");
  Employee emp = new Employee(1, "John", initialAddress);
  System.out.println("The original object is emp which is as follows:");
  System.out.println(emp);
  System.out.println("\n Copying from emp to empCopy now.");
  Employee empCopy = new Employee(emp);
  System.out.println("The empCopy object is as follows:");
  System.out.println(empCopy);
  System.out.println("\n--Changing the detail of the copied object now.--");
  empCopy.id = 10;
  empCopy.name = "Sam";
  empCopy.empAddress.address = "123, xyz Road, Canada";

  System.out.println("\nNow the emp object is as follows:");
  System.out.println(emp);
  System.out.println("\nAnd the empCopy object is as follows:");
  System.out.println(empCopy);

 }
}
```

Output

Here is the output. Notice the bold lines.

```
***A simple copy constructor demo***

The original object is emp which is as follows:
Employee detail: Id: 1 Name: John Address: 21, abc Road, USA

 Copying from emp to empCopy now.
The empCopy object is as follows:
Employee detail: Id: 1 Name: John Address: 21, abc Road, USA
```

--Changing the detail of the copied object now.--

Now the emp object is as follows:
Employee detail: Id: 1 Name: John Address: 21, abc Road, USA

And the empCopy object is as follows:
Employee detail: Id: 10 Name: Sam Address: 123, xyz Road, Canada

Analysis

Notice the final portion of the output. It shows that when you incorporate a change, it is properly reflected in the copied object only.

This chapter showed you multiple implementations of prototype design patterns and discussed the difference between a shallow copy and a deep copy. You also learned the use of a user-defined copy constructor. Now you can move to the next chapter and continue learning another interesting pattern.

CHAPTER 6

Builder Pattern

This chapter covers the Builder pattern.

GoF Definition

It separates the construction of a complex object from its representation so that the same construction processes can create different representations.

Concept

The Builder pattern is useful for creating complex objects that have multiple parts. The object creation process should be independent of these parts. In addition, you should be able to use the same construction process to create different representations of the objects. This pattern is one of those design patterns that are relatively tough to understand on the very first attempt. Once you see the code and analyze the structure, they become easy. So, keep reading.

Before you move forward, let me show you a code snippet and analyze the potential difficulties. Here is a sample class A with a constructor that has many parameters:

```
Class A{

  A(int arg1, int arg2, double arg3,int arg4,B b, C c){
        // Some code to initialize
  }
        // Remaining code is skipped
}
```

Now go through the following points:

© Vaskaran Sarcar 2022
V. Sarcar, *Java Design Patterns*, https://doi.org/10.1007/978-1-4842-7971-7_6

- You need to supply a B class object and a C class object. So, to construct an A class instance, you need to create a B class object and a C class object before you call the A class constructor. So, you consider the B object and the C object as parts of an A object. If you need to make a final object from various parts, the Builder pattern is a good choice.

- You can see that you also need to supply three integer arguments. Since these arguments are similar, understanding and using them can be challenging if you do not follow proper naming (for example, you need to remember their order of appearance). But even proper naming won't help if you see a compiled version of the code. In that case, to understand them, you need to refer to the code documentation. This is why passing too many arguments in a method or constructor is not a recommended practice in general. It is better if you pass a minimum number of arguments (preferably one or zero) at a time. The Builder pattern can help you write better code in a similar case.

As per the GoF book, four different players are involved in this pattern. They have the relationships shown in Figure 6-1.

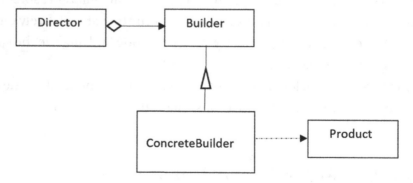

Figure 6-1. *A sample of the Builder pattern*

Here, the Product is the complex object under consideration, and it is the final outcome. In the upcoming examples, vehicles are the products. The Car and MotorCycle classes are used to make the concrete products, cars and motorcycles, respectively. These classes inherit from the Vehicle class.

The `Builder` is an interface that contains the methods to build different parts of a product. The `ConcreteBuilder` implements the `Builder` interface and assembles these parts. In other words, the `ConcreteBuilder` object builds the internal representations of a `Vehicle` instance, and it can have a method that can be called to get this `Vehicle` instance. (As said before, vehicles are the products in the upcoming examples.)

The `Director` is responsible for creating the final object using the `Builder` interface. It is important to note that the `Director` decides the sequence of steps to build the product. You can safely assume that the `Director` can vary the sequence to make different products.

Real-Life Example

To complete an order for a computer, different hardware parts are assembled based on customer preferences. For example, one customer can opt for a 1000GB hard disk with an Intel processor, and another customer can choose a 500GB hard disk with an AMD processor. Here the computer is the final `Product`, the customer plays the role of the `Director,` and the seller/assembler plays the role of the `ConcreteBuilder.`

Computer World Example

The classical GoF book considers an example when a typical application tries to convert one text format to another text format, such as converting from Rich Text Format (RTF) to ASCII. Typically, there is a reader and a converter. The reader parses the document and converts the document to the target format using a converter. This converter has specialized subclasses that perform different types of conversions and assemble the object using an abstract interface. In this example, the converter plays the role of a *builder* and the reader plays the role of a *director*. Here are a few more examples:

- The `Java.util.Calendar.Builder` class is an example in this category. But it is available from `Java 8` onwards only.

- You can also consider the `java.lang.StringBuilder` class as a close example in this context. But you need to remember that the GoF definition also says that when using this pattern, you can use the same construction process to make different representations. In this context, this example does not fully qualify for the GoF's definition.

Implementation

In demonstration 1, `Builder` is used for the `Builder` interface and `CarBuilder` and `MotorCycleBuilder` are two `ConcreteBuilders`. `Car` and `MotorCycle` are the concrete products. The `Director` class has its usual meaning: it instructs a builder to make a product. In demonstration 1, `CarDirector` and `MotorCycleDirector` are the concrete directors that inherit from the abstract class `Director`. Let's examine them one by one.

Start with the `Builder` interface, which defines the possible methods to build different parts for a vehicle:

```
interface Builder {
    void addBrandName();

    void buildBody();

    void insertWheels();

    // The following method is used to
    // retrieve the object that is constructed.
    Vehicle getVehicle();
}
```

`CarBuilder` and `MotorCycleBuilder` implement this interface. They provide the implementation as per their needs. Here is a sample:

```
// The CarBuilder builds cars.
class CarBuilder implements Builder {
    Car car;

    public CarBuilder() {
        car=new Car("Ford");
    }
    @Override
    public void addBrandName() {
        car.add(" Adding the car brand: " + car.brandName);
    }
    @Override
    public void buildBody() {
```

```
        car.add(" Making the car body.");
    }

    @Override
     public void insertWheels() {
        car.add(" 4 wheels are added to the car.");
    }

    @Override
    public Vehicle getVehicle() {
        return car;
    }
}
```

CarDirector and the MotorCycleDirector inherit from the abstract class Director. They provide the step-by-step process for building a vehicle. Here is a sample with supporting comments:

```
// Director class
abstract class Director {
    // Director knows how to use/instruct the
    // builder to create a vehicle.
    public abstract Vehicle instruct(Builder builder);
}

/**
 * The CarDirector directs the
 * car's instantiation steps.
 */

class CarDirector extends Director {
    // The car director follows
    // its own sequence:
    // Make body-> add wheels->then add the brand name.
    public Vehicle instruct(Builder builder) {
        builder.buildBody();
        builder.insertWheels();
```

```
        builder.addBrandName();
        return builder.getVehicle();
    }
}
```

Inside the client code, you make one car and one motorcycle. Notice that you create the builder object before a `Director` object uses it. The `Director` instance invokes the `instruct(...)` method to instruct a builder object on how to assemble a product. Here is the sample for making a car:

```
// Making a car
Builder builder = new CarBuilder();
Director director = new CarDirector();
Vehicle vehicle=director.instruct(builder);
vehicle.showProduct();
```

The `Vehicle` is an abstract class that is easy to understand. Notice the use of a linked list data structure to combine different parts of a vehicle. Here is its definition:

```
abstract class Vehicle {
    /*
     * You can use any data structure that you prefer.
     * I have used LinkedList<String> in this case.
     */

    private LinkedList<String> parts;

    public Vehicle() {
        parts = new LinkedList<String>();
    }

    public void add(String part) {
        // Adding parts
        parts.addLast(part);
    }

    public void showProduct() {
        System.out.println("These are the construction sequences:");
```

```
        for (String part : parts)
            System.out.println(part);
    }
}
```

The Car and MortorCycle classes extend this Vehicle class and are used to get a final product such as a car or a motorcycle.

Now you can go through the complete demonstration.

Class Diagram

Figure 6-2 shows the class diagram.

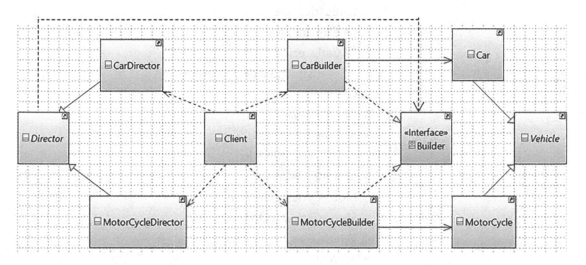

Figure 6-2. *Class diagram*

Package Explorer View

Figure 6-3 shows the high-level structure of the program.

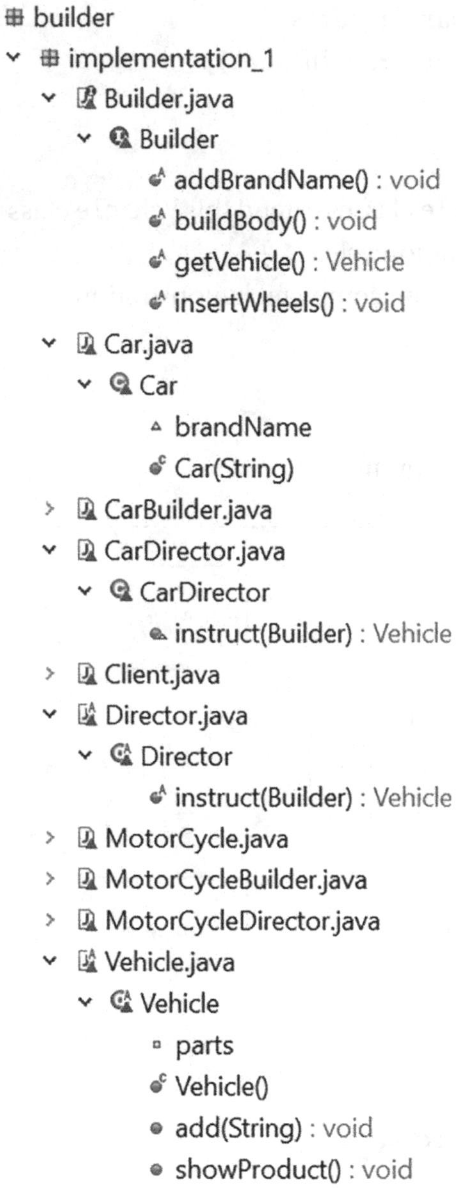

⊞ builder
⌄ ⊞ implementation_1
  ⌄ 📗 Builder.java
    ⌄ 🆀 Builder
      ⚬ addBrandName() : void
      ⚬ buildBody() : void
      ⚬ getVehicle() : Vehicle
      ⚬ insertWheels() : void
  ⌄ 📄 Car.java
    ⌄ 🆀 Car
      △ brandName
      ⚬ Car(String)
  › 📄 CarBuilder.java
  ⌄ 📄 CarDirector.java
    ⌄ 🆀 CarDirector
      ⚬ instruct(Builder) : Vehicle
  › 📄 Client.java
  ⌄ 📄 Director.java
    ⌄ 🆀 Director
      ⚬ instruct(Builder) : Vehicle
  › 📄 MotorCycle.java
  › 📄 MotorCycleBuilder.java
  › 📄 MotorCycleDirector.java
  ⌄ 📄 Vehicle.java
    ⌄ 🆀 Vehicle
      ▫ parts
      ⚬ Vehicle()
      ● add(String) : void
      ● showProduct() : void

Figure 6-3. *Package Explorer view*

Note   This program has many parts. To make the diagram short and simple, I just expand `Car`, `CarBuilder`, and `CarDirector` along with the necessary parts. You can also refer to the class diagram (Figure 6-2) if you need it. I follow the same mechanism for other snapshots of the book, so when a snapshot is really big, I expand/show only the important parts and make it short.

Demonstration 1

Here's the complete implementation. All parts of the program are stored inside the package named `jdp3e.builder.implementation_1`.

Note   If you want to reuse some of these parts (e.g., `Vehicle.java`, `Car.java`, and `MotorCycle.java`), you can change their respective visibility to `public` and import these parts in a different demonstration. To execute a program, I put all these parts in the same folder, so I generally choose `package-private` visibility. This same comment applies to all programs in this book.

```java
// Builder.java
// This is the common interface
interface Builder {

    void addBrandName();

    void buildBody();

    void insertWheels();

    // The following method is used to
    // retrieve the object that is constructed.
    Vehicle getVehicle();
}
```

// CarBuilder.java

```java
// The CarBuilder builds cars.

class CarBuilder implements Builder {

    Car car;

    public CarBuilder() {
        car=new Car("Ford");
    }
    @Override
    public void addBrandName() {
        car.add(" Adding the car brand: " + car.brandName);
    }
    @Override
    public void buildBody() {
        car.add(" Making the car body.");
    }
    @Override
    public void insertWheels() {
        car.add(" 4 wheels are added to the car.");
    }

    @Override
    public Vehicle getVehicle() {
        return car;
    }

}
```

// MotorCycleBuilder.java

```java
// The MotorCycleBuilder builds motorcycles.

class MotorCycleBuilder implements Builder {

    MotorCycle motorCycle;

    public MotorCycleBuilder() {
     motorCycle=new MotorCycle("Honda");
    }
```

```java
        @Override
        public void addBrandName() {
         motorCycle.add(" Adding the brand name: " +
                            motorCycle.brandName);
        }

        @Override
        public void buildBody() {
         motorCycle.add(" Making the body of the motorcycle.");
        }

        @Override
        public void insertWheels() {
         motorCycle.add(" 2 wheels are added to the motorcycle.");
        }

        @Override
        public Vehicle getVehicle() {
             return motorCycle;
        }
}
```

// Vehicle.java

```java
/**
 * The Vehicle class is used to create the products.
 * Making the class abstract, so that
 * you cannot instantiate from it directly.
 */
import java.util.LinkedList;
abstract class Vehicle {
    /*
     * You can use any data structure that you prefer.
     * I have used LinkedList<String> in this case.
     */

    private LinkedList<String> parts;
```

```java
        public Vehicle() {
            parts = new LinkedList<String>();
        }

        public void add(String part) {
            // Adding parts
            parts.addLast(part);
        }

        public void showProduct() {
            System.out.println("These are the construction sequences:");
            for (String part : parts)
                System.out.println(part);
        }
}
```

// Car.java

```java
class Car extends Vehicle{
    String brandName;
    public Car(String brandName) {
        this.brandName=brandName;
        System.out.println("\nWe are about to make a " +
                            brandName+ " car.");
    }
}
```

// MotorCycle.java

```java
class MotorCycle extends Vehicle{
    String brandName;
    public MotorCycle(String brandName) {
        this.brandName=brandName;
        System.out.println("\nWe are about to make a " +
                            brandName+ " motorcycle.");
    }
}
```

// Director.java

```java
abstract class Director {
    // Director knows how to use/instruct the
    // builder to create a vehicle.
    public abstract Vehicle instruct(Builder builder);

}
```

// CarDirector.java

```java
/**
 * The CarDirector directs the
 * car's instantiation steps.
 */

class CarDirector extends Director {
    // The car director follows
    // its own sequence:
    // Make body-> add wheels->then add the brand name.
    public Vehicle instruct(Builder builder) {
        builder.buildBody();
        builder.insertWheels();
        builder.addBrandName();
        return builder.getVehicle();
    }
}
```

// MotorCycleDirector.java

```java
/**
 *  The motorcycle director directs the
 *  motorcycle's instantiation steps.
 */
```

```java
class MotorCycleDirector extends Director {
    // The motor cycle director follows
    // its own sequence:
    // Add brand name-> make body-> insert wheels.
    public Vehicle instruct(Builder builder) {
        builder.addBrandName();
        builder.buildBody();
        builder.insertWheels();
        return builder.getVehicle();
    }
}
```

// Client.java

```java
class Client {

    public static void main(String[] args) {
        System.out.println("*** Builder Pattern Demonstration. ***");

        // Making a car

        Builder builder = new CarBuilder();
        Director director = new CarDirector();
        Vehicle vehicle=director.instruct(builder);
        vehicle.showProduct();

        // Making a motorcycle

        builder = new MotorCycleBuilder();
        director = new MotorCycleDirector();
        vehicle=director.instruct(builder);
        vehicle.showProduct();
    }

}
```

```
*** Builder Pattern Demonstration. ***

We are about to make a Ford car.
These are the construction sequences:
 Making the car body.
 4 wheels are added to the car.
 Adding the car brand: Ford

We are about to make a Honda motorcycle.
These are the construction sequences:
 Adding the brand name: Honda
 Making the body of the motorcycle.
 2 wheels are added to the motorcycle.
```

Q&A Session

6.1 What is the advantage of using a Builder pattern?

Here are some advantages:

- You direct the builder to build the objects step by step, and you promote encapsulation by hiding the details of the complex construction process. The director can retrieve the final product from the builder when the whole construction is over. In general, at a high level, you seem to have only one method that makes the complete product, but other internal methods are involved in the creation process. So, you have finer control over the construction process.

- Using this pattern, the same construction process can produce different products.

- In short, by changing the type of a builder, you change the internal representation of the product.

6.2 What are the drawbacks associated with a Builder pattern?

Here are some challenges:

- It is not suitable if you want to deal with mutable objects (which can be modified later).

- You may need to duplicate some portion of the code. These duplications may cause a performance impact in some contexts.

- To create more products, you need to create more concrete builders.

6.3 In demonstration 1, Builder is an interface. Could you use an abstract class instead of the interface in the illustration of this pattern?

Yes. You could use an abstract class instead of an interface in this example.

6.4 How do you decide whether to use an abstract class or an interface in an application?

If you want to have some centralized or default behaviors, an abstract class is a better choice. In those cases, you can provide some default implementation. On the other hand, the interface implementation starts from scratch and indicates some kind of rules/contracts such as what is to be done, but it does not enforce the "how" part upon you. Also, interfaces are preferred when you try to implement the concept of multiple inheritance.

Remember that if you need to add a new method in an interface, then you need to track down all the implementations of that interface, and you need to put the concrete implementation for that method in all those places. In such a case, an abstract class is a better choice because you can add a new method in an abstract class with a default implementation, and the existing code can run smoothly.

Java has taken special care on this last point. Java 8 introduced the use of the `default` keyword in the interface. From Java 8 onwards, you can prefix the word `default` before your intended method signature and provide a default implementation. Interface methods are public by default, so you do not need to mark them by the keyword `public`.

Here are the summarized suggestions from the ORACLE Java documentation (`https://docs.oracle.com/javase/tutorial/java/IandI/abstract.html`). You should give preferences to abstract class for the following scenarios:

- You want to share code among multiple closely related classes.

- The classes that extend the abstract class can have many common methods or fields, or they require non-public access modifiers inside them.

- You want to use non-static or/and non-final fields that enable you to define methods that can access and modify the state of the object to which they belong.

On the other hand, you should give preferences to interfaces for these scenarios:

- You expect that several unrelated classes are going to implement your interface. For example, the interfaces `Comparable` and `Cloneable` can be implemented by many unrelated classes.

- You express your concern only to specify the behavior of a particular data type, but it does not matter how the implementer implements it.

- You want to use the concept of multiple inheritance in your application.

6.5 Why are you using a separate class for the director? You could use the client code to play the role of the director.

No one restricts you from doing that. In the preceding implementation, I wanted to separate this role from the client code. But in the upcoming demonstration, I use the client as a director.

6.6 What do you mean by *client code*?

A client is any class that uses another class (or interface). In the previous program, the class that contains the `main()` method is the client code. In most parts of the book, with the words *client code*, I mean the same.

6.7 You have talked several times about varying steps. I can see that the car director and the motorcycle director follow a different sequence of steps. Is this correct?

Yes. It is a good find. The upcoming implementation is even better. This demonstration uses method chaining to vary the steps inside the client code. It is very useful in this kind of design.

Alternative Implementation

Now I'll show you an alternative implementation. Here are the key characteristics of the modified implementation:

- The client code itself plays the role of a director in this implementation.

- This time I show you the use of method chaining to make a product with varying steps.

- Similar to the previous example, `Builder` represents the builder interface but the return type of the first three methods is changed (earlier it was void; now it is `Builder`). Notice the following interface with the changes in bold:

```
interface Builder {

    Builder addBrandName();

    Builder buildBody();

    Builder insertWheels();

    // The following method is used to
    // retrieve the object that is constructed.
    Vehicle getVehicle();
}
```

- Just like demonstration 1, the `CarBuilder` and `MotorCycleBuilder` classes implement all the methods defined in the interface. Here is a sample with the key changes in bold:

```
class CarBuilder implements Builder {

Car car;

public CarBuilder() {
car=new Car("Ford");}
@Override
public Builder addBrandName() {
```

```
        // Starting with brand name
        car.add(" Adding the car brand:" + car.brandName);
        return this;
    }
    @Override
    public Builder buildBody() {
        car.add(" Making the car body.");
        return this;
    }

    public Builder insertWheels() {
        car.add(" 4 wheels are added to the car.");
        return this;
    }

    @Override
    public Vehicle getVehicle() {
        return car;
     }
    }
```

- Notice that these methods are similar to the previous demonstration but there is one major change: their return type is Builder. Since the return type is Builder, now you can apply **method chaining**. Before you assemble the parts (using the getVehicle() method) and display the complete product (using the showProduct() class),you can vary these steps. This is why, inside main(), you'll see code segments like the following:

```
// Construction Steps:
// Make body-> add wheels->then add the brand name.
        Vehicle vehicle=builder.buildBody()
                .insertWheels()
                .addBrandName()
                .getVehicle()
        vehicle.showProduct();
```

Since most of the parts are similar to the previous implementation, let's directly jump into the next demonstration.

Demonstration 2

Here is the alternative implementation for the Builder pattern. All the parts are stored inside package `jdp3e.builder.implementation_2`.

// Builder.java

```
import java.util.LinkedList;

// The common interface
interface Builder {

    Builder addBrandName();

    Builder buildBody();

    Builder insertWheels();

    // The following method is used to
    // retrieve the object that is constructed.
    Vehicle getVehicle();
}
```

// CarBuilder.java

```
// The CarBuilder builds cars.

class CarBuilder implements Builder {

    Car car;

    public CarBuilder() {
        car=new Car("Ford");
    }

    @Override
    public Builder addBrandName() {
        // Starting with brand name
```

```java
        car.add(" Adding the car brand: " + car.brandName);
        return this;
    }

    @Override
    public Builder buildBody() {
        car.add(" Making the car body.");
        return this;
    }

    @Override
    public Builder insertWheels() {
        car.add(" 4 wheels are added to the car.");
        return this;
    }

    @Override
    public Vehicle getVehicle() {
        return car;
    }

}
```

// **MotorCycleBuilder.java**

```java
// The MotorCycleBuilder builds motorcycles.

class MotorCycleBuilder implements Builder {

    MotorCycle motorCycle;

    public MotorCycleBuilder() {
        motorCycle=new MotorCycle("Honda");    }

    @Override
    public Builder addBrandName() {
        motorCycle.add(" Adding the brand name: " +
                         motorCycle.brandName);
        return this;
    }
```

```java
    @Override
    public Builder buildBody() {
        motorCycle.add(" Making the body of the motorcycle.");
        return this;
    }

    @Override
    public Builder insertWheels() {
        motorCycle.add(" 2 wheels are added to the motorcycle.");
        return this;
    }

    @Override
    public Vehicle getVehicle() {
        return motorCycle;
    }
}
```

// Vehicle.java

```java
/**
 * The Vehicle class is used to create the products.
 *  Making the class abstract, so that
 *  you cannot instantiate from it directly.
 */

abstract class Vehicle {
    /*
     * You can use any data structure that you prefer.
     * I have used LinkedList<String> in this case.
     */
    private LinkedList<String> parts;

    public Vehicle() {
        parts = new LinkedList<String>();
    }
```

```java
    public void add(String part) {
        // Adding parts
        parts.addLast(part);
    }

    public void showProduct() {
        System.out.println("These are the construction sequences:");
        for (String part : parts)
            System.out.println(part);
    }
}
```

// **Car.java**

```java
class Car extends Vehicle{
    String brandName;
    public Car(String brandName) {
        this.brandName=brandName;
        System.out.println("\nWe are about to make a " +
                            brandName+ " car.");
    }
}
```

// **MotorCycle.java**

```java
class MotorCycle extends Vehicle{
    String brandName;
    public MotorCycle(String brandName) {
        this.brandName=brandName;
        System.out.println("\nWe are about to make a " +
                            brandName+ " motorcycle.");
    }
}
```

// Client.java

```java
/**
 * The client is the director now.
 */

class Client {
 public static void main(String[] args) {
        System.out.println("*** Builder Pattern Demo2(Using
                            method chaining) ***");

        // Making a car
        Builder builder = new CarBuilder();
        // Construction Steps:
        // Make body-> add wheels->then add the brand name.
        Vehicle vehicle=builder.buildBody()
                .insertWheels()
                .addBrandName()
                .getVehicle();
        vehicle.showProduct();

        // Making a motorcycle
        builder = new MotorCycleBuilder();
        // Add brand name-> make body-> insert wheels.
        vehicle=builder.addBrandName()
            .buildBody()
            .insertWheels()
            .getVehicle();
        vehicle.showProduct();

    }
}
```

Output

Here's the output, which is the same except for the first line:

*** Builder Pattern Demo2(Using method chaining)***

We are about to make a Ford car.
These are the construction sequences:
 Making the car body.
 4 wheels are added to the car.
' Adding the car brand: Ford

We are about to make a Honda motorcycle.
These are the construction sequences:
 Adding the brand name: Honda
 Making the body of the motorcycle.
 2 wheels are added to the motorcycle.

Analysis

Examine the `main()` method closely. You can see that the director (client, in this example) creates two different products using the builders and each time it follows a different sequence of steps. Using this process, you can make an efficient and flexible application.

Q&A Session Continued

6.8 When should I consider using a Builder pattern?

As mentioned, if you need to make a complex object that involves various steps of the construction process and at the same time the products need to be immutable, the Builder pattern is a good choice.

Note   In the second edition of this book, I promoted immutability inside demonstration 2. There I used the `final` keyword for the concrete products. Also, there was a class called `ProductClass`. Inside this class, the attributes were marked with `private` keywords and there were no setter methods. Based on feedback, in this edition I show you two different demonstrations that are closely related. With some simple modifications, you can switch between them and understand the intent of the Builder pattern easily.

6.9 What is the key benefit associated with immutable objects?

Once constructed, they can be safely shared, and most importantly, they are thread-safe, so you save lots of synchronization costs in a multithreaded environment.

In these examples, cars and motorcycles are the final products. Instead of using these products, I could use closely related products whose internal representations are quite different, such as sports cars and standard cars, or something similar. In fact, this pattern could be described using concrete products only. Also, to reduce the code size, I could use only one director to avoid the use of an abstract class. But I want you to think about this pattern from all possible angles. So, the overall code size is relatively big, but I hope that you have a clear understanding of this pattern now.

CHAPTER 7

Singleton Pattern

This chapter covers the Singleton pattern.

GoF Definition

It ensures that a class has only one instance and provides a global point of access to it.

Concept

Let's assume you have a class called A and you need to create an object from it. Normally what do you do? You guess it right; you simply use the following line of code: A obA = new A();

But let's look at it closely. If you keep using the new keyword ten more times, you'll have ten more objects. Right? But in a real-world scenario, unnecessary object creation is a big concern (particularly when constructor calls are truly expensive), so you need to restrict this. In a situation like this, the Singleton pattern comes into the picture. It restricts the use of new like this and ensures that you do not have more than one instance of the class.

In short, this pattern says that a particular class should have only one instance. You can create an instance if it is not available; otherwise, you should use an existing instance to serve your need. Following this approach, you can avoid creating multiple objects.

Real-Life Example

Let's assume that you have a sports team, and your team is participating in a tournament. Your team needs to play against multiple opponents throughout the tournament. At the beginning of each match, as per the rules of the game, the captains

© Vaskaran Sarcar 2022
V. Sarcar, *Java Design Patterns*, https://doi.org/10.1007/978-1-4842-7971-7_7

of the two sides must go for a coin toss. So, if your team does not have a captain, you need to elect someone as a captain first. Prior to each game and each coin toss, you may not repeat the process of electing a captain if you have already nominated a person as a captain of your team for this tournament. Notice that in this example, selecting a captain is like creating a new object. Having that captain for the rest of the season is like reusing the same object that was created at the beginning.

Computer World Example

In some software systems, you may decide to maintain only one file system so that you can use it for the centralized management of resources. This approach can help you to implement caching mechanisms effectively. This pattern can also be used to maintain a thread pool in a multithreading environment. Here is another example for you:

- Once you learn about eager initialization in this chapter, you'll recognize that the `java.lang.Runtime` class follows this pattern.

Implementation

A Singleton pattern can be implemented in many different ways. Each approach has its pros and cons. We'll examine some of them.

The first demonstration takes a simple approach. Let's go through the notable characteristics of this approach:

- The `Captain` class is implemented as a singleton where its constructor is private. So, you cannot instantiate this class outside. For example, inside the client code, you cannot write something like the following:

```
Captain captain = new Captain(); // error
```

- This construct will help you refer to the only instance that can exist in the system.

- The private constructor also ensures that the `Captain` class cannot be extended. So, subclasses cannot misuse the concept. Thus, the following line of code also produces a compile-time error:

176

```
// We cannot extend Captain class.
// The constructor is private in this case.
class B extends Captain{} // error
```

- getCaptain() is responsible for the Captain instance creation. This method is synchronized, which means that multiple threads cannot involve in the instantiation process at the same time. It enables you to force each thread to wait for its turn to access this method. So, thread-safety is ensured.

- Although it was not strictly necessary for this implementation, I marked the Captain class as final to guard a specific scenario. I discuss the reason in the Q&A session.

Note   Synchronization is a costly operation and once the instance is created, it is an additional overhead. I discuss some alternative methods in the upcoming sections. Each has its pros and cons.

Class Diagram

Figure 7-1 shows the class diagram for the illustration of the Singleton pattern.

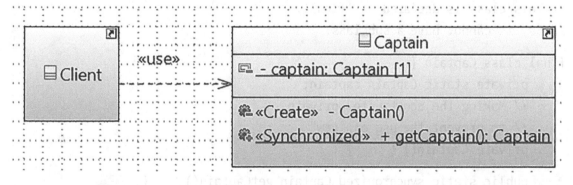

Figure 7-1.   *Class diagram*

Package Explorer View

Figure 7-2 shows the high-level structure of the program.

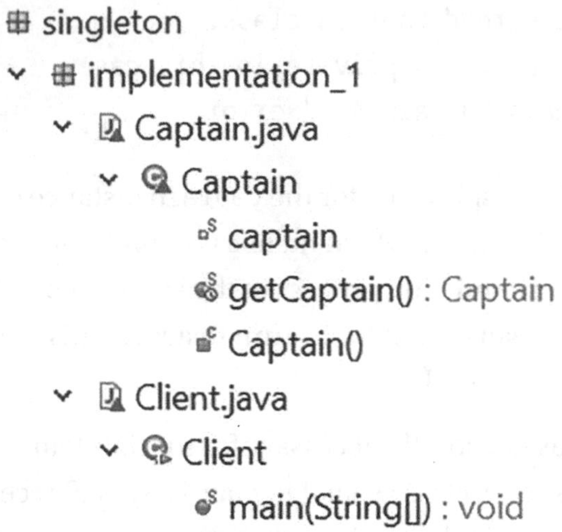

```
# singleton
  ∨ # implementation_1
    ∨ ▣ Captain.java
      ∨ ⓠ Captain
          ◦ˢ captain
          ⓔˢ getCaptain() : Captain
          ⓔᶜ Captain()
    ∨ ▣ Client.java
      ∨ ⓠ Client
          ⓔˢ main(String[]) : void
```

Figure 7-2. *Package Explorer view*

Demonstration 1

Now go through the following implementation. There are supportive comments for your easy understanding. All parts of the program are stored inside the package named jdp3e.singleton.implementation_1.

// Captain.java

```java
// This class is declared as 'final'.
// So, it cannot have a subclass.

final class Captain {
    private static Captain captain;
    // Making the constructor private
    // to prevent the use of "new"
    private Captain() {      }

    public static synchronized Captain getCaptain()     {

        // Lazy initialization
        if (captain == null) {
         captain = new Captain();
         System.out.println("\tA new captain is elected for your team.");
        }
```

```
        else {
            System.out.println("\tYou already have a captain for your team.");
            System.out.println("\tSend him for the toss.");
        }
        return captain;
    }
}
```

// Client.java

```
class Client {
    public static void main(String[] args) {
        System.out.println("***Singleton Pattern Demo***\n");
        System.out.println("Trying to make a captain for your team.");
        Captain captain1 = Captain.getCaptain();
        System.out.println("Trying to make another captain for your team:");
        Captain captain2 = Captain.getCaptain();
        if (captain1 == captain2){
            System.out.println("Both captain1 and captain2 are the same.");
        }
    }
}
```

Output

When you execute this program, you'll see the following output:

```
***Singleton Pattern Demo***

Trying to make a captain for your team.
    A new captain is elected for your team.
Trying to make another captain for your team:
    You already have a captain for your team.
    Send him for the toss.
Both captain1 and captain2 are the same.
```

Analysis

In demonstration 1, you saw a common way to implement the Singleton pattern. If you analyze further, you will see that the overall process can be boiled down into the following steps:

- Make the constructor `private`.

- Use a `public static` getter method that returns the static instance of the Singleton class.

Q&A Session

7.1 Why do you use the `synchronized` keyword? Looks like I can write the same program without using it.

This approach can work in a single-threaded environment. But consider a multithreaded environment where two (or more) threads may try to evaluate the following code at the same time:

```
if (captain == null)
```

If they see that the instance has not been created yet, each of them will try to create a new instance. As a result, you may end up with multiple instances of the class.

7.2 Why do you use the term *lazy initialization* in the code?

It's a technique that you use to delay the object creation process. The basic idea is that you should create the object only when it is truly required. This method is useful when object creation is a costly operation. So, using lazy initialization, you delay the object creation process to avoid expensive processes to create an object.

7.3 In short, if I need to create synchronized code, I can use the `synchronized` keyword in Java. Is my understanding correct?

Yes, JVM ensures this. Internally it uses locks on a class or an object to ensure that only one thread is accessing the data. Depending on an implementation, you may see the use of synchronized methods as well as synchronized statements.

7.4 Why are multiple object creations a big concern?

Here are some important points that you can remember:

- Object creations in the real world can be costly if you are working with resource-intensive objects.

- In some applications, you may need to pass a common object to multiple places.

7.5 Why are you making the class final? You have a private constructor that itself could prevent the inheritance. Is my understanding correct?

Subclassing can be prevented in various ways. Yes, in this example, since the constructor is already marked with the `private` keyword, it is not needed. But if you make the `Captain` class final, as shown in the example, this approach can be considered a better practice. This approach can be effective when you consider a nested class.

For example, let's modify the private constructor body to examine the number of instances (of the `Captain` class) created. Let's further assume that in the above example, you have a non-static nested class (called an inner class in Java) like the following. (All changes are shown in bold. I have also placed this code in a separate package named `jdp3e.singleton.implementation_2`. It can help you test the code directly once you download it from the Apress website).

```
package jdp3e.singleton.implementation_2;

class Captain {
    private static Captain captain;
    static int numberOfInstance = 0;
    // Making the constructor private
    // to prevent the use of "new"

    private Captain() {
        numberOfInstance++;
        System.out.println("Number of instances at this
                        moment=" + numberOfInstance);
    }

    public static synchronized Captain getCaptain() {
        // Lazy initialization
        if (captain == null) {
```

```
        captain = new Captain();
        System.out.println("\tA new captain is elected for your team.");
    } else {
        System.out.println("\tYou already have a
                                captain for your team.");
        System.out.println("\tSend him for the toss.");
    }
    return captain;
}

// A non-static nested class (inner class)
public class CaptainDerived extends Captain {
    // Some code
}
}
```

Now add an additional line of code (shown in bold) inside the main() method:

```
import jdp3e.singleton.implementation_2.Captain;

class Client {
    public static void main(String[] args) {
        System.out.println("***Singleton Pattern Demo***\n");
        System.out.println("Trying to make a captain for your team.");
        // Constructor is private. We cannot use "new"
         // here.
        // Captain captain = new Captain(); // error
        Captain captain1 = Captain.getCaptain();
        System.out.println("Trying to make another captain for your team:");
        Captain captain2 = Captain.getCaptain();
        if (captain1 == captain2){
            System.out.println("Both captain1 and captain2 are the same.");

        }
```

```
Captain.CaptainDerived derived1=captain1.new
                              CaptainDerived();
Captain.CaptainDerived derived2=captain1.new
                              CaptainDerived();
}

}
```

When you execute the program, you can see the following output:

```
***Singleton Pattern Demo***

Trying to make a captain for your team.
Number of instances at this moment=1
    A new captain is elected for your team.
Trying to make another captain for your team:
    You already have a captain for your team.
    Send him for the toss.
Both captain1 and captain2 are the same.
Number of instances at this moment=2
Number of instances at this moment=3
```

Have you noticed that the total number of instances is increasing? So, although in my original demonstration I could exclude the use of the `final` keyword, I kept it to guard against this type of situation, which may arise due to a modification of the original implementation.

7.6 When should I use the Singleton pattern?

Here are some common use cases where you'll find this pattern useful:

- To work with a centralized system (for example, consider a database).

- To maintain a common log file.

- To maintain a thread pool in a multithreaded environment.

- To implement a caching mechanism or device drivers and so forth.

Alternative Implementations

There are many approaches to implementing a Singleton design pattern. Each has its pros and cons. You have seen an example. Let's discuss some alternative approaches.

Demonstration 2: Eager Initialization

In eager initialization, an object of the singleton class is always instantiated at the beginning. The following code snippet shows such an example:

```java
class Captain {
    // Early initialization
    private static final Captain CAPTAIN_INSTANCE =
                                        new Captain();

    // Making the constructor private
     // to prevent the use of "new"
     private Captain() {
      System.out.println("\tNew captain is elected for your team.");
     }

    // Global point of access.
    public static Captain getCaptain(){
    System.out.println("\tYou already have a captain for your team.");
    System.out.println("\tSend him for the toss.");
    return CAPTAIN_INSTANCE;
  }
}
```

Analysis

This approach has the following pros and cons.

Pros:

- This approach is straightforward and cleaner.

- It is opposite to lazy initialization but it is thread-safe.

- There is a small lag time when the application is already in execution mode because all kinds of stuff is already loaded in memory.

Cons:

- The application will take longer to start (compared to lazy initialization) because everything needs to be loaded first. To examine this, let's add a dummy method (shown in bold) in the singleton class. Notice that in the main method, I invoke only this dummy method. Now examine the output.

```java
class Captain {
    // Early initialization
    private static final Captain CAPTAIN_INSTANCE =
                                      new Captain();

     // Making the constructor private
     // to prevent the use of "new"
     private Captain() {
      System.out.println("\tA new captain is elected
                        for your team.");
     }

     // Global point of access.
     public static Captain getCaptain(){
     System.out.println("\tYou already have a captain for your team.");
     System.out.println("\tSend him for the toss.");
     return CAPTAIN_INSTANCE;
     }
     public static void dummyMethod(){
     System.out.println("It is a dummy method");
  }

}
```

```java
// Client.java
class Client {

    public static void main(String[] args) {
        System.out.println("***Singleton Pattern Demo
                    using Eager Initialization***\n");
        Captain.dummyMethod();

        // Remaining code is omitted
    }
}
```

Now run this program segment and notice the output:

```
***Singleton Pattern Demo using Eager Initialization***
```

A new captain is elected for your team.
```
It is a dummy method
```

Note that "New captain is elected for your team" has appeared in this output, although you may have no intention of dealing with it.

Demonstration 3: Bill Pugh's Solution

In the earlier days (prior to Java 5), there were many issues when dealing with singleton classes. To overcome those situations, Bill Pugh came up with a different approach using a static nested helper class:

```java
class Captain {
    private Captain() {
        System.out.println("\tNew captain is elected for your team.");
    }

    // The helper class
    private static class SingletonHelper {
     // This nested class is referenced after
       // the getCaptain() method is called.
```

```java
    private static final Captain CAPTAIN_INSTANCE =
                            new Captain();
    }

    public static Captain getCaptain() {
        return SingletonHelper.CAPTAIN_INSTANCE;
    }
}
```

Analysis

This method does not use the synchronization technique and eager initialization. Notice that the SingletonHelper class comes into consideration only when someone invokes the getCaptain() method. And this approach will not create any unwanted output if you call any dummyMethod() inside the main() method, as shown in the previous case.

Note   In all these different approaches of implementing a Singleton Pattern, the main() method is essentially the same. So, for brevity, I have not added this segment repeatedly in these discussions. But it is in the full code on the GitHub/Apress website. If interested, you can download the full implementations from there.

Demonstration 4: Enum Singleton

Joshua Bloch is an American software engineer and famous technical author. He shows us that we can use enum type(s) to implement a Singleton design pattern. I encourage you to watch his talk at www.youtube.com/watch?v=pi_I7oD_uGI#t=28m50s (particularly, listen to the talk from 29:00-32:00). He explains why an apparently good-looking singleton class can be broken by an intelligent hacker if the class has a non-transient field.

So, what is the suggestion? Here is a sample implementation for you:

```java
// ENUM Singleton
enum Captain{
    INSTANCE;
```

```
    public synchronized void getCaptain()        {
        System.out.println("\tYou already have a captain for your team.");
        System.out.println("\tSend him for the toss.");
    }
}
```

The previous code can be used effectively in the following client code:

```
class Client {
    public static void main(String[] args) {
        System.out.println("***Singleton Pattern Demo using enum type***\n");
        Captain.INSTANCE.getCaptain();
    }
}
```

When you run this program, you get the following output:

```
***Singleton Pattern Demo using enum type***

    You already have a captain for your team.
    Send him for the toss.
```

Analysis

An enum-based Singleton class is easy to write compared to other traditional approaches. But at the same time, you need to keep in mind the restrictions that are associated with an enum type. Some of these restrictions can be tricky depending on the implementation.

The further details of each of these techniques and other approaches are beyond the scope of the book. The reason is simple: the book is very fat and you still have a long path to cover. At the same time, I also believe that you have got the idea behind the Singleton design pattern. I encourage you to read the online article www.journaldev.com/1377/java-singleton-design-pattern-best-practices-examples. Here you can learn more about various implementations of this pattern in brief.

Q&A Session Continued

7.7 I have one last question for you. I have some concerns about the example of eager initialization. Following the definition, it appears to me that it is also not exactly "eager." I understand that this class will be loaded by the JVM only when it is referenced by some code during the execution of the application. That way this is also lazy initialization. Is this understanding correct?

Yes, to some extent your observation is correct. There is a debate on this point. In short, it is *eager* compared to the previous approaches. You have seen that when you called the dummyMethod() only, still you instantiated the singleton, although you did not need it. So, in a context like this, it is *eager*, but it is *lazy* in a sense that the singleton instantiation will not occur until the class is initialized. So, the degree of laziness is the key concern here.

Lastly, I must say that "performance vs. laziness" is always a concern with this pattern, and some developers always question those areas. But the truth is that this pattern can be found in many applications. Let's finish the chapter with an Erich Gamma quote from an interview in 2009 (https://www.informit.com/articles/article.aspx?p=1404056):

> *"When discussing which patterns to drop, we found that we still love them all. (Not really—I'm in favor of dropping Singleton. Its use is almost always a design smell.)"*
>
> Erich Gamma

CHAPTER 8

Proxy Pattern

This chapter covers the Proxy pattern.

GoF Definition

It provides a surrogate or placeholder for another object to control access to it.

Concept

There are situations where you want to restrict direct communication between an intended object and the outside world. There are various reasons for this. For example, you may be promoting additional securities, you need to improve the response time, you may have some resource constraints, or the final product is still in the development phase.

Proxies can be of different types, but fundamentally they are substitutes (or placeholders) for an original object. As a result, when a client interacts with a proxy object, it appears that it is directly talking to the actual object. So, using this pattern, you may want to use a class that can perform as an interface to the original one.

Real-Life Example

Consider the case when a particular teacher in a school is absent due to some unavoidable circumstances. The school authority can send another teacher as a replacement to teach the classes. Consider an example from a different domain, say ATMs. An ATM implementation can hold proxy objects for bank information that actually exists on a remote server.

© Vaskaran Sarcar 2022
V. Sarcar, *Java Design Patterns*, https://doi.org/10.1007/978-1-4842-7971-7_8

Computer World Example

In the programming world, creating multiple instances of a complex object can be costly. This is because you may need resources that are not easily available or allocatable. In such a situation, you can create multiple proxy objects that can point to the original object. This mechanism can help you to save computer/system memory and improve the performance of your application.

Another very common use of a proxy is when users do not want to disclose the true IP address of their machine; instead, they want to make it anonymous. Here are few more examples:

- In the `java.lang.reflect` package, the `Proxy` class and the `InvocationHandler` interface support a similar concept.

- The package `java.rmi.*` also provides methods through which an object in one Java virtual machine can invoke methods on an object that resides in a different Java virtual machine.

- You can see this pattern in other domains, too. For example, .NET developers often use a Windows Communication Foundation (WCF) framework for building service-oriented applications. There you may notice the use of WCF client proxies, which a client application uses to communicate with the service. You can also configure a REST API to work behind a proxy server to promote authorized communication.

Implementation

This chapter offers two demonstrations. In the first program, `Subject` is an abstract class with an abstract method called `doSomeWork()`. It has the following definition:

```
public abstract class Subject {
    public abstract void doSomeWork();
}
```

ConcreteSubject is a concrete class that inherits from Subject and provides the implementation for the doSomeWork() method. It looks like the following:

```
// The ConcreteSubject class
class ConcreteSubject extends Subject {
    ConcreteSubject(){}
    @Override
    public void doSomeWork() {
        System.out.println("The doSomeWork() is executed.");
    }
}
```

Let's assume you want to restrict the client from directly invoking the method in ConcreteSubject. (Consider the cases discussed in the computer world examples for the reasons behind this). So, you make a proxy class called ProxySubject. In your implementation, the ProxySubject class contains the same-named method doSomeWork() and a client can use this method using a Proxy instance. When a client calls the doSomeWork() method of the proxy object, the call propagates to the doSomeWork() method in the ConcreteSubject object. This gives the clients a feeling that they have invoked the method from the ConcreteSubject directly. This is why the ProxySubject class looks like the following:

```
/**
 * This is the proxy class.
 * It invokes the doSomeWork() from
 * the ConcreteSubject.
 */
public class ProxySubject extends Subject {
    private Subject subject;

    public ProxySubject() {
        // We create only one instance
        // of the ConcreteSubject
        if (subject == null) {
            subject = new ConcreteSubject();
        }
    }
```

```
    @Override
    public void doSomeWork() {
        System.out.println("Proxy call is happening now.");
        subject.doSomeWork();
    }
}
```

Class Diagram

Figure 8-1 shows the class diagram.

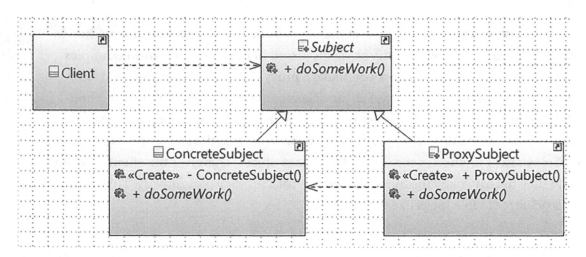

Figure 8-1. *Class diagram*

Package Explorer View

Figure 8-2 shows the high-level structure of the program.

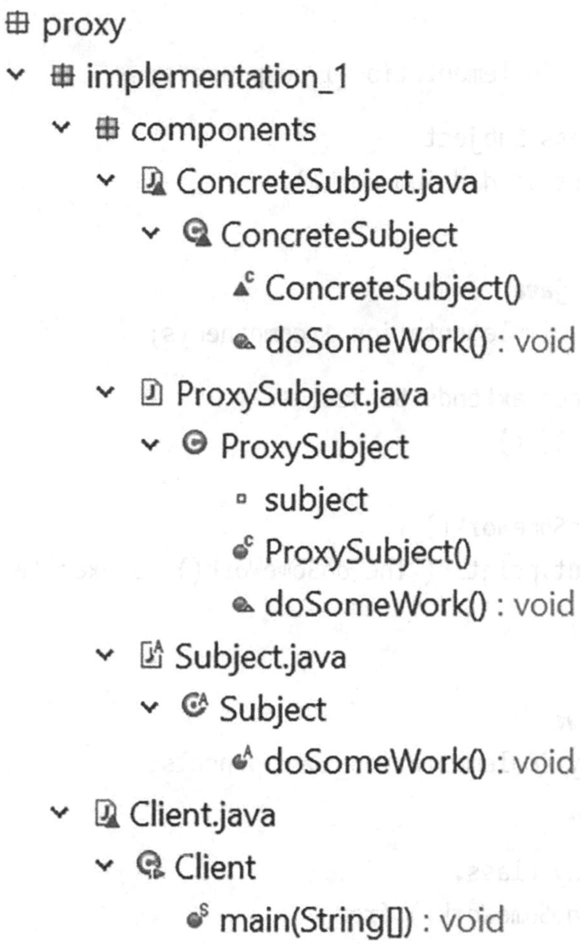

⊞ proxy
  ⌄ ⊞ implementation_1
    ⌄ ⊞ components
      ⌄ ▣ ConcreteSubject.java
        ⌄ ⊘ ConcreteSubject
          ▵ᶜ ConcreteSubject()
          ⬤ doSomeWork() : void
      ⌄ ▣ ProxySubject.java
        ⌄ ⊙ ProxySubject
          ▫ subject
          ⬥ᶜ ProxySubject()
          ⬤ doSomeWork() : void
      ⌄ ▣ Subject.java
        ⌄ ⊘ Subject
          ⬥ᴬ doSomeWork() : void
    ⌄ ▣ Client.java
      ⌄ ⊘ Client
        ⬥ˢ main(String[]) : void

Figure 8-2. *Package Explorer view*

Demonstration 1

The client code is stored inside the package jdp3e.proxy.implementation_1. The
remaining code is stored inside the package jdp3e.proxy.implementation_1.
components.

Notice that the ConcreteSubject class and its constructor have package-private
visibility. This is why inside the client code you cannot directly make an instance of
ConcreteSubject so you are forced to use the ProxySubject class.

Lastly, there's only one instance of ConcreteSubject. If needed, you can reuse the same instance and avoid unnecessary object creation. This part is optional, but you know that it is a better practice. Here's the complete implementation:

// Subject.java
```
package jdp3e.proxy.implementation_1.components;

public abstract class Subject {
    public abstract void doSomeWork();
}
```

// ConcreteSubject.java
```
package jdp3e.proxy.implementation_1.components;

class ConcreteSubject extends Subject {
    ConcreteSubject(){}
    @Override
    public void doSomeWork() {
        System.out.println("The doSomeWork() is executed.");
    }
}
```

// ProxySubject.java
```
package jdp3e.proxy.implementation_1.components;

/**
 * This is the proxy class.
 * It invokes the doSomeWork() from
 * the ConcreteSubject.
 */
public class ProxySubject extends Subject {
    private Subject subject;

    public ProxySubject() {
        // We create only one instance
        // of the ConcreteSubject
```

```
        if (subject == null) {
            subject = new ConcreteSubject();
        }
    }

    @Override
    public void doSomeWork() {
        System.out.println("The proxy call is happening now.");
        subject.doSomeWork();
    }
}
```

// Client.java

```
package jdp3e.proxy;
import jdp3e.proxy.implementation_1components.*;
/**
 * The client is talking to a ConcreteSubject
 * instance through a proxy method.
 */
class Client {
    public static void main(String[] args) {
        System.out.println("***Proxy Pattern Demo***\n");
        // ConcreteSubject has package-private visibility
        // So, you cannot make an instance of it here.
        //Subject cs = new ConcreteSubject();//Error

        Subject proxy = new ProxySubject();
        proxy.doSomeWork();
    }
}
```

Output

Here's the output of the program:

```
***Proxy Pattern Demo***

The proxy call is happening now.
The doSomeWork() is executed.
```

Q&A Session

8.1 What are the different types of proxies?

These are the common types of proxies:

- *Remote proxies*: These proxies can hide an object that sits in a different address space.

- *Virtual proxies*: These proxies are used to perform optimization techniques such as creating a heavy object on an on-demand basis.

- *Protection proxies*: These proxies generally deal with different access rights.

- *Smart reference*: These proxies can perform additional housekeeping when an object is accessed by a client. A typical operation may include counting the number of references to an object at a particular moment in time.

8.2 Why do you separate the client code from the rest of the code? Is it necessary?

It is a better practice in the sense that you do not allow a client to access the ConcreteSubject directly. This class and its constructor have package-private visibility. So, the clients are forced to use the Proxy class.

8.3 Using the lazy instantiation process, you may create unnecessary objects in a multithreaded application. Is this correct?

Yes. In this book, I present simple illustrations only, so I ignore that part. In the discussions of the Singleton pattern in Chapter 7, I analyze alternative approaches that tell you how to work in a multithreaded environment. You can always refer to those discussions in situations like this. (For example, in this particular scenario, you could implement a smart proxy to ensure that a particular object is locked before you grant access to the object).

8.4 Can you give an example of a remote proxy?

Suppose you want to call a method of an object, but the object is running in a different address space (for example, in a different location or on a different computer). How can you proceed? With the help of remote proxies, you can call the method on the proxy object, which in turn will forward the call to the actual object that is running on the remote machine. (You can refer to demonstration 1 as an example of this category in this context if the actual method exists on a different computer and you connect to it via a proxy object over a network). This type of need can be realized through different well-known mechanisms such as ASP.NET, CORBA, COM/DCOM, or Java's RMI.

Figure 8-3 shows a simple remote proxy structure.

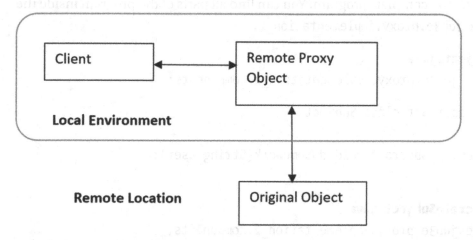

Figure 8-3. *A simple remote proxy diagram*

8.5 When can you use a virtual proxy?

They can be used to preserve some memory from being allocated to an object. If the actual object creation is an expensive operation, you can create a light copy of the intended object with the most important details and supply it to the user. The expensive object will be created only when it is truly needed. For example, you can use the concept to avoid loading an extremely large image unnecessarily for better application performance.

8.6 When can you use a protection proxy?

In an organization, the security team can implement a protection proxy to block internet access to specific websites. Demonstration 2 can help you understand this better.

Demonstration 2

Consider the following example, which is a modified version of the Proxy pattern implementation described earlier. For simplicity, let's assume you have only three registered users who can exercise the proxy method doSomeWork(String user). You can see that this time this method accepts a String parameter. You use this parameter to validate a registered user. If an unwanted user (say Robin) tries to invoke the method, the system will reject this request. When the system rejects this kind of unwanted access, there is no point in making a proxy object. In the upcoming example, all registered users are initialized in the proxy class constructor.

Here's the complete program. You can find all parts of the program inside the package jdp3e.proxy.implementation_2.

// Subject.java

```
package jdp3e.proxy.implementation_2.components;

public abstract class Subject
{
    public abstract void doSomeWork(String user);
}
```

// ConcreteSubject.java

```
package jdp3e.proxy.implementation_2.components;

// ConcreteSubject class
class ConcreteSubject extends Subject
{
    @Override
    public void doSomeWork(String user)
    {
        System.out.println(user+ " invokes the method-doSomeWork().");
    }
}
```

// ProxySubject.java

```
package jdp3e.proxy.implementation_2.components;
```

```java
import java.util.ArrayList;
import java.util.List;

/**
 * @author V.Sarcar
 * This is the proxy class.
 * It invokes the doSomeWork() from
 * the ConcreteSubject.
 */
public class ProxySubject extends Subject {
  private Subject subject;
  //String[] registeredUsers;
  String currentUser;
  List<String> registeredUsers;
  //Or, simply create this mutable list in one step
  //List<String> registeredUsers=new
  // ArrayList<String>(Arrays.asList( "Admin","Kate","Sam"));
   public ProxySubject () {

     // We need to create only one instance
     // of the ConcreteSubject.
     if (subject == null)      {
      subject= new ConcreteSubject();
     }

     // Initialize the registered users:
     registeredUsers = new ArrayList<String>();
     registeredUsers.add("Admin");
     registeredUsers.add("Kate");
     registeredUsers.add("Sam");
}
 @Override
 public void doSomeWork(String user) {
  System.out.println("\n The proxy call is happening now.");
  System.out.println(user+" wants to invoke a proxy method.");
   if (registeredUsers.contains(user)){
```

```
        // Allow the registered user to invoke the method
        subject.doSomeWork(user);
        } else {

            System.out.println("Sorry, "+ user+ ",
                            you do not have access rights.");
        }
    }

}
```

// Client.java
```java
package jdp3e.proxy.implementation_2;
import jdp3e.proxy.implementation_2.components.Subject;
import jdp3e.proxy.implementation_2.components.ProxySubject;

/**
 * @author V.Sarcar
 * The client is talking to a ConcreteSubject instance
 * through a proxy method.
 */
class Client {
    public static void main(String[] args) {
        System.out.println("***Modified Proxy Pattern Demonstration.***");
        // Admin is an authorized user
        Subject proxy = new ProxySubject();
        proxy.doSomeWork("Admin");
        // Robin is an unauthorized user
        proxy.doSomeWork("Robin");

    }
}
```

Output

Here's the modified output for you:

```
***Modified Proxy Pattern Demonstration.***

 The proxy call is happening now.
Admin wants to invoke a proxy method.
Admin invokes the method-doSomeWork().

 The proxy call is happening now.
Robin wants to invoke a proxy method.
Sorry, Robin, you do not have access rights.
```

8.7 It looks like proxies act like decorators (in Chapter 9). Is this correct?

Sometimes a proxy implementation can have similarities to a decorator, but you should not forget the true intent of a proxy. Decorators focus on adding responsibilities, whereas proxies focus on controlling access to an object. So, if you remember their purpose, in most cases you will be able to distinguish proxies from decorators.

Remember the following: In general, proxies work on the same interface but decorators can work on extended interfaces.

8.8 When should I think of designing a proxy?

As said earlier in the chapter, here are some important use cases where proxies can help you:

- You are writing test cases for a scenario that is still in the development phase or very hard to reproduce. For example, when you want to evaluate a particular behavior of an application that can be seen in a customer environment only, but you also recognize that when the application is running, the probability of getting the behavior is very low. In such a case, you can mimic the customer environment behavior in your proxy object and execute your test cases to evaluate this behavior.

- You want to hide the complexity and enhance the security of the system.

8.9 What are the cons associated with proxies?

Here are some factors that you should keep in mind while using this pattern:

- The overall response time can be an issue because you are not directly talking to the actual object.

- You need to maintain an additional layer for the proxies.

- Lastly, a proxy can hide the actual responses from objects. For example, consider the case when a proxy method modifies the original exception thrown by a method. Debugging and fixing such a case is not straightforward.

CHAPTER 9

Decorator Pattern

This chapter covers the Decorator pattern, which is also known as the Wrapper pattern.

GoF Definition

It attaches additional responsibilities to an object dynamically. Decorators provide a flexible alternative to subclassing for extending functionality.

Concept

An alternative to inheritance is composition. It is quite common in programming and often gives you a better payoff. This chapter shows a useful case study on this topic using some wrappers.

So, what is a wrapper(or a decorator)? ***A wrapper is like a topping that surrounds an object. The enclosing object is often called a decorator, which conforms to the interface of the component that it decorates. In programming, you often use a wrapper to add functionalities dynamically.*** This is a powerful technique because you can add or discard a wrapper as per your need, and it does not hamper the functionalities of the original object.

Say you need to work on a piece of code and add new features. Someone coded it before and you cannot change the existing code. This scenario is common in software industries when you need to enhance a feature to attract new customers, but you cannot alter the existing workflow of the software to support the existing customers. You understand that in this case, since you were not a part of the team that wrote the first version of the software, you do not have exclusive control from the beginning. Wrappers are useful in similar situations. As said before, in this case, you can add new functionality on top of the existing functionality to support new customers. In fact, by using different types of wrappers you can support different types of customers.

© Vaskaran Sarcar 2022
V. Sarcar, *Java Design Patterns*, https://doi.org/10.1007/978-1-4842-7971-7_9

This pattern is most effective when you add decorators dynamically. It's interesting to note since decorators are often added dynamically, it is perfectly fine if you do not want them in a later phase of development, because the original object can still work for you. The upcoming example will make the concept clearer to you.

Real-Life Example

Consider a group of people who each want to build a home. Each person has a different budget and mindset. So, this group visits a home builder to get cost estimates. For simplicity, let's assume that they have the following options:

- They can either make a basic home with standard facilities or they can make an advanced home with additional facilities. For illustration purposes, let's refer to these homes as `BasicHome` and `AdvancedHome`, respectively.

- The builder gives them options of a playground, a swimming pool, or both. Let's call them luxuries. Each luxury means additional cost to the buyer.

Based on their budget, a customer can opt for various options and thus the final price will vary. Most importantly, a customer who opts for a `BasicHome` today can upgrade their home tomorrow by adding a playground or a swimming pool (or both). Each luxury (playground or swimming pool) acts as a decorator in this example.

Computer World Example

The I/O Streams implementations in the .NET Framework, .NET Core, and Java use the concept of the Decorator pattern.

- For example, notice the use of the Decorator pattern in the I/O Streams implementations in both .NET Framework and Java. For example, the `java.io.BufferedOutputStream` class can decorate any `java.io.OutputStream` object.

- Similarly, in the C# programming language, notice the use of the `BufferedStream` class, which inherits from the `Stream` class. If you look closely, you'll notice the presence of two overloaded constructors in this class; each takes a Stream (parent class) as a parameter. (This construct is similar to the upcoming demonstration.)

In general, when you see this kind of construct, there is a possibility that you are seeing a Decorator pattern.

Implementation

Let's continue the discussion of the real-life example. Your job is to write a program that mimics a similar case. Before you see the program, let's analyze the different approaches.

Using Subclassing

If you want to provide a solution using inheritance, first try to understand the problems that are associated with it. Assume that you start with the following structure:

```
class Home {
    // Some code
}
class PlayGround extends Home {
    // Some code
}
class SwimmingPool extends PlayGround {
    // Some code
}
```

This is not a recommended approach, because to get a swimming pool, you first get a playground, which a customer may not want. Due to similar logic, the following structure is not a good choice either:

```
class Home {
    // Some code
}
Class SwimmingPool extends Home {
    // Some code
}
```

```
class PlayGround extends SwimmingPool {
    // Some code
}
```

This time, to get a playground you first get a swimming pool that a customer may not want. *So, implementing a multilevel inheritance, in this case, is not a good idea!*

Now let's assume that you start with a hierarchical inheritance where SwimmingPool and PlayGround both inherit from the Home class, as shown in Figure 9-1.

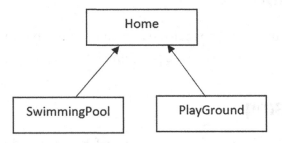

Figure 9-1. *A hierarchical inheritance*

Now you need a home with a swimming pool and a playground, so you end up with the design shown in Figure 9-2.

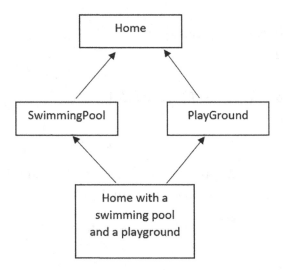

Figure 9-2. *A class needs to inherit from multiple base classes. It causes the diamond problem in Java*

But you know that *you cannot have multiple base classes in Java.* So, any construct like the following will raise the following compilation error:

```
class Home extends SwimmingPool, PlayGround // Error
{

}
```

Now you understand that using simple subclassing, in this case, is not a good idea. What are the alternatives? Let's continue investigating.

You may proceed with an interface for the luxuries. For example, you can opt for the following interface:

```
interface Luxury {
    void addPlayGround();
    void addSwimmingPool();
}
```

Now you can have a class that can implement this interface. For example, here is a Home class that extends the BasicHome class and implements the Luxury interface:

```
class Home extends BasicHome implements Luxury {
    public void addPlayGround(){
        // Some code
    }

    public void addSwimmingPool(){
        // Some code
    }
}
```

But again, a customer may opt for a home with one of these luxuries, but not both. In that case, if a method is not needed, you write

```
throw new NotImplementedException();
```

The problem associated with this is discussed in the context of the Liskov Substitution Principle (LSP) in Chapter 1. To avoid this, you may follow the Interface Segregation Principle (ISP) and segregate the Luxury interface. Yes, this time it will work! But in this chapter, let's search for an alternative approach.

Using Object Composition

Let's see how a wrapper can help. ***Using a wrapper, you surround an object with another object.*** It forwards the requests to the original component and can perform additional operations before or after those requests. ***You can add an unlimited number of responsibilities with this concept.*** The following figures will help you understand this.

Figure 9-3 shows a home (basic or advanced) surrounded by a playground.

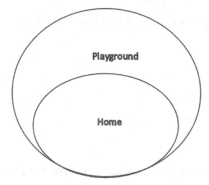

Figure 9-3. *The home is surrounded by a playground*

Figure 9-4 shows a home surrounded by a swimming pool.

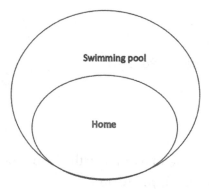

Figure 9-4. *The home is surrounded by a swimming pool*

Figure 9-5 shows the home surrounded by a playground and swimming pool. Here you first surround the home with a playground and then you surround both with a swimming pool.

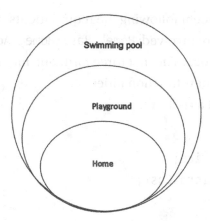

Figure 9-5. *The home is surrounded by a playground and a swimming pool*

Figure 9-6 shows the home surrounded by a swimming pool and a playground again. But this time you change the order; you first surround the home with a swimming pool, and then you surround both with a playground.

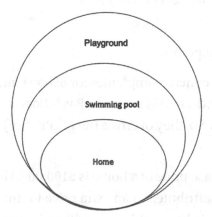

Figure 9-6. *The home is surrounded by a swimming pool. Later you surround both with a playground*

Following the same technique, you can add two more playgrounds or swimming pools.

Let's implement this concept following the requirements you have. In the upcoming demonstration, six players are involved: `Home`, `BasicHome`, `AdvancedHome`, `Luxury`, `PlayGround`, and `SwimmingPool`. The first three form one inheritance hierarchy and the last three are created to add new functionalities.

The `Home` class is defined as follows:

```
abstract class Home {
    public double basePrice;
    public double additionalCost;

    public Home() {
     // Minimum home price is $100000
     this.basePrice = 100000.0;
     this.additionalCost = 0.0;
    }

    public abstract double getPrice();
}
```

Here are some important points:

- You can see that a concrete implementor of `Home` must implement the `getPrice()` methods. In this example, `BasicHome` and `AdvancedHome` inherit from `Home`. So, they override the `getPrice()` method as per their needs.

- Assume that the base price of a home is $100,000. Using the `additionalPrice` attribute, set an extra price for the advanced home. Currently, for a basic home, this cost is $0 and for an advanced home, this cost is $25,000.

- Assume that once the home is built, there is no need for an immediate modification. One can add the luxuries later.

- Once a home is built, you can opt for a playground or a swimming pool for an existing home, or you may want both. So, the `PlayGround` and `SwimmingPool` classes appear in this example. In the client class, there are eight different scenarios to demonstrate the power of this design pattern. There you see a client can opt for different homes with different facilities in different orders.

- Although it was not strictly needed, to share the common code, both the Playground class and SwimmingPool class inherit from the abstract class Luxury, which has the following structure:

```
abstract class Luxury extends Home {
    protected Home home;
    public double luxuryCost;

    public Luxury(Home home) {
        this.home = home;
    }

    @Override
    public double getPrice() {
        return home.getPrice();
    }
}
```

- Like the additionalPrice attribute, you can set a luxury cost using the luxuryCost attribute. You use it inside the constructors.

- Notice that Luxury holds a reference of Home. So, the concrete decorators (PlayGround or SwimmingPool in this example) can decorate an instance of Home.

- Now let's look into the structure of a concrete decorator, say PlayGround, which is as follows:

```
class PlayGround extends Luxury {
    public PlayGround(Home home) {
     super(home);
     this.luxuryCost = 20000;
     System.out.println(" For a playground, you pay an
                        extra $" + this.luxuryCost);
    }
```

```
        @Override
        public double getPrice() {
                return home.getPrice() + luxuryCost;
        }
    }
```

- You can see that when you get this facility, you pay an additional $20,000. You initialize this value inside the constructor.

- Most importantly, notice that how the final price is calculated. It calls a Home instance price and then adds the luxury cost. The original Home hierarchy is not touched.

- The SwimmingPool class works similarly, but you have to pay more for this. (Yes, I assume that a swimming pool costs more than a playground in this case).

Class Diagram

Figure 9-7 shows the most important parts of the class diagram.

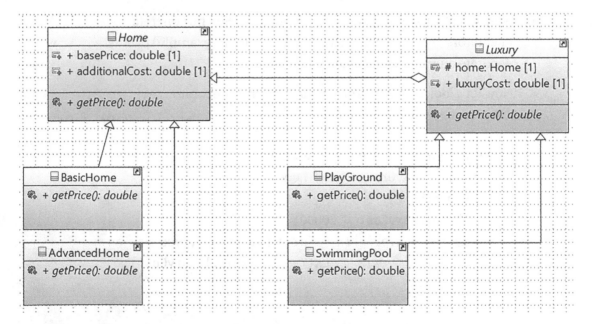

Figure 9-7. *Class diagram (without the client class)*

Package Explorer View

Figure 9-8 shows the high-level structure of the program.

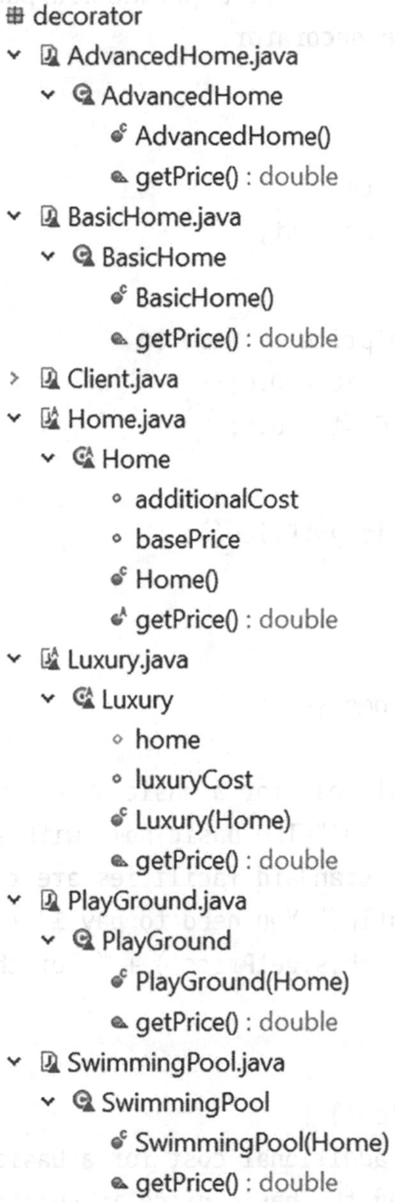

```
# decorator
  v  AdvancedHome.java
     v  @ AdvancedHome
          @ AdvancedHome()
          @ getPrice() : double
  v  BasicHome.java
     v  @ BasicHome
          @ BasicHome()
          @ getPrice() : double
  >  Client.java
  v  Home.java
     v  @ Home
          o additionalCost
          o basePrice
          @ Home()
          @ getPrice() : double
  v  Luxury.java
     v  @ Luxury
          o home
          o luxuryCost
          @ Luxury(Home)
          @ getPrice() : double
  v  PlayGround.java
     v  @ PlayGround
          @ PlayGround(Home)
          @ getPrice() : double
  v  SwimmingPool.java
     v  @ SwimmingPool
          @ SwimmingPool(Home)
          @ getPrice() : double
```

Figure 9-8. *Package Explorer view*

215

Demonstration

Here is the complete demonstration for you. In the client code, you see many different scenarios to show the effectiveness of this application. All parts of the program can be seen inside the package jdp3e.decorator.

// Home.java

```java
abstract class Home {
    public double basePrice;
    public double additionalCost;

    public Home() {
        // Minimum home price is $100000
        this.basePrice = 100000.0;
        this.additionalCost = 0.0;
    }

    public abstract double getPrice();
}
```

// BasicHome.java

```java
class BasicHome extends Home {
    public BasicHome() {
        // No additional cost for a basic home.
        System.out.println(" The basic home with some
                        standard facilities are ready.");
        System.out.println(" You need to pay $" +
                        this.getPrice() + " for this.");
    }

    @Override
    public double getPrice() {
        // There is no additional cost for a basic home
        // So, returning the basic price is sufficient.
        return basePrice;
    }
}
```

```
// AdvancedHome.java

class AdvancedHome extends Home {
    public AdvancedHome() {
        additionalCost = 25000;
        System.out.println(" It becomes an advanced home
                            with more facilities.");
        System.out.println(" You need to pay $" +
                            this.getPrice() + " for this.");
    }

    @Override
    public double getPrice() {
        return basePrice + additionalCost;
    }
}
```

```
// Luxury.java

abstract class Luxury extends Home {
    protected Home home;
    public double luxuryCost;

    public Luxury(Home home) {
        this.home = home;
    }

    @Override
    public double getPrice() {
        return home.getPrice();
    }
}
```

```
// PlayGround.java

class PlayGround extends Luxury {
    public PlayGround(Home home) {
        super(home);
        this.luxuryCost = 20000;
```

```java
            System.out.println(" For a playground, you pay an
                            extra $" + this.luxuryCost);
    }

    @Override
    public double getPrice() {
        return home.getPrice() + luxuryCost;
    }
}
```

// SwimmingPool.java

```java
class SwimmingPool extends Luxury {
    public SwimmingPool(Home home) {
        super(home);
        this.luxuryCost = 55000;
        System.out.println(" For a swimming pool, you pay
                            an extra $" + this.luxuryCost);
    }

    @Override
    public double getPrice() {
        return home.getPrice() + luxuryCost;
    }
}
```

// Client.java

```java
class Client {
    public static void main(String[] args) {
        System.out.println("***Using wrappers in different scenarios.***\n");
        System.out.println("Scenario-1: Making a basic home
                            with standard facilities.");
        Home home = new BasicHome();
        System.out.println("Total cost: $" +
                            home.getPrice());
```

```java
System.out.println("\nScenario-2: Making a basic
                    home. Then adding a playground.");
home = new BasicHome();
home = new PlayGround(home);
System.out.println("Total cost: $" +
                    home.getPrice());

System.out.println("\nScenario-3: Making a basic
                    home. Then adding two
                    playgrounds one-by-one.");
home = new BasicHome();
home = new PlayGround(home);
home = new PlayGround(home);
System.out.println("Total cost: $" +
                    home.getPrice());

System.out.println("\nScenario-4: Making a basic
                    home. Then adding one additional
                    playground and swimming pool.");
home = new BasicHome();
home = new PlayGround(home);
home = new SwimmingPool(home);
System.out.println("Total cost: $" +
                    home.getPrice());

System.out.println("\nScenario-5: Adding a swimming
                    pool and then a playground
                    to a basic home.");
home = new BasicHome();
home = new SwimmingPool(home);
home = new PlayGround(home);
System.out.println("Total cost: $" +
                    home.getPrice());

System.out.println("\nScenario-6: Making an
                    advanced home now.");
home = new AdvancedHome();
```

```
            System.out.println("Total cost: $" +
                            home.getPrice());

            System.out.println("\nScenario-7: Making an
                            advanced home. Then adding one
                            additional playground to it.");
            home = new AdvancedHome();
            home = new PlayGround(home);
            System.out.println("Total cost: $" +
                            home.getPrice());

            System.out.println("\nScenario-8: Making an
                            advanced home. Then adding one
                            additional playground and one swimming
                            pool to it.");
            home = new AdvancedHome();
            home = new PlayGround(home);
            home = new SwimmingPool(home);
            System.out.println("Total cost: $" +
                            home.getPrice());

    }
}
```

Output

***Using wrappers in different scenarios. ***

Scenario-1: Making a basic home with standard facilities.
 The basic home with some standard facilities are ready.
 You need to pay $100000.0 for this.
Total cost: $100000.0

Scenario-2: Making a basic home. Then adding a playground.
 The basic home with some standard facilities are ready.
 You need to pay $100000.0 for this.
 For a playground, you pay an extra $20000.0
Total cost: $120000.0

Scenario-3: Making a basic home. Then adding two playgrounds one by one.
  The basic home with some standard facilities are ready.
  You need to pay $100000.0 for this.
  For a playground, you pay an extra $20000.0
  For a playground, you pay an extra $20000.0
Total cost: $140000.0

Scenario-4: Making a basic home. Then adding one additional playground and swimming pool.
  The basic home with some standard facilities are ready.
  You need to pay $100000.0 for this.
  For a playground, you pay an extra $20000.0
  For a swimming pool, you pay an extra $55000.0
Total cost: $175000.0

Scenario-5: Adding a swimming pool and then a playground to basic home.
  The basic home with some standard facilities are ready.
  You need to pay $100000.0 for this.
  For a swimming pool, you pay an extra $55000.0
  For a playground, you pay an extra $20000.0
Total cost: $175000.0

Scenario-6: Making an advanced home now.
  It becomes an advanced home with more facilities.
  You need to pay $125000.0 for this.
Total cost: $125000.0

Scenario-7: Making an advanced home. Then adding one additional playground to it.
  It becomes an advanced home with more facilities.
  You need to pay $125000.0 for this.
  For a playground, you pay an extra $20000.0
Total cost: $145000.0

Scenario-8: Making an advanced home. Then adding one additional playground and one swimming pool to it.
  It becomes an advanced home with more facilities.
  You need to pay $125000.0 for this.

```
For a playground, you pay an extra $20000.0
For a swimming pool, you pay an extra $55000.0
Total cost: $200000.0
```

Q&A Session

9.1 You say that composition promotes dynamic behavior in this design. You also say that it is better than inheritance in this example. Can you throw some more light on this discussion?

When a derived class inherits from a base class, it actually inherits the behavior of the base class at that time only. Although different subclasses can extend the parent class in different ways, this type of binding is known at compile time. So, this method is static in nature. But by using the concept of composition, as in the previous example, you implement dynamic behaviors.

Notice carefully: a decorator object is designed in such a way that it has the same interface as the underlying object. It allows a client object to interact with the decorated object in the same way as it would with the underlying object. This is the reason: a decorator object contains a reference to the actual object. When a client sends a request, the decorated objects forward this request to the underlying object. But it can add functionality before or after forwarding the request to the actual object. This ensures that you add behavior at runtime without modifying the original object structure.

When you design a parent class, you may not have enough visibility about what kind of additional responsibilities your clients may want in some later phase. Since the constraint is that you cannot modify the existing code, in this case, object composition not only outclasses inheritance but also ensures that you are not introducing bugs in the old architecture.

Lastly, in this context, you must try to remember one key design principle that says *classes should be open for extension but closed for modification*.

9.2 What are the key advantages of using a decorator?

Here are some key advantages:

- The existing structure is untouched, so you do not introduce bugs in that part of the code.

- New functionalities can be added to an existing object easily.

- You can not only add a behavior to an interface, but you can alter the behavior too.

- You do not need to predict/implement all the supported functionalities at once (for example, in the initial design phase). You can develop incrementally. For example, you can add decorator objects one by one to support your needs. If you make a complex class first and then want to extend the functionalities, that will be a tedious process.

9.3 How is the overall design pattern different from inheritance?

You can add or alter or remove responsibilities by simply attaching or detaching decorators. But with simple inheritance techniques, you need to create new classes for new responsibilities. So, it is possible that you will end up with a complex system. In this context, read the discussion of the subtopic "Using Subclassing" under "Implementation" in this chapter. You can also revisit Q&A 9.1 in this context.

9.4 I notice that you have created the classes with a single responsibility. Is this beneficial?

Yes. It makes the Decorator pattern more efficient because you can simply add or remove a responsibility dynamically one at a time.

9.5 What are the disadvantages associated with this pattern?

I believe that if you are careful, there are no significant disadvantages. But if you create too many decorators in the system, it can be hard to maintain and debug. So, in that case, they create unnecessary complexities.

9.6 In the example, the **Luxury** class is abstract, but there is no abstract method in it. How is this possible?

In Java, you can have an abstract class without any abstract method in it, but the reverse is not true. So, if a class contains at least one abstract method, it means that the class itself is incomplete and you are forced to mark it with abstract keyword.

Let's revisit the Luxury class and notice the bold line:

```
abstract class Luxury extends Home {
    protected Home home;
    public double luxuryCost;
```

```
    public Luxury(Home home) {
        this.home = home;
    }

    @Override
    public double getPrice() {
        return home.getPrice();
    }
}
```

In the bold line of code, you delegate a task. In addition, you want to use and instantiate the concrete decorators only. So, in this example, you cannot simply instantiate the Luxury instance because it is marked with the abstract keyword.

9.7 Is it mandatory to use decorators for dynamic binding only?

No. You can use the concept for both static and dynamic binding. But dynamic binding is its strength, so I concentrated on that here. The GoF definition also focuses on dynamic binding only.

9.8 In simple words, you are using decorators to wrap the core architecture. Is this understanding correct?

Yes. These are wrapper codes to extend the core functionalities of the application. But the original architecture is untouched when you use them.

9.9 Can you throw some light on how BufferedOutputStream plays the role of a decorator?

Consider the following code segment, which we often see:

```
import java.io.BufferedOutputStream;
import java.io.FileNotFoundException;
import java.io.FileOutputStream;
import java.io.OutputStream;

class JDKExample {

    public static void main(String[] args) throws
                            FileNotFoundException {
        OutputStream stream;
        stream = new FileOutputStream("somefile.txt");
```

```
        stream =new BufferedOutputStream(stream);
        // Some other code
    }
  }
```

Now investigate further. You see the following:

```
public class BufferedOutputStream extends FilterOutputStream {

  public BufferedOutputStream(OutputStream out) {
      this(out, 8192);
  }
// Remaining code skipped
}
```

It means the BufferedOutputStream inherits from FilterOutputStream. Now look into this class:

```
public class FilterOutputStream extends OutputStream {
    /**
     * The underlying output stream to be filtered.
     */
    protected OutputStream out;
    public FilterOutputStream(OutputStream out) {
        this.out = out;
    }
    // remaining code skipped
}
```

You also see that the FileOutputStream class extends the OutputStream class. Here is a sample code segment:

```
public class FileOutputStream extends OutputStream {
    // Remaining code skipped
}
```

So, the overall structure can be simplified with the diagram in Figure 9-9.

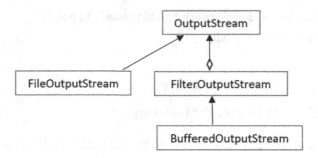

Figure 9-9. *A hierarchical inheritance*

Now you understand the following:

- The Luxury class plays the role of FilterOutputStream (an abstract decorator).

- The PlayGround and SwimmingPool classes play the role of BufferedOutputStream (a concrete decorator).

- The Home class plays the role of the OutputStream (the abstract class).

- BasicHome and AdvancedHome play the role of FileOutputStream (the concrete class that inherits from the abstract class) .

CHAPTER 10

Adapter Pattern

This chapter covers the Adapter pattern.

GoF Definition

It converts the interface of a class into another interface that clients expect. The Adapter pattern lets classes work together that could not otherwise because of incompatible interfaces.

Concept

From the GoF definition, you can guess that this pattern deals with at least two incompatible inheritance hierarchies. In a domain-specific system, the clients know how to invoke methods in software. These methods can follow an inheritance hierarchy. Now assume that you need to upgrade your system and need to follow a new inheritance hierarchy. When you do that, you do not want to force your clients to learn the new way to access the software. So, what can you do? The solution is simple: you write an adapter that accepts client requests and translates these requests into a form that the methods in the new hierarchy can understand. As a result, clients can enjoy the updated software without any hassle. By using this pattern, you make two incompatible interfaces compatible so that they can work together.

There are two types of adapters: class adapters and object adapters. I'll cover both types in this chapter.

© Vaskaran Sarcar 2022
V. Sarcar, *Java Design Patterns*, https://doi.org/10.1007/978-1-4842-7971-7_10

Real-Life Example

A common use of this pattern is when you use an electrical outlet adapter/AC power adapter on international travel. These adapters act as middlemen so that an electronic device, say a laptop that accepts a U.S. power supply, can be plugged into a European power outlet.

Even a translator who converts one language to another can be considered to be following this pattern in real life.

Let's consider a situation where you have two different shapes (say Shape1 and Shape2), neither of which is a rectangle, and they look like those in Figure 10-1.

Figure 10-1. *Before using an adapter*

Let's further assume that you need to form a rectangle by combining these two shapes. How can you proceed? Ok, one simple solution is to bring in another bounded X-shaped figure like the one shown in Figure 10-2 (which is filled with colors here).

Figure 10-2. *An adapter*

Then you can attach these three shapes as shown in Figure 10-3.

Figure 10-3. *After using an adapter*

228

In programming, you can think of Shape1 and Shape2 as two different interfaces that can't work together unless you combine them to form a rectangle using this X-shaped figure. ***The X-shaped figure is playing the role of an adapter in this scenario.***

Computer World Example

Suppose you have an application that can be broadly classified into two parts: the user interface (UI or the front end) and the database (the back end). Through the user interface, clients can pass some specific type of data or objects. Your database is compatible with those objects and can store them smoothly. Over a period of time, you may realize that you need to upgrade your software to make your clients happy. So, you may want to allow some other type of object to also pass through the UI. But in this case, the first issue will come from your database because it cannot store the new type of object. In such a situation, you can use an adapter that will take care of the conversion of these new objects to a compatible form that your existing database can accept and store. Here is another example for you:

- In Java, you can consider the `java.io.InputStreamReader` class and the `java.io.OutputStreamWriter` class as examples of this pattern. They adapt an existing `InputStream`/`OutputStream` object to a Reader/Writer interface. They are object adapters. You will learn about class adapters and object adapters shortly.

Note   `Reader` and `Writer` are abstract classes in Java. When we use polymorphic code, we often use the term "interface" as a supertype, but not as a Java interface. So, you should not assume that the term "interface" is limited to Java interfaces only.

Implementation

In the upcoming example, there are two hierarchies, one for rectangles and one for triangles. There are two methods in the interface called `RectInterface`: `calculateArea()` and `aboutMe()`. The `Rectangle` class implements this interface and forms the first hierarchy as follows:

```
package jdp3e.adapter;

interface RectInterface {
    void aboutMe();
    double calculateArea();
}

class Rectangle implements RectInterface {
    double length;
    public double width;

    public Rectangle(double length, double width) {
        this.length = length;
        this.width = width;
    }

    @Override
    public void aboutMe() {
        System.out.println("Shape type: Rectangle.");
    }

    @Override
    public double calculateArea() {
        return length * width;
    }
}
```

The TriInterface interface has two methods called calculateTriangleArea()
and aboutTriangle(). The Triangle class implements this interface and forms another
hierarchy as follows:

```
interface TriInterface {

    void aboutTriangle();
    double calculateTriangleArea();
}

class Triangle implements TriInterface {
    double baseLength;
    double height;
```

```java
    public Triangle(double length, double height) {
        this.baseLength = length;
        this.height = height;
    }

    @Override
    public double calculateTriangleArea() {
        return 0.5 * baseLength * height;
    }

    @Override
    public void aboutTriangle() {
        System.out.println("Shape type: Triangle.");
    }
}
```

These two hierarchies are easy to understand. Now, suppose *you need to calculate the area of a triangle using the Rectangle hierarchy.*

How can you proceed? Yes, you guess it right: you need to use an adapter to solve this problem. Here is an example:

```java
/*
 * Adapter is implementing RectInterface.
 * So, it needs to implement
 * all the methods defined
 * in the target interface.
 */
class Adapter implements RectInterface {
    TriInterface triangle;

    public Adapter(TriInterface triangle) {
        this.triangle = triangle;
    }

    @Override
    public void aboutMe() {
        triangle.aboutTriangle();
    }
```

```
    @Override
    public double calculateArea() {
        return triangle.calculateTriangleArea();
    }
}
```

Notice the beauty of using the adapter. You are not making any changes to any hierarchy. By using an `Adapter` instance, you use the methods of `RectInterface` to calculate the area of a triangle. It is because although you are using the `aboutMe()` and `calculateArea()` methods of the `RectInterface` at a high level, inside those methods you are invoking the methods of `TriInterface`.

Note   In this example, the `Adapter` adapts `TriInterface` to the `RectInterface`, so the client can use the incompatible `TriInterface` methods in the `RectInterface` hierarchy.

Apart from this advantage, you can also extend the benefit of using an adapter. For example, suppose you need to have a large number of rectangles in an application, but there is a constraint on the number of rectangles you can create. (For simplicity, let's assume that you are allowed to create a maximum of 5 rectangles and 10 triangles, but when the application runs, in certain scenarios, you may need to supply 10 rectangles.) In those cases, using this pattern, you can use some of the triangle objects that can behave like rectangle objects. How? Well, when using the adapter, although you call `calculateArea()`, it invokes `calculateTriangleArea()`. This approach shows that you can modify the method body as per your needs. For example, in your application, let's assume that each rectangle object has a length of 20 units and a width of 10 units, whereas each triangle object has a base of 20 units and a height of 10 units. So, each rectangle object has an area of 20*10=200 square units and each triangle object has an area of 0.5*20*10=100 square units. Now you can simply multiply each triangle area by 2 to get an equivalent rectangle area and substitute (or use) it where a rectangle area is needed. I believe that this makes sense to you.

Finally, you need to keep in mind that this technique suits best when you deal with objects that are not exactly the same but very similar.

Note   In the context of the previous point, you should not attempt to convert a circle area to a rectangle area (or do a similar type of conversion), because they are totally different shapes. In this example, I am talking about triangles and rectangles because they have similarities.

Class Diagram

Figure 10-4 shows the class diagram for the important parts of the program. Notice that the Adapter class holds an adaptee (TriInterface) reference.

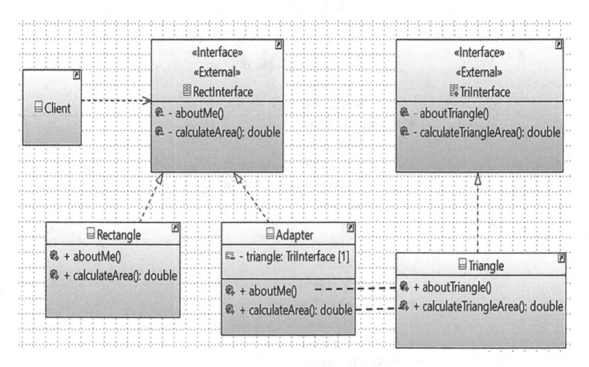

Figure 10-4. *Class diagram*

233

Package Explorer View

Figure 10-5 shows the high-level structure of the program.

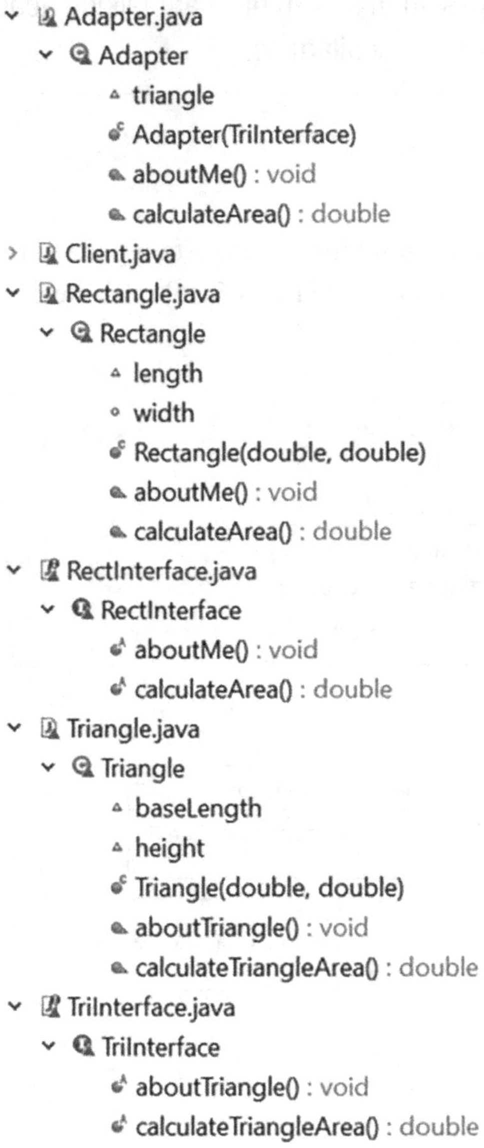

- ∨ 🗋 Adapter.java
  - ∨ ⬢ Adapter
    - ▵ triangle
    - ⚡ Adapter(TriInterface)
    - ⬟ aboutMe() : void
    - ⬟ calculateArea() : double
- ＞ 🗋 Client.java
- ∨ 🗋 Rectangle.java
  - ∨ ⬢ Rectangle
    - ▵ length
    - ○ width
    - ⚡ Rectangle(double, double)
    - ⬟ aboutMe() : void
    - ⬟ calculateArea() : double
- ∨ 🗋 RectInterface.java
  - ∨ ⬢ RectInterface
    - ⚡ aboutMe() : void
    - ⚡ calculateArea() : double
- ∨ 🗋 Triangle.java
  - ∨ ⬢ Triangle
    - ▵ baseLength
    - ▵ height
    - ⚡ Triangle(double, double)
    - ⬟ aboutTriangle() : void
    - ⬟ calculateTriangleArea() : double
- ∨ 🗋 TriInterface.java
  - ∨ ⬢ TriInterface
    - ⚡ aboutTriangle() : void
    - ⚡ calculateTriangleArea() : double

Figure 10-5. *Package Explorer view*

Demonstration 1

Here's the implementation. All parts of the program are stored in the `jdp3e.adapter` package.

// **RectInterface.java**

```java
interface RectInterface {

    void aboutMe();
    double calculateArea();
}
```

// **Rectangle.java**

```java
class Rectangle implements RectInterface {
    double length;
    public double width;

    public Rectangle(double length, double width) {
        this.length = length;
        this.width = width;
    }

    @Override
    public void aboutMe() {
        System.out.println("Shape type: Rectangle.");
    }

    @Override
    public double calculateArea() {
        return length * width;
    }
}
```

// **TriInterface.java**

```java
interface TriInterface {

    void aboutTriangle();
    double calculateTriangleArea();
}
```

// Triangle.java

```java
class Triangle implements TriInterface {
    double baseLength; // base
    double height; // height

    public Triangle(double length, double height) {
        this.baseLength = length;
        this.height = height;
    }

    @Override
    public double calculateTriangleArea() {
        return 0.5 * baseLength * height;
    }

    @Override
    public void aboutTriangle() {
        System.out.println("Shape type: Triangle.");
    }
}
```

// Adapter.java

```java
/*
 * Adapter is implementing RectInterface.
 * So, it needs to implement
 * all the methods defined
 * in the target interface.
 */
class Adapter implements RectInterface {
    TriInterface triangle;

    public Adapter(TriInterface triangle) {
        this.triangle = triangle;
    }

    @Override
    public void aboutMe() {
        triangle.aboutTriangle();
```

```
        }

        @Override
        public double calculateArea() {
            return triangle.calculateTriangleArea();
        }
}

// Client.java

import java.util.ArrayList;
import java.util.List;

class Client {
    public static void main(String[] args) {
        System.out.println("***Adapter Pattern Demo***\n");

        // A rectangle instance
        RectInterface rectangle = new Rectangle(20, 10);

        // A triangle instance
        TriInterface triangle = new Triangle(20, 10);

        // Using the adapter for the triangle object
        RectInterface adapter = new Adapter(triangle);

        // Holding all objects inside a list
        // It helps you traverse the list in
        // an uniform way.
        List<RectInterface> rectangleObjects = new
                            ArrayList<RectInterface>();
        rectangleObjects.add(rectangle);
        // rectangleObjects.add(triangle);//Error
        rectangleObjects.add(adapter); // No error

        System.out.println("Processing the following objects:\n");
        for (RectInterface rectObject : rectangleObjects) {
            System.out.println("Area: " +
                getDetails(rectObject) + " square units.\n");
        }
    }
```

```
    /*
     * The following method does not
     * know whether it gets a rectangle,
     * or a triangle through the adapter.
     */
    static double getDetails(RectInterface rectangle) {
        rectangle.aboutMe();
        return rectangle.calculateArea();
    }
}
```

Output

Here's the output:

Adapter Pattern Demo

Processing the following objects:

Shape type: Rectangle.
Area: 200.0 square units.

Shape type: Triangle.
Area: 100.0 square units.

Analysis

First, consider the following segment of code:

```
// rectangleObjects.add(triangle);//Error
rectangleObjects.add(adapter); // No error
```

The commented line says that you cannot directly add the Triangle instance into the list of rectangles. But using an adapter, you can do this. This is the real power of using an adapter.

Secondly, note the use of the following code segment with comments inside the client code:

```
/*
 * The following method does not
 * know whether it gets a rectangle,
 * or a triangle through the adapter.
 */
static double getDetails(RectInterface rectangle) {
 rectangle.aboutMe();
 return rectangle.calculateArea();
}
```

This segment is optional. I use it to show a usage where you can invoke both methods in one call. Notice that this method was supposed to process the rectangle objects. Now you can see that using an adapter, you can help this method to process a triangle object too.

Types of Adapters

The GoF described two types of adapters: class adapters and object adapters.

Object Adapters

Object adapters adapt through object composition, as shown in Figure 10-6. So, the adapter discussed so far is an example of an object adapter.

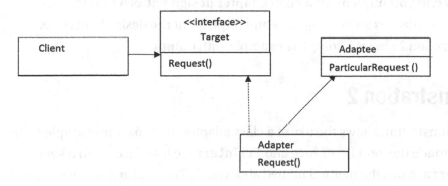

Figure 10-6. *Object adapter*

In the example, `Adapter` is the adapter that implements `RectInterface` (Target interface). `TriInterface` is the `Adaptee` interface. Notice that the adapter holds the adaptee instance. You can see that it accepts the adaptee as a constructor argument to make use of composition.

Class Adapters

Class adapters adapt through subclassing and support multiple inheritance. But you know that Java does not support multiple inheritance through classes. So, you need interfaces to implement the concept.

Figure 10-7 shows the typical class diagram for class adapters, which support multiple inheritance.

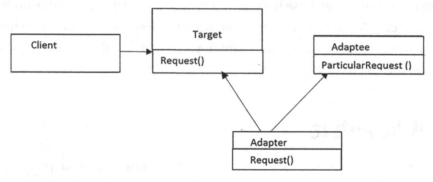

Figure 10-7. *Class adapter*

Q&A Session

10.1 How can you implement a class adapter design pattern in C#?

You can subclass an existing class and implement the desired interface. Demonstration 2 shows a complete example with output.

Demonstration 2

This demonstration shows the use of a class adapter. To make the example short and simple, I made the `RectInterface` and `TriInterface` interfaces with a single method. `RectInterface` has the method named `aboutMe()`. The `Rectangle` class implements this interface, and thus the following hierarchy is formed:

```
interface RectInterface {
    void aboutMe();
}

class Rectangle implements RectInterface {
    public void aboutMe() {
        System.out.println("Shape type: Rectangle.");
    }
}
```

TriInterface has the method aboutTriangle(). The Triangle class implements this interface and the following hierarchy is formed:

```
interface TriInterface {
    void aboutTriangle();
}

class Triangle implements TriInterface {
    public void aboutTriangle(){
        System.out.println("Shape type: Triangle.");
    }
}
```

Now comes the class adapter, which uses the concept of multiple inheritance using a concrete class and an interface. The attached comments will help you understand the code easily.

```
/*
 * Adapter is implementing RectInterface.
 * So, it needs to implement all the methods
 * defined in the target interface.
 */
class Adapter extends Triangle implements RectInterface{
    public void aboutMe() {
        // Invoking the adaptee method
        aboutTriangle();
    }
}
```

Now you can go through the complete demonstration. It's in a separate folder called implementation_2 inside the package jdp3e.adapter. So, when you download the source code from the Apress website, you can see all parts of the program inside the package jdp3e.adapter.implementation_2.

// RectInterface.java

```java
interface RectInterface {
    void aboutMe();
}
```

// Rectangle.java

```java
class Rectangle implements RectInterface {
    public void aboutMe() {
        System.out.println("Shape type: Rectangle.");
    }
}
```

// TriInterface.java

```java
interface TriInterface {
    void aboutTriangle();
}
```

// Triangle.java

```java
class Triangle implements TriInterface {
    public void aboutTriangle(){

        System.out.println("Shape type: Triangle.");
    }
}
```

// Adapter.java

```java
/*
 * Adapter is implementing RectInterface.
 * So, it needs to implement all the methods
 * defined in the target interface.
 */
```

```java
class Adapter extends Triangle implements RectInterface{
    public void aboutMe() {
        // Invoking the adaptee method
        this.aboutTriangle();
    }
}
```

// Client.java

```java
class Client {

    public static void main(String[] args) {
        System.out.println("***Class Adapter Demo.***\n");
        RectInterface rectangle = new Rectangle();
        System.out.println("Initially, printing the details of
                           both shapes.\n");
        System.out.println("The rectangle.AboutMe() says:");
        rectangle.aboutMe();

        TriInterface triangle = new Triangle();
        System.out.println("The triangle.Triangle() says:");
        triangle.aboutTriangle();

        System.out.println("\nNow using the adapter.");
        RectInterface adapter = new Adapter();
        System.out.println("The adapter.aboutMe() says:");
        adapter.aboutMe();
    }
}
```

Output

Here is the output:

Class Adapter Demo.

Initially, printing the details of both shapes.

```
The rectangle.AboutMe() says:
Shape type: Rectangle.
The triangle.Triangle() says:
Shape type: Triangle.

Now using the adapter.
The adapter.aboutMe() says:
Shape type: Triangle.
```

Analysis

This approach may not be suitable in all scenarios. For example, you may need to adapt a method that is not specified in a Java interface. In this case, object adapters are better.

But there is an advantage, too. A class adapter is often called a two-way adapter. Why? Let's add a few lines of code inside the client as follows:

```java
class Client {

    public static void main(String[] args) {
        // Previous codes skipped

        // 2-way adapter
        System.out.println("\nTesting a two-way adapter.");
        Adapter adapter2 = new Adapter();
        showAdapter(adapter2);
        showAdaptee(adapter2);
    }

    private static void showAdapter(RectInterface adapter) {
        adapter.aboutMe();

    }
    private static void showAdaptee(TriInterface adaptee) {
        adaptee.aboutTriangle();
    }
}
```

Note the following points:

- You can pass adapter2 to the method showAdapter(...), which expects a RectInterface (Adapter interface) argument from you.

- Again, notice that the Adapter class extends from TriInterface. It means you can pass adapter2 to the method showAdaptee(...) that expects a TriInterface (Adaptee interface) argument.

10.2 Which one do you prefer, class adapters or object adapters?

In most cases, I prefer compositions over inheritances. Object adapters use compositions and are more flexible. Also, in many cases, it is challenging to implement a true class adapter when you need to adapt a specific method from the adaptee interface but there is no close match for it in the target interface. Apart from this, consider the case when the adaptee class (such as Triangle in the example) and the target class are both concrete classes and you cannot inherit from them. In this case, the object adapter is the only solution you have. Lastly, a class adapter can expose some unrelated methods (since you extend from the adaptee and implement the target interface). People can misuse them.

10.3 "...it is challenging to implement a true class adapter when you need to adapt a specific method from an adaptee interface but there is no close match for that in the target interface?" Can you please elaborate?

In my examples, the target interface methods and adaptee interface methods are similar. For example, RectInterface has aboutMe() and TriInterface has aboutTriangle(). What are they doing? They are indicating whether it is a rectangle or a triangle. Aren't they? Now suppose there is no such method called aboutMe() in RectInterface but aboutTriangle() still exists in TriInterface. In a case like this, if you need to adapt the aboutTriangle() method, you need to analyze how to proceed. In this example, aboutTriangle() is a simple method but in real-world programming, the method can be much more complex and there can be a dependency associated with that, too. So, when you do not have a corresponding target method, you may find challenges in adapting the method from an adaptee.

10.4 It appears to me that the clients are unaware of the presence of adapters in the code. Is this understanding correct?

Correct. I made this implementation to show you that clients need not know that their requests are translated through an adapter to an adaptee. But if you want to show a message, you could simply add a console message in your adapter in demonstration 2 as follows:

245

```
class Adapter extends Triangle implements RectInterface {
    public void aboutMe() {
        // Invoking the adaptee method
        // For Q&A
        System.out.println("Using an adapter now.");
        aboutTriangle();
    }
}
```

10.5 What happens if the target interface and adaptee interface method signature differ?

It's not a problem at all. If an adapter method has a few parameters, you can invoke the adaptee method with some additional dummy parameters.

In the reverse scenario (if the adapter method has more parameters than the adaptee method), obviously using those additional parameters you can add some functionality before you transfer the call to the adaptee method.

Lastly, when the method parameters are incompatible, you may need to apply the casting mechanism (if possible).

10.6 It appears to me that I can instantiate an adaptee class directly inside the constructor of the object adapter class. Is this correct?

It can work, but it is not a preferred solution. Notice that when you do this, you are promoting tight coupling with the specific adaptee class. But notice this code in demonstration 1:

```
class Adapter implements RectInterface {
    TriInterface triangle;

    public Adapter(TriInterface triangle) {
        this.triangle = triangle;
    }
    // The remaining code skipped
}
```

Using this construct, you can pass any subclass of TriInterface to the adapter. This is an efficient solution.

10.7 What are the drawbacks associated with this pattern?

I do not see any big challenges. I believe that an adapter's job is simple and straightforward. You need to write some additional code, but the payoff is great, particularly for those legacy systems that cannot be changed but you still want to use them for their stability and simplicity.

I suggest you make adapters as simple as possible. When you use class adapters, you may think that you can override the adaptee behavior. But this practice is discouraged because in this case there is a behavior change between the adapter and the adaptee. It may impose an unnecessary burden when someone needs to debug your code later.

CHAPTER 11

Facade Pattern

This chapter covers the Facade pattern.

GoF Definition

It provides a unified interface to a set of interfaces in a subsystem. The Facade pattern defines a higher-level interface that makes the subsystem easier to use.

Concept

This pattern is a great promoter of loose coupling. Using this pattern, you emphasize the abstraction and hide the complex details by exposing a simple interface.

Consider a simple case. Let's say an application has multiple classes and each consists of multiple methods. A client can make a product using a combination of methods from these classes, but they need to remember which classes to pick and which methods to use with the calling sequence of these constructs. It can be ok for a developer, but it makes a client's life difficult. It is also challenging if there are lots of variations among these products.

To overcome this, you can use the Facade pattern. This pattern provides the client a user-friendly, simple interface to use, so that all the inner complexities (like which methods to invoke and what should be the calling sequence or series of steps to follow) are hidden. As a result, a client can simply concentrate on the final outcome(s).

In short, facades provide you with an entry point to access various methods across different classes in a structured manner. If you enforce a rule that does not allow you access to the individual methods directly, and instead you access them through your facade only, then the facade is called an **opaque** facade; otherwise, it is a **transparent** facade. At the time of this writing, you cannot tag the keyword `static` with a top-level class in Java. The Java Language Specification (Java SE 17 Edition) says that the modifier

249

© Vaskaran Sarcar 2022
V. Sarcar, *Java Design Patterns*, https://doi.org/10.1007/978-1-4842-7971-7_11

`static` pertains only to member classes and local classes. But depending on the programming language, you can make a top-level static class. For example, C# allows this, but there are restrictions such as you are allowed to use static data and methods inside the static class. So, depending on the programming language, you can make a top-level static class with static methods to avoid direct instantiation of a facade class. And when you use a similar concept, we say that you are using a **static** facade.

Real-World Example

Suppose you are planning to host a birthday party with 300 guests. Nowadays you can hire a party organizer and let them know the key information such as the party type, date and time of the party, number of attendees, and so on. The organizer will do the rest for you. You do not need to worry about how they will decorate the party room, how they manage the food in buffet style, and so on.

Consider another example. Suppose a customer requests a loan from a bank. In this case, the customer is only interested in knowing whether the loan is approved or not. They do not care about the inner background verification processes conducted at the bank's end. You'll see this as a sample case study in this chapter.

Computer World Example

Think about a case when you use a method from a library (in the context of a programming language). You don't worry about how the method is implemented in the library. You just call the method for easy usage.

You can consider the `java.net.URL` class as an example of a Facade pattern implementation. Here you can see the user-friendly and simplified methods that reduce the inner complexity of interacting with different methods that belong to different classes. Let's examine the concept:

- Investigate the shorthand methods `openStream()` or `getContent()` in this class. The `openStream()` method returns `openConnection().getInputStream()` and the `getContent()` method returns `openConnection.getContent()`. When you see the definition of `openConnection()`, you see that it is another method defined in the `java.net.URL` class and this method returns `handler.openConnection(this)`. What is this handler? It is an `URLStreamHandler` object. So, you can see that invoking `openStream()` simplifies the invoking of other methods that belong to different classes.

- Similarly, you can consider another method called `setURLStreamHandlerFactory(...)`. It uses the `URLStreamHandler` and the `URLStreamHandlerFactory` instances inside its definition.

The upcoming demonstration will make the overall concept clearer to you.

Implementation

Consider a case when a person applies for a loan from a bank. The bank officials must do some background verification before they grant the loan to the customer. This background verification is a complex process that consists of various subprocesses. The bank officials can visit a customer's property, too, before they consider the loan application. If the applicant satisfies all criteria, he can get a loan. But here is the key: the applicants do not know the details of the background verification. They are interested only in the final outcome: whether they get the loan. The final decision is made by the bank officials only. In the upcoming example, you will see such a process. For simplicity, let's make the following assumptions about approving a loan to a customer:

- The loan applicant or customer must have some assets. If the asset value is less than the loan amount he wants, he cannot get the loan.

- If the customer has an existing loan, he cannot get a new loan.

- If the above points do not apply to a customer, he can get a loan.

Your job is to make an application that is based on these assumptions. Here is sample output for better clarity:

Case 1:
```
Bob's current asset value: $5000,
He claims loan amount: $20,000
He has an existing loan.
```

Expected Outcome: Bob cannot get the loan for the following reasons:

- Insufficient balance.

- An old loan exists.

Case 2:
Jack's current asset value: $70,000,
He claims loan amount: $30,000
He has no existing loan.

Expected Outcome: Jack can get the loan.

Case 3:
Tony's current asset value: $125000,
He claims loan amount: $50,000
He has an existing loan.

Expected Outcome: Tony cannot get the loan for the following reason:

- An old loan exists.

Let's build the application now. As per the requirements, in the upcoming example, you see three classes: Person, Asset, and LoanStatus. This class has a constructor that takes three parameters: name, assetValue, and previousLoanExist. Here is the Person class:

```
class Person {
    String name;
    double assetValue;
    boolean previousLoanExist;

    public Person(String name, double assetValue, boolean
                                    previousLoanExist) {
        this.name = name;
        this.assetValue = assetValue;
        this.previousLoanExist = previousLoanExist;
    }
}
```

In this client code, you see three loan applicants Bob, Jack, and Tony. They are the instances of Person class:

```
// Person-1
Person person = new Person("Bob", 5000, true);
// Person-2
person = new Person("Jack", 70000, false);
// Person-3
person = new Person("Tony", 125000, true);
```

Now see the Asset class. This class has the method hasSufficientAssetValue to verify whether the current asset value is greater than or equal to the claim amount. Here is the Asset class:

```
class Asset {
  public boolean hasSufficientAssetValue(Person person,
                                         double claimAmount) {
  System.out.println("Verifying " + person.name + "'s asset value.");
  return person.assetValue >= claimAmount ? true : false;
  }
}
```

Now see the LoanStatus class. This class has the method hasPreviousLoans to verify whether a person has an existing loan.

```
class LoanStatus {
  public boolean hasPreviousLoans(Person person) {
  System.out.println("Verifying " + person.name + "'s previous
                  loan(s) status.");
  return person.previousLoanExist ? true : false;
  }
}
```

Notice the conditional operators in the bodies of these methods. You could use an if-else chain also. You can use either option to make the methods hasSufficientAssetValue and hasPreviousLoans work.

Class Diagram

Figure 11-1 shows the class diagram. Notice that the LoanApprover class plays the role of the facade. Here you can see the visibility and parameter type(s) of a method too.

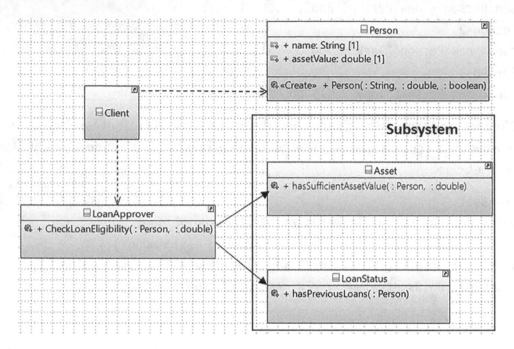

Figure 11-1. *Class diagram*

Package Explorer View

Figure 11-2 shows the high-level structure of the program. From this view, you can see that at a high level, the subsystem classes (Asset and LoanStatus) are segregated from the facade class (LoanApprover) and the client code.

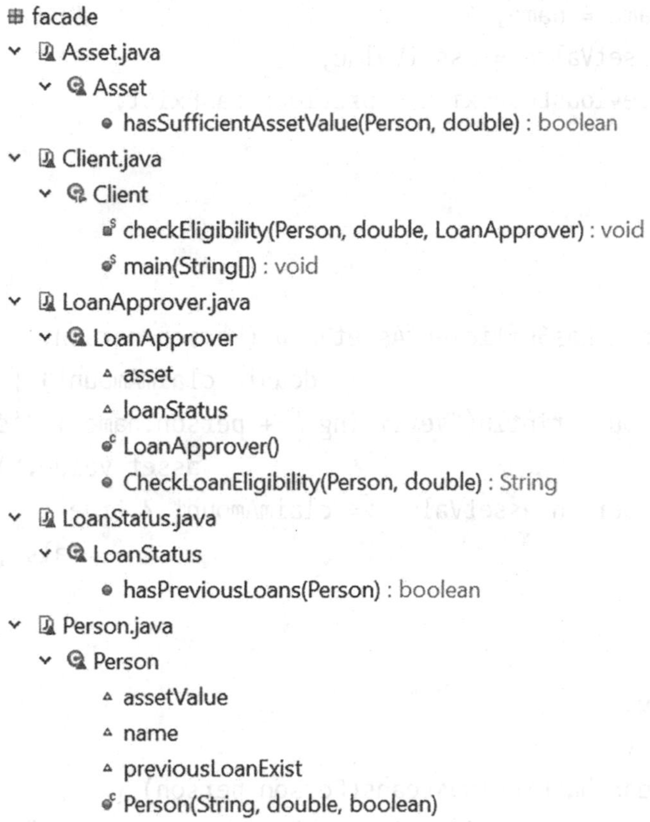

```
# facade
∨  Asset.java
   ∨  Asset
        • hasSufficientAssetValue(Person, double) : boolean
∨  Client.java
   ∨  Client
        ⚲ checkEligibility(Person, double, LoanApprover) : void
        ⚲ main(String[]) : void
∨  LoanApprover.java
   ∨  LoanApprover
        ▵ asset
        ▵ loanStatus
        ⚲ LoanApprover()
        • CheckLoanEligibility(Person, double) : String
∨  LoanStatus.java
   ∨  LoanStatus
        • hasPreviousLoans(Person) : boolean
∨  Person.java
   ∨  Person
        ▵ assetValue
        ▵ name
        ▵ previousLoanExist
        ⚲ Person(String, double, boolean)
```

Figure 11-2.   *Package Explorer view*

Demonstration

Here's the full implementation. You can download the code from the `jdp3e.facade` package.

// Person.java

```java
class Person {
    String name;
    double assetValue;
    boolean previousLoanExist;

    public Person(String name, double assetValue, boolean
                                previousLoanExist) {
```

```java
            this.name = name;
            this.assetValue = assetValue;
            this.previousLoanExist = previousLoanExist;
        }
}

// Asset.java
class Asset {
    public boolean hasSufficientAssetValue(Person person,
                                    double claimAmount) {
        System.out.println("Verifying " + person.name + "'s
                                            asset value.");
        return person.assetValue >= claimAmount ? true :
                                                    false;

    }
}

// LoanStatus.java
class LoanStatus {
    public boolean hasPreviousLoans(Person person) {
        System.out.println("Verifying " + person.name + "'s
                            previous loan(s) status.");
        return person.previousLoanExist ? true : false;
    }
}

// LoanApprover.java
class LoanApprover {
    Asset asset;
    LoanStatus loanStatus;

    public LoanApprover() {
        asset = new Asset();
        loanStatus = new LoanStatus();
    }

    public String CheckLoanEligibility(Person person,
                                    double claimAmount) {
```

```java
        String status = " Approved";
        String reason = "";
        System.out.println("\nChecking the loan approval
                            status of " + person.name);

        System.out.println("[The current asset value: " +
                            person.assetValue + ",\n claim
                            amount: " + claimAmount
                               +",\n existing loan?: " +
                            person.previousLoanExist + "]\n");

        if (!asset.hasSufficientAssetValue(person,
                              claimAmount)) {
            status = " Not approved.";
            reason += "\nInsufficient balance.";
        }

        if (loanStatus.hasPreviousLoans(person)) {
            status = " Not approved.";
            reason += "\nAn old loan exists.";
        }

        // Collecting the remarks (if any).
        String remarks = String.format("%nRemarks if
                        any:%s", reason);
        // Combining the final result with remarks using
         // the  format() method.
        String result = String.format("%s %s", status, remarks);
        // Same as:
        // String result=status+"\nRemarks if any:"+reason;

        return result;
    }
}

// Client.java
class Client {
```

```java
    public static void main(String[] args) {
        System.out.println("***Simplifying the usage of a
                        complex system using a facade.***");
        // Using a facade
        LoanApprover loanApprover = new LoanApprover();

        // Person-1
        Person person = new Person("Bob", 5000, true);
        checkEligibility(person, 20000, loanApprover);
        System.out.println("--------");

        // Person-2
        person = new Person("Jack", 70000, false);
        checkEligibility(person, 30000, loanApprover);
        System.out.println("--------");

        // Person-3
        person = new Person("Tony", 125000, true);
        checkEligibility(person, 125000, loanApprover);
        System.out.println("--------");
    }

    private static void checkEligibility(
                        Person person,
                        double claimAmount,
                        LoanApprover approver) {
      String approvalStatus =
       approver.CheckLoanEligibility(person, claimAmount);
      System.out.println(person.name + "'s application
                        status:" + approvalStatus);
    }
}
```

Output

Here's the output:

```
***Simplifying the usage of a complex system using a facade.***
```

```
Checking the loan approval status of Bob
[The current asset value: 5000.0,
 claim amount: 20000.0,
 existing loan?: true ]

Verifying Bob's asset value.
Verifying Bob's previous loan(s) status.
Bob's application status: Not approved.
Remarks if any:
Insufficient balance.
An old loan exists.
--------

Checking the loan approval status of Jack
[The current asset value: 70000.0,
 claim amount: 30000.0,
 existing loan?: false ]

Verifying Jack's asset value.
Verifying Jack's previous loan(s) status.
Jack's application status: Approved
Remarks if any:
--------

Checking the loan approval status of Tony
[The current asset value: 125000.0,
 claim amount: 125000.0,
 existing loan?: true ]

Verifying Tony's asset value.
Verifying Tony's previous loan(s) status.
Tony's application status: Not approved.
Remarks if any:
An old loan exists.
--------
```

Analysis

This demonstration shows you that a facade provides the following benefits:

- You make a simplified interface for your client, and you reduce the number of objects that a client needs to deal with. Notice that a client does not need to create any subsystem instances (for example, an `Asset` or `LoanStatus` instance) to know the final result. Instead, there is a loan approver instance that is the only point of contact to know the status of an application.

- In the future, if there are any new criteria to get a loan, let the loan approver take the responsibility of handling the situation. I believe that you value this point.

- If there is a big number of subsystems, managing those subsystems with a facade can make communication easier.

- Have you noticed that inside the client code you do not expose your background verification logic? I believe that you value this point too.

Q&A Session

11.1 What are the key advantages of using the Facade pattern?

Here are some advantages:

- If your system consists of many subsystems, managing those subsystems becomes tough, and clients will find it difficult to communicate separately with each of these subsystems. In a case like this, facade patterns are handy. Instead of presenting complex subsystems, you present one simplified interface to clients. This approach also supports weak coupling by separating the client code from the subsystems.

- It reduces the number of objects that a client needs to access.

11.2 The facade class uses compositions in this example. Is this necessary?

Yes. By using this approach you can access the intended methods in each subsystem.

11.3 Can you access each of the subsystems directly?

Yes, you can. The Facade pattern does not restrict you from doing this. But in this case, the code may look dirty, and you may lose the benefits associated with the Facade pattern. In this context, note that since the client can directly access the subsystem, it is called a **transparent** facade. But when you restrict that usage and force them to use a LoanApprover instance only to know whether they can get the loan, it is an **opaque** facade.

11.4 How is the Facade pattern different from the Adapter design pattern?

In the Adapter pattern, you try to alter an interface so that your clients do not see the difference between the interfaces. By contrast, the Facade pattern simplifies the interface. So, a client can interact with a simple interface instead of using a complex subsystem.

11.5 There should be only one facade for a complex subsystem. Is this correct?

Nope. You can create any number of facades for a subsystem.

11.6 Can you add new stuff/additional code with a facade?

Yes, you can. Note the use of simple statements inside the LoanApprover class to enable you to see messages like the following:

```
Checking the loan approval status of Jack
[The current asset value: 70000.0,
 claim amount: 30000.0,
 existing loan?: false ]
```

11.7 What are the challenges associated with this pattern?

Here are some challenges:

- Subsystems are connected to the facade layer. So, you need to take care of an additional layer of coding (thus increasing your codebase).

- When the internal structure of a subsystem changes, you need to incorporate the changes in the facade layer also.

- Developers need to learn about this new layer, whereas some of them are aware of how to use the subsystems/APIs efficiently.

11.8 In a different programming language such as C#, I have seen static facade classes. Can I make the same in Java?

In many examples, there is only one facade and you may not need to initialize the facade class. In those cases, it makes sense if you make the facade class static. But remember that Java does not allow you to create a top-level static class, whereas in C#, it is allowed but there are restrictions.

You can refer to the Java 16 language specification in this context at `https://docs. oracle.com/javase/specs/jls/se16/jls16.pdf` which says the following:

The modifier static pertains only to member classes and local classes. It further repeats the same: *It is a compile-time error if a local class or interface declaration has the modifier static (§8.1.1)*

Note   Java 17 is released now. This language specification tells the same. This specification is available at the following link: `https://docs.oracle.com/ javase/specs/jvms/se17/jvms17.pdf`.

CHAPTER 12

Flyweight Pattern

This chapter covers the Flyweight pattern.

GoF Definition

It uses sharing to support large numbers of fine-grained objects efficiently.

Concept

This pattern may look simple but if you do not identify the core concepts, the implementations may appear to be complex. So, I'll start with a very basic and detailed explanation before you implement this pattern. Let's start.

Sometimes you need to handle lots of objects that are very similar (but not the same). But the constraint is that you cannot create all of them to lessen resource and memory usage. The Flyweight pattern is made to handle these scenarios.

So how do you do this? Ok, to understand this, let's quickly revisit the fundamentals of object-oriented programming. A class is a template or blueprint, and an object is an instance of it. An object can have states and behaviors. For example, if you are familiar with the game of football (or soccer, as it's known in the United States), you can say that Ronaldo or Beckham are objects from the Footballer class. You may notice that they have states like "playing state" or "non-playing state." In the playing state, they can show different skills (or behaviors)—they can run, they can kick, they can pass the ball, and so forth. To begin with object-oriented programming, you can ask the following questions:

- What are the possible states of my objects?
- What are the different functions (behaviors) they can perform in those states?

© Vaskaran Sarcar 2022
V. Sarcar, *Java Design Patterns*, https://doi.org/10.1007/978-1-4842-7971-7_12

Once you get the answers to these questions, you are ready to proceed. Now come back to the Flyweight pattern. Here your job is to identify the following:

- What are the states of my objects?

- Which parts of these states can be changed?

Once you identify the answers, you break the states into two parts called *intrinsic* (which does not vary) and *extrinsic* (which can vary). If you make objects with intrinsic states, you can share them. For the extrinsic part, the user or client needs to pass in the information. So, whenever you need to have an object, you can get the object with the intrinsic state(s) and then you can configure the object on the fly by passing the extrinsic state(s). This technique reduces unnecessary object creations and memory usage.

Now verify your understanding in the following paragraph, which is extremely important. Let's see what GoF said about flyweights:

> *A flyweight is a shared object that can be used in multiple contexts simultaneously. The flyweight acts as an independent object in each context—it's indistinguishable from an instance of the object that's not shared. Flyweights cannot make assumptions about the context in which they operate. The key concept here is the distinction between intrinsic and extrinsic states. The intrinsic state is stored in the flyweight; it consists of information that's independent of the flyweight's context, thereby making it sharable. The extrinsic state depends on and varies with the flyweight's context and therefore can't be shared. Client objects are responsible for passing extrinsic state to the flyweight when it needs it.*

Real-Life Example

Suppose you have a pen. You can use different ink refills to write with different colors. So, the pen without the refill can be considered the flyweight with intrinsic data, and the refills can be considered the extrinsic data in this example. Now consider the case when you have many similar pens with different ink fills. For simplicity, assume that you have some pens with red refills and some pens with green refills and you want to distribute these pens among the kids. Later you identify that the kids like red pens more than green pens. So, you replace the green refills with red refills to make more red pens and distribute them among the kids to make them happy.

Consider another example. Suppose a company needs to print business cards for its employees. In this case, what is the starting point? The print department can create a common template where the company logo, address, and other details are already printed (intrinsic) and later the company adds the particular employee details (extrinsic) on the cards.

Computer World Example

Consider a computer game where you see a large number of participants whose core structures are the same, but their appearances vary (for example, they may have different states, colors, weapons, and so on). Therefore, when the game runs, if you want to store all of these objects with all of these variations/states, the memory requirement will be huge. So, instead of storing all these objects, you can design the application in such a way that you will create one of these instances with the states that don't vary among objects and your client can maintain remaining variations/states. When you successfully implement the concept, you can say that you have followed the flyweight pattern in your application. Here are few more examples:

- In Java, you may notice the use of this pattern when you use wrapper classes like java.lang.Integer, java.lang.Short, java.lang.Byte, and java.lang.Character where the static method valueof() replicates a factory method. (It is worth remembering that some wrapper classes such as java.lang.Double do not use the same concept.) This method checks whether an object is present in the cache. If it is found in the cache, it is returned.

- A String pool in JVM is another example of a flyweight. When you call the intern() method, it can return a cached object, too.

- Similarly, the string interning in a .NET application follows this pattern.

Implementation

The following example shows the usage of three different types of vehicles called Car, Bus, and FutureVehicle (let's assume we'll see them in 2050). In this application, you assume that a client may want to use a large number of objects from these classes with different colors that they like. You also assume that the basic structure of a car (or bus, etc.) does not vary.

When a client requests a particular vehicle, the application will not create an object from scratch if it previously created an instance of that type of vehicle; instead, it'll prepare the existing one (without `color`) to serve the needs of the client. Just before delivering the product, it'll paint the vehicle with the `color` that the client prefers. Now look into the implementation strategies, which are as follows.

First, you create an interface for flyweights. This interface is made to provide common method(s) that accept extrinsic state(s) of flyweights. In your example, `color` is supplied by clients, so it is treated as an extrinsic state. This is why you see the following code segment:

```
interface Vehicle {
    // Color comes from client. It is extrinsic.
    void aboutMe(String color);
}
```

Most often you will see a factory that will supply the flyweights to the client. This factory caches flyweights and provides methods to get them. In a shared flyweight object, you add intrinsic state(s) and implement the method(s) if necessary. You can have unshared flyweights, too. In these cases, you can ignore the extrinsic states that are passed by a client.

In the upcoming example, `VehicleFactory` is the factory that supplies the flyweights with intrinsic states. Notice that a `Map` object is used to store the `key/value` pairs to store vehicles with a specific type. Initially, there are no objects inside the factory, but once it starts receiving requests for vehicles, it will create the vehicles and cache them for future use. Notice that "One `car is ready`," "One `bus is ready`," and "One `future vehicle(Vehicle 2050) is ready`" are supplied by the factory inside the flyweight objects during the object creation phase. They are the intrinsic states of the vehicles and they don't vary across the products.

In addition, there is a method called `totalObjectsCreated()` that is used to track the number of truly unique objects in the application. The following code segment shows this factory class:

```
class VehicleFactory {
    Map<String, Vehicle> vehicles = new HashMap<String,
                                            Vehicle>();
```

```
/**
 * To count different types of vehicles
 * in a given moment.
 */

public int totalObjectsCreated() {
    return vehicles.size();
}

public synchronized Vehicle
        getVehicleFromFactory(String vehicle)
                        throws Exception {
    Vehicle vehicleType = vehicles.get(vehicle);
    if (vehicleType != null) {
        // Using the existing type
        System.out.println("\n\t Using an existing vehicle now.");
    } else {
        switch (vehicle) {
        case "car":
            System.out.println("Making a car for the first time.");
            vehicleType = new Car("One car is ready");
            vehicles.put("car", vehicleType);
            break;
        case "bus":
            System.out.println("Making a bus for the first time.");
            vehicleType = new Bus("One bus is ready");
            vehicles.put("bus", vehicleType);
            break;
        case "future":
            System.out.println("Making a future
                    vehicle for the first time.");
            vehicleType = new FutureVehicle("One
                    future vehicle(Vehicle 2050) is ready");
            vehicles.put("future", vehicleType);
            break;
```

```
                  default:
                      throw new Exception("Unknown vehicle type.");
                  }
              }
          return vehicleType;
      }
  }
```

Let's see a concrete flyweight class now. Here is one of these classes (the others are similar). The associated comments will help you understand it better. Notice how the method aboutMe() is used to show the intrinsic and extrinsic states of the vehicle.

Note   The comments are here for your easy reference. In the demonstration, I removed them to avoid repetition. But when you download the code from the Apress website, you get them again.

```java
// A shared flyweight implementation

class Car implements Vehicle {
    /**
     * This is an intrinsic state:
     * 1.It is not supplied by client.
     * 2.It is independent of the flyweight's context.
     * 3.This can be shared across.
     * 4.These data are often immutable.
     */
    private String description;

    /**
     * The VehicleFactory will supply this
     * inside the flyweight object.
     */
    public Car(String description) {
        this.description = description;
    }
```

```
    // Client supplies the color
    @Override
    public void aboutMe(String color) {
        System.out.print(description + " with " + color
                            + " color.");
    }
}
```

From this code segment, you can see that the description is supplied during the object creation process (the Flyweight factory does this), but the color will be supplied by the clients. In this example, the colors are drawn at random using a method called getRandomColor(). This method has the following definition:

```
/**
 * Get a random color. Here I consider
* two colors only-red and green.
*/
static String getRandomColor() {
 Random r = new Random();
 int random = r.nextInt();
 if (random % 2 == 0) {
  return "red";
   } else {
    return "green";
   }
}
```

So, inside the main()method, note the code segments like the following: vehicle.aboutMe(getRandomColor());

Lastly, the FutureVehicle is considered as an unshared flyweight in this example. So, in this class, the aboutMe(...) method ignores the String parameter. As a result, it always produces vehicles with a blue color and ignores the client's preferences. Here is the code segment with comments that reflects the same:

```
// Client cannot choose color for FutureVehicle.
// It is an unshared flyweight.
// So, we ignore the client's input.
```

```
@Override
public void aboutMe(String color) {
  System.out.print(description + " with " + "blue
                    (default) color.");
}
```

Class Diagram

Figure 12-1 shows the class diagram.

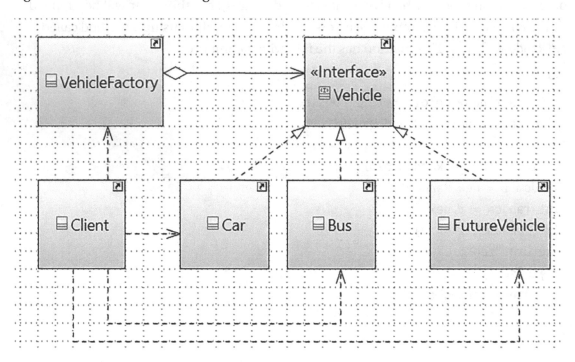

Figure 12-1.   *Class diagram*

Package Explorer View

Figure 12-2 shows the high-level structure of the program. Since it's a big diagram, let's move to the next page.

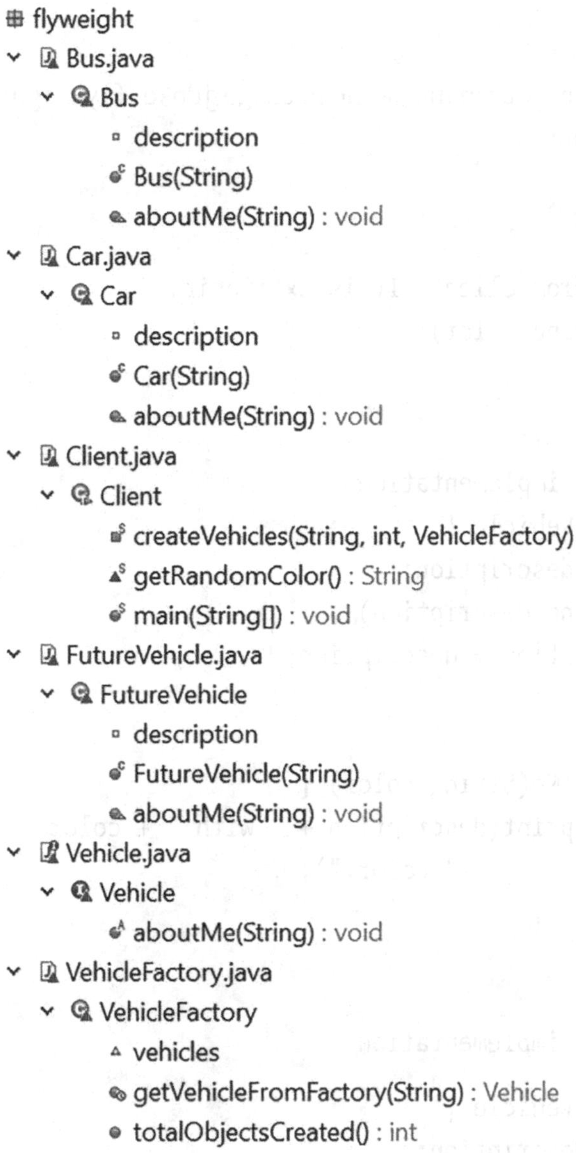

⊞ flyweight

∨ 📄 Bus.java

  ∨ 🅠 Bus

    ▫ description

    🔩 Bus(String)

    🔩 aboutMe(String) : void

∨ 📄 Car.java

  ∨ 🅠 Car

    ▫ description

    🔩 Car(String)

    🔩 aboutMe(String) : void

∨ 📄 Client.java

  ∨ 🅠 Client

    🔩 createVehicles(String, int, VehicleFactory) : void

    🔺 getRandomColor() : String

    🔩 main(String[]) : void

∨ 📄 FutureVehicle.java

  ∨ 🅠 FutureVehicle

    ▫ description

    🔩 FutureVehicle(String)

    🔩 aboutMe(String) : void

∨ 📄 Vehicle.java

  ∨ 🅠 Vehicle

    🔩 aboutMe(String) : void

∨ 📄 VehicleFactory.java

  ∨ 🅠 VehicleFactory

    🔺 vehicles

    🔩 getVehicleFromFactory(String) : Vehicle

    ● totalObjectsCreated() : int

Figure 12-2. Package Explorer view

Demonstration

All parts of the program are stored inside the package jdp3e.flyweight. Here's the complete implementation:

```
// Vehicle.java
interface Vehicle {
    // Color comes from client. It is extrinsic.
    void aboutMe(String color);
}
```

```
// Car.java
// A shared flyweight implementation
class Car implements Vehicle {
    private String description;
    public Car(String description) {
        this.description = description;
    }
    @Override
    public void aboutMe(String color) {
        System.out.print(description + " with " + color
                        + " color.");
    }
}
```

```
// Bus.java
// A shared flyweight implementation

class Bus implements Vehicle {
    private String description;

    public Bus(String description) {
        this.description = description;
    }
    @Override
    public void aboutMe(String color) {
        System.out.print(description + " with " + color
                        + " color.");
```

```
    }
}
```

// FutureVehicle.java

```java
// An unshared flyweight implementation

class FutureVehicle implements Vehicle {
    private String description;

    public FutureVehicle(String description) {
        this.description = description;
    }

    // Client cannot choose color for FutureVehicle.
    // It is an unshared flyweight.
    // So, we ignore the client's input.

    @Override
    public void aboutMe(String color) {
        System.out.print(description + " with " + "a
                         blue (default) color.");
    }
}
```

// VehicleFactory.java

```java
import java.util.HashMap;
import java.util.Map;

class VehicleFactory {
    Map<String, Vehicle> vehicles = new HashMap<String,
                                    Vehicle>();

    /**
     * To count different types of vehicles
     * in a given moment.
     */
```

```java
    public int totalObjectsCreated() {
        return vehicles.size();
    }

    public synchronized Vehicle
     getVehicleFromFactory(String vehicle)
                                throws Exception {
        Vehicle vehicleType = vehicles.get(vehicle);
        if (vehicleType != null) {
            // Using the existing type
            System.out.println("\n\t Using an existing vehicle now.");
        } else {

            switch (vehicle) {
            case "car":
                System.out.println("Making a car for the first time.");
                vehicleType = new Car("One car is ready");
                vehicles.put("car", vehicleType);
                break;
            case "bus":
                System.out.println("Making a bus for the first time.");
                vehicleType = new Bus("One bus is ready");
                vehicles.put("bus", vehicleType);
                break;
            case "future":
                System.out.println("Making a future
                    vehicle for the first time.");
                vehicleType = new FutureVehicle("One
                    future vehicle(Vehicle 2050) is ready");
                vehicles.put("future", vehicleType);
                break;
            default:
                throw new Exception("Unknown vehicle type.");
            }
```

```
        }
        return vehicleType;
    }
}
```

// Client.java

```java
import java.util.Random;

class Client {

    public static void main(String[] args) throws
                                    Exception {
        System.out.println("***Flyweight Pattern Demo.***\n");
        VehicleFactory vehicleFactory = new
                                VehicleFactory();

        // Making 3 cars
        createVehicles("car", 3, vehicleFactory);

        // Making 5 Buses
        createVehicles("bus", 5, vehicleFactory);

        // Making 2 future vehicles
        createVehicles("future", 2, vehicleFactory);

    }

    /**
     * We are trying to get the 5 vehicles.
     * Note that: we need not create additional
     * vehicles if we have already created one of these
     * categories.
     */
    private static void createVehicles(String
      vehicleType, int count, VehicleFactory factory)
                                throws Exception {
        int distinctVehicles;
```

```
        for (int i = 0; i < count; i++) {
         Vehicle vehicle =
         factory.getVehicleFromFactory(vehicleType);
         vehicle.aboutMe(getRandomColor());
        }
        distinctVehicles =
         factory.totalObjectsCreated();
        System.out.println("\n\tDistinct vehicles in
             this application: " + distinctVehicles);
        System.out.println("------------");

    }

    /**
     * Get a random color. Here I consider
     * two colors only-red and green.
     */
    static String getRandomColor() {
        Random r = new Random();

        int random = r.nextInt();
        if (random % 2 == 0) {
            return "red";
        } else {
            return "green";
        }
    }

}
```

Output

Here's a possible output (because the color is generated at random). This is from the first run on my machine. I marked a few lines bold to show the unique number of vehicles at a given time.

```
***Flyweight Pattern Demo.***

Making a car for the first time.
One car is ready with green color.
    Using an existing vehicle now.
One car is ready with green color.
    Using an existing vehicle now.
One car is ready with red color.
```
Distinct vehicles in this application: 1
```
------------
Making a bus for the first time.
One bus is ready with green color.
    Using an existing vehicle now.
One bus is ready with red color.
    Using an existing vehicle now.
One bus is ready with green color.
    Using an existing vehicle now.
One bus is ready with green color.
    Using an existing vehicle now.
One bus is ready with red color.
```
Distinct vehicles in this application: 2
```
------------
Making a future vehicle for the first time.
One future vehicle(Vehicle 2050) is ready with a blue (default) color.
    Using an existing vehicle now.
One future vehicle(Vehicle 2050) is ready with a blue (default) color.
```
Distinct vehicles in this application: 3
```
------------
```

Here's another probable output (because the color is generated at random). This is from the second run on my machine.

```
***Flyweight Pattern Demo.***

Making a car for the first time.
One car is ready with green color.
    Using an existing vehicle now.
```

One car is ready with green color.
        Using an existing vehicle now.
One car is ready with green color.
    Distinct vehicles in this application: 1

Making a bus for the first time.
One bus is ready with green color.
        Using an existing vehicle now.
One bus is ready with green color.
        Using an existing vehicle now.
One bus is ready with green color.
        Using an existing vehicle now.
One bus is ready with green color.
        Using an existing vehicle now.
One bus is ready with green color.
    Distinct vehicles in this application: 2

Making a future vehicle for the first time.
One future vehicle(Vehicle 2050) is ready with a blue (default) color.
        Using an existing vehicle now.
One future vehicle(Vehicle 2050) is ready with a blue (default) color.
    Distinct vehicles in this application: 3

Note   Remember that the outputs vary because the colors are picked at random in this example.

Analysis

Notice that the application creates an object if and only if the object is not available at that moment. Once it creates an object, it caches the object for future reuse.

Q&A Session

12.1 Can you highlight the key differences between a Singleton pattern and a Flyweight pattern?

Singleton helps you to maintain at most one object that is required in the system. In other words, once the required object is created, you cannot create more of it. You need to reuse the existing object.

Normally, a Flyweight pattern concerns heavy but similar objects (where all states are not exactly the same) because they may occupy big blocks of memory. So, you try to create a smaller set of template objects that can be configured on the fly to make these heavy objects. These smaller and configurable objects are called flyweights. You can reuse them in your application when you deal with many large objects. This approach helps you reduce the consumption of big chunks of memory. Basically, flyweights make *one look like many*. This is why the GoF tells us the following: "A flyweight is a shared object that can be used in multiple contexts simultaneously. The flyweight acts as an independent object in each context—it's indistinguishable from an instance of the object that's not shared."

Figure 12-3 shows you how to visualize the core concepts of the Flyweight pattern before using flyweights.

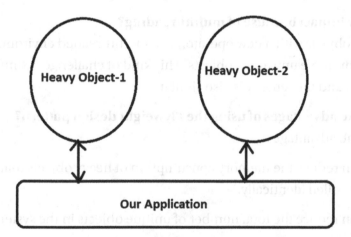

Figure 12-3. *Before using flyweights*

Figure 12-4 shows the design after using flyweights.

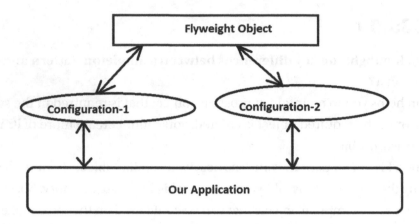

Figure 12-4. *After using flyweights*

So, from Figure 12-4, you can see that the Heavy-Object1 can be created when you apply Configuration-1 to the Flyweight Object. Similarly, Heavy-Object2 can be created when you apply Configuration-2 to the Flyweight Object. You can see that instance-specific contents (like color in the previous demonstration) can be passed to the flyweights to make these heavy objects. So, note in this example that the flyweight object acts like a common template that can be configured as per the need.

12.2 Is there any impact because of multithreading?

If you create objects with a new operator, in a multithreaded environment you may end up creating multiple unwanted objects. This kind of challenge is similar to the Singleton pattern and the remedy is also similar.

12.3 What are the advantages of using the Flyweight design pattern?

Here are some advantages:

- You can reduce the memory consumption of heavy objects that can be controlled identically.

- You can reduce the total number of unique objects in the system.

- You can maintain centralized states of many "virtual" objects.

12.4 What are the challenges associated with using the Flyweight design pattern?

Here are some challenges:

- In this pattern, you need to spend some time configuring these flyweights. This configuration time can impact the overall performance of the application.

- To create flyweights, you extract a common template class from existing objects. This additional layer of programming can be tricky and sometimes hard to debug and maintain.

12.5 Can you have a non-shareable flyweight interface?

Yes, a flyweight interface does not enforce that it needs to be shareable always. So, in some cases, you may have non-shareable flyweights only. In our example, the FutureVehicle class is made to demonstrate this case. You can see that its instances are always made with a blue color. For this vehicle, it doesn't matter whatever color (red or green or any other color) a client supplies to it as an extrinsic state.

12.6 Since the intrinsic data of flyweights is the same, you try to share them. Is this correct?

Yes. Notice that the strings "One car is ready," "One bus is ready," or "One future vehicle(Vehicle 2050) is ready" are supplied by the factory inside the flyweights during the flyweight (with the intrinsic state) object creation phase.

12.7 How do clients handle the extrinsic data of these flyweights?

They need to pass that information (the states) to the flyweights.

12.8 This means that extrinsic data is not shareable. Is this correct?

Yes. It's very important to understand this before you implement this pattern.

12.9. What is the role of VehicleFactory in this implementation?

It caches flyweights and provides a method to get them. In this example, there are multiple objects with an intrinsic state that can be shared. I believe that storing them in a central place is a good idea.

12.10 Can I implement the factory class as a singleton?

Yes, you can. In fact, you may see this in many applications. In addition, you'll see some of those applications instantiate all possible objects at the beginning. For example, you may try to initialize all different types of vehicles inside the VehicleFactory's constructor. When you do that, you always start with three distinct vehicle objects at the beginning. But the problem is, if you do not need bus, car, or Vehicle2050, you unnecessarily waste memory for the object(s).

On the contrary, in the shown demonstration, if any object is not available, the factory class creates it and caches it for future use. So, my vote is for this kind of demonstration unless you modify such an implementation keeping this potential drawback in mind.

In short, whenever you use this pattern, you create an object, fill in all the required state information, and give it to your client. Each time a client requests an object, your application should check whether it can reuse an existing object (with required states filled) or not. Thus you can reduce unnecessary object creations and save memory consumption.

12.11 You said that `java.lang.Integer` is an example of flyweight. Can you please elaborate?

Let me show you a partial snapshot from the Eclipse IDE of the `valueOf(...)` method inside the `Integer` class (see Figure 12-5).

```
 * This method will always cache values in the range -128 to 127,
 * inclusive, and may cache other values outside of this range.
 *
 * @param   i an {@code int} value.
 * @return an {@code Integer} instance representing {@code i}.
 * @since   1.5
 */
@IntrinsicCandidate
public static Integer valueOf(int i) {
    if (i >= IntegerCache.low && i <= IntegerCache.high)
        return IntegerCache.cache[i + (-IntegerCache.low)];
    return new Integer(i);
}
```

Figure 12-5. *The definition of the valueOf(...) method inside the Integer class*

Have you noticed the method description? Can you identify the words such as "IntrinsicCandidate" and "cache" here? What does the method do? It checks whether the integer argument belongs to a particular range. If it is in the range, you get a cached object.

(You may note that `public Integer(int value){...}` is deprecated since Java 9. It is reflected inside the snapshot too.)

You can also investigate the definition of the `intern()` method of String in the same way to get the following information:

"A pool of strings, initially empty, is maintained privately by the class String. When the intern method is invoked, if the pool already contains a string equal to this String object as determined by the equals(Object) method, then the string from the pool is returned. Otherwise, this String object is added to the pool, and a reference to this String object is returned."

CHAPTER 13

Composite Pattern

This chapter covers the Composite pattern.

GoF Definition

It composes objects into tree structures to represent part-whole hierarchies.
The Composite pattern lets clients treat individual objects and compositions of objects uniformly.

Concept

Consider a shop that sells different kinds of dried fruit such as cashews, dates, and walnuts. Each item has a certain price. Let's assume that you can purchase individual items or you can purchase gift packs (or boxed items) which are composed of different dried fruit items. In this case, the cost of a gift pack is the sum of the individual parts (component). The composite pattern is useful in a similar situation where you want to treat both the individual parts and the combination of the parts in the same way so that you can process them uniformly.

In object-oriented programming, a composite is an object with a composition of one or more similar objects, where each of these objects has similar functionality. (This is also known as a "has-a" relationship among objects.) So, the usage of this pattern

© Vaskaran Sarcar 2022
V. Sarcar, *Java Design Patterns*, https://doi.org/10.1007/978-1-4842-7971-7_13

is common in tree-structured data. When you implement this pattern in such a data structure, you do not need to discriminate between a branch and the leaf nodes of the tree. You can achieve the following goals using this pattern:

- You can compose objects into a tree structure to represent a part-whole hierarchy.

- You can access both the composite objects (branches) and the individual objects (leaf nodes) uniformly. As a result, you can reduce the complexity of the code and make the application less error prone.

Real-Life Example

Apart from the previous example, you can also think of an organization that consists of many departments. In general, an organization has many employees. Some of these employees are grouped to form a department and those departments can be further grouped to build the final structure of the organization.

Computer World Example

This pattern is common in various UI frameworks where you need to add other UI controls such as a button or a textbox in a container. Here are some examples:

- I mentioned that a tree data structure can follow this concept where the clients can treat the leaves of the tree and the non-leaves (branches of the tree) in the same way. So, when you see hierarchical data, it's a clue that a composite pattern can be useful. XML files are very common examples where you notice such tree structures.

- In Java, note the use of the generic Abstract Window Toolkit (AWT) container object. It is a component that can contain other AWT components. For example, in the `java.awt.Container` class (which extends `java.awt.Component`) you can see overloaded versions of the `add (...)` method. These methods accept another `Component` object to proceed further.

Note   When you traverse a tree, you often use the concept of the Iterator design pattern, covered in Chapter 18 of this book.

Implementation

This example represent a college organization. Let's assume you have a principal and two heads of departments (HODs), one for Computer Science and Engineering (CSE) and one for Mathematics (Math). In the Mathematics department, there are currently two lecturers (or teachers), and in the Computer Science and Engineering department there are three lecturers (or teachers). The tree structures for this organization look like Figure 13-1.

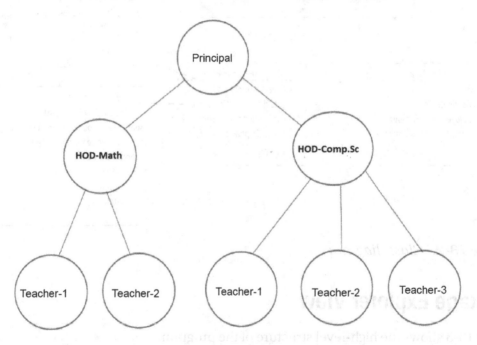

Figure 13-1. *A college organization with a Principal, two HODs and five Lecturers*

Let's also assume that at the end of the year, one lecturer from the CSE department resigns. The following example considers the mentioned scenarios.

Class Diagram

Figure 13-2 shows the class diagram.

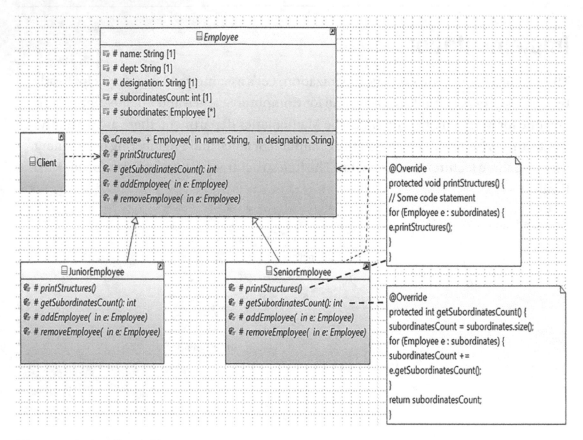

Figure 13-2.   *Class diagram*

Package Explorer View

Figure 13-3 shows the high-level structure of the program.

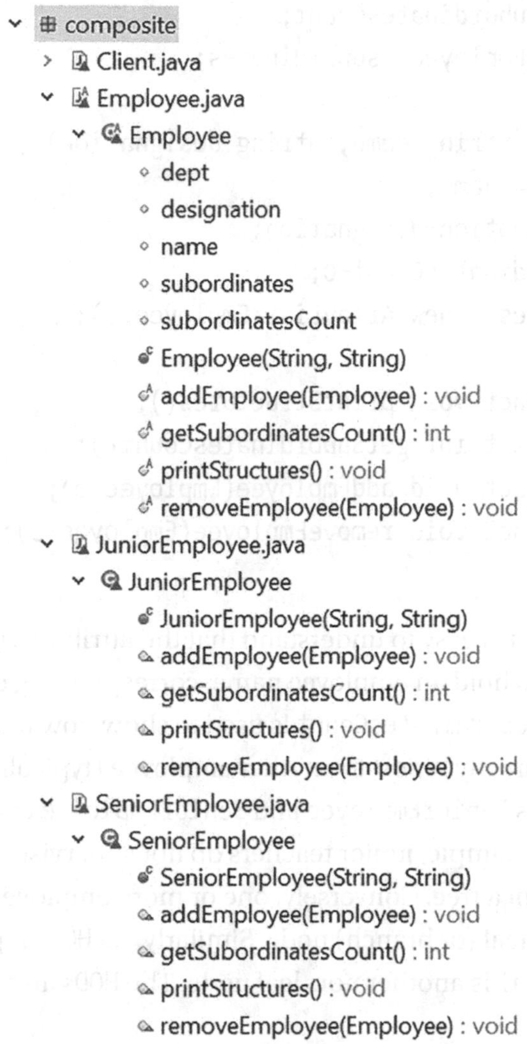

```
∨  ⊞ composite
   >  ⌕ Client.java
   ∨  ⌕ Employee.java
      ∨  ⓒ Employee
         ○ dept
         ○ designation
         ○ name
         ○ subordinates
         ○ subordinatesCount
         ⚘ Employee(String, String)
         ⚹ addEmployee(Employee) : void
         ⚹ getSubordinatesCount() : int
         ⚹ printStructures() : void
         ⚹ removeEmployee(Employee) : void
   ∨  ⌕ JuniorEmployee.java
      ∨  ⓒ JuniorEmployee
         ⚘ JuniorEmployee(String, String)
         ⚬ addEmployee(Employee) : void
         ⚬ getSubordinatesCount() : int
         ⚬ printStructures() : void
         ⚬ removeEmployee(Employee) : void
   ∨  ⌕ SeniorEmployee.java
      ∨  ⓒ SeniorEmployee
         ⚘ SeniorEmployee(String, String)
         ⚬ addEmployee(Employee) : void
         ⚬ getSubordinatesCount() : int
         ⚬ printStructures() : void
         ⚬ removeEmployee(Employee) : void
```

Figure 13-3. Package Explorer view

Demonstration

This demonstration starts with the abstract class Employee that has four abstract methods. It looks like the following:

```
abstract class Employee {
    protected String name;
    protected String dept;
    protected String designation;
```

```
    protected int subordinatesCount;
    protected List<Employee> subordinates;
    // Constructor
    public Employee(String name, String designation) {
        this.name = name;
        this.designation=designation;
        this.subordinatesCount=0;
        subordinates = new ArrayList<Employee>();
    }
    protected abstract void printStructures();
    protected abstract int getSubordinatesCount();
    protected abstract void addEmployee(Employee e);
    protected abstract void removeEmployee(Employee e);
}
```

As per their names, it is easy to understand that the attributes name, dept, and designation are used to hold an employee name, corresponding department, and designation. The field subordinatesCount is used to show how many employees (or lecturers or teachers) directly report to another employee (typically a senior teacher).

The concrete classes JuniorEmployee and SeniorEmployee extend this Employee class. In the upcoming example, junior teachers do not supervise any other teacher so they act like leaf nodes of a tree. Conversely, one or more employees can report to a HOD, so it is treated as a non-leaf (or branch) node. Similarly, all HODs report to the Principal. This is why the Principal is another non-leaf node. The HODs and the Principal are senior employees.

Here is the code segment to form a department. The comments are for your easy understanding.

```
System.out.println("Forming Mathematics department.");
System.out.println("A HOD with two lectureres are here.\n");
// Teachers of Mathematics directly
// reports to HOD-Mathematics
hodMaths.addEmployee(mathTeacher1);
hodMaths.addEmployee(mathTeacher2);
```

The SeniorEmployee class maintains the subordinate list. It has two additional methods called addEmployee(...) and removeEmployee(...). These methods are used to add an employee to the list or remove an employee from the list, respectively.

Now go through the complete implementation and refer to the supportive comments. All parts of the program are stored inside the package jdp3e.composite.

// Employee.java

```java
import java.util.ArrayList;
import java.util.List;

    abstract class Employee {
    protected String name;
    protected String dept;
    protected String designation;
    protected int subordinatesCount;
    protected List<Employee> subordinates;
    // Constructor
    public Employee(String name, String designation) {
        this.name = name;
        this.designation=designation;
        this.subordinatesCount=0;
        subordinates = new ArrayList<Employee>();
    }
    protected abstract void printStructures();
    protected abstract int getSubordinatesCount();
    protected abstract void addEmployee(Employee e);
    protected abstract void removeEmployee(Employee e);
}
```

// SeniorEmployee.java
```java
// It is a non-leaf node
class SeniorEmployee extends Employee {
    public SeniorEmployee(String name, String designation) {
        super(name, designation);
    }
```

```java
    @Override
    protected void printStructures() {
        System.out.println("\t" + this.name + " is a " +
                            this.designation);
        for (Employee e : subordinates) {
            e.printStructures();
        }
    }

    @Override
    protected int getSubordinatesCount() {
        subordinatesCount = subordinates.size();
        for (Employee e : subordinates) {
            subordinatesCount += e.getSubordinatesCount();
        }
        return subordinatesCount;
    }

    @Override
    protected void addEmployee(Employee e) {
        subordinates.add(e);
    }

    @Override
    protected void removeEmployee(Employee e) {
        subordinates.remove(e);
    }
}

// JuniorEmployee.java
class JuniorEmployee extends Employee{
    public JuniorEmployee(String name, String designation) {
        super(name, designation);
    }

    @Override
    protected void printStructures(){
        System.out.println("\t\t"+this.name + " is a " +
```

```
                                    this.designation);
    }
    @Override
    protected int getSubordinatesCount(){
        return subordinatesCount; //Always 0
    }

    @Override
    protected void addEmployee(Employee e) {
        // Empty method
    }

    @Override
    protected void removeEmployee(Employee e) {
        // Empty method
    }

}
```

// Client.java
(Refer to the comments for your easy reference)

```
class Client {

    public static void main(String[] args) {
        System.out.println("***Composite Pattern
    Demonstration.***");

        Employee hodMath = formMathDept();
        Employee hodCompSc = formComputerScDept();
        Employee principal = formPrincipal(hodMath,
                                        hodCompSc);

        /*
        Printing the leaf-nodes and branches
        in the same way i.e.
        in each case, we are calling
        printStructures() method.
        */
```

```java
System.out.println("The details of the Principal object:");
// Prints the complete college structure
principal.printStructures();

System.out.println("\n The details of the
                HOD(Computer Sc.) object:");
// Prints the details of Computer Science
// department
hodCompSc.printStructures();

System.out.println("\n The details of the
                HOD(Mathematics) object:");
// Prints the details of Mathematics department
hodMath.printStructures();

// Leaf node
System.out.println("\n  The structure of a Junior
                    employee(leaf node):");
hodMath.subordinates.get(0).printStructures();

// Current management details
displayManagementDetail(principal,
    hodCompSc,hodMath);

System.out.println("\nThe lecturer Mr.
    C.Jones(cseTeacher2) resigns.");
hodCompSc.removeEmployee(
            hodCompSc.subordinates.get(1));
System.out.println("The organization has the
                    following members now:");
principal.printStructures();

// Current management details
displayManagementDetail(principal,
                    hodCompSc,hodMath);

System.out.println("Testing the structure of some
                    junior employee's:");
```

```
        Employee juniorMathTeacher1=
                        hodMath.subordinates.get(0);
        Employee juniorCSETeacher1=
                    hodCompSc.subordinates.get(0);
        System.out.println("The Lecturer( M.Jacob) manages
            "+ juniorMathTeacher1.getSubordinatesCount()+
            " employee(s).");
        System.out.println("The Lecturer( C.Kate) manages
            "+ juniorCSETeacher1.getSubordinatesCount()+
            " employee(s).");

    }

    private static Employee formComputerScDept() {

        System.out.println("Forming Computer Science department.");
        System.out.println("A HOD with three lecturers is here.\n");
        Employee cseTeacher1 = new JuniorEmployee
                            ("C.Kate", "Lecturer");
        Employee cseTeacher2 = new JuniorEmployee
                            ("C.Jones", "Lecturer");
        Employee cseTeacher3 = new JuniorEmployee
                            ("C.Proctor", "Lecturer");

        Employee hodCompSc = new SeniorEmployee
                        ("Mr. V.Sarcar", "HOD(CSE)");

        // Teachers of Computer Science
        // directly reports to HOD-CSE
        hodCompSc.addEmployee(cseTeacher1);
        hodCompSc.addEmployee(cseTeacher2);
        hodCompSc.addEmployee(cseTeacher3);
        return hodCompSc;
    }

    private static Employee formMathDept() {
        System.out.println("Forming Mathematics department.");
        System.out.println("A HOD with two lecturers is here.\n");
```

```java
            // Two lecturers other than HOD work
            // in the Mathematics department.
            Employee mathTeacher1 = new JuniorEmployee
                                    ("M.Jacob", "Lecturer");
            Employee mathTeacher2 = new JuniorEmployee
                                    ("M.Rustom", "Lecturer");

            Employee hodMath = new SeniorEmployee("Mrs.S.Das",
                                "HOD(Math)");
            // Teachers of Mathematics directly
            // reports to HOD-Mathematics
            hodMath.addEmployee(mathTeacher1);
            hodMath.addEmployee(mathTeacher2);
            return hodMath;

    }

    private static Employee formPrincipal(Employee hodMath,
                                Employee hodCompSc) {

        System.out.println("Forming the top-level management.");
        System.out.println("A principal with two HOD's is here.\n");
        // Principal of the college
        Employee principal = new
                SeniorEmployee("Dr.S.Som","Principal");
        /*
         The Principal is on top of the college.
         The HOD(Mathematics) and
         HOD(Computer Science) directly report
         to him.
         */
        principal.addEmployee(hodMath);
        principal.addEmployee(hodCompSc);

        return principal;
    }
```

```
    private static void displayManagementDetail(
        Employee principal,
        Employee hodCompSc,
        Employee hodMaths) {
        System.out.println("\n---The current management
                    status summary:---");
        System.out.println("The Principal manages "+
                    principal.getSubordinatesCount()+ "
                    employee(s).");
        System.out.println("The HOD(Computer Sc.) manages
                    "+ hodCompSc.getSubordinatesCount()+ "
                    employee(s).");
        System.out.println("The HOD(Mathematics) manages "+
                    hodMaths.getSubordinatesCount()+ "
                    employee(s).");

        System.out.println("--------");
    }
}
```

Output

Here's the output:

```
***Composite Pattern Demonstration.***
Forming Mathematics department.
A HOD with two lecturers is here.

Forming Computer Science department.
A HOD with three lecturers is here.

Forming the top-level management.
A principal with two HOD's is here.

The details of the Principal object:
    Dr.S.Som is a Principal
    Mrs.S.Das is a HOD(Math)
```

```
        M.Jacob is a Lecturer
        M.Rustom is a Lecturer
  Mr. V.Sarcar is a HOD(CSE)
        C.Kate is a Lecturer
        C.Jones is a Lecturer
        C.Proctor is a Lecturer

 The details of the HOD(Computer Sc.) object:
    Mr. V.Sarcar is a HOD(CSE)
        C.Kate is a Lecturer
        C.Jones is a Lecturer
        C.Proctor is a Lecturer

 The details of the HOD(Mathematics) object:
    Mrs.S.Das is a HOD(Math)
        M.Jacob is a Lecturer
        M.Rustom is a Lecturer

  The structure of a Junior employee(leaf node):
        M.Jacob is a Lecturer

---The current management status summary:---
The Principal manages 7 employee(s).
The HOD(Computer Sc.) manages 3 employee(s).
The HOD(Mathematics) manages 2 employee(s).
--------

The lecturer Mr. C.Jones(cseTeacher2) resigns.
The organization has the following members now:
    Dr.S.Som is a Principal
    Mrs.S.Das is a HOD(Math)
        M.Jacob is a Lecturer
        M.Rustom is a Lecturer
  Mr. V.Sarcar is a HOD(CSE)
        C.Kate is a Lecturer
        C.Proctor is a Lecturer
```

```
---The current management status summary:---
The Principal manages 6 employee(s).
The HOD(Computer Sc.) manages 2 employee(s).
The HOD(Mathematics) manages 2 employee(s).
--------
Testing the structure of some junior employee's:
The Lecturer( M.Jacob) manages 0 employee(s).
The Lecturer( C.Kate) manages 0 employee(s).
```

Analysis

Before you move to the next section, let me remind you what I told you in the introduction of this book: *"Anything that is the latest today will be old (or outdated) tomorrow. But the core constructs (or features) are evergreen. All new features are built on top of these universal features. So, I like to write code that is compatible with a wide range of versions using the basic language constructs."*

But you may have a different thought. For example, if you are a lambda lover, you may want to replace the code snippet

```
for (Employee e: subordinates) {
            e.printStructures();
        }
```

with

```
subordinates.forEach(Employee :: printStructures);
```

You may refactor your code accordingly for similar segments. But lambda support comes in Java 8, not before that. If you ask me which one is better, my answer is that it's your choice. If my code is readable enough, easy to understand, can serve my purpose, and can run in a wide range of Java versions, I am OK with that. The same comment applies to all code in this book.

Q&A Session

13.1 What are the advantages of using the Composite design pattern?

Here are some advantages:

- In a tree-like structure, you can treat both the composite objects (branch nodes) and the individual objects (leaf nodes) uniformly. Notice that in this example, I use two common methods, `printStructures()` and `getSubordinatesCount()`, to print the structure of the organization and get the employee count from both the composite object structure (`Principal` or `HODs`) and the single object structure (leaf nodes like *M.Jacob*.)

- It is common to implement a part-whole hierarchy using this design pattern.

- You can easily add a new component to the architecture or delete an existing component from the architecture.

13.2 What are the challenges associated with using the Composite design pattern?

Here are some disadvantages:

- If you want to maintain the ordering of child nodes (for example, if the parse trees are represented as components), you may need to take special care.

- If you are dealing with immutable objects, you cannot simply delete them.

- If you keep adding new nodes, maintenance can become difficult over time. Sometimes you may want to deal with a composite that has special components. This kind of constraint may cause additional development costs because you may need to provide a dynamic checking mechanism to support the concept.

13.3 In this example, you used a list data structure. Are other data structures OK to use?

Absolutely. There is no universal rule. You are free to use your preferred data structure. The GoF also confirmed that it is not necessary to use a general-purpose data structure.

13.4 How can you connect the Iterator design pattern to a Composite design pattern?

When you go through the example again, you will notice that if you want to examine a composite object architecture, you needed to iterate over the objects. This is why you see the following code segment in the `printStructure()` method:

```
for (Employee e: subordinates) {
            e.printStructures();
}
```

The `getSubordinatesCount()` method also uses a similar code snippet:

```
for (Employee e : subordinates) {
  subordinatesCount += e.getSubordinatesCount();
}
```

In addition, if you want to do special activities with some branches, you may need to iterate over the leaf nodes and non-leaf nodes.

13.5 In your implementation, the addEmployee() and removeEmployee() methods in the JuniorEmployee class are empty. You could use them for senior employees only. Is this understanding correct?

Nice observation. Even the GoF discussed this. It is true that when you put the `addEmployee(...)` and `removeEmployee(...)` methods in the abstract class, the leaf nodes (junior employees) have these addition and removal operations. Since a junior employee does not manage any other employee, the presence of these methods is not meaningful enough for them. So, if you throw an exception instead of making the method body empty, you need to take special care when you use polymorphic code.

Notice that in this case, you need to update the client code as well. For example, now you cannot write

```
Employee hodMaths = new SeniorEmployee("Mrs.S.Das","HOD(Math)");
hodMaths.addEmployee(mathTeacher1);
```

But you can go ahead with

```
SeniorEmployee hodMaths = new SeniorEmployee("Mrs.S.Das","HOD(Math)");
hodMaths.addEmployee(mathTeacher1);
```

This is why, in this case, I opt for transparency over safety. Obviously, you promote more safety if you block the meaningless operations in the leaf nodes. This is why GoF also mentioned that this kind of decision involves a trade-off between safety and transparency.

13.6 I want to use an abstract class instead of an interface. Is this allowed?

In most cases, the simple answer is yes. But you need to understand the difference between an abstract class and an interface. In a typical scenario, you will find one of them may be more useful than the other one. Since throughout the book I present only simple and easy-to-understand examples, you may not see much difference between these two.

In Q&A Session 6.4 of Chapter 6, which covers the Builder pattern, I discuss how to decide between an abstract class and an interface.

CHAPTER 14

Bridge Pattern

This chapter covers the Bridge pattern. You'll see two different implementations.

GoF Definition

It decouples an abstraction from its implementation so that the two can vary independently.

Concept

This pattern is also known as the Handle/Body pattern. Using it, you decouple an implementation class from an abstract class by providing a bridge between them.

This bridge interface makes the functionality of concrete classes independent from the interface implementer classes. You can alter different kinds of classes structurally without affecting each other. This pattern initially may seem to be complicated, which is why, in this chapter, I've provided you with two different implementations containing lots of explanations. The concept will be clearer to you when you go through the examples.

Real-Life Example

In a software product development company, the development team and the marketing team both play crucial roles. Normally, the marketing team does a market survey and gathers customer requirements. The development team implements those requirements in the product to fulfill customer needs. Any change (say, in the operational strategy) in one team should not have a direct impact on the other team. In this case, you can think of the marketing team as playing the role of the bridge between the clients of the product and the development team of the software organization.

301

© Vaskaran Sarcar 2022
V. Sarcar, *Java Design Patterns*, https://doi.org/10.1007/978-1-4842-7971-7_14

Computer World Example

GUI frameworks can use the Bridge pattern to separate abstractions from the platform-specific implementation. For example, using this pattern, you can separate a window abstraction from a window implementation for Linux or macOS.

In Java, you may notice the use of JDBC, which provides a bridge between your application and a particular database. For example, the `java.sql.DriverManager` class and the `java.sql.Driver` interface can form a bridge pattern where the first one plays the role of abstraction and the second one plays the role of implementors. There are many concrete implementors such as `com.mysql.cj.jdbc.Driver` and `oracle.jdbc.driver.OracleDriver`.

Note   The online link `https://dev.mysql.com/doc/connector-j/8.0/en/connector-j-api-changes.html` confirms that the name of the class that implements `java.sql.Driver` in MySQL Connector/J has changed from `com.mysql.jdbc.Driver` to `com.mysql.cj.jdbc.Driver`. The old class name has been deprecated.

In my other book, *Interactive Object-Oriented Programming in Java* (Second Edition, Apress, 2020), I have a chapter on database programming. Here are some lines from it for your immediate reference.

`DriverManager`: This *class* manages a set of JDBC drivers. It matches the connection request from a Java application with the proper database driver. (It is important to note that JDBC 2.0 provides an alternate way to connect to a data source. The use of a `DataSource` object is a recommended way to connect a data source.)

`Driver`: This is an *interface* to handle the communication with the database server. Each driver must provide a class that will implement this interface. Each `Driver` class should be small and standalone so that it can be loaded without vast supporting code. When a `Driver` class is loaded, you should create an instance of itself and register with `DriverManager`.

In that chapter, to connect to a MySQL database, I used the following lines:

```
Class.forName("com.mysql.cj.jdbc.Driver").newInstance();
Connection connectionOb = DriverManager.getConnection(
            "jdbc:mysql://localhost:3306/test",
            "root", "admin");
```

Similarly, to connect with an Oracle database, you can use the following line of code:

```
Class.forName("oracle.jdbc.driver.OracleDriver").newInstance();
```

To connect with a MS SQL Server, use the following line of code:

```
Class.forName("com.microsoft.jdbc.sqlserver.SQLServerDriver").
newInstance();
```

Connection: This *interface* provides the methods to connect a database. Your SQL statements execute, and the results are returned within the context of a connection. All communication with the database passes through the connection object.

getConnection(): This method attempts to make a connection to the given database URL. Multiple overloaded versions are available for this method.

Implementation

Suppose you need to design a piece of software for a seller who sells different electronic items. For simplicity, let's assume the seller is currently selling televisions and DVD players, and they sell them both online and offline (in different showrooms). To implement this, you start with the designs shown in Figure 14-1 or Figure 14-2.

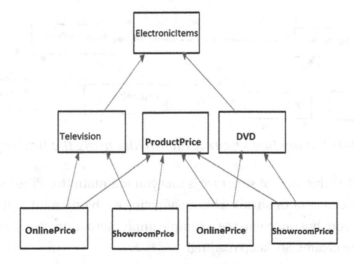

Figure 14-1. Approach 1

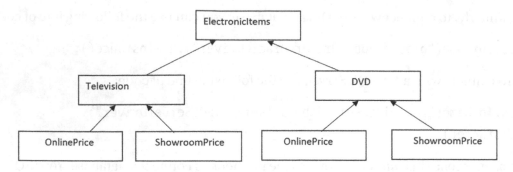

Figure 14-2. *Approach 2*

On further analysis, you discover that approach 1 is messy and difficult to maintain.

In the beginning, approach 2 looks cleaner, but if you want to include new prices such as ThirdPartyPrice, FestiveTimePrice, and so on, or if you want to include new electronic items like air conditioners, refrigerators, and so on, you will face new challenges because the elements are tightly coupled in this design. But in a real-world scenario, this kind of enhancement is often required.

So, you need to start with a loosely coupled system for future enhancements, so that either of these two hierarchies (electronics items and their prices) can grow independently. The Bridge pattern is perfect for such a scenario. When you use the Bridge pattern, the structure may look like the one in Figure 14-3.

Figure 14-3. *Maintaining two separate hierarchies using the Bridge pattern*

The idea behind this kind of structure is that you maintain two different inheritance hierarchies. They can grow or shrink without affecting each other. Initially, it may sound strange to you, but once you see a sample implementation, the idea behind this philosophy will be clearer. So, keep reading!

Before I show you a sample implementation, let's start with the most common class diagram of a Bridge pattern, shown in Figure 14-4.

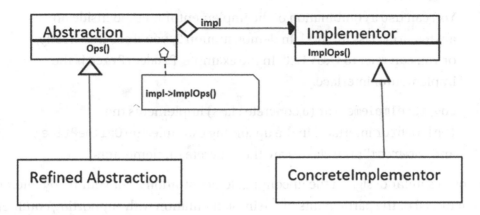

Figure 14-4. *A classic Bridge pattern*

In this class diagram,

- Abstraction defines the abstract interface and maintains the Implementor reference. In this example, it is an abstract class, but don't assume that you need an abstract class or interface to define an abstraction. The word "abstraction" here is used regarding the methods that are used to remove the complexity. These methods simply hide the inner details of their working mechanism from the client code. In the example, ElectronicItem plays the role of abstraction. The common operations are placed inside this abstraction class.

- RefinedAbstraction (a concrete class) extends the interface defined by Abstraction. Remember that it is optional if you do not start with an abstract class or an interface. In the example, the Television and DVD classes are the concrete abstractions.

- Implementor defines the interface for implementation classes. The interface methods don't have to correspond to the abstraction methods exactly. Typically, they include the primitive operations, and Abstraction defines the high-level operation based on these primitives. Also, note that there need not be a one-to-one mapping between an abstraction class method and an implementor method.

You can use a combination of the implementor method inside an abstraction class method. In demonstration 2, you'll see this clearly, or you can refer to Q&A 12.8. In the example, `ProductPrice` is the implementor interface.

- `ConcreteImplementor` (a concrete class) implements the `Implementor` interface. In the upcoming example, the `OnlinePrice` and `ShowroomPrice` classes are the concrete implementors.

I follow a similar design in the upcoming demonstrations. For your ready reference, I also point out all of the participants in the implementation with supporting comments.

Class Diagram

Figure 14-5 shows the important parts of the class diagram for the upcoming demonstration (demonstration 1). I do not show the full method signatures in order to make the diagram short and simple. But an important note is added and separate hierarchies are marked so that you can notice the heart of the design.

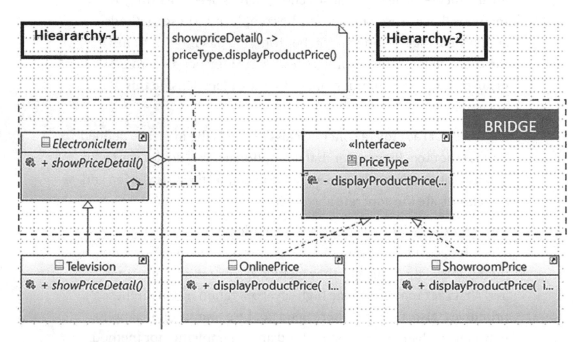

Figure 14-5.   *Class diagram*

Package Explorer View

Figure 14-6 shows the structure of the program.

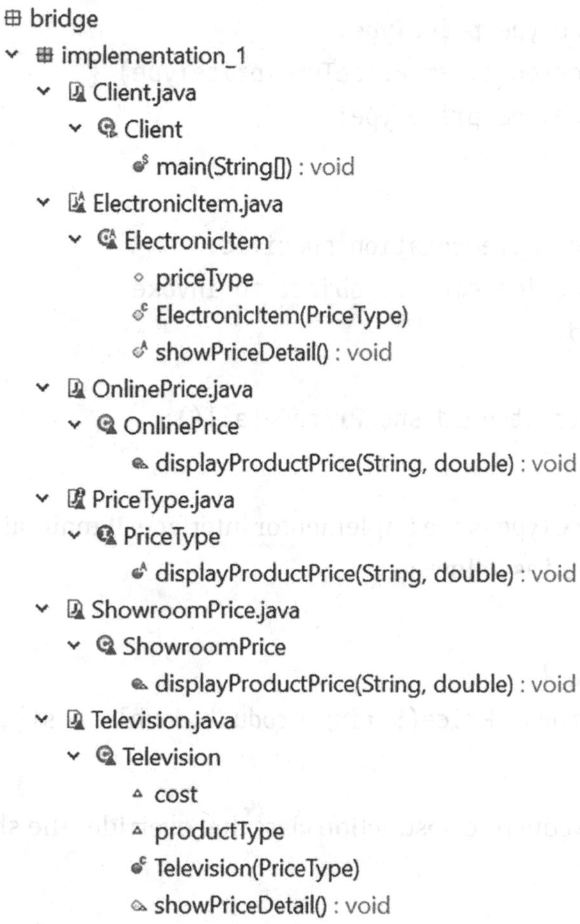

Figure 14-6. *Package Explorer view*

Demonstration 1

The package `jdp3e.bridge.implementation_1` contains all parts of the program. In this example, `ElectronicItem` is the abstraction class. It is placed in hierarchy-1. This class is defined as follows:

```java
// Abstraction
abstract class ElectronicItem {

    // Composition - implementor
    protected PriceType priceType;
    protected ElectronicItem(PriceType priceType) {
        this.priceType=priceType;
    }
    /*
     * This method implementation specific.
     * We'll use an implementor object to invoke
     * this method.
     */
    protected abstract void showPriceDetail();
}
```

The interface PriceType is the implementor interface. It maintains the second hierarchy and is defined as follows:

```java
// Implementor
interface PriceType {
    void displayProductPrice(String product,double cost);
}
```

Television is the concrete abstraction class that overrides the showPriceDetail() method as follows:

```java
// Refined Abstraction
class Television extends ElectronicItem{

    String productType;
    double cost;

    public Television(PriceType priceType) {
        super(priceType);
        this.productType="television";
        this.cost=2000;
    }
```

```
/*
 * Implementation specific:
 * We are delegating the implementation
 * to the Implementor object.
 */

@Override
protected void showPriceDetail() {
    priceType.displayProductPrice(productType,cost);
}
}
```

With the supporting comments, you can see that inside the showPriceDetail() method, you invoke the displayProductPrice(...) method from the other hierarchy and pass the information about the product type.

The concrete implementors (OnlinePrice and ShowroomPrice) catch this information and use it in the displayProductPrice(...) method. Both concrete implementors are similar. For your immediate reference, here's one of them:

```
// This is ConcreteImplementor-1
class OnlinePrice implements PriceType {
    @Override
    public void displayProductPrice(String productType,
                                    double cost) {
        System.out.println("The " + productType + "'s
                            online price is $"+ cost*.9);
    }
}
```

Notice that in the previous code segment, the price is a little bit less (a 10% discount) if a product is purchased online.

Now go through the complete demonstration, which is as follows:

// PriceType.java
```
interface PriceType {
    void displayProductPrice(String product,double cost);
}
```

```java
// OnlinePrice.java      // This is ConcreteImplementor-1

class OnlinePrice implements PriceType {
    @Override
    public void displayProductPrice(String productType,
                                     double cost) {
        System.out.println("The " + productType + "'s
                            online price is $"+ cost*.9);
    }
}
```

```java
// ShowroomPrice.java     // This is ConcreteImplementor-2

class ShowroomPrice implements PriceType {
    @Override
    public void displayProductPrice(String productType,
                                     double cost) {
        System.out.println("The " + productType + "'s
                            showroom price is $"+ cost);
    }
}
```

```java
// ElectronicItem.java
abstract class ElectronicItem {

    // Composition - implementor
    protected PriceType priceType;
    protected ElectronicItem(PriceType priceType) {
        this.priceType=priceType;
    }
    /*
     * This method implementation specific.
     * We'll use an implementor object to invoke
     * this method.
     */
    protected abstract void showPriceDetail();

}
```

// Television.java

```java
class Television extends ElectronicItem{
    /*
     * Implementation specific:
     * Delegating the task
     * to the Implementor object.
     */
    String productType;
    double cost;

    public Television(PriceType priceType) {
        super(priceType);
        this.productType="television";
        this.cost=2000;
    }

    /*
     * Implementation specific:
     * We are delegating the implementation
     * to the Implementor object.
     */

    @Override
    protected void showPriceDetail() {
        priceType.displayProductPrice(productType,cost);
    }
}
```

// Client.java

```java
class Client {
    public static void main(String[] args) {
        System.out.println("***Bridge Pattern Demo.***");

        System.out.println("Verifying the market price of a television.");
        // Verifying online price
        ElectronicItem eItem = new Television(new
                                        OnlinePrice());
```

```
        eItem.showPriceDetail();
        //System.out.println("----------");

        // Verifying the offline/showroom price
        eItem = new Television(new ShowroomPrice());
        eItem.showPriceDetail();
    }
}
```

Output

Here's the output:

```
***Bridge Pattern Demo.***
Verifying the market price of a television.
The television's online price is $1800.0
The television's showroom price is $2000.0
```

Additional Implementation

I include an additional implementation in this chapter to help you explore the flexibility of this pattern. To maintain the previous example, in this example, again I use constructors, not getter-setter methods. It's just a choice. Before I show you the flexibility, let's assume the following:

- The seller can sell either a television or a DVD.

- The seller can provide a discount on a sale in the festive season.

- The seller can provide a double discount for a DVD sale, but he does not wish to provide the same for a television purchase.

- The seller can also send a thank you message once the product is purchased.

As per these new requirements, let's make some changes to the earlier implementation. Let's analyze these changes one by one.

How should you start? You guess it right: you start with the implementor hierarchy. This time the PriceType interface needs some additional methods. The concrete implementors provide the implementation details. So, here is the PriceType interface with the new methods shown in bold:

```
// Implementor
interface PriceType {
    void displayProductPrice(String product,double cost);
    // Additional method(s) in implementation-2
    void festiveSeasonDiscount(int percentage);
    void sayThanks();
}
```

Since these additional methods are added in the PriceType interface, the concrete implementors need to implement these methods. Here is such an implementation. It is from the OnlinePrice class implementor:

```
class OnlinePrice implements PriceType{
    @Override
    public void displayProductPrice(String productType,
                                    double cost) {
        System.out.println("The " + productType + "'s
                            online cost is $"+ cost*.9);
    }

    @Override
    public void festiveSeasonDiscount(int percentage) {
        System.out.println(" You can get a maximum of " +
                percentage + "% discount in festive season.");
    }

    @Override
    public void sayThanks() {
        System.out.println("Thank you for your interest in our product.");
    }
}
```

Now concentrate on the abstraction hierarchy. Here showPriceDetail() can exist for both televisions and DVDs. So, you can place this method in the abstract class ElectronicItem. Note that since the method is NOT abstract now, there is no need to make this class abstract. But you still make the ElectronicItem class abstract, so that a client cannot instantiate this class directly. In addition, this time there are two new methods that call the corresponding implementor methods. Here is the ElectronicItem class for demonstration 2 with the important changes in bold:

```
// Abstraction
// Making the class abstract,
// so that you cannot instantiate it
// inside the client code.
abstract class ElectronicItem {
    protected String productType;
    protected double cost;
    // Composition - implementor
    protected PriceType priceType;

    protected ElectronicItem(PriceType priceType) {
        this.priceType = priceType;
    }

    protected void showPriceDetail() {
        priceType.displayProductPrice(productType,cost);
    }

    // Additional methods for demonstration-2
    protected void giveDiscount() {
            priceType.festiveSeasonDiscount(5);
    }

    protected void conveyThanks() {
            priceType.sayThanks();
    }
}
```

The subclasses of ElectronicsItem *can use all of these methods as-is, but they can provide additional functionalities as well.* As per the new design, the Television class can use the showPriceDetail() method that is defined in its parent class. Also, it does not offer a double discount. So, you do not need to define any new method inside the following class:

```
class Television extends ElectronicItem{
        public Television(PriceType priceType) {
        super(priceType);
         this.productType="television";
         this.cost=2000;
     }

    // No additional methods exist for Television
}
```

A seller can provide double discounts on a DVD sold in a festive season and they can also send thanks message for the purchase. Note that the DVD class may need another method to provide the double discount (normal discount + additional discount). But you cannot add this method in the abstraction class ElectronicItem, because in that case, the Television class will also have this method. To accommodate this, in this implementation, add the following method in the DVD class:

```
// Specific method in the DVD class

    public void getDoubleDiscountWithThanks() {
        getDiscount(10); //10% discount
        getDiscount(5); // Additional 5% discount
        conveyThanks();
    }
```

Note You can see that inside the getDoubleDiscountWithThanks() method, you use the getDiscount(...) and conveyThanks() methods of ElectronicItem. This means you are coding in terms of "superclass abstraction." This structure helps to vary the abstraction and implementation independently. In short, using this pattern, you maintain two separate but connected hierarchies that can vary independently.

Notice that a client he wants. This method is coded in the superclass abstraction and the other inheritance hierarchy is unaffected due to the addition of this DVD class. Let's cross verify the key goal again.

Due to the addition of the DVD class in hierarchy-1, you do not need to change ShowroomPrice or OnlinePrice, which are placed in a different hierarchy (hierarchy-2). Similarly, if you add a separate class, say SpecialDayPrice in the PriceType interface in hierarchy-2, you do not need to make changes in hierarchy-1. Obviously, in this case, you ensure that SpecialDayPrice adheres to the PriceType contract.

Note   In short, here you separate the methods that clients use from how these methods are implemented.

Now do a crosscheck of your understanding with the following class diagram. Then directly follow the complete demonstration and output. I don't show the package explorer view for this modified implementation, which is easy to understand with the preceding discussions and the following class diagram.

Class Diagram

Figure 14-7 shows the modified class diagram. Again, this figure shows the most important parts of the class diagram for demonstration 2. I do not show the full method signatures in order to make the diagram short and simple. But an important note is added and separate hierarchies are marked so that you can notice the important parts. You can see that the ElectronicItem, Television, and DVD classes are placed in hierarchy-1 and the interface PriceType and the classes OnlinePrice and ShowroomPrice are placed in hierarchy-2.

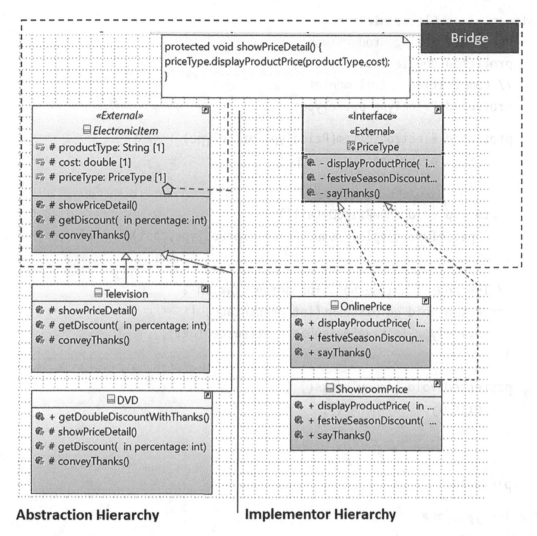

Figure 14-7. *Class diagram for demonstration 2*

Demonstration 2

Download the package jdp3e.bridge.implementation_2 to see all parts of the modified program. Here is the complete implementation:

```
// Abstraction
// Making the class abstract,
// so that you cannot instantiate it
```

// ElectronicItem.java

```java
abstract class ElectronicItem {
    protected String productType;
    protected double cost;
    // Composition - implementor
    protected PriceType priceType;

    protected ElectronicItem(PriceType priceType) {
        this.priceType = priceType;
    }

    protected void showPriceDetail() {
        priceType.displayProductPrice(productType,cost);
    }

    // The additional methods for demonstration-2
    protected void getDiscount(int percentage) {
        priceType.festiveSeasonDiscount(percentage);
    }

    protected void conveyThanks() {
        priceType.sayThanks();
    }
}

// Implementor
```

// PriceType.java
```java
interface PriceType {
    void displayProductPrice(String product,double cost);
    // The additional method(s) in implementation-2
    void festiveSeasonDiscount(int percentage);
    void sayThanks();
}
```

// OnlinePrice.java
```java
class OnlinePrice implements PriceType{
    @Override
    public void displayProductPrice(String productType,
                                    double cost) {
```

```java
        System.out.println("The " + productType + "'s
                            online cost is $"+ cost*.9);
    }

    @Override
    public void festiveSeasonDiscount(int percentage) {
        System.out.println("You can get a maximum of " +
                percentage + "% discount in festive season.");
    }

    @Override
    public void sayThanks() {
        System.out.println("Thank you for your interest in our product.");
    }
}
```

```java
// ShowroomPrice.java
class ShowroomPrice implements PriceType {
    @Override
    public void displayProductPrice(String productType,
                                          double cost) {
        System.out.println("The " + productType + "'s
                            showroom price is $"+ cost);
    }

    @Override
    public void festiveSeasonDiscount(int percentage) {
        System.out.println("You can get a maximum of " +
                            percentage + "% discount in the
                            festive seasons.");
    }

    @Override
    public void sayThanks() {
        System.out.println("Thank you for your interest in our product.");
    }
}
```

// Television.java
```java
class Television extends ElectronicItem{
    /*
     * Implementation specific:
     * Delegating the task
     * to the Implementor object.
     */

    public Television(PriceType priceType) {
        super(priceType);
         this.productType="television";
         this.cost=2000;
     }

    // No additional method exists for Television
}
```

// DVD.java
```java
class DVD extends ElectronicItem {
    /*
     * Implementation specific:
     * Delegating the task
     * to the Implementor object.
     */

    public DVD(PriceType priceType) {
        super(priceType);
         this.productType="DVD";
         this.cost=3000;
     }

    // Specific method in the DVD class
    public void getDoubleDiscountWithThanks() {
        getDiscount(10); //10% discount
        getDiscount(5); // Additional 5% discount
        conveyThanks();
     }
}
```

// Client.java

```java
class Client {
    public static void main(String[] args) {
        System.out.println("***Alternative Implementation
                            of Bridge Pattern.***");

        System.out.println("Verifying the market price of a television.");
        // Verifying online price
        ElectronicItem eItem = new Television(new
                                OnlinePrice());
        eItem.showPriceDetail();

        // Verifying the offline/showroom price
        eItem = new Television(new ShowroomPrice());
        eItem.showPriceDetail();
        eItem.getDiscount(7);
        eItem.conveyThanks();
        //Error: the following method is DVD specific.
        //eItem.getDoubleDiscountWithThanks();

        System.out.println("----------");

        System.out.println("Verifying the market price of a DVD.");
        // Verifying online price
        eItem = new DVD(new OnlinePrice());
        eItem.showPriceDetail();

        // Verifying the offline/showroom price
        eItem = new DVD(new ShowroomPrice());
        eItem.showPriceDetail();

        //Checking the DVD specific method
        ((DVD)eItem).getDoubleDiscountWithThanks();
    }
}
```

Output

Here's the new output:

```
***Alternative Implementation of Bridge Pattern.***
Verifying the market price of a television.
The television's online cost is $1800.0
The television's showroom price is $2000.0
 You can get a maximum of 7% discount in the festive seasons.
Thank you for your interest in our product.
----------
Verifying the market price of a DVD.
The DVD's online cost is $2700.0
The DVD's showroom price is $3000.0
 You can get a maximum of 10% discount in the festive seasons.
 You can get a maximum of 5% discount in the festive seasons.
Thank you for your interest in our product.
```

Q&A Session

14.1 How can this pattern make my programming life easier?

In this chapter, the two examples show you

- How to avoid the tight coupling between the items and their corresponding prices

- How to maintain two different hierarchies where both of them can be extended without impacting each other

- How to deal with multiple objects where implementations are shared among themselves

14.2 You could use simple subclassing instead of using this kind of design. Is this correct?

No. With simple subclassing, your implementations cannot vary dynamically. Your implementations may seem to behave differently, but actually they are bound to the abstraction at compile time.

14.3 Can I use getter-setter methods instead of a constructor inside the Abstraction class?

Yes. In fact, some developers prefer getter-setter methods over constructors, because you can set a new value for an attribute later. In the previous edition of this book, I showed both usages. In this book, I modified the example in demonstration 1 to focus on the required enhancement in demonstration 2.

14.4 What are the key advantages of using a Bridge design pattern?

Here are some advantages:

- Implementations are not bound to abstractions.

- The abstractions and implementations can grow independently.

- It simply means that the concrete classes are independent of the interface implementer classes. In other words, changes in one of them do not affect the other. So, you can also vary the abstraction and the implementation hierarchies in different ways.

14.5 What are the challenges associated with this pattern?

Here are some challenges:

- The overall structure is complex.

- Here you do not directly invoke a method. Instead, the abstraction layer delegates the work to the implementation layer. So, you may notice a slight performance impact when you execute an operation.

14.5 I see similarities between a Bridge design pattern and an Adapter design pattern. Am I right?

Sometimes the Bridge pattern is confused with the Adapter pattern—most accurately, with an Object Adapter design pattern. In cases like this, it is tough if you try to match a design pattern after seeing an implementation. Instead, it can be beneficial if you start from the beginning and try to understand the intent of the design.

Remember that the key purpose of an Adapter pattern is to deal with incompatible interfaces only and we assume that those interfaces already exist.

14.6 Do you mean that an adapter can be beneficial for me when I need to support legacy code but I want to implement the new features as well?

Yes.

14.7 When you explained the implementor interface before demonstration 1, you said, "...there need not be a one-to-one mapping between an abstraction class method and an implementor method." Can you please elaborate?

See the following method definitions:

```
protected void getDiscount(int percentage) {
    priceType.festiveSeasonDiscount(percentage);
}

protected void conveyThanks() {
    priceType.sayThanks();
}
public void getDoubleDiscountWithThanks() {
    getDiscount(10); // 10% discount
    getDiscount(5); // Additional 5% discount
    conveyThanks();
}
```

From these method definitions, you can notice the following points:

- The getDiscount() method invokes the festiveSeasonDiscount() method and the conveyThanks() method invokes the sayThanks() method but these methods belong to a different inheritance hierarchy.

- Notice the getDoubleDiscountWithThanks() method now. Using this method, you invoke multiple methods from a different inheritance hierarchy.

14.8 "You can use a combination of the implementor method when you use an abstraction class method. In demonstration 2, you'll see this clearly." Can you please elaborate?

It is already shown. Notice the following method in demonstration 2:

```
// Specific method in the DVD class
public void getDoubleDiscountWithThanks() {
    getDiscount(10); //10% discount
    getDiscount(5); // Additional 5% discount
    conveyThanks();
}
```

You can see that when a client calls this method, it invokes two different implementor methods together.

Note   Remember that a high-level abstraction method can include multiple implementor methods, but clients may not be aware of this.

CHAPTER 15

Template Method Pattern

This chapter covers the Template Method pattern.

GoF Definition

It defines the skeleton of an algorithm in an operation, deferring some steps to subclasses. The Template Method pattern lets subclasses redefine certain steps of an algorithm without changing the algorithm's structure.

Concept

Using this pattern, you begin with the minimum or essential structure of an algorithm. Then you defer some responsibilities to the subclasses. As a result, the derived class can redefine some steps of an algorithm without changing the flow of the algorithm.

Simply put, this design pattern is useful when you implement a multistep algorithm but allow customization through subclasses. Here you keep the outline of the algorithm in a separate method referred to as a **template method**. The container class of this template method is often referred to as the **template class**.

It is important to note that some amount of implementation may not vary across the subclasses. As a result, you may see some default implementations in the template class. Only the specific details are implemented in a subclass. So, using this approach, you write a minimum amount of code in a subclass.

© Vaskaran Sarcar 2022
V. Sarcar, *Java Design Patterns*, https://doi.org/10.1007/978-1-4842-7971-7_15

Real-Life Example

When you order a pizza, the chef of the restaurant can use a basic mechanism to prepare the pizza, but they may allow you to select the final materials. For example, a customer can opt for different toppings such as bacon, onions, extra cheese, or mushrooms. So, just before the delivery of the pizza, the chef can include these choices.

Computer World Example

Suppose you have been hired to design an online engineering degree course. In general, the first semester of the course is the same for all students. For subsequent semesters, you need to add new papers or subjects to the application based on the course opted by a student.

The Template Method pattern makes sense when you want to avoid duplicate code in your application but allow subclasses to change specific details of the parent class workflow to bring varying behavior to the application. (However, you may not want to override the parent class methods entirely to make radical changes in the subclasses. In this way, the pattern differs from simple polymorphism.)

Here is an built-in example for you:

- The `removeAll()` method of `java.util.AbstractSet` can be considered as an example of a Template Method pattern. (You can refer to Q&A 15.9 for additional information).

Implementation

Let's assume that each engineering student needs to pass the courses on Mathematics and soft skills (such as communication skills, people management skills, and so on) in their initial semester to obtain their degrees. Later you will add some special papers to their courses based on their chosen paths (computer science or electronics).

To serve the purpose, a template method `displayCourseStructure()` is defined in an abstract class `BasicEngineering`.

Note   You will see that the `displayCourseStructure()` method calls the other methods in sequential order. You can think of them as the steps of the overall algorithm.

It has the following structure. The supporting comments are kept for your easy understanding.

```
abstract class BasicEngineering {

    // The "Template Method"
    // Making the method final to prevent overriding.

    public final void displayCourseStructure() {
        /*
         * The course needs to be completed
         * in the following sequence:
         * 1.Mathematics
         * 2.Soft skills
         * 3.Subclass-specific paper
         */

        // Common Papers:
        courseOnMathematics();//Step-1
        courseOnSoftSkills(); //Step-2

        // Course-specific Paper:
        courseOnSpecialPaper();//Step-3
    }

    private void courseOnMathematics() {
        System.out.println("1. Mathematics");
    }

    private void courseOnSoftSkills() {
        System.out.println("2. Soft Skills");
    }

    /*
```

```
 * The following method will vary.
 * It will be overridden by the
 * derived classes.
 */

public abstract void courseOnSpecialPaper();
}
```

Notice that subclasses of BasicEngineering cannot alter (or override) the flow of the displayCourseStructure() method but they can override the SpecialPaper() method to include course-specific details and make the final course list different from each other.

The concrete classes ComputerScience and Electronics are the subclasses of BasicEngineering and they take the opportunity to override the courseOnSpecialPaper() method. The following code segment shows such a sample from the ComputerScience class:

```
// The concrete derived class: ComputerScience
class ComputerScience extends BasicEngineering {

    @Override
    public void courseOnSpecialPaper() {
        System.out.println("3. Object-Oriented Programming");
    }
}
```

Class Diagram

Figure 15-1 shows the important parts of the class diagram.

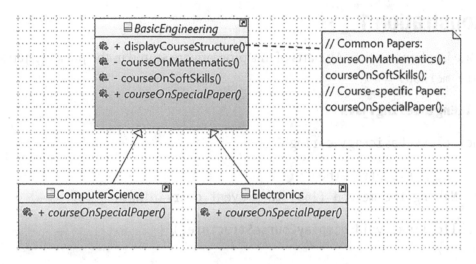

Figure 15-1. *Class diagram*

Package Explorer View

Figure 15-2 shows the high-level structure of the program.

```
▦ template_method
  ⌄ 🗓 BasicEngineering.java
    ⌄ ⓒ BasicEngineering
        ▪ courseOnMathematics() : void
        ▪ courseOnSoftSkills() : void
        ⊿ courseOnSpecialPaper() : void
        ⊿ displayCourseStructure() : void
  ⌄ 🗓 Client.java
    ⌄ ⓒ Client
        ⊿ main(String[]) : void
  ⌄ 🗓 ComputerScience.java
    ⌄ ⓒ ComputerScience
        ▪ courseOnSpecialPaper() : void
  ⌄ 🗓 Electronics.java
    ⌄ ⓒ Electronics
        ▪ courseOnSpecialPaper() : void
```

Figure 15-2. *Package Explorer view*

Demonstration 1

Here's the implementation. All parts of this program are stored in the package jdp3e.
template_method.

// BasicEngineering.java

```java
abstract class BasicEngineering {

    // The "Template Method"
    // Making the method final to prevent overriding.

    public final void displayCourseStructure() {
        /*
         * The course needs to be completed in the
         * following sequence:
         * 1.Mathematics
         * 2.Soft skills
         * 3.Subclass-specific paper
         */

        // Common Papers:
        courseOnMathematics();
        courseOnSoftSkills();

        // Course-specific Paper:
        courseOnSpecialPaper();
    }

    private void courseOnMathematics() {
        System.out.println("1. Mathematics");
    }

    private void courseOnSoftSkills() {
        System.out.println("2. Soft skills");
    }

    /*
     * The following method will vary.
     * It will be overridden by the
```

```
 * derived classes.
 */

public abstract void courseOnSpecialPaper();
}
```

// ComputerScience.java

// The concrete derived class: ComputerScience

```java
class ComputerScience extends BasicEngineering {

    @Override
    public void courseOnSpecialPaper() {
        System.out.println("3. Object-Oriented Programming");
    }
}
```

// Electronics.java

// The concrete derived class: Electronics

```java
class Electronics extends BasicEngineering {

    @Override
    public void courseOnSpecialPaper() {
        System.out.println("3. Digital Logic and Circuit Theory");
    }
}
```

// Client.java

```java
class Client {
    public static void main(String[] args) {

        System.out.println("***Template Method Pattern
            Demonstration.***\n");
        BasicEngineering preferrredCourse = new
                        ComputerScience();
```

```
        System.out.println("Computer Science course structure:");
        preferrredCourse.displayCourseStructure();
        System.out.println();
        preferrredCourse = new Electronics();
        System.out.println("Electronics course structure:");
        preferrredCourse.displayCourseStructure();

    }

}
```

Output

Here's the output:

```
***Template Method Pattern Demonstration.***

Computer Science course structure:
1. Mathematics
2. Soft skills
3. Object-Oriented Programming

Electronics course structure:
1. Mathematics
2. Soft skills
3. Digital Logic and Circuit Theory
```

Q&A Session

15.1 In this pattern, subclasses can simply redefine the methods based on their needs. Is this correct?

Yes.

15.2 In the abstract class BasicEngineering, only one method is abstract and the other two methods are concrete. What is the reason behind this?

I want the subclasses to override only the courseOnSpecialPaper() method here. Other methods are common to both courses, and they do not need to be overridden by the subclasses.

15.3 Suppose you want to add more methods in the BasicEngineering class, but you want to work on those methods if and only if your derived classes need them. Otherwise, you ignore them. This type of situation is common in some Ph.D. programs where some courses are mandatory, but if a student has certain qualifications, the student may not need to attend the lectures for those subjects. Can you design this kind of situation with the Template Method pattern?

Yes, you can. Basically, you want to use a hook, which is a method that can help you to control some kind of flow in an algorithm.

What is a hook in programming? In very simple words, a hook helps you execute some code before or after existing code. It can help you extend the behavior of a program at runtime. A hook method can provide some default behavior that a subclass can override if necessary. Often, they do nothing by default.

To demonstrate this, let's add a few lines of code in the BasicEngineering class. Notice the bold lines in the following code segments:

```
// The previous code skipped
// The template method

public final void displayCourseStructure() {
 /*
 * The course needs to be completed
 * in the following sequence:
 * 1.Mathematics
 * 2.Soft skills
 * 3.Subclass-specific paper
 * 4.Additional paper, if any
 */

// Common Papers:
courseOnMathematics();//Step-1
courseOnSoftSkills(); //Step-2
```

```
// Course-specific Paper:
courseOnSpecialPaper();//Step-3

if (isAdditionalPaperNeeded()){
    courseOnAdditionalPaper();//Step-4 (if required)
}
// The remaining code skipped
```

Where the hook method is defined as:

```
/* A hook method.
* By default, an additional
* subject is needed.
*/
boolean isAdditionalPaperNeeded(){
 return true;
}
```

These two code segments tell us that when you invoke the template method, by default the method courseOnAdditionalPaper() will be executed. It is because isAdditionalPaperNeeded() returns true, which in turn makes the if condition inside the template method true. But in the upcoming demonstration, the Electronics class overrides this method as follows:

```
@Override
boolean isAdditionalPaperNeeded() {
   return false;
}
```

So, when you instantiate an Electronics instance and call the template method, you can see that courseOnAdditionalPaper() is NOT called at the end. Let's go through the complete program and output now.

Demonstration 2

Here's the modified implementation. The classes in this demonstration are in package jdp3e.template_method.hook_example. It helps you to get everything immediately when you download the source code from the Apress website.

// BasicEngineering.java

```java
abstract class BasicEngineering {

    // The "Template Method"
    // Making the method final to prevent overriding.

    public final void displayCourseStructure() {
        /*
         * The course needs to be completed
         * in the following sequence:
         * 1.Mathematics
         * 2.Soft skills
         * 3.Subclass-specific paper
         * 4.Additional paper,if any
         */

        // Common Papers:
        courseOnMathematics();//Step-1
        courseOnSoftSkills(); //Step-2

        // Course-specific Paper:
        courseOnSpecialPaper();//Step-3

        if (isAdditionalPaperNeeded()){
            // Step-4 (if required)
            courseOnAdditionalPaper();
        }
    }

    private void courseOnMathematics() {
        System.out.println("1. Mathematics");
    }

    private void courseOnSoftSkills() {
        System.out.println("2. Soft skills");
    }
```

```java
    /*
     * The following method will vary.
     * It will be overridden by the
     * derived classes.
     */

    public abstract void courseOnSpecialPaper();

    // Include an additional subject
    // if required.

    private void courseOnAdditionalPaper()
    {
        System.out.println("4. Compiler construction.");
    }

    /* A hook method.
     * By default, an additional
     * subject is needed.
     */
    boolean isAdditionalPaperNeeded(){
        return true;
    }

}
```

// ComputerScience.java

```java
// The concrete derived class: ComputerScience

class ComputerScience extends BasicEngineering {

    @Override
    public void courseOnSpecialPaper() {
        System.out.println("3. Object-Oriented Programming");
    }
}
```

// Electronics.java

```java
// The concrete derived class: Electronics

class Electronics extends BasicEngineering {

    @Override
    public void courseOnSpecialPaper() {
        System.out.println("3.Digital Logic and Circuit Theory");
    }
    /*
     * Overriding the hook method.
     * The additional paper is not needed
     * for the Electronics students.
     */

    @Override
    boolean isAdditionalPaperNeeded() {
        return false;
    }

}
```

// Client.java

```java
class Client {
public static void main(String[] args) {

System.out.println("***Template Method Pattern with a hook
                    method.***\n");
  BasicEngineering preferrredCourse = new ComputerScience();
  System.out.println("Computer Science course structure:");
  preferrredCourse.displayCourseStructure();
  System.out.println();
  preferrredCourse = new Electronics();
  System.out.println("Electronics course structure:");
  preferrredCourse.displayCourseStructure();
 }
}
```

Output

Here's the modified output:

```
***Template Method Pattern with a hook method.***

Computer Science course structure:
1. Mathematics
2. Soft skills
3. Object-Oriented Programming
4. Compiler construction.

Electronics course structure:
1. Mathematics
2. Soft skills
3. Digital Logic and Circuit Theory
```

Note   You may prefer an alternative approach. For example, you could directly include the default method called `courseOnAdditionalPaper()` in `BasicEngineering`. After that, you could override the method in the `Electronics` class and make the method body empty. But is it a good idea to use an empty method in this example? I do not think so. For example, consider a case when you have many subclasses and most of them override the superclass method and you are forced to make this method empty in each of them. You may say, instead of making a method body empty, you will throw an exception and indicate that it is not a valid method for a particular subclass. If you think like this, I suggest you recollect the LSP principle and its importance. This is why using a hook method can provide you with a better alternative in certain scenarios.

15.4 It looks like this pattern is similar to the Builder pattern. Is this correct?

No. Don't forget the core intent; the Template Method pattern is a behavioral design pattern, whereas the Builder pattern is a creational design pattern. In the Builder pattern, the client/customer is the boss. They control the order of the algorithm. In the Template Method pattern, you (or the developers) are the boss. You put your code in a central location (the abstract class `BasicEngineering.cs` in this example), and you have absolute control over the flow of the execution, which cannot be altered by the client. For example, you can see that "Mathematics" and "Soft skills" always appear at the top following the execution order in the template method `displayCourseStructure()`. The clients need to obey this flow.

If you alter the flow in your template method, other participants will also follow the new flow.

15.5 What are the key advantages of using a Template Method design pattern?

Here are some key advantages:

- You can control the flow of the algorithms. Clients cannot change this.

- Common operations are in a centralized location. For example, in an abstract class, the subclasses can redefine only the varying parts so that you can avoid redundant code.

15.6 What are the key challenges associated with a Template Method design pattern?

The disadvantages can be summarized as follows:

- The client code cannot direct the sequence of steps. If you want that type of functionality, use the Builder pattern (refer to Chapter 6).

- A subclass can override a method defined in the parent class (in other words, hiding the original definition in the parent class), which can go against the Liskov Substitution Principle.

- Having more subclasses means more scattered code and difficult maintenance.

15.7 What will happen if a subclass tries to override the other parent methods in the `BasicEngineering` **class?**

This pattern suggests not to do that. When you use this pattern, you should not override all the parent methods entirely to bring a radical change in the subclasses. In this way, it differs from simple polymorphism.

15.8 It will be helpful if you explain some built-in template methods in Java.

Consider the `removeAll()` method of `java.util.AbstractSet`. It has the following definition:

```
public boolean removeAll(Collection<?> c) {
        Objects.requireNonNull(c);
        boolean modified = false;

        if (size() > c.size()) {
            for (Object e : c)
                modified |= remove(e);
        } else {
            for (Iterator<?> i = iterator(); i.hasNext(); ) {
                if (c.contains(i.next())) {
                    i.remove();
                    modified = true;
                }
            }
        }
        return modified;
    }
```

Have you noticed the use of the size() method? On further investigation, you'll see that size() is present in the parent class AbstractCollection and it has the following definition:

```
public abstract int size();
```

Apart from this, there are many non-abstract methods in the java.util. AbstractMap and java.util.AbstractSet classes, which can also be considered as examples of the Template Method pattern. For example, notice the definition of the following method in the AbstractMap<K,V> class:

```
public int size() {
        return entrySet().size();
    }
```

You can see that the previous method uses another method named entrySet(), which is defined as an abstract method in AbstractMap<K,V> as follows:

```
public abstract Set<Entry<K,V>> entrySet();
```

CHAPTER 16

Observer Pattern

This chapter covers the Observer pattern.

GoF Definition

It defines a one-to-many dependency between objects so that when one object changes state, all its dependents are notified and updated automatically.

Concept

In this pattern, there are two types of objects. One is an observer and the other is the subject. What is an observer? In simple words, it is an object that needs to be informed when interesting stuff happens in another object. The object about whom an observer is interested is called the subject.

Normally many observers observe a particular subject. Since the observers are interested in the changes in a subject, they register themselves to get the notifications from the subject. When they lose interest in the subject, they simply unregister from the subject. Sometimes this model is referred to as the Publisher-Subscriber (Pub-Sub) model.

The whole idea can be summarized as follows: using this pattern, an object (subject) can send notifications to multiple observers (a set of objects) at the same time. Observers can decide how to respond/react to these notifications. You can visualize the scenarios with the following diagrams.

In step 1, three observers request notifications from a subject (see Figure 16-1).

© Vaskaran Sarcar 2022

V. Sarcar, *Java Design Patterns*, https://doi.org/10.1007/978-1-4842-7971-7_16

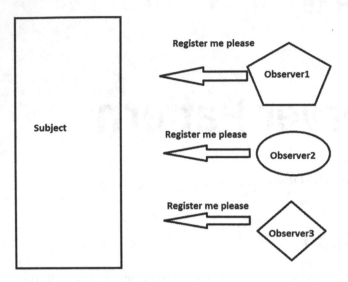

Figure 16-1. *Step 1*

In step 2, the subject can grant the requests; in other words, a connection is established (Figure 16-2).

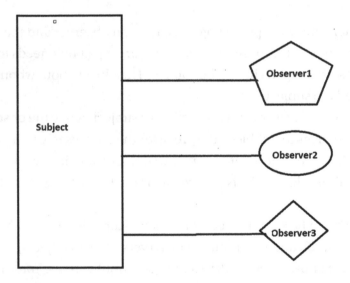

Figure 16-2. *Step 2*

In step 3, the subject sends notifications to the registered users (see Figure 16-3).

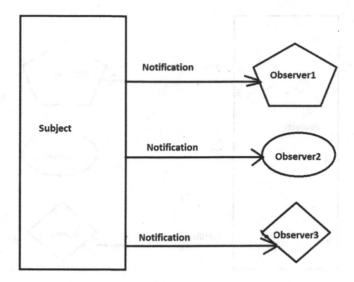

Figure 16-3. *Step 3*

In step 4 (optional), Observer2 does not want to get further notifications and requests to unregister themselves (or the subject doesn't want to keep Observer2 in their notification list due to some specific reason, so they unregister Observer2). So, the connection between the subject and Observer2 is lost (see Figure 16-4).

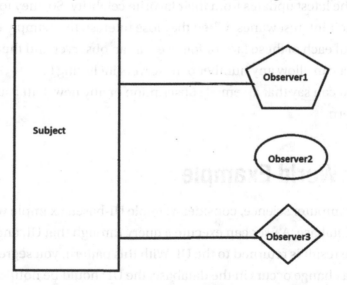

Figure 16-4. *Step 4*

In step 5, from now on, only Observer1 and Observer3 get notifications from the subject (see Figure 16-5).

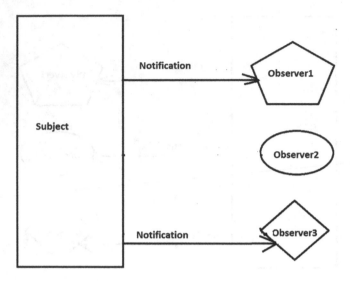

Figure 16-5. *Step 5*

Real-Life Example

Think about a celebrity who has many followers on social media. Each of these followers wants to get all the latest updates from their favorite celebrity. So, they follow the celebrity until their interest wanes. When they lose interest, they simply unfollow that celebrity. Think of each of these fans or followers as an observer and the celebrity as the subject. A subject can allow any number of observers including 0.

Similarly, you can say that an email subscription or any newsletter subscription follows this pattern.

Computer World Example

In the world of computer science, consider a simple UI-based example where the UI is connected to a database. A user can execute a query through that UI, and after searching the database, the result is returned to the UI. With this pattern, you segregate the UI from the database. If a change occurs in the database, the UI should be notified so that it can update its display according to the change.

To simplify this scenario, assume that you are the person responsible for maintaining a particular database in your organization. Whenever there is a change made to the database, you want to get a notification so that you can take action if necessary.

You can see the presence of this pattern in any event-driven software. Modern languages like Java and C# have built-in support for handling these events following this pattern. These constructs will make your life easier. In this context, note the following points:

- In Java programming, you see the use of event listeners. These listeners are nothing but observers only. Before Java 9, there were readymade constructs such as the `Observable` class and the `Observer` interface. `Observable` can have multiple observers who need to implement the `Observer` interface.

- On further investigation, you see that the `Observer` interface has an update method as follows: `void update(Observable o, Object arg)`. This method is invoked whenever a change occurs in the observed object. Your application needs to call the `Observable` object's `notifyObservers()` method to notify the change of the observers. The methods `addObserver(Observer o)` and `deleteObserver(Observer o)` are used to add an observer and delete an observer, similar to our register and unregister methods.

- This `Observable` class was used to represent the observable objects or "data" in the model-view paradigm. Java developers used to subclass it to represent an object that the application wants to have observed.

Note   Java 9 onwards they are deprecated. The Eclipse IDE shows the following description: This class (`Observable`) and the `Observer` interface have been deprecated. The event model supported by `Observer` and `Observable` is quite limited, the order of notifications delivered by `Observable` is unspecified, and state changes are not in one-for-one correspondence with notifications. For a richer event model, consider using `java.beans` package. For reliable and ordered messaging among threads, consider using one of the concurrent data structures in the `java.util.concurrent` package. For reactive streams style programming, see the `java.util.concurrent.Flow` API.

- Following the previous suggestion, let's investigate the alternatives. In Java 9 onwards, the `Flow` class is introduced. Here you see the presence of static interfaces such as `Publisher<T>`, `Subscriber<T>`, and `Subscription`. These constructs can be used as an alternative to the Observer design pattern.

- If you are already familiar with the .NET Framework, you know that in C#, you already have generic `System.IObservable<T>` and `System.IObserver<T>` interfaces where the generic type parameter is used to provide notifications.

Implementation

In this example, you see two inheritance chains, one for the subject and one for the observers. The observer hierarchy starts with the `Observer` interface. Two concrete types of `Employee` and `Customer` implement this interface. *I created two different types of observers to demonstrate that they need not belong to the same class. Consider a real-world example. A company has both employees and customers who can purchase the company stocks. As a result, they like to get alerts when the stock price changes. In this case, both customers and employees are the observers and the company is the subject.*

Inside the client code, you'll see four observer instances (`roy, kevin, bose,` and `jacklin`). There are two subject instances too; one is for `ABC Ltd.` and the other is for the `XYZ Co.` Let us call them as `abcLtd` and `xyzCo`, respectively.

Each subject maintains a list of all of its registered users. The observers receive a notification when the stock price changes in the subject(s).

Initially, three observers (`Roy, Kevin,` and `Bose`) register themselves to get notifications from `ABC Ltd.` (when the stock price is $5). So, in the initial phase, all of them received notifications. Later `Kevin` loses interest. When the subject becomes aware of this, it removes `Kevin` from its observer list. At this time, only `Roy` and `Bose` receive notifications (when the stock price is $50). But `Kevin` changes his mind later and wants to get notifications again, so the company `ABC Ltd.` registers him again. This is why, when the stock price jumps to $100, all three observers receive notifications.

Later you see another company named `XYZ Co.` `Roy` and `Jacklin` are registered in its observer list. So, when this company sets its stock price to $500, both `Roy` and `Jacklin` receive the notification.

Now, look into the code. Here is the Observer interface, which has the following definition:

```
interface Observer {
    void getNotification(Company company);
    String getObserverName();
}
```

Two concrete classes named Employee and Customer are used to show that you can have different types of observers. These classes implement the Observer interface. They are similar. Here is one of them:

```
//Observer type-1: These are employees

class Employee implements Observer {
    String nameOfObserver;

    public Employee(String name) {
        this.nameOfObserver = name;
    }

    @Override
    public void getNotification(Company company) {
        System.out.print(nameOfObserver + " has received an
                            alert from " +company.getName());
        System.out.println("The current stock price is:$" +
                            company.getStockPrice());
    }

    @Override
    public String getObserverName() {
        return nameOfObserver;
    }

}
```

To represent subjects, let's start with an abstract class. Notice that this class contains three methods called register(...), unRegister(...), and notifyRegisteredUsers(). As per the names, these methods are used to register an observer, unregister an observer, and notify all registered observers, respectively. In addition, this class maintains a list of observers. The following code segment with supporting comments help you understand this class:

```java
abstract class Company {

    List<Observer> observerList = new ArrayList<Observer>();

    // Name of the subject
    private String name;

    public Company(String name) {
        this.name = name;
    }
    public String getName() {
        return this.name;
    }

    // For the stock price
    private int stockPrice;

    public int getStockPrice() {
        return this.stockPrice;
    }

    public void setStockPrice(int stockPrice) {
        this.stockPrice = stockPrice;
        // The stock price is changed.
        // So notify observer(s).
        notifyRegisteredUsers();
    }

    // To register an observer
    abstract void register(Observer o);

    // To Unregister an observer
    abstract void unRegister(Observer o);
```

```
    // To notify registered users
    abstract void notifyRegisteredUsers();

}
```

Concrete class SpecificCompany extends the Company class and provides the specific implementations as follows:

```
class SpecificCompany extends Company {
    public SpecificCompany (String name) {
        super(name);
    }

    @Override
    void register(Observer anObserver) {
        observerList.add(anObserver);
        System.out.println(this.getName()+ " registers "+
                        anObserver.getObserverName());
    }
    @Override
    void unRegister(Observer anObserver) {
        observerList.remove(anObserver);
        System.out.println(this.getName()+ " unregisters "+
                        anObserver.getObserverName());
    }

    // Notify all registered observers.

    @Override
        public void notifyRegisteredUsers() {
            for(Observer observer: observerList) {
                observer.getNotification(this);
            }
        }
}
```

There's a constructor inside the subject. The constructor is as follows:

```
public Company(String name) {
  this.name = name;
}
```

This constructor represents different subjects. So, inside client code, you will see the following lines with comments:

```
System.out.println("Working with the company: Abc Ltd.\n");
Company abcLtd = new SpecificCompany("ABC Ltd.");
// Remaining code skipped
```

The remaining code is easy to understand. You can follow the supportive comments if required.

Note   In this example, the subject is responsible for registering and/or unregistering an observer. It is because I closely follow the built-in Java constructs where the subject (Observable class) does the same, but the Observer interface has only the update method. It means that the Observable class is only responsible for the observer's registration or unregistration. But you can make an application that allows an observer to register themselves to get a notification from a subject, too. You will see a discussion on this topic later.

Class Diagram

Figure 16-6 shows the class diagram.

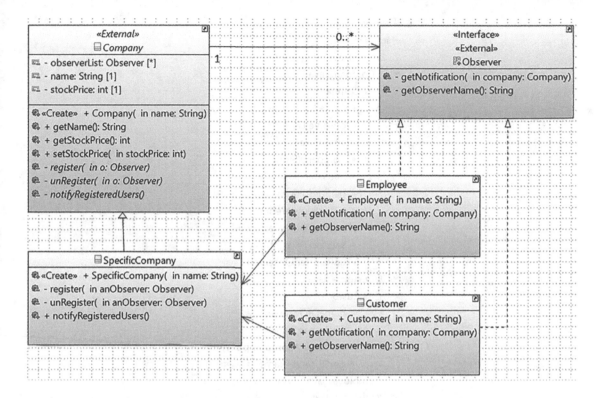

Figure 16-6. *The class diagram*

Package Explorer View

Figure 16-7 shows the high-level structure of the program. Employee.java is similar to Customer.java. To make the diagram short, I did not expand it again in the Package Explorer.

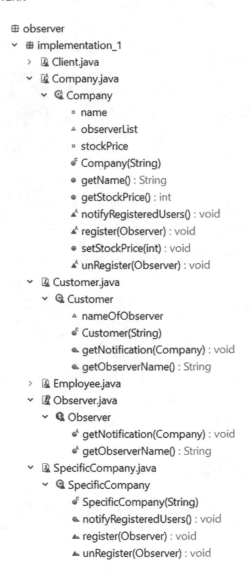

Figure 16-7. *Package Explorer view*

Demonstration

All the classes and the `Observer` interface are stored inside the package jdp3e.observer. implementation_1. Here's the complete demonstration:

// Observer.java

```
interface Observer {
```

```java
        void getNotification(Company company);
        String getObserverName();
}
```

// Employee.java

```java
// Observer type-1: These are employees

class Employee implements Observer {
    String nameOfObserver;

    public Employee(String name) {
        this.nameOfObserver = name;
    }

    @Override
    public void getNotification(Company company) {
        System.out.print(nameOfObserver + " has received an
                            alert from " +company.getName());
        System.out.println("The current stock price is:$" +
                            company.getStockPrice());
    }

    @Override
    public String getObserverName() {
        return nameOfObserver;
    }

}
```

// Customer.java

```java
// Observer type-2: These are customers
class Customer implements Observer {
    String nameOfObserver;

    public Customer(String name) {
        this.nameOfObserver = name;
    }
```

```java
    @Override
    public void getNotification(Company company) {
        System.out.print(nameOfObserver + " is notified
                        from " +company.getName());
        System.out.println("Its current stock price is:$"
                        + company.getStockPrice());

    }
    @Override
    public String getObserverName() {
        return nameOfObserver;
    }
}
```

// Company.java

```java
import java.util.ArrayList;
import java.util.List;

abstract class Company {

    List<Observer> observerList = new ArrayList<Observer>();

    // Name of the subject
    private String name;

    public Company(String name) {
        this.name = name;
    }
    public String getName() {
        return this.name;
    }

    // For the stock price
    private int stockPrice;

    public int getStockPrice() {
        return this.stockPrice;
    }
```

```java
    public void setStockPrice(int stockPrice) {
        this.stockPrice = stockPrice;
        // The stock price is changed.
        // So,notify observer(s).
        notifyRegisteredUsers();
    }

    // To register an observer
    abstract void register(Observer o);

    // To Unregister an observer
    abstract void unRegister(Observer o);

    // To notify registered users
    abstract void notifyRegisteredUsers();

}
```

// SpecificCompany.java

```java
class SpecificCompany extends Company {
    public SpecificCompany (String name) {
        super(name);
    }

    @Override
    void register(Observer anObserver) {
        observerList.add(anObserver);
        System.out.println(this.getName()+ " registers "+ anObserver.
        getObserverName());
    }

    @Override
    void unRegister(Observer anObserver) {
        observerList.remove(anObserver);
        System.out.println(this.getName()+ " unregisters "+ anObserver.
        getObserverName());
    }
```

```
        // Notify all registered observers.
        @Override
            public void notifyRegisteredUsers() {
                for(Observer observer: observerList) {
                    observer.getNotification(this);
                }
            }
        }
}
```

// Client.java

```
class Client {
    public static void main(String[] args) {
        System.out.println("***Observer Pattern Demonstration.***\n");
        // We have 4 different observers.
        Observer roy = new Employee("Roy");
        Observer kevin = new Employee("Kevin");
        Observer bose = new Customer("Bose");
        Observer jacklin = new Customer("Jacklin");
        System.out.println("Working with the company: Abc Ltd.\n");

        Company abcLtd = new SpecificCompany("ABC Ltd. ");
        // Registering the observers - Roy, Kevin, Bose
        abcLtd.register(roy);
        abcLtd.register(kevin);
        abcLtd.register(bose);
        System.out.println(" ABC Ltd.'s current stock price is $5.");
        abcLtd.setStockPrice(5);
        System.out.println("-----");

        // Kevin doesn't want to get further notification.
        System.out.println("\nABC Ltd. is removing Kevin
                        from the observer list now.");
        abcLtd.unRegister(kevin);
        // No notification is sent to Kevin any more.
```

```
System.out.println("\n ABC Ltd.'s new stock price is $50.");
abcLtd.setStockPrice(50);
System.out.println("-----");

System.out.println("\nKevin registers again to get
                    notification from ABC Ltd.");
abcLtd.register(kevin);

System.out.println("\n ABC Ltd.'s new stock price is $100.");
abcLtd.setStockPrice(100);
System.out.println("-----");

System.out.println("\n Working with another company: XYZ Co.");

// Creating another company
Company xyzCo = new SpecificCompany("XYZ Co. ");
// Registering the observers-Roy and Jacklin
xyzCo.register(roy);
xyzCo.register(jacklin);
System.out.println("\nXYZ Co.'s new stock price is $500.");
xyzCo.setStockPrice(500);

    }
}
```

Output

Here's the output:

Observer Pattern Demonstration.

Working with the company: Abc Ltd.

ABC Ltd. registers Roy
ABC Ltd. registers Kevin
ABC Ltd. registers Bose
 ABC Ltd.'s current stock price is $5.
Roy has received an alert from ABC Ltd. The current stock price is:$5

Kevin has received an alert from ABC Ltd. The current stock price is:$5
Bose is notified from ABC Ltd.Its current stock price is:$5

ABC Ltd. is removing Kevin from the observer list now.
ABC Ltd. unregisters Kevin

 ABC Ltd.'s new stock price is $50.
Roy has received an alert from ABC Ltd. The current stock price is:$50
Bose is notified from ABC Ltd.Its current stock price is:$50

Kevin registers again to get notifications from ABC Ltd.
ABC Ltd. registers Kevin

 ABC Ltd.'s new stock price is $100.
Roy has received an alert from ABC Ltd. The current stock price is:$100
Bose is notified from ABC Ltd.Its current stock price is:$100
Kevin has received an alert from ABC Ltd. The current stock price is:$100

Working with another company: XYZ Co.
XYZ Co. registers Roy
XYZ Co. registers Jacklin

XYZ Co.'s new stock price is $500.
Roy has received an alert from XYZ Co. The current stock price is:$500
Jacklin is notified from XYZ Co. Its current stock price is:$500

Q&A Session

16.1 If I have only one observer, then I may not need to set up the interface. Is this correct?

Yes. But if you want to follow the pure object-oriented programming guidelines, you should prefer interfaces (or abstract classes) instead of using a concrete class. Aside from this point, usually you have multiple observers and you implement them following the contracts. That's where you get the benefit from this kind of design.

16.2 Can you have different observers that may vary?

Yes. This is why, in the demonstration, I showed different types of observers, such as employees and customers. These observers also work with different subjects (i.e., companies).

16.3 Can you add or remove observers at runtime?

Yes. Notice that at the beginning of the program, to get notifications, Kevin registers himself. In between, he unregisters himself and then reregisters again.

16.4 It appears to me that there are similarities between the Observer pattern and the Chain of Responsibility pattern (Chapter 17). Is this understanding correct?

In an Observer pattern, all registered users get notifications in parallel, but in a Chain of Responsibility pattern, objects in the chain are sequentially notified one by one, and this process continues until an object handles the notification fully (or reaches at the end of the chain). I show the comparisons with diagrams in the "Q&A Session" section of the Chain of Responsibility pattern (see Q&A 17.7 in Chapter 17).

16.5 Does this model support one-to-many relationships?

Yes, the GoF definition confirms this. Since a subject can send notifications to multiple observers, this kind of dependency depicts a one-to-many relationship.

16.6 I read previous editions of this book. I understand that before Java 9, you could use the ready-made constructs (for example, `Observable` class and `Observer` interface, etc.). Instead of using them, why did you use custom code to model an Observer Design pattern?

You cannot change ready-made functionalities, but I believe that when you try to implement the concept yourself, you gain an understanding that can help you to better use those ready-made constructs. Let's consider some typical scenarios:

- In Java, `Observable` is a concrete class and it does not implement an interface. We know that programming to an interface is always better than programming to a concrete class when you try implementing polymorphic code.

- You also remember that Java does not allow multiple inheritance through classes. So, when you extend the `Observable` class, you have to keep in mind the restriction. So, it may limit the reuse potential.

- The signature of the `setChanged` method in `Observable` is as follows:

  ```
  protected void setChanged().
  ```

  This means to use it, you needed to subclass the `Observable` class. This violates one of the key design principles that says to *prefer composition over inheritance.*

- Finally, I told you that the `Observable` class and the `Observer` interface have been deprecated since Java 9.

Similarly, if you are familiar with the C# programming language, you may see the use of System.IObservable<T> and System.IObserver<T> interfaces. What does this mean? It tells us that you need to be familiar with generic programming. Not only that, if you give a closer look at these interfaces, you will see the following:

```
public interface IObservable<out T>
public interface IObserver<in T>
```

This simply means that you need to be familiar with covariance and contravariance in C#, too. In the beginning, these concepts may seem to be difficult to understand. In *Getting Started with Advanced C#,* I discuss these concepts in detail with code examples.

16.7 What are the key benefits of the Observer pattern?

Here are some key advantages:

- Subjects (companies, in this example) and their registered users (observers) make up a loosely coupled system. They do not need to know each other explicitly. Typically, a subject does not care how an observer reacts to the notification event.

- You do not need to make changes in the subject when you add or remove an observer from its notification lists.

- You can add or remove observers at runtime independently.

16.8 What are the key challenges associated with an Observer pattern?

Here are some key challenges when you implement (or use) this pattern:

- Undoubtedly, memory leak is the greatest concern when you handle events in Java or a similar language such as C#. It is also referred to as the *lapsed listener problem*. In simple words, consider a case when an observer registers with a subject to get event notifications but forgets to unregister the same. It causes some live references to stay in the computer memory. The garbage collector does not collect them and as a result, you see the impact of memory leaks.

- The order of notification is not dependable.

- As the number of observers increases, each update operation becomes costly.

16.9 I have a concern: I see that in your demonstration, the subject is registering and unregistering the observers. But in a real-world application, I want to give these observers more freedom. They should be able to register and unregister themselves, too. How can I make such an application?

It is easy. Let's add two additional methods in the `Observer` interface as follows (notice the changes in bold):

```
interface Observer {
    void getNotification(Company company);
    void registerTo(Company company);
    void unregisterFrom(Company company);
    String getObserverName();
}
```

Here is a sample implementation of a concrete observer:

```
// Observer type-1: These are employees

class Employee implements Observer {
    String nameOfObserver;

    public Employee(String name) {
        this.nameOfObserver = name;
    }
```

```
@Override
public void getNotification(Company company) {
    System.out.print(nameOfObserver + " has received an alert from "
    +company.getName());
    System.out.println("The current stock price is:$" + company.
    getStockPrice());
}

@Override
public void registerTo(Company company) {
    company.register(this);
    System.out.println(this.nameOfObserver+ "
                       registered himself/herself to "+
                       company.getName());

}

@Override
public void unregisterFrom(Company company) {
    company.unRegister(this);
    System.out.println(this.nameOfObserver+ "
                       unregistered himself/herself
                       from "+ company.getName());

}

@Override
public String getObserverName() {
    return nameOfObserver;
}
}
```

No changes are made in the subject hierarchy. Inside the client code, now an observer can register or unregister themselves. Notice the changes in bold in the following code:

```
// Observers

Observer roy = new Employee("Roy");
Observer kevin = new Employee("Kevin");
//other codes, if any

// Observers register themselves
roy.registerTo(xyzCo);
kevin.registerTo(xyzCo);
//some other code

// An observer unregisters himself
roy.unregisterFrom(xyzCo);
//some other code
```

Note   I have not put in the validations whether an observer is already registered (or unregistered) to a subject. I leave this kind of exercise for you because our focus is on the design patterns only. I kept an additional implementation on the Apress site to demonstrate how an observer can register to a subject or unregister from the subject. If you want to see this implementation, you can refer to the package jdp3e.observer.implementation_2.

CHAPTER 17

Chain of Responsibility Pattern

This chapter covers the Chain of Responsibility pattern.

GoF Definition

It avoids coupling the sender of a request to its receiver by giving more than one object a chance to handle the request. It chains the receiving objects and passes the request along the chain until an object handles it.

Concept

In this pattern, you form a chain of objects where you pass the responsibility of a task from one object to another and so forth until an object accepts the responsibility of completing the task. Each object in the chain can handle a particular kind of request. If an object cannot handle the request fully, it passes the request to the next object in the chain. This process may continue until the end of the chain. This kind of request-handling mechanism gives you the flexibility to add a new processing object (handler) or shuffle their order in the chain. Figure 17-1 shows such a chain with N number of handlers.

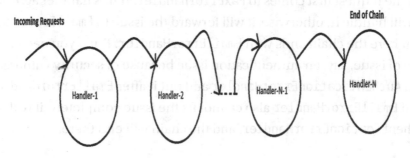

***Figure 17-1.** Chain of Responsibility pattern*

© Vaskaran Sarcar 2022
V. Sarcar, *Java Design Patterns*, https://doi.org/10.1007/978-1-4842-7971-7_17

Real-Life Example

Most software organizations have customer care representatives who take feedback from customers and forward any issues to the appropriate departments in the organization. However, not all of these departments will start fixing the issue simultaneously. The department that seems to be responsible will take a look at the issue first, and if those employees believe that the issue should be forwarded to another department, they will forward it.

You may see a similar scenario when a patient visits a hospital. Doctors from one department can refer the patient to a different department for further diagnosis if they think it's needed.

You can consider a mobile company organization, too. For example, in India, the Vodafone mobile company runs a customer care department. If you have a complaint about the service, you first raise the issue to the customer care department. If they fail to solve your problem, you can escalate it to a nodal officer. If you are not satisfied with the solution given by the nodal officer, you can further escalate the issue to an appellate officer.

Computer World Example

Consider a software application (say, a printer) that can send e-mails and faxes. As a result, any customer can report either fax issues or e-mail issues, so you need to have two different types of error handlers. Let us call them `EmailErrorHandler` and `FaxErrorHandler`. You can safely assume that `EmailErrorHandler` will handle e-mail errors only and will not fix fax errors. In the same manner, `FaxErrorHandler` will handle fax errors and will not care about e-mail errors.

You can form a chain like this: whenever your application finds an error, it will raise a ticket and forward the error with the hope that one of those handlers will handle it. Let's assume that the request first comes to `FaxErrorhandler`. If this handler agrees that it is a fax issue, it will handle it; otherwise, it will forward the issue to `EmailErrorHandler`.

Note that here the chain ends with `EmailErrorHandler`. But if you need to handle another type of issue, say, an authentication issue because of security vulnerabilities, you can make an `AuthenticationErrorHandler` and put it after `EmailErrorHandler` in the chain. Now if `EmailErrorHandler` also cannot fix the issue completely, it will forward the issue to `AuthenticationErrorHandler`, and the chain will end there.

```
POINTS TO REMEMBER
```

This is just an example; you are free to place these handlers in any order you'd like. The bottom line is that the processing chain may end in either of these two scenarios:

- A handler can process the request completely.

- You have reached the end of the chain.

Here is another example for you:

- Java's exception handling mechanism can be considered as a variation of this pattern. Consider a program that has a `try` block followed by multiple `catch` blocks. You know that each `catch` block is an exception handler that handles the type of exception indicated by its argument. But you cannot place them arbitrarily. To avoid the compile-time errors, you need to arrange these `catch` blocks from "more specific" to "more general" type. If there is no `catch` block to handle the exception, then the current thread (the thread that encountered the exception) is terminated. In this context, it is important to note that the online link `https://docs.oracle.com/javase/tutorial/essential/exceptions/catch.html` also says: "Exception handlers can do more than just print error messages or halt the program. They can do error recovery, prompt the user to make a decision, or propagate the error up to a higher-level handler using chained exceptions."

Implementation

In the following example, you'll write the program for the computer world example just discussed. In this example, you need to process different messages that may come from either e-mail or fax. The beginning of the program has the following segments of code to describe the error messages:

```
class Message {
    public String text;

    public Message(String msg) {
```

```
        text = msg;
    }
}
```

Then you use a handler interface that looks like the following:

```
interface Handler {
    void handleMessage(Message message);
    void nextErrorHandler(Handler nextReceiver);
}
```

The FaxErrorHandler and EmailErrorHandler classes implement this interface. They are the concrete handlers in this program. It is important to note that to demonstrate a very simple use case, you could use the following code segment in FaxErrorHandler:

```
if (message.text.contains("fax"))
{
  System.out.println("FaxErrorHandler processed the issue :" + message.text);
}
else if (nextReceiver != null)
{
    nextReceiver.HandleMessage(message);
}
```

POINTS TO REMEMBER

In the previous code segment, you can see that if a message contains the word "fax," then FaxErrorHandler will handle it; otherwise, it will pass the issue to the next handler. Similarly, in the upcoming example, if a message contains the word "email," then EmailErrorHandler will handle the message and so forth. But what happens if both "email" and "fax" are included in a message? I have taken care of this case in the upcoming example, but for simplicity, you can ignore the case using this segment of code.

In a real-world problem, one error may cause another error, so it is possible when an error occurs in the fax code base, the same error propagates to the email codebase (if they share a common codebase). As a result, a common fix can solve both issues. In the upcoming example, I show when you should be concerned about the issue and how to pass it to the next handler. So, in the beginning, you may ignore the individual pillar complexities.

Actually, an organization may prefer to implement an AI-based mechanism to analyze an issue first, and then based on the symptoms they can forward the issue to a particular department. But at the core, you may see the use of this pattern.

To demonstrate a case where a message contains both "email" and "fax," let's use a relatively complex structure for FaxErrorHandler. How does it work? Read the following points:

- If the error message contains the word "fax" but not "email," after fixing the issue, it will not pass the error to the email handler.

- If the error message contains both the words "email" and "fax," it will fix the fax issue and then it will pass it to the email handler so that the email team can verify the fix and can add additional code if they think it's necessary.

- If the error message does not contain either "email" or "fax," the issue will ultimately be forwarded to the unknown handler.

EmailErrorHandler and FaxErrorHandler are similar. Let's pick one of them for your easy reference (the associated comments can be your guide):

```java
class FaxErrorHandler implements Handler {
    private Handler nextHandler;

    @Override
    public void nextErrorHandler(Handler nextHandler) {
        this.nextHandler = nextHandler;
    }

    @Override
    public void handleMessage(Message message) {
        if (message.text.contains("fax")) {
            // Error message contains both- 'fax' and 'email'
            if (message.text.contains("email")) {
                System.out.println("-FaxErrorHandler
                    fixed the fax issue: " + message.text);
                System.out.println("--Now
                    EmailErrorHandler needs to cross verify it.");
```

```
                    if (nextHandler != null) {
                        nextHandler.handleMessage(message);
                    }

                }
                // It's a fax error only.
                else {
                    System.out.println("FaxErrorHandler
                        processed  the issue: " + message.text);
                }
            }
            // Neither a fax issue nor an email issue
            else {
                if (nextHandler != null) {
                    nextHandler.handleMessage(message);
                }
            }
        }
    }
}
```

Now if you have a message that contains both "email" and "fax" like "Neither fax nor email is working properly," this relatively complex structure can help you to get the following output where you can see that both teams worked on the defect:

```
-FaxErrorHandler fixed the fax issue: Neither email nor fax is working
properly.
--Now EmailErrorHandler needs to cross verify it.

-EmailErrorHandler fixed the email issue: Neither email nor fax is working
properly.
--Now FaxErrorHandler needs to cross verify it.
```

At the end of this chain, there is an UnknownErrorHandler that simply says the issue is neither from Email nor from Fax, so consult the expert developers to tackle the issue.

```
class UnknownErrorHandler implements Handler {
    private Handler nextHandler;
```

```java
    @Override
    public void nextErrorHandler(Handler nextHandler) {
        this.nextHandler = nextHandler;
    }

    @Override
    public void handleMessage(Message message) {
        if (!(message.text.contains("fax") || message.text.
        contains("email"))) {
            System.out.println("Unknown error occurs.Consult experts
            immediately.");
        } else if (nextHandler != null) {
            nextHandler.handleMessage(message);
        }
    }
}
```

The forming of the error handler objects is quite straightforward. From the following code segment and supportive comments, you can easily understand how to set a starting point and make a chain of handlers:

```java
// Set the root handler/ starting point
Handler rootHandler=faxHandler;
// Making the following chain:
// FaxErrorHandler->EmailErrorHandler->UnknownHandler->End.
rootHandler.nextErrorHandler(emailHandler);
emailHandler.nextErrorHandler(unknownHandler);
unknownHandler.nextErrorHandler(null);
```

Why use rootHandler? If you form a new chain by putting these handlers in a different order, you do not need to make any change inside the client code, which is as follows (you just need to tell which one is rootHandler at that point):

```java
System.out.println("Handling different types of errors.");
System.out.println("\nError-1:");
rootHandler.handleMessage(msg1);
System.out.println("\nError-2:");
rootHandler.handleMessage(msg2);
```

```
System.out.println("\nError-3:");
rootHandler.handleMessage(msg3);
System.out.println("\nError-4:");
rootHandler.handleMessage(msg4);
System.out.println("\nError-5:");
rootHandler.handleMessage(msg5);
System.out.println("\nError-6:");
rootHandler.handleMessage(msg6);
```

Class Diagram

Figure 17-2 shows the class diagram.

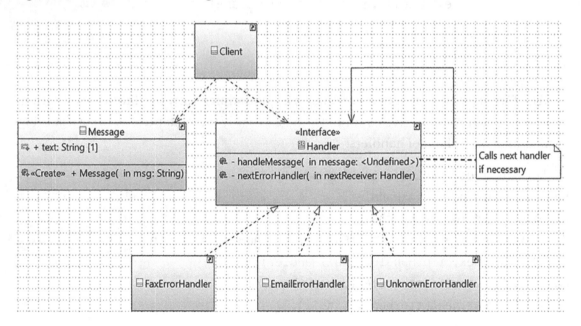

Figure 17-2. *Class diagram*

Package Explorer View

Figure 17-3 shows the high-level structure of the program.

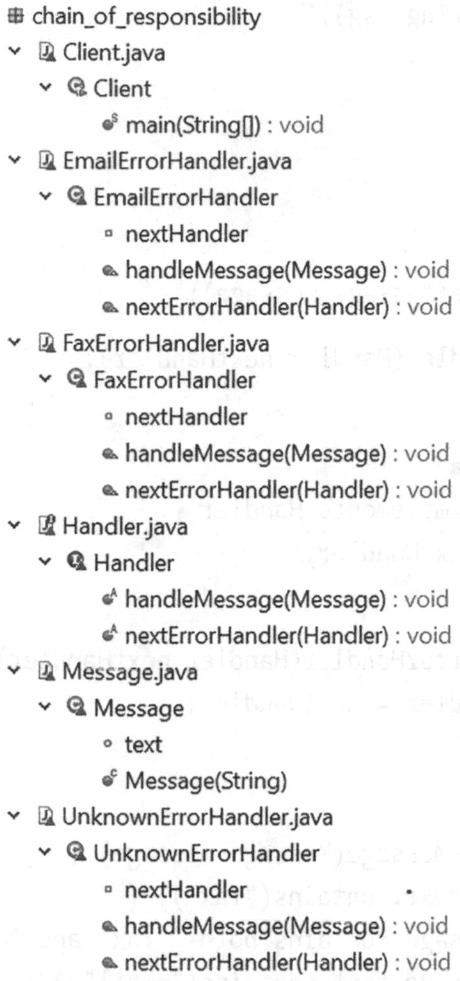

⊞ chain_of_responsibility
∨ ▣ Client.java
   ∨ ⓠ Client
         ✦ main(String[]) : void
∨ ▣ EmailErrorHandler.java
   ∨ ⓠ EmailErrorHandler
         ▫ nextHandler
         ◬ handleMessage(Message) : void
         ◬ nextErrorHandler(Handler) : void
∨ ▣ FaxErrorHandler.java
   ∨ ⓠ FaxErrorHandler
         ▫ nextHandler
         ◬ handleMessage(Message) : void
         ◬ nextErrorHandler(Handler) : void
∨ ▣ Handler.java
   ∨ ⓠ Handler
         ✦ handleMessage(Message) : void
         ✦ nextErrorHandler(Handler) : void
∨ ▣ Message.java
   ∨ ⓠ Message
         ○ text
         ✦ Message(String)
∨ ▣ UnknownErrorHandler.java
   ∨ ⓠ UnknownErrorHandler
         ▫ nextHandler
         ◬ handleMessage(Message) : void
         ◬ nextErrorHandler(Handler) : void

Figure 17-3. *Package Explorer view*

Demonstration

Here's the complete program. All parts of the program are stored inside the package
jdp3e.chain_of_responsibility.

// Message.java

```
class Message {
    public String text;
```

```java
    public Message(String msg) {
        text = msg;
    }
}
```

// Handler.java
```java
interface Handler {
    void handleMessage(Message message);

    void nextErrorHandler(Handler nextHandler);
}
```

// FaxErrorHandler.java
```java
class FaxErrorHandler implements Handler {
    private Handler nextHandler;

    @Override
    public void nextErrorHandler(Handler nextHandler) {
        this.nextHandler = nextHandler;
    }

    @Override
    public void handleMessage(Message message) {
        if (message.text.contains("fax")) {
        // Error message contains both- 'fax' and 'email'
            if (message.text.contains("email")) {
                System.out.println("-FaxErrorHandler
                    fixed the fax issue: " + message.text);
                System.out.println("--Now
                    EmailErrorHandler needs to cross verify it.");
                if (nextHandler != null) {
                    nextHandler.handleMessage(message);
                }

            }
```

```java
            // It's a fax error only.
            else {
                System.out.println ("FaxErrorHandler
                    processed the issue: " + message.text);
            }
        }
        // Neither a fax issue nor an email issue
        else {
            if (nextHandler != null) {
                nextHandler.handleMessage(message);
            }
        }
    }
}
```

// EmailErrorHandler.java
```java
class EmailErrorHandler implements Handler {
    private Handler nextHandler;

    @Override
    public void nextErrorHandler(Handler nextHandler) {
        this.nextHandler = nextHandler;
    }

    @Override
    public void handleMessage(Message message) {
        if (message.text.contains("email")) {
        // Error message contains both-'email' and 'fax'
            if (message.text.contains("fax")) {
                System.out.println("-EmailErrorHandler
                    fixed the email issue: " +
                    message.text);
                System.out.println("--Now
                    FaxErrorHandler needs to cross verify it.");
                if (nextHandler != null) {
                    nextHandler.handleMessage(message);
                }
```

```
            }
            // It's an email error only.
            else {
                System.out.println("EmailErrorHandler
                    processed the issue: "+ message.text);
            }
        }
        // Neither a fax issue nor an email issue
        else {
            if (nextHandler != null) {
                nextHandler.handleMessage(message);
            }
        }
    }
}
```

```
// UnknownErrorHandler.java
class UnknownErrorHandler implements Handler {
    private Handler nextHandler;

    @Override
    public void nextErrorHandler(Handler nextHandler) {
        this.nextHandler = nextHandler;
    }

    @Override
    public void handleMessage(Message message) {
        if (!(message.text.contains("fax") ||
            message.text.contains("email"))
            ) {
            System.out.println("An unknown error
                occurs. Consult experts immediately.");
        } else if (nextHandler != null) {
            nextHandler.handleMessage(message);
        }
    }
}
```

```java
// Client.java
class Client {

    public static void main(String[] args) {
        System.out.println("***Chain of Responsibility Pattern Demo***\n");

        // Objects of the chains
        Handler faxHandler = new FaxErrorHandler();
        Handler emailHandler = new EmailErrorHandler();
        Handler unknownHandler = new UnknownErrorHandler();
        // The root handler/ starting point
        Handler rootHandler;

        // Making the following chain:
        // FaxErrorHandler->EmailErrorHandler-
        //  >UnknownHandler->End.
        rootHandler = faxHandler;
        rootHandler.nextErrorHandler(emailHandler);
        emailHandler.nextErrorHandler(unknownHandler);
        unknownHandler.nextErrorHandler(null);

        // Different error messages
        Message msg1 = new Message("The fax is going slow.");
        Message msg2 = new Message("The emails are not reaching
                                    destinations.");
        Message msg3 = new Message("Sometimes the BCC field
                                    is disabled in emails.");
        Message msg4 = new Message("The fax is not reaching destinations.");
        Message msg5 = new Message("Neither email nor fax is working
                                    properly.");
        Message msg6 = new Message("Users cannot login into the system.");

        System.out.println("Handling different types of errors.");
        System.out.println("\nError-1:");
        rootHandler.handleMessage(msg1);
        System.out.println("\nError-2:");
        rootHandler.handleMessage(msg2);
        System.out.println("\nError-3:");
```

```
            rootHandler.handleMessage(msg3);
            System.out.println("\nError-4:");
            rootHandler.handleMessage(msg4);
            System.out.println("\nError-5:");
            rootHandler.handleMessage(msg5);
            System.out.println("\nError-6:");
            rootHandler.handleMessage(msg6);
    }
}
```

Output

Here's the output:

Chain of Responsibility Pattern Demo

Handling different types of errors.

Error-1:
FaxErrorHandler processed the issue: The fax is going slow.

Error-2:
EmailErrorHandler processed the issue: The emails are not reaching
destinations.

Error-3:
EmailErrorHandler processed the issue: Sometimes the BCC field is disabled
in emails.

Error-4:
FaxErrorHandler processed the issue: The fax is not reaching destinations.

Error-5:
-FaxErrorHandler fixed the fax issue: Neither email nor fax is working
properly.
--Now EmailErrorHandler needs to cross verify it.

-EmailErrorHandler fixed the email issue: Neither email nor fax is working properly.
--Now FaxErrorHandler needs to cross verify it.

Error-6:
An unknown error occurs. Consult experts immediately.

Q&A Session

17.1 What are the advantages of using the Chain of Responsibility design pattern?

Some notable advantages are as follows:

- You have more than one object to handle a request. (Notice that if a handler cannot handle the whole request, it can forward the responsibility to the next handler in the chain.)

- The nodes of the chain can be added or removed dynamically. Also, you can shuffle their order. For example, in the previous application, if you see that most issues are e-mail issues, then you may place EmailErrorHandler as the first handler to save the average processing time of the application.

- A handler does not need to know how the next handler in the chain will handle the request. It can focus on its own handling mechanism only.

- In this pattern, you are decoupling the senders (of requests) from the receivers.

17.2 What are the challenges associated with using the Chain of Responsibility design pattern?

The following points talk about some challenges:

- There is no guarantee that the request will be handled because you may reach the end of the chain but not found any explicit receiver to handle the request. (I agree that depending upon the situation, this can be an advantage too. Consider the case when the Java exception handlers handle an exception on behalf of you.)

- Debugging becomes tricky with this kind of design.

- If there are many handlers, you need to be careful about placing them in the proper order to improve the overall response time.

17.3 How can you handle the scenario where you have reached the end of the chain but no handler handled the request?

One simple solution is through try-catch (or try-finally or try-catch-finally) blocks. If there is no handler to handle the request, you can raise an exception with the appropriate messages and catch the exception in the catch block to draw attention to it (or handle it in a different way).

The GoF talked about Smalltalk's automatic forwarding mechanism (doesNotUnderstand) in a similar context. If a message cannot find a proper handler, it will be caught in doesNotUnderstand implementations that can be overridden to forward the message in the object's successor, log it in some file, and store it in a queue for later processing, or you can simply perform any other intended operations. But note that, by default, this method raises an exception that needs to be handled properly.

17.4 In short, I can say that a handler either handles the request fully or passes it to the next handler. Is this correct?

Yes.

17.5 Can you give me a demo of making a different chain?

See the following code block with supporting comments:

```
// Making a different chain:
// EmailErrorHandler->FaxErrorHandler->UnknownHandler->End.
rootHandler = emailHandler;
rootHandler.nextErrorHandler(faxHandler);
faxHandler.nextErrorHandler(unknownHandler);
unknownHandler.nextErrorHandler(null);
```

once you run the code now, you'll see the following output:

```
***Chain of Responsibility Pattern Demo***

Handling different types of errors.

Error-1:
FaxErrorHandler processed the issue: The fax is going slow.
```

Error-2:
EmailErrorHandler processed the issue: The emails are not reaching
destinations.

Error-3:
EmailErrorHandler processed the issue: Sometimes the BCC field is disabled
in emails.

Error-4:
FaxErrorHandler processed the issue: The fax is not reaching destinations.

Error-5:
-EmailErrorHandler fixed the email issue: Neither email nor fax is working
properly.
--Now FaxErrorHandler needs to cross verify it.
-FaxErrorHandler fixed the fax issue: Neither email nor fax is working
properly.
--Now EmailErrorHandler needs to cross verify it.

Error-6:
An unknown error occurs. Consult experts immediately.

Notice inside Error-5 now the email issue is fixed first and then the fax issue is fixed.
This is the power of this pattern. You can shuffle your handlers as per your need.

**17.6 In your demonstration, a Message instance contains a String. So, it appears to
me, instead of using the Message instances, you could use simple strings inside the
client code to reduce the overall code size. Am I right?**

Nice observation. You are correct. But I want you to note that a message instance
may contain different things, such as ids and priorities. In the previous version of the
book, I used message priorities. This time I made the implementation simpler, but I want
you to follow the structure when you need to include additional information in an error
message. This comment applies to all similar implementations in this book.

17.7 It appears to me that there are similarities between the Observer pattern (Chapter 16) and the Chain of Responsibility pattern. Is this correct?

In an Observer pattern, all registered users can get notifications at the same time, but in the case of the Chain of Responsibility pattern, objects in the chain are notified one by one, which can happen until an object handles the notification fully. Figure 17-4 and Figure 17-5 summarize the difference.

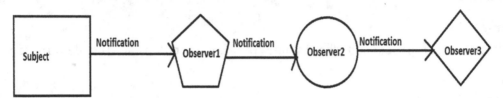

Figure 17-4. *Chain of Responsibility pattern*

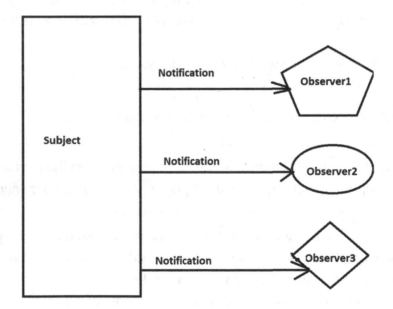

Figure 17-5. *Observer pattern*

In Figure 17-4, I assume that Observer3 was able to process the notification completely. So, it is the end node of the chain.

CHAPTER 18

Iterator Pattern

This chapter covers the Iterator pattern.

GoF Definition

It provides a way to access the elements of an aggregate object sequentially without exposing its underlying representation.

Concept

Iterators are generally used to traverse a container (or a collection of objects) to access its elements without knowing how the data are stored internally. It is very useful when you need to traverse different kinds of collection objects in a standard and uniform way. Figure 18-1 shows a sample and the most common diagram for an Iterator pattern.

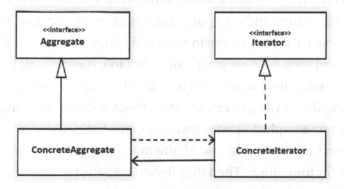

Figure 18-1. *A sample diagram for an Iterator pattern*

The participants are as follows:

- **Iterator**: It is an interface that is used to access or traverse elements.

© Vaskaran Sarcar 2022
V. Sarcar, *Java Design Patterns*, https://doi.org/10.1007/978-1-4842-7971-7_18

- ConcreteIterator: It implements the Iterator interface methods. It can also keep track of the current position in the traversal of the aggregate.

- Aggregate: It defines an interface that can create an Iterator object.

- ConcreteAggregate: It implements the Aggregate interface. It returns an instance of the ConcreteIterator.

POINTS TO NOTE

- This pattern is frequently used to traverse the nodes of a tree-like structure. So, in many examples, you may notice the use of the Iterator pattern with the Composite pattern.

- The role of an iterator is not limited to traversing. This role can vary to support different requirements. For example, you can filter the elements in various ways.

- Clients cannot see the actual traversal mechanism. A client program only uses the iterator methods that are public in nature.

Real-Life Example

Suppose there are two companies, Company A and Company B. Company A stores its employee records (such as each employee's name, address, salary details, and so on) in a linked list data structure, and Company B stores its employee data in an array. One day the two companies decide to merge to form a big organization. The Iterator pattern is handy in such a situation because you do need not to write the code from scratch. In a situation like this, you can have a common interface through which you can access the data for both companies so you can call those methods without rewriting the code.

Consider another example. Suppose your company has decided to promote some employees based on their performances. All the managers get together and set a common criterion for promotion. Then they iterate over the records of the employees one by one to mark the potential candidates for promotion.

Consider an example from a different domain. When you store songs in your preferred audio device, say an MP3 player or your mobile device, you can iterate over them through various button presses or swipe movements. The basic idea is to provide you with some mechanism so that you can go through your list smoothly.

Computer World Example

Go through the following bullet points. They are common examples of the Iterator pattern.

- You may have already used Java's built-in Iterator interface, `java.util.Iterator`. When you use interfaces like `java.util.Iterator` or `java.util.Enumeration`, you basically use this pattern. The concepts of iterators and enumerators have existed for a long time. In simple words, enumerators can produce the next element based on a criterion whereas using iterators, you cycle a sequence from a starting point to the endpoint. In Java, you can treat an `Iterator` as an improved version of an `Enumeration`, because the JDK documentation says the following: `Iterator` takes the place of `Enumeration` in the Java Collections Framework. Iterators differ from enumerations in two ways:

  - `Iterator`s allow the caller to remove elements from the underlying collection during the iteration with well-defined semantics.

  - Method names have been improved.

- The `java.util.Scanner` class that implements `Iterator<String>` also follows this pattern. It allows you to iterate over an input stream.

Implementation

In this chapter, you will see three different implementations of the Iterator pattern. I start with an example that follows the core theory of this pattern. In the next example, I modify the example using Java's in-built support of the Iterator pattern. In the third and final example, I show you the usage of this pattern with a different data structure. In the first two examples, I use the String data type, but in the final example, I use a complex data type. Before you start, note the structure of the program in the Package Explorer view for an immediate reference.

Similar to the real-world example, let's assume that in a particular college, a student of the Arts department needs to study four subjects: English, History, Geography, and Psychology. These subjects are stored in an array data structure.

The administrative department does not interfere with how a department maintains the records for its students. It is simply interested in getting the data from each department and wants to access the data uniformly. Now assume you are a member of the administrative department and at the beginning of a new session, you want to write a program to advertise the curriculum using the iterators. Let's see how to implement it in the upcoming demonstration.

The Iterator pattern enables a client object to traverse through a collection of objects (often termed as a container) without having the container reveal how the data is stored internally. This is why, to implement this pattern, you should remember the following points:

- This pattern suggests you have a container object that provides a public interface in the form of an `Iterator` object so that different client objects can access its contents.

- An `Iterator` object contains public methods to allow a client object to navigate through the list of objects within the container.

Let's assume that your iterator currently supports four basic methods named `first()`, `next()`, `currentItem()`, and `hasNext()`. As per their naming,

- The `first()` method reset the pointer to the first element before you start traversing a data structure.

- The `next()` method returns the next element in the container.

- The `currentItem()` method returns the current element of the container where the iterator is pointing at a particular point of time.

- The `hasNext()` method validates whether any next element is available for further processing or not. So, the `hasNext()` method helps you to decide whether you have reached the end of your container or not.

This is why in the upcoming demonstration you see an Iterator that acts as a common interface. It is defined as follows:

```
interface Iterator {
    void first();
    String next();
    String currentItem();
    boolean hasNext();
}
```

Any class that implements this interface must provide the concrete implementations for these methods. ArtsIterator does the same. You may notice that these implementations purely depend on the underlying data structure. For example, you need to define the currentItem() method differently if you use a LinkedList data structure instead of an array data structure (you'll get the idea when you see the third implementation in this chapter).

To print the curriculum, you need two of these methods, hasNext() and next(). But you also see the use of the first() and currentItem() methods. I mention all four methods and provide sample implementations for them because they are very common in different Iterator pattern implementations.

There is another interface called Department that has one method, as follows:

```
interface Department {
        Iterator createIterator();
}
```

The Arts department uses an array data structure. This is why you see the following class in demonstration 1:

```
class ArtsDepartment implements Department{

    private String[] subjects;

    public ArtsDepartment() {
        subjects = new String[] { "1.English",
                                  "2.History",
                                  "3.Geography",
                                  "4.Psychology"
                                  };
    }
```

```
public Iterator createIterator() {
    return new ArtsIterator(subjects);
}
}
```

Class Diagram

Figure 18-2 shows the class diagram. In the upcoming example, you will see that an ArtsDepartment object creates an ArtsIterator object. This is why I edited the dashed line with an arrowhead (which is used to denote a "usage" link in Papyrus) and attach the tag <<create>> to it for a better understanding.

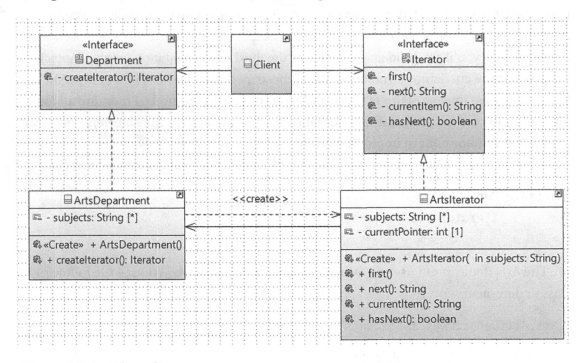

Figure 18-2. *Class diagram*

Package Explorer View

Figure 18-3 shows the high-level structure of the program.

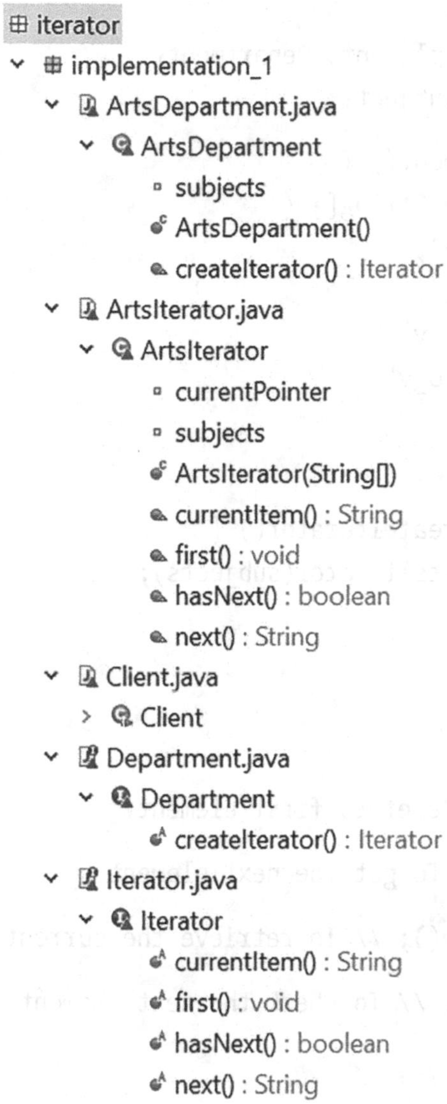

```
⊞ iterator
  ∨  ⊞ implementation_1
      ∨  ▣ ArtsDepartment.java
          ∨  ⬤ ArtsDepartment
                 ▫ subjects
                 ⚙ ArtsDepartment()
                 ⬤ createIterator() : Iterator
      ∨  ▣ ArtsIterator.java
          ∨  ⬤ ArtsIterator
                 ▫ currentPointer
                 ▫ subjects
                 ⚙ ArtsIterator(String[])
                 ⬤ currentItem() : String
                 ⬤ first() : void
                 ⬤ hasNext() : boolean
                 ⬤ next() : String
      ∨  ▣ Client.java
          >  ⬤ Client
      ∨  ▣ Department.java
          ∨  ⬤ Department
                 ⬥ createIterator() : Iterator
      ∨  ▣ Iterator.java
          ∨  ⬤ Iterator
                 ⬥ currentItem() : String
                 ⬥ first() : void
                 ⬥ hasNext() : boolean
                 ⬥ next() : String
```

Figure 18-3. *Package Explorer view*

Demonstration 1

All parts of this demonstration are stored inside the package `jdpe3e.iterator.`
`implementation_1`. Here's the implementation:

`// Department.java`
```
interface Department {
    Iterator createIterator();
}
```

```java
// ArtsDepartment.java
class ArtsDepartment implements Department{
    private String[] subjects;

    public ArtsDepartment() {
        subjects = new String[] {
            "1. English",
            "2. History",
            "3. Geography",
            "4. Psychology"
        };
    }

    public Iterator createIterator() {
        return new ArtsIterator(subjects);
    }
}

// Iterator.java
interface Iterator {
    void first(); // Reset to first element

    String next(); // To get the next element

    String currentItem(); // To retrieve the current element

    boolean hasNext(); // To check the next element.
}

// ArtsIterator.java
class ArtsIterator implements Iterator {
    private String[] subjects;

    private int currentPointer;

    public ArtsIterator(String[] subjects) {
        this.subjects = subjects;
        currentPointer = 0;
    }
```

```java
    @Override
    public void first() {
        currentPointer = 0;
    }

    @Override
    public String next() {
        // System.out.println("Currently pointing to: "+
        // this.currentItem());
        return subjects[currentPointer++];
    }

    @Override
    public String currentItem() {
        return subjects[currentPointer];
    }

    @Override
    public boolean hasNext() {

        if (currentPointer >= subjects.length)
            return false;
        return true;

    // return currentPointer >= subjects.length? false: true;
    }
}

// Client.java
class Client {
    public static void main(String[] args) {
        System.out.println("***Iterator Pattern Demonstration-1***\n");
        Department arts = new ArtsDepartment();

        Iterator artsIterator = arts.createIterator();
        System.out.println("Iterating over the Arts subjects:\n");
        while (artsIterator.hasNext()) {
            System.out.println(artsIterator.next());
        }
```

```
        // Moving back to first element
        artsIterator.first();
        System.out.println("\nThe pointer moves to -> " +
                            artsIterator.currentItem());
    }
}
```

Output

Here's the output:

```
***Iterator Pattern Demonstration-1***

Iterating over the Arts subjects:

1. English
2. History
3. Geography
4. Psychology

The pointer moves to -> 1. English
```

Additional Comments

I want you to note the following comments:

- You can see that the Iterator interface methods hasNext(), next(), first(), and currentItem() are common methods for a client. Any class that implements this interface must provide implementations following its internal data structure, but from the client's point of view, it does not matter because they can uniformly invoke these methods. Since ArtsDepartment uses an array, these implementations are based on the array data structure. If another class uses a different data structure, say a List or a LinkedList, you need to update the code accordingly. Demonstration 3 shows such an example.

- Some developers prefer to use a conditional operator instead of an if-else chain. This choice is up to you. I commented out this alternative approach inside the hasNext() method for reference.

- Additional use of the currentItem() method is shown with commented code inside the next() method. If you want to test it, you can uncomment the line.

Demonstration 2

Now you'll see another implementation using Java's built-in Iterator interface that supports the Iterator pattern.

- Here you use Java's built-in support for the Iterator pattern. Note the inclusion of the following line at the beginning of the program:

  ```
  import java.util.Iterator;
  ```

- If you open the source code, you will see that Iterator<E> interface has three methods named hasNext(), next(), and remove(), as follows:

  ```
  boolean hasNext();
  E next();
  default void remove() {
    throw new UnsupportedOperationException("remove");
  }
  ```

- You can see that remove() has a default implementation. So, in the following example, you need to override the hasNext() and next() methods only.

- Here you are using Java's Iterator interface so there is no need to define your iterator interface.

- In this program, the ArtsIterator class implements Iterator<String>. You do not need to write ArtsIterator<String>. It is because the type parameter is already mentioned in the generic interface. Java allows you to write this type of code.

- To maintain the similarity with demonstration 1, you use two more methods, `first()` and `currentItem()`, inside the `ArtsIterator` class. So, when you call these methods inside the client code, you need to typecast properly.

- In this modified implementation, key changes are shown in bold.

Since the overall concept and intent are similar to demonstration 1, you can jump directly to demonstration 2. All parts of the programs are stored inside the `jdp3e.iterator.implementation_2` package. Here's the complete implementation:

Do not forget to import `java.util.Iterator` at the beginning of these files. To avoid repetition, I excluded them.

```java
// Department.java
interface Department {
    Iterator<String> createIterator();
}

// ArtsDepartment.java
class ArtsDepartment implements Department {
    private String[] subjects;

    public ArtsDepartment() {
        subjects = new String[] { "1. English",
                                  "2. History",
                                  "3. Geography",
                                  "4. Psychology" };
    }

    @Override
    public Iterator<String> createIterator() {
        return new ArtsIterator(subjects);
    }
}
```

```java
// ArtsIterator.java
class ArtsIterator implements Iterator<String> {
    private String[] subjects;
    private int currentPointer;

    public ArtsIterator(String[] papers) {
        this. subjects = papers;
        currentPointer = 0;
    }

    public void first() {
        currentPointer = 0;
    }

    public String currentItem() {
        return subjects [currentPointer];
    }

    @Override
    public boolean hasNext() {
        if (currentPointer >= subjects.length)
            return false;
        return true;
    }

    @Override
    public String next() {
        return subjects [currentPointer ++];
    }
}
```

```java
// Client.java
class Client {

    public static void main(String[] args) {
        System.out.println("***Iterator Pattern Demonstration-2.***");

        Department arts = new ArtsDepartment();
```

```
Iterator<String> artsIterator =
                    arts.createIterator();
System.out.println("Iterating over the Arts subjects:\n");
while (artsIterator.hasNext()) {
    System.out.println(artsIterator.next());
}
// Moving back to first element
((ArtsIterator) artsIterator).first();

String pointer= ((ArtsIterator)artsIterator).
                    currentItem();
System.out.println("\nThe pointer moves to -> " + pointer);
    }
}
```

Output

Here's the output:

```
***Iterator Pattern Demonstration-2.***
Iterating over the Arts subjects:

1. English
2. History
3. Geography
4. Psychology

The pointer moves to -> 1. English
```

Q&A Session

18.1 What is the Iterator pattern used for?

The following includes some usage:

- You can traverse an object structure without knowing its internal details. As a result, if you have a collection of different subcollections (for example, your container is mixed with arrays, lists, linked lists, and so on), you can still traverse the overall collection and deal with the elements in a universal way without knowing the internal details or differences among them.

- You can traverse a collection in different ways. If they are designed properly, multiple traversals are also possible in parallel.

18.2 What are the key challenges associated with this pattern?

You must make sure that no accidental modification has taken place during the traversal procedure.

18.3 But to deal with the challenge mentioned earlier, you can simply make a backup and then proceed. Am I right?

Making a backup and re-examining it later is a costly operation.

18.4 Throughout the discussion, you talked about collections. What is a collection?

It is a group of individual objects that are presented in a single unit. You may often see the use of interfaces like `java.util.Collection` and `java.util.Map` in Java programs. They are common interfaces for Java's collection classes and they are introduced from JDK 1.2 onwards.

Before collections, you had choices like arrays and vectors to store or manipulate a group of objects. But these classes do not have a common interface. The way you access elements in an array is quite different from the way you access the elements of a vector. This is why it's difficult to write a common algorithm to access different elements from these different implementations. Also, many of these methods are final, so you can't extend them.

The collection framework was introduced to address this kind of difficulty. At the same time, it provides high-performance implementations to make programmers' lives easier.

18.5 In the modified implementation, why am I not seeing the `@Override` annotation for the methods **first()** and **currentItem()**?

These two methods are not present in the `java.util.Iterator` interface. The built-in Iterator interface has the methods `hasNext()` and `next()`. So, I use the `@Override` annotation for these methods only. Lastly, there is another method called `remove()` in this interface. This method has a default implementation. Since I have not used it, I did not need to modify this method.

18.6 In these implementations, I am seeing that you are using an array of Strings to store and manipulate data. Can you show an Iterator pattern implementation that uses a relatively complex data type and a different data structure?

To make these examples simple, I use strings and an array data structure only. You can always choose your preferred data structure and apply the same process when you consider a complex data type. For example, consider the following illustration (demonstration 3) with these key characteristics:

- Here I use a relatively complex data type named `Employee`. Each employee object has three fields: a name, an identification number(id), and salary. To reduce the code size, I do not use any setter methods in this class, but I use getter methods.

- This time, instead of using an array, I use a different data structure named `LinkedList` in the following implementation. So, I need to include the following line in this implementation:

  ```
  import java.util.LinkedList;
  ```

- I follow the same approach as the previous example.

Demonstration 3

Here is another demonstration of the Iterator pattern. All parts of the programs are stored inside the `jdp3e.iterator.implementation_3` package. Here's the complete implementation:

```
// Employee.java
/**
 * This is the Employee class.
 * This class has getter methods,
 * but no setter methods.
 */

class Employee {
    private String name;
    private int id;
    private double salary;
```

```java
    public Employee(String name, int id, double salary) {
        this.name = name;
        this.id = id;
        this.salary = salary;
    }

    public String getName() {
        return name;
    }

    public int getId() {
        return id;
    }

    public double getSalary() {
        return salary;
    }

    @Override
    public String toString() {
        return "Employee Name: " + this.getName() + ", ID:
                " + this.getId() + " and salary: $" +
                this.getSalary();
    }
}
```

// **Database.java**

```java
import java.util.Iterator;

interface Database {
    Iterator<Employee> createIterator();
}
```

// **EmployeeDatabase.java**

```java
import java.util.LinkedList;

class EmployeeDatabase implements Database {
    private LinkedList<Employee> employeeList;
```

```java
        public EmployeeDatabase() {
            employeeList = new LinkedList<Employee>();
            employeeList.add(new Employee("Ron", 1, 1000.25));
            employeeList.add(new Employee("Jack", 2, 2000.5));
            employeeList.add(new Employee("Sufi", 3, 3000.75));
            employeeList.add(new Employee("Jian", 4, 2550.0));
            employeeList.add(new Employee("Alex", 5, 753.83));
        }

        public EmployeeIterator createIterator() {
            return new EmployeeIterator(employeeList);
        }
}
```

// EmployeeIterator.java

```java
import java.util.Iterator;
import java.util.LinkedList;

class EmployeeIterator implements Iterator<Employee> {
    private LinkedList<Employee> employeeList;
    private int currentPointer;

    public EmployeeIterator(LinkedList<Employee>
                            employeeList) {
        this.employeeList = employeeList;
        currentPointer = 0;
    }

    public void first() {
        currentPointer = 0;
    }

    public Employee currentItem() {
        return employeeList.get(currentPointer);
    }
```

```java
    @Override
    public Employee next() {
        return employeeList.get(currentPointer ++);
    }

    @Override
    public boolean hasNext() {
        if (currentPointer >= employeeList.size())
            return false;
        return true;
    }
}
```

// Client.java

```java
import java.util.Iterator;
class Client {
    public static void main(String[] args) {

        System.out.println("***Iterator Pattern Demonstration-3***");
        Database employeesList = new EmployeeDatabase();

        Iterator<Employee> employeeIterator =
                        employeesList.createIterator();
        System.out.println("Iterating over the employee list:\n");

        while (employeeIterator.hasNext()) {
            System.out.println(employeeIterator.next());
        }

        // Moving back to first element
        // artsIterator.first();
         ((EmployeeIterator) employeeIterator).first();

        Employee pointer = ((EmployeeIterator)
                        employeeIterator).currentItem();
        System.out.println("\nThe pointer moves to -> " + pointer);
    }
}
```

```
***Iterator Pattern Demonstration-3***
Iterating over the employee list:

Employee Name: Ron, ID: 1 and salary: $1000.25
Employee Name: Jack, ID: 2 and salary: $2000.5
Employee Name: Sufi, ID: 3 and salary: $3000.75
Employee Name: Jian, ID: 4 and salary: $2550.0
Employee Name: Alex, ID: 5 and salary: $753.83

The pointer moves to -> Employee Name: Ron, ID: 1 and salary: $1000.25
```

CHAPTER 19

Command Pattern

This chapter covers the Command pattern.

GoF Definition

It encapsulates a request as an object, thereby letting you parameterize clients with different requests, queue or log requests, and support undoable operations.

Concept

Using this pattern, you encapsulate a method invocation process. Here an object can invoke an operation through some crystalized method, and it does not worry about how to perform the intended operation. This pattern is often used in a multithreaded environment. It's one of those patterns that is normally tough to understand by merely reading the description. The concept becomes clearer when you see the implementations. So, stay with me and keep reading until you see demonstration 1.

In general, four terms are important here: *invoker, client, command,* and *receiver,* which are as follows:

- The command object consists of the action(s) that a receiver will perform.

- A *command* object can invoke a method of the receiver in a way that is specific to that receiver's class. The *receiver* then starts processing the job (or the action).

- A command object is separately passed to the *invoker* object to invoke the command. The invoker object contains those crystallized methods through which a client can perform a job without worrying about how the actual job is performed by the target receiver.

© Vaskaran Sarcar 2022
V. Sarcar, *Java Design Patterns*, https://doi.org/10.1007/978-1-4842-7971-7_19

- The *client* object holds the invoker object and the command objects. The client must decide which commands to execute before it passes the appropriate command to the invoker object.

Real-Life Example

When you draw a picture, you may need to redraw (undo) some parts of it to make it better.

Computer World Example

In general, you can observe this pattern in the menu system of an editor or integrated development environment (IDE). For example, you can use the Command pattern to support an Undo operation or the Undo all previous operations in a software application. Here is another common example:

- When you use the java.lang.Runnable interface and use the run() method to invoke the target receiver's method, you use Command design pattern.

It is interesting to note that Microsoft also used this pattern in Windows Presentation Foundation (WPF). The article named "The Command Pattern in .NET" from the Visual Studio Magazine site (https://visualstudiomagazine.com/articles/2012/04/10/command-pattern-in-net.aspx) describes it in detail:

> *"The command pattern is well suited for handling GUI interactions. It works so well that Microsoft has integrated it tightly into the Windows Presentation Foundation (WPF) stack. The most important piece is the ICommand interface from the System.Windows.Input namespace. Any class that implements the ICommand interface can be used to handle a keyboard or mouse event through the common WPF controls. This linking can be done either in XAML or in a code-behind."*

Note   Implementations for undos vary and can be complex. The Memento design pattern (covered in Chapter 20) also supports undo operations and you may need to use both design patterns in your application to implement a complex undo operation.

Implementation

Game is the receiver class in the upcoming example. It has three methods and one constructor. It has the following definition:

```
class Game {
    String gameName;

    public Game(String name) {
        this.gameName = name;
    }

    public void start() {
        System.out.println(gameName + " is on.");
    }

    public void displayScore() {
        System.out.println("The score is changing from time to time.");
    }

    public void stop() {
        System.out.println("The game of " + gameName + " is stopped.");
    }
}
```

GameStartCommand and GameStopCommand are two concrete classes to represent commands. These two classes implement the common interface Command, which is as follows (the associated comments tell the purposes of these methods):

```
interface Command {

    // To execute a command
    void executeCommand();

    // To undo last command execution
    void undoPreviousCommand();
}
```

407

First, look at the concrete command class named GameStopClass. Notice that the concrete command class stores the receiver (Game) as an instance variable. It also uses the receiver's actions inside its method bodies.

```java
class GameStopCommand implements Command {
    private Game game;

    public GameStopCommand(Game game) {
        this.game = game;
    }

    @Override
    public void executeCommand() {
        System.out.println("Finishing the game.");
        game.stop();
    }

    @Override
    public void undoPreviousCommand() {
        System.out.println("Undoing the stop command.");
        game.start();
        game.displayScore();
    }
}
```

Here RemoteControlInvoker is the invoker class.

Note   I append the word "Invoker" for your easy understanding. I agree that RemoteControl can be a better choice when you write real-world code.

It has the following definition:

```java
class RemoteControlInvoker {
    Command currentCommand, lastCommandPerformed;

    public void setCommand(Command command) {
        this.currentCommand = command;
    }
```

```
public void executeSelectedCommand() {
    currentCommand.executeCommand();
    lastCommandPerformed = currentCommand;
}

public void undoCommand() {
    // Undo the last command executed
    lastCommandPerformed.undoPreviousCommand();
}
}
```

How can a client use this pattern? At a high level, there are the following steps:

Step 1: A client uses a receiver object to create a command object.

```
Game gameName = new Game("Golf");
// Command to start the game
GameStartCommand gameStartCommand = new
                            GameStartCommand(gameName);
```

Step 2: Next, it sets the command to an invoker and uses the executeSelectedCommand() method to execute the command.

```
System.out.println("Starting the game using a command.");
invoker.setCommand(gameStartCommand);
invoker.executeSelectedCommand();
```

Now investigate the method body of the executeSelectedCommand() method, which is as follows:

```
currentCommand.executeCommand();
// Remaining code skipped
```

It means that the call is delegated to the target receiver's (Game class object in this example) executeCommand(). I kept some console messages for your easy reference.

One last point: notice the executeMethod() of GameStartClass:

```
public void executeCommand() {
 System.out.println("Game is about to start.");
 game.start();
 game.displayScore();
}
```

You can see that a particular command doesn't restrict itself to perform a single action only; instead, based on your needs, you can perform a series of actions on a target receiver and encapsulate them in a command object.

POINTS TO NOTE

The examples in this chapter show simple demonstrations of undo operations. The implementation of an undo depends on the specification and can be complex in some scenarios. For demonstration 1, an undo call simply undoes the last command that was performed successfully. If you notice the executeCommand() and undoPreviousCommand() methods of the GameStartCommand and GameStopCommand classes, you will see that they are just doing the opposite, so when a client invokes an undo operation using GameStopCommand, the game will start again and display the score details (which is a simple console message in this example), but if the client invokes the undo operation using GameStartCommand, the game will finish immediately. It is similar to switching on a light and switching off the same light, or adding a number to a target number and, as a reverse case, subtracting the same number from the resultant number again.

Class Diagram

Figure 19-1 shows the class diagram.

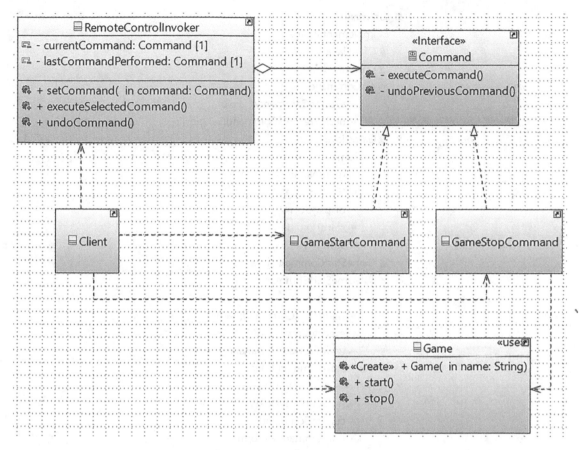

Figure 19-1. *Class diagram*

Package Explorer View

Figure 19-2 shows the high-level structure of the program. To make the diagram short,
I did not expand GameStopCommand, which has a similar structure as GameStartCommand.
(The implementation_2 folder is used for the next demonstration).

```
⊞ command
> ⊞ implementation_2
> 🔲 Client.java
∨ 🔲 Command.java
    ∨ ⓠ Command
        ✦ executeCommand() : void
        ✦ undoPreviousCommand() : void
∨ 🔲 Game.java
    ∨ ⓠ Game
        △ gameName
        ✦ Game(String)
        ● displayScore() : void
        ● start() : void
        ● stop() : void
∨ 🔲 GameStartCommand.java
    ∨ ⓠ GameStartCommand
        ▫ game
        ✦ GameStartCommand(Game)
        ● executeCommand() : void
        ● undoPreviousCommand() : void
> 🔲 GameStopCommand.java
∨ 🔲 RemoteControlInvoker.java
    ∨ ⓠ RemoteControlInvoker
        △ currentCommand
        △ lastCommandPerformed
        ● executeSelectedCommand() : void
        ● setCommand(Command) : void
        ● undoCommand() : void
```

Figure 19-2. Package Explorer view

Demonstration 1

Here's the complete program. All the classes and interfaces are stored in the package
jdp3e.command.

// Game.java
```
class Game {
    String gameName;
```

```java
    public Game(String name) {
        this.gameName = name;
    }

    public void start() {
        System.out.println(gameName + " is on.");
    }

    public void displayScore() {
        System.out.println("The score is changing from time to time.");
    }

    public void stop() {
        System.out.println("The game of " + gameName + " is stopped.");
    }
}
```

```java
// Command.java
interface Command {
    // To execute a command
    void executeCommand();

    // To undo last command execution
    void undoPreviousCommand();
}
```

```java
// GameStartCommand.java
class GameStartCommand implements Command {
    private Game game;

    public GameStartCommand(Game game) {
        this.game = game;
    }

    @Override
    public void executeCommand() {
        System.out.println("The game is about to start.");
        game.start();
        game.displayScore();
    }
```

413

```java
    @Override
    public void undoPreviousCommand() {
        System.out.println("Undoing the start command.");
        game.stop();
    }
}
```

```java
// GameStopCommand.java
class GameStopCommand implements Command {
    private Game game;

    public GameStopCommand(Game game) {
        this.game = game;
    }

    @Override
    public void executeCommand() {
        System.out.println("Finishing the game.");
        game.stop();
    }

    @Override
    public void undoPreviousCommand() {
        System.out.println("Undoing the stop command.");
        game.start();
        game.displayScore();
    }
}
```

```java
// RemoteControlInvoker.java (Invoker)
class RemoteControlInvoker {
    Command currentCommand, lastCommandPerformed;

    public void setCommand(Command command) {
        this.currentCommand = command;
    }
```

```java
    public void executeSelectedCommand() {
        currentCommand.executeCommand();
        lastCommandPerformed = currentCommand;
    }

    public void undoCommand() {
        // Undo the last command executed
        lastCommandPerformed.undoPreviousCommand();
    }
}

// Client.java
class Client {
    public static void main(String[] args) {
        System.out.println("***Command Pattern Demonstration.***\n");

        // Receiver
        Game gameName = new Game("Golf");

        // Command objects:

        // Command to start the game
        GameStartCommand gameStartCommand = new
                        GameStartCommand(gameName);
        // Command to stop the game
        GameStopCommand gameStopCommand = new
                        GameStopCommand(gameName);

        // Invoker
        RemoteControlInvoker invoker = new
                        RemoteControlInvoker();

        System.out.println("---Testing Scenario-1---\n");

        System.out.println("Starting the game using a command.");
        invoker.setCommand(gameStartCommand);
        invoker.executeSelectedCommand();
        System.out.println("\nUndoing the previous command now.");
        invoker.undoCommand();
```

```
        System.out.println("\n---Testing Scenario-2---\n");

        System.out.println("Starting the game again.");
        invoker.setCommand(gameStartCommand);
        invoker.executeSelectedCommand();
        System.out.println("\nIssueing a stop command now.");
        invoker.setCommand(gameStopCommand);
        invoker.executeSelectedCommand();
        System.out.println("\nUndoing the previous command now.");
        invoker.undoCommand();
    }
}
```

Output

Here's the output:

```
***Command Pattern Demonstration.***

---Testing Scenario-1---

Starting the game using a command.
The game is about to start.
Golf is on.
The score is changing from time to time.

Undoing the previous command now.
Undoing the start command.
The game of Golf is stopped.

---Testing Scenario-2---

Starting the game again.
The game is about to start.
Golf is on.
The score is changing from time to time.
```

Issuing a stop command now.
Finishing the game.
The game of Golf is stopped.

Undoing the previous command now.
Undoing the stop command.
Golf is on.
The score is changing from time to time.

Q&A Session

19.1 The GoF definition starts with "Encapsulate a request." How are you implementing the encapsulation in demonstration 1?

Notice that the command object contains the set of actions that target a specific receiver. When you set the command and invoke the executeSelectedCommand() on the invoker object, the intended actions are performed at the receiver's end. From the invoker's point of view, it simply knows that if it calls the executeSelectedCommand(), the requests will be processed by the target receiver. This method encapsulates the actions needed to get the final result/outcome from a target object/receiver.

In the next demonstration, you will also see that an invoker can handle different types of objects that can be placed in different inheritance hierarchies. For example, in this implementation, notice the use of commands to start a game or stop a game. How does this work? You set commands to start or stop a game first so that the invoker can handle the game. Let's assume you want to handle a number generator in a similar way, which means you tell the invoker to handle a number generator to increase or decrease a number. It means that you want an invoker to handle a different type of object without knowing about the target receiver. The Command pattern allows you to implement a similar type of implementation. In this case, at the top level, from an invoker perspective, it simply invokes the corresponding methods of the target receiver(s).

19.2 Following the GoF definition, how did you parameterize other objects with different requests?

Notice the following method in the RemoteControlInvoker class:

```
public void setCommand(Command command) {
    this.currentCommand = command;
}
```

You can see that this method can be parameterized with different commands. Here is a partial segment of testing scenario-2 inside the client code, which is as follows:

```
System.out.println("Starting the game again.");
invoker.setCommand(gameStartCommand);
invoker.executeSelectedCommand();
System.out.println("\nIssueing a stop command now.");
invoker.setCommand(gameStopCommand);
invoker.executeSelectedCommand();
```

Notice that you first set GameStartCommand in the invoker and later replace it with GameStopCommand. The invoker object invokes the executeSelectedCommand() in both cases. It is possible because the invoker knows that all these commands can be executed using this method.

19.3 In this example, you are dealing with a single receiver only. How can you deal with multiple receivers?

No one restricts you from creating a new class and following the implementation that is shown in demonstration 1. In demonstration 2, you'll see such an implementation.

But before I show you demonstration 2, I want you to notice another point in this context. In demonstration 1, you create a Game class object using the following line:

```
Game gameName = new Game("Golf");
```

Since the Game class constructor accepts a String parameter, you could also pass a different value and create a different Game object. For example, if you append the following code segment inside the client code

```
System.out.println("\n-----Testing Scenario-3-----");
System.out.println("Playing a different game now.\n");

// Receiver
gameName = new Game("Soccer");
// Command to start the game
gameStartCommand = new GameStartCommand(gameName);
// Command to stop the game
gameStopCommand = new GameStopCommand(gameName);
```

```
System.out.println("Starting the game using a command.");
invoker.setCommand(gameStartCommand);
invoker.executeSelectedCommand();
System.out.println("\nUndoing the previous command now.");
invoker.undoCommand();
```

you get the following output:

```
-----Testing Scenario-3-----
Playing a different game now.

Starting the game using a command.
The game is about to start.
Soccer is on.
The score is changing from time to time.

Undoing the previous command now.
Undoing the start command.
The game of Soccer is stopped.
```

19.4 Can I ignore the use of the invoker object?

The invoker plays an important role. Its usage is explained in Q&A 19.1. Most of the time, programmers try to encapsulate data and the corresponding methods in object-oriented programming. But using the Command pattern, you try to encapsulate command objects. In other words, you implement encapsulation from a different perspective.

I told you earlier that when executeSelectedCommand() of the invoker object is called, the intended actions are performed at the receiver's end. From the outside, no other objects have a clue about how it happens; they simply know that if they call this method, their requests will be processed. So, simply put, an invoker contains some crystalized method through which a client can perform a job without worrying how the actual job is performed at the receiver's end. This approach makes sense when you deal with a complex set of commands.

Let's review the terms again. To invoke a receiver's method, you create command objects. You execute those commands through an invoker that calls the actual methods of the receiver. Using this approach, you decouple the caller and the receiver. So, the invoker is actually the middleman who helps you implement a nice object-oriented design. If your program is very short and simple, you may feel that this invoker class is not mandatory. For example, consider a case in which a command object has only one method to execute and so you try to dispense with an invoker to invoke the method. But invokers may play an important role when you want to handle different objects that reside in different inheritance hierarchies. It also helps you keep track of a series of commands in a log file (or in a queue).

19.5 Why would you want to keep track of these logs?

You may want to create undo or redo operations.

19.6 What are the key advantages associated with the Command pattern?

Here are some advantages:

- The Command pattern decouples the sender and receiver objects. In other words, it helps you decouple an object making a request from an object that receives the request and performs the intended action. Notice that an invoker can work with a receiver without directly knowing about it. In addition, a client also does not know how a middleman (invoker) fulfils its needs.

- An invoker can handle different types of objects that perform different types of works. Demonstration 2 will make this point clear to you.

- You can create macro commands (these are sequences of multiple commands and can be invoked together. Here's an example: for a macro command, you can create a class that has a constructor to accept a list of commands. And in its executeCommand() method, you can invoke executeCommand() of these commands sequentially using a loop.

- New commands can be added without affecting the existing system.

- Most importantly, you can support the undo (and redo) operations.

- It should be noted that once you create a command object, it does not mean that the computation starts immediately. You can schedule it for later or place it in a job queue and execute it later.

19.7 What are the challenges associated with the Command pattern?

Here are some disadvantages:

- To support more commands, you need to create more classes. So, maintenance can be difficult as time goes on.

- Handling errors or making a decision about what to do with return values when an erroneous situation occurs becomes tricky. A client may want to know about them. But since you decouple the caller from a target receiver, this kind of situation is difficult to handle. The challenge becomes significant in a multithreaded environment where an invoker can run on a different thread.

19.8 In demonstration 1, you undo only the last command. Is there any way to implement undo on all of the previous commands? Also, how can you log requests?

Good question. You can simply maintain a stack that can store the commands, and then you can pop the items from the stack and invoke the undo() method. In Chapter 20 on the Memento pattern, which is similar to this pattern, I discuss more about undos and I show various implementations. For now, let me show you a simple example in which you can undo all the previous commands. Demonstration 2 is made for that. It's a simple extension of demonstration 1, so I show you the high-level class diagram. I omit the Package Explorer view, which is straightforward. You can directly jump into the implementation.

You asked another question on how to log the requests. In demonstration 2, when you maintain a list to store the commands that execute, you use this list to support undo all commands using a single method invocation. The same list can serve as a history of commands, which you can print in your target location. For example, you can make a separate file to maintain the details each time a command executes. Later you can retrieve the file for a detailed look if necessary.

Modified Implementation

This example shows a way to invoke multiple undo operations. There is no change in the Game class hierarchy, but some small changes are made to the invoker class. Here are some important points:

- Inside the invoker class, you maintain an ArrayList object(savedCommands) to store all the commands that you execute. Whenever a command is executed, it is added to this list.

- In this example, once you call an undo operation, you remove it from the saved command list too.

- Here you also see a method called undoAllStoredCommand() that is used to iterate over the savedCommand list and call the corresponding undo operations.

- Finally, you clear the stored commands from this list.

The invoker is shown with key changes in bold as follows:

```
import java.util.ArrayList;

class RemoteControlInvoker {
    Command currentCommand, lastCommandPerformed;
    ArrayList<Command> savedCommands = new
                            ArrayList<Command>();

    public void setCommand(Command command) {
        this.currentCommand = command;
    }

    public void executeCommand() {
        currentCommand.executeCommand();
        savedCommands.add(currentCommand);
        lastCommandPerformed = currentCommand;
    }

    public void undoCommand() {
        // Undo the last command executed
        lastCommandPerformed.undoPreviousCommand();
        // Remove it from saved command list
        savedCommands.remove(lastCommandPerformed);
    }

    public void undoAllStoredCommands() {
      for (int i = savedCommands.size(); i > 0; i--) {
        // Get a restore point and undo previous commands
        (savedCommands.get(i - 1)).undoPreviousCommand();
        }
```

```
    // Removing everything from the
    // saved list now.
        savedCommands.clear();
    }
}
```

The NumberGenerator class represents the new receiver class. Note the following assumptions:

- When you initialize an instance of this class, you start with the number 0.

- The incrementNumber() method increments a number by 1 and the decrementNumber() method does the opposite. But you cannot go beyond 0.

This class has the following definition:

```
// Receiver-2
class NumberGenerator {
    private int currentNumber;

    public NumberGenerator() {
        currentNumber = 0;
        System.out.println("The initial number is: " + currentNumber);
        System.out.println("You can increase it, but you
                            cannot decrease it further.");
    }

    public int getMyNumber() {
        return currentNumber;
    }

    public void setMyNumber(int currentNumber) {
        this.currentNumber = currentNumber;
    }

    public void incrementNumber() {
        System.out.println(" Received an
                increment number request.");
        int presentNumber=getMyNumber();
        setMyNumber(currentNumber + 1);
```

```
            System.out.println(presentNumber + " + 1 = " + getMyNumber());
        }

    public void decrementNumber() {
            System.out.println(" Received a decrement number request.");
            int presentNumber = this.currentNumber;
            // We started with number 0.
            // We'll not decrease further.
            if (presentNumber > 0) {
                setMyNumber(this.currentNumber - 1);
                System.out.println(presentNumber + " - 1 =" +
                                        this.currentNumber);
                System.out.println(" The number is decremented.");
            } else {
                System.out.println("Nothing more to decrement.");
            }
        }
    }
}
```

The AdditionCommand class is a concrete Command class that is used to target NumberGenerator. Notice that it stores the receiver (NumberGenerator) as an instance variable. Here is the AdditionCommand class:

```
class AdditionCommand implements Command {
    private NumberGenerator numberGenerator;
    public AdditionCommand(NumberGenerator receiver){
        this.numberGenerator = receiver;
    }
    @Override
    public void executeCommand() {
        numberGenerator.incrementNumber();
    }
    @Override
    public void undoPreviousCommand() {
        numberGenerator.decrementNumber();
    }
}
```

In the same way, you can make another class, say SubtractionCommand if you want. Since I do not use such a class in this implementation, I leave this exercise for you. The remaining code is easy to understand, so go through demonstration 2 now.

Class Diagram

Figure 19-3 shows the new class diagram. To make it short, I don't show the client in this diagram.

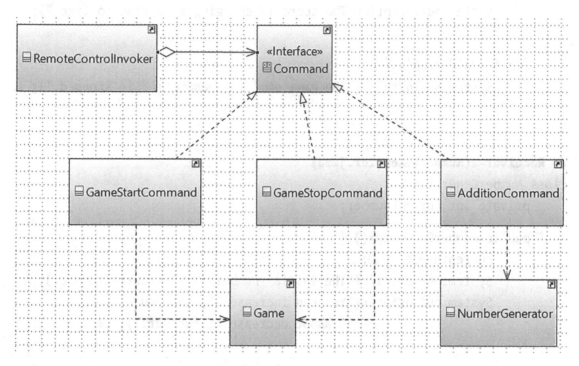

Figure 19-3. *Class diagram showing the key participants in demonstration 2*

Demonstration 2

Here is the complete program. All participants are stored inside a new package, jdp3e. command.implementation_2.

```
import java.util.ArrayList;
// Receiver- 1(Game.java)
class Game {
    String gameName;
```

```java
    public Game(String name) {
        this.gameName = name;
    }

    public void start() {
        System.out.println(gameName + " is on.");
    }

    public void displayScore() {
        System.out.println("The score is changing from time to time.");
    }

    public void stop() {
        System.out.println("The game of " + gameName + " is stopped.");
    }
}

// Receiver-2(NumberGenerator.java)
class NumberGenerator {
    private int currentNumber;

    public NumberGenerator() {
        currentNumber = 0;
        System.out.println("The initial number is: " + currentNumber);
        System.out.println("You can increase it, but you
                            cannot decrease it further.");
    }

    public int getMyNumber() {
        return currentNumber;
    }

    public void setMyNumber(int currentNumber) {
        this.currentNumber = currentNumber;
    }
```

```java
    public void incrementNumber() {
        System.out.println(" Received an increment number request.");
        int presentNumber=getMyNumber();
        setMyNumber(currentNumber + 1);
        System.out.println(presentNumber + " + 1 = " + getMyNumber());
    }

    public void decrementNumber() {
        System.out.println(" Received a decrement number request.");
        int presentNumber = this.currentNumber;
        // We started with number 0.
        // We'll not decrease further.
        if (presentNumber > 0) {
            setMyNumber(this.currentNumber - 1);
            System.out.println(presentNumber + " - 1 =" +
                                    this.currentNumber);
            System.out.println(" The number is decremented.");
        } else {
            System.out.println("Nothing more to decrement...");
        }
    }
}
```

```java
// Command.java
interface Command {

    // To execute a command
    void executeCommand();

    // To undo last command execution
    void undoPreviousCommand();
}
```

```java
// GameStartCommand.java
class GameStartCommand implements Command {
    private Game game;
```

```java
    public GameStartCommand(Game game) {
        this.game = game;
    }

    @Override
    public void executeCommand() {
        System.out.println("Game is about to start.");
        game.start();
        game.displayScore();
    }

    @Override
    public void undoPreviousCommand() {
        System.out.println("Undoing the start command.");
        game.stop();
    }
}

// GameStopCommand.java
class GameStopCommand implements Command {
    private Game game;

    public GameStopCommand(Game game) {
        this.game = game;
    }

    @Override
    public void executeCommand() {
        System.out.println("Finishing the game.");
        game.stop();
    }

    @Override
    public void undoPreviousCommand() {
        System.out.println("Undoing the stop command.");
        game.start();
        game.displayScore();
    }
}
```

```java
// AdditionCommand.java
class AdditionCommand implements Command {
    private NumberGenerator numberGenerator;
    public AdditionCommand(NumberGenerator receiver){
        this.numberGenerator = receiver;
    }
    @Override
    public void executeCommand() {
        numberGenerator.incrementNumber();
    }
    @Override
    public void undoPreviousCommand() {
        numberGenerator.decrementNumber();
    }
}
```

```java
// RemoteControlInvoker.java
import java.util.ArrayList;

class RemoteControlInvoker {
    Command currentCommand, lastCommandPerformed;
    ArrayList<Command> savedCommands = new
                        ArrayList<Command>();

    public void setCommand(Command command) {
        this.currentCommand = command;
    }

    public void executeCommand() {
        currentCommand.executeCommand();
        savedCommands.add(currentCommand);
        lastCommandPerformed = currentCommand;
    }

    public void undoCommand() {
        // Undo the last command executed
        lastCommandPerformed.undoPreviousCommand();
```

```java
            // Remove it from saved command list
            savedCommands.remove(lastCommandPerformed);
    }

    public void undoAllStoredCommands() {
      for (int i = savedCommands.size(); i > 0; i--) {
          // Get a restore point and undo previous commands
          (savedCommands.get(i - 1)).undoPreviousCommand();
          }
          // Removing everything from the saved list
          savedCommands.clear();

    }
}
// Client.java
class Client {
    public static void main(String[] args) {
        System.out.println("***Command Pattern Demonstration-2.***\n");

        // Client holds both the Invoker
        // and Command Objects.

        RemoteControlInvoker invoker = new
                                RemoteControlInvoker();

        System.out.println("-----Testing the game scenarios-----\n");

        // Initializing a receiver
        Game gameName = new Game("Golf");

        // Initializing commands to start and stop a game.
        GameStartCommand gameStartCommand = new
                                GameStartCommand(gameName);
        GameStopCommand gameStopCommand = new
                                GameStopCommand(gameName);

        System.out.println("Starting the game.");
        invoker.setCommand(gameStartCommand);
        invoker.executeCommand();
```

```
System.out.println("\nIssueing a stop command now.");
invoker.setCommand(gameStopCommand);
invoker.executeCommand();
// System.out.println("\nUndoing the previous command now.");
// invoker.undoCommand();

System.out.println("\n---Testing the number scenarios---\n");

// Initializing a receiver
NumberGenerator numberGenerator = new
                                NumberGenerator();
// Initializing commands to start and stop a game.
AdditionCommand addNumberCommand = new
                AdditionCommand(numberGenerator);
invoker.setCommand(addNumberCommand);
System.out.println("\nWe'll test a series of do/undo
                    operations now.**");

System.out.println("Incrementing a number three times.");
invoker.executeCommand();
invoker.executeCommand();
invoker.executeCommand();
System.out.println("Undoing the last command only.");
invoker.undoCommand();

System.out.println("Calling the undoAllStoredCommands() now.");
invoker.undoAllStoredCommands();
    }
}
```

Output

Here's the new output:

Command Pattern Demonstration-2.

-----Testing the game scenarios -----

Starting the game.
The game is about to start.
Golf is on.
The score is changing from time to time.

Issuing a stop command now.
Finishing the game.
The game of Golf is stopped.

-----Testing the number scenarios-----

The initial number is: 0
You can increase it, but you cannot decrease it further.

We'll test a series of do/undo operations now.**
Incrementing a number three times.
 Received an increment number request.
0 + 1 = 1
 Received an increment number request.
1 + 1 = 2
 Received an increment number request.
2 + 1 = 3
Undoing the last command only.
 Received a decrement number request.
3 - 1 =2
 The number is decremented.
Calling the undoAllStoredCommands() now.
 Received a decrement number request.
2 - 1 =1
 The number is decremented.
 Received a decrement number request.

```
1 - 1 =0
 The number is decremented.
Undoing the stop command.
Golf is on.
The score is changing from time to time.
Undoing the start command.
The game of Golf is stopped.
```

CHAPTER 20

Memento Pattern

This chapter covers the Memento pattern.

GoF Definition

Without violating encapsulation, the Memento pattern captures and externalizes an object's internal state so that the object can be restored to this state later.

Concept

As per the dictionary, the word *memento* is used as a reminder of past events. Following the object-oriented way, you can also track (or save) the states of an object. So, whenever you want to restore an object to its previous state, you can consider using this pattern.

In this pattern, you commonly see three participants called memento, originator, and caretaker (often used as a client). The workflow can be summarized as follows: the originator object has an internal state, and a client can set a state in it. To save the current internal state of the originator, a client (or caretaker) requests a memento from it. A client can also pass a memento (which it holds) back to the originator to restore a previous state. Following the proper approach, these saving and restoring operations do not violate encapsulation.

Real-Life Example

You can see a classic example of the Memento pattern in the states of a finite state machine. It is a mathematical model, but one of its simplest applications is a turnstile. A turnstile has rotating arms, which initially are locked. When you go through it (for example, after putting some coins in), the locks open and the arms rotate. Once you pass through, the arms return to a locked state.

435

© Vaskaran Sarcar 2022
V. Sarcar, *Java Design Patterns*, https://doi.org/10.1007/978-1-4842-7971-7_20

You can also consider a game application that has many difficulty levels. If it is a long-running game, it's useful if you can pause at a certain level and later resume the game. If you want, you can directly jump to a preferred level, too.

Note   Using the real-world examples, sometimes it is tough to differentiate between the patterns. For example, the turnstile example can be used in the context of the State pattern (Chapter 22), too. But once you go through the State pattern, you'll understand that the state in the State pattern is not used like a memento. In a State pattern, you deal with an object's behavior in a particular state. But you can use a memento to transform an object into a desired state to enable that particular behavior. Let's analyze a case study: when a television is in its switched-on mode, you can switch between channels; otherwise, you cannot change the channels. But you can switch off the television by pressing the power button on a remote control. So, in this case, a power button press helps a television to change between its states, which in turn shows different behaviors of a television in those states.

Computer World Example

In a drawing application, you may need to revert to an older state. You can also consider the transactions in a database where you may need to roll back a specific transaction. Memento patterns can be used in those scenarios. Here is another example:

- Consider a Java Swing example. You may see the use of the
  JTextField class, which extends the abstract class JTextComponent
  and provides undo support mechanism. The Java documentation
  at https://docs.oracle.com/en/java/javase/16/docs/api/
  java.desktop/javax/swing/text/JTextComponent.html says
  the following about this capability: "Support for an edit history
  mechanism is provided to allow undo/redo operations. The text
  component does not itself provide the history buffer by default
  but does provide the UndoableEdit records that can be used in
  conjunction with a history buffer to provide the undo/redo support.

The support is provided by the Document model, which allows one to attach `UndoableEditListener` implementations." In this case an implementation of `javax.swing.undo.UndoableEdit` acts like a memento and an implementation of `javax.swing.text.Document` acts like an originator and `javax.swing.undo.UndoManager` acts as a caretaker.

`java.io.Serializable` is often referred to as an example of a memento but it should be noted that though you can serialize a memento object, it is not a mandatory requirement for the Memento design pattern.

Implementation

Before you proceed further, here are some important suggestions from the GoF:

- You see three important players (memento, originator, and caretaker) in this design implementation.

- A memento is an object that stores the internal state of another object. We call this "another object" as the memento's originator. It means the originator has an internal state which is our concern.

- The originator initializes the memento with its current state. Ideally, the originator that produces the memento can access its internal state.

- Only the originator can store and retrieve necessary information from the memento. This memento is "opaque" to other objects.

- A caretaker class is the container of mementos. This class is used for the memento's safekeeping, but it never operates or examines the content of a memento. A caretaker can get the memento from the originator.

- A caretaker first asks the originator for a memento object. Then it can set a new state to it. Next, if it wants, it can save the memento. To reset an originator's state, it passes back a memento object to the originator.

- The originator uses the memento to restore its internal state.

- The caretaker sees a *narrow* interface to the memento. It can only pass the memento to other objects. The originator, in contrast, sees a *wide* interface, one that lets it access all the data necessary to restore itself to its previous state. Ideally, only the originator that produced the memento is permitted to access the memento's internal state.

Note   In short, the caretaker is not allowed to make any changes to a memento. It simply passes the memento to an originator. From its standpoint, it sees a narrow interface to the memento. On the contrary, the originator sees a wide interface because it has full access to the memento. The originator uses this facility to restore its previous state.

A Memento design pattern can have varying implementations using different techniques. In this chapter, you'll see two demonstrations. Demonstration 1 is relatively simple and easy to understand. It is improved upon in Demonstration 2. In both implementations, I **don't** use a separate caretaker class. Instead, I use the client code to play the role of the caretaker.

In the upcoming example, the Originator class has a field called state. This variable represents the current state of an Originator object, which is your main concern. In addition, the Originator class has three methods called setState(...), restoreMemento(...), and getMemento().

The first one is used to set a new state of an originator. It is defined as follows (remember that you are setting a state, but not saving this state yet):

```
public void setState(String newState) {
 this.state = newState;
 System.out.println(" Originator's current state is: " + state);
}
```

The second one is used to restore the originator to a previous state. This state is contained in a memento (that comes as a method argument) from the caretaker. A caretaker sends this memento object that it saved earlier. This method is defined as follows:

```
public void restore(Memento memento) {
this.state = memento.state;
System.out.println("Restored to state: " + state);
}
```

The third one is used to supply a memento in response to a caretaker's request. It contains the current state of the Originator object. It is defined as follows:

```
public Memento getMemento() {
  Memento currentMemento = new Memento(state);
  return currentMemento;
}
```

To keep the memento class short and simple, there's only one variable. To match the originator state, it's called state as well. In many other applications, you may see a memento class with the getter-setter methods (or, at least a getter method). You don't use them here because you're omitting the use of an access modifier for this field. This variable has package-private visibility, which means that other classes in the same package can access it, so it is slightly more open than private visibility but not as much as protected visibility. You can guess the reason behind this design: you do not want an arbitrary object to set a new value or access the internal state of the memento. In addition, you make this field final so that this value cannot be modified later. (You'll see an additional discussion on this in Q&A 20.1). You make this class public so that the caretaker/client can see it from outside of the package. Here is the Memento class:

```
public class Memento {

    // package-private visibility with final keyword
    final String state;//prevents editing the state later
    // package-private visibility
      Memento(String state) {
          this.state = state;
      }

}
```

Keep in mind that in this example, the client class acts as the caretaker that is responsible for the memento's safe keeping, but it never operates on the content of a memento. Here the caretaker holds an Originator object and asks for memento objects from it. So, you see the following lines inside the client code:

```
Originator originator = new Originator();
memento = originatorObject.getMemento();
```

This caretaker also saves and holds the mementos in a list. So, you see the following lines of code inside the client code:

```
List<Memento> savedMementos = new ArrayList<Memento>();
```

This time you create a separate method to mark the checkpoints (or snapshots) and save them into the savedMementos list. This is optional. (I use it to avoid code duplication inside the client code and promote the Don't Repeat Yourself (DRY) principle.) Here is the method definition:

```
private static void saveSnapShot(Originator originator, String checkPoint,
List<Memento> savedMementos) {
    // Setting a new state
    originator.setState(checkPoint);
    // Get the current state from the
    // originator through a memento
    Memento memento = originator.getMemento();
    System.out.println(".Saving this checkpoint.");
    savedMementos.add(memento);
}
```

Now you understand why you see the following line when you create the first snapshot (marked with Snapshot #0):

```
saveSnapShot(originator, "Snapshot #0", savedMementos);
```

In the same way, you create and save other snapshots except the last one. For the last snapshot (Snapshot #4), you see the following line where the client simply sets a new state to the originator but does not save this state:

```
originator.setState("Snapshot #4");
```

Finally, notice that inside Client.java,there are additional import statements because you use the List and ArrayList data structures to store mementos. You know that the ArrayList class implements the List interface. In this example, you could use ArrayList only, but you know programming to an interface is a better practice. This is the reason for the line

```
List<Memento> savedMementos = new ArrayList<Memento>();
```

instead of the line

```
ArrayList<Memento> savedMementos = new ArrayList<Memento>();
```

The remaining code is easy to understand. So, let's proceed.

Class Diagram

Figure 20-1 shows the class diagram. The originator creates mementos, so you see the <<create>> tag with the usage edge in the diagram.

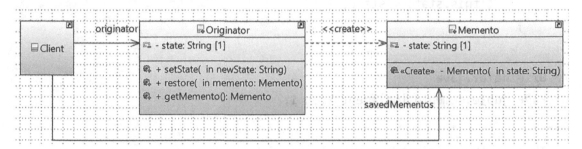

Figure 20-1. *Class diagram*

Package Explorer View

Figure 20-2 shows the high-level structure of the program. You can see that Memento. java and Originator.java are placed inside implementation_1, but Client.java is placed outside of the folder.

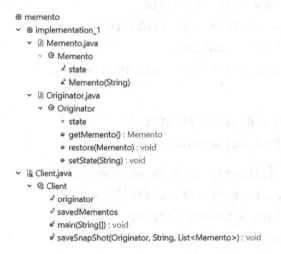

Figure 20-2. *Package Explorer view*

441

Demonstration 1

Here is the complete implementation:

```java
// Memento.java
package jdp3e.memento.implementation_1;

public class Memento {
    final String state;
        Memento(String state) {
            this.state = state;
    }
 }
```

```java
// Originator.java
package jdp3e.memento.implementation_1;

/**
 * This is the originator class. As per GoF:
 * 1. It creates a memento that contains a snapshot of
 *    its current internal state.
 * 2. It uses a memento to restore its internal state.
 */
class Originator {
    private String state;

    // Setting a new internal state
    public void setState(String newState) {
        this.state = newState;
        System.out.print("The current state is " + state);
    }

    // Back to an old state (Restore)
    public void restore(Memento memento) {

        // The following line is ok due
        // to package-private visibility
        this.state = memento.state;
        System.out.println("Restored to state: " + state);
    }
```

```java
        // Originator (which contains its current state)
        // will supply the memento in response to the
        // caretaker's request.
    public Memento getMemento() {
        Memento currentMemento = new Memento(state);
        return currentMemento;
    }
}
```

// Client.java

```java
package jdp3e.memento;
import java.util.ArrayList;
import java.util.List;
import jdp3e.memento.implementation_1.Memento;
import jdp3e.memento.implementation_1.Originator;

/**
 * This is the caretaker class. As per GoF:
 * 1. This class is responsible for memento's safe-keeping.
 * 2. Never operates or Examines the content of a Memento.
 */

class Client {
    static Originator originator;
    static List<Memento> savedMementos;

    public static void main(String[] args) {
        System.out.println("***Memento Pattern Demonstration-1.***\n");

        originator = new Originator();

        // This list stores the checkpoints
        savedMementos = new ArrayList<Memento>();
        // Snapshot #0
        saveSnapShot(originator, "Snapshot #0", savedMementos);
        // Snapshot #1
        saveSnapShot(originator, "Snapshot #1", savedMementos);
```

```java
        // Snapshot #2
        saveSnapShot(originator, "Snapshot #2", savedMementos);
        // Snapshot #3
        saveSnapShot(originator, "Snapshot #3", savedMementos);
        // Snapshot #4. Taking a snapshot,
        // but not adding as a restore point.
        originator.setState("Snapshot #4");

        // Undo's
        // Roll back everything...
        System.out.println("\n\nStarted restoring process...");
        for (int i = savedMementos.size(); i > 0; i--) {
            // Get a restore point
            originator.restore(savedMementos.get(i - 1));
        }

        // Redo's
        System.out.println("\nPerforming redo's now.");

        // Restore starts from "Snapshot #1" now.
        for (int i = 2; i <= savedMementos.size(); i++) {
            // Get a restore point
            originator.restore(savedMementos.get(i - 1));
        }

        // Restoring to any specified checkpoint
        System.out.println("\nRestoring to Snapshot #1.");
        originator.restore(savedMementos.get(1));
    }

    private static void saveSnapShot(Originator
            originator,String checkPoint, List<Memento>
                                        savedMementos) {
        // Setting a new state
        originator.setState(checkPoint);
        // Get the current state from the
        // originator through a memento
```

```
        Memento memento = originator.getMemento();
        System.out.println(". Saving this checkpoint.");
        savedMementos.add(memento);
    }
}
```

Note   In Java, the `java.util` and `java.awt` packages define a type called List. So, do not forget to use the correct one, which is shown here. In addition, when you download the source code from the Apress website, you'll see additional code comments that I already discussed. I kept them from your immediate reference.

Output

Here's the output:

```
***Memento Pattern Demonstration-1.***

The current state is Snapshot #0. Saving this checkpoint.
The current state is Snapshot #1. Saving this checkpoint.
The current state is Snapshot #2. Saving this checkpoint.
The current state is Snapshot #3. Saving this checkpoint.
The current state is Snapshot #4

Started restoring process...
Restored to state: Snapshot #3
Restored to state: Snapshot #2
Restored to state: Snapshot #1
Restored to state: Snapshot #0

Performing redo's now.
Restored to state: Snapshot #1
Restored to state: Snapshot #2
Restored to state: Snapshot #3

Restoring to Snapshot #1.
Restored to state: Snapshot #1
```

Analysis

Per the concept of this program, you can use three different variations of undo operations:

- You can just go back to the previous restore point.

- You can go back to your specified restore point directly using the index property. For example, to go back directly to Snapshot #1, you use the following code snippet:

```
// Restoring to any specified checkpoint
System.out.println("\nRestoring to Snapshot #1.");
originator.restore(savedMementos.get(1));
```

- You can revert all restore points (which is shown using a for loop and the index property).

Note   If an application is using a Memento pattern and there is a state that is a mutable reference type, you may see the implementation of the deep copy technique to store the state inside the Memento object. You learned about deep copies when I discussed the Prototype pattern in Chapter 5.

Q&A Session

20.1 What will happen if I put the client class with the originator and memento class inside the same package? I also see you make the state field final inside the Memento class. Can you explain the reason behind this design?

In this case, the following line inside the client code will not cause any compilation error:

```
Memento m1=new Memento("test");
```

This means that the client (who plays the role of the caretaker in this example) can create the mementos with an arbitrary state.

Not only that, if I do not mark the state field in the Memento class with the final keyword, the following line can also work too (if the state field in the Memento class is public):

```
m1.state="arbitrary state";
```

So, the client cannot edit/change this state if it is marked final in the Memento class.

20.2 What are the key advantages of using the Memento design pattern?

Here are some advantages:

- The biggest advantage is that you can always discard the unwanted changes and restore them to an intended or stable state.

- You do not compromise the encapsulation associated with the key objects that are participating in this model.

- You can maintain high cohesion.

- It provides an easy recovery technique.

20.3 What are the key challenges associated with the Memento design pattern?

Here are some disadvantages:

- Having more mementos requires more storage. They also put an additional burden on a caretaker.

- The previous point increases maintenance costs.

- You cannot ignore the time it takes to save these states, which can decrease the overall performance of the application.

It is useful to note that in a language such as C# or Java, you may prefer to use serialization/deserialization techniques instead of directly implementing the Memento design pattern. Each technique has its own pros and cons, but you can combine both techniques in your application.

20.4 I am confused. To support undo operations, which pattern should I prefer, Memento or Command?

The GoF says that they are related patterns. They also said: Commands can use mementos to maintain state for undoable operations. So, it primarily depends on how you want to handle the situation. Suppose you are adding 25 to an integer. After this

447

addition operation, you can undo it by doing a reverse operation. In simple words, 50 + 25 = 75, so to go back, you do 75 – 25 = 50. In this type of operation, you do not need to store the previous state.

But consider a situation where you may need to store the state of your objects before the operation. In this case, you use Memento. For example, in a paint application, you can avoid the cost of undoing some painting operations by storing the list of objects before executing the commands. This stored list can be treated as mementos, and you can keep this list with the associated commands. A similar concept applies to a long-running game application that has multiple levels and in which you may save your last performance level. So, a particular application can use both patterns to support undo operations.

In the end, you must remember that storing a memento object is mandatory in the Memento pattern so that you can revert back to a previous state, but in the case of the Command pattern, it is not necessary to store the commands. Once you execute a command, its job is done. Particularly so, if you do not support undo operations, you may not be interested to store these commands at all.

20.5 I see that mementos are intended not to be read/updated by a client or a caretaker. Why do we need this constraint for a memento class?

If you allow a memento to be read or updated by others (except the originators), you expose the originator's state to the outside world, which means the encapsulation is broken.

20.6 I understand that by using the package-private visibility you avoid the use of getter/setter methods. But in many applications, I notice the use of a getter method inside a Memento class. Does it not violate the encapsulation?

There is a lot of discussion and debate about whether you should use getter/setter or not, particularly when you consider encapsulation. I believe that it depends on how much strictness you want to impose. For example, if you provide getters/setters for all fields without any reason, that is surely a bad design. The same thing applies when you use all the public fields inside the objects. But sometimes the accessor methods are really required and useful. In this book, I aim to encourage you to learn design patterns via simple examples. If I need to consider each minute detail like this, you may lose interest in this subject.

20.7 In many applications, I notice that the memento class is presented as an inner class of Originator. Why are you not following that approach?

A Memento design pattern can be implemented in many different ways (for example, using package-private visibility or using object serialization techniques). But in each case, if you analyze the key aim, you will find that once the memento instance is created by an originator, except its creator, no one else (including caretaker/client) is allowed to access the internal state. A caretaker's job is to store the memento instance (restore points, in our example) and supply them when you are in need.

In demonstration 1, I show a simple way to implement a Memento design pattern. If you wish to see an alternative implementation and prefer to implement the memento class as an inner class of the originator, consider using demonstration 2.

Additional Implementation

Here is an alternative implementation of the Memento design pattern. These are the important changes in this program:

- This time Memento is an inner class. It is nested inside the Originator class.

- The Memento class constructor is private. I made this change because I put the caretaker class (Client2.java) in the same package. As a result, the caretaker class cannot instantiate the Memento class. In short, you cannot use the following lines inside the client code. I kept some supporting comments before each line of code for your easy understanding.

```
// Client can't create the mementos
// and access the state
```

```
// Error, because the Memento class is not visible now
// Memento m1=new Memento("test");
// Error, because Memento constructor is private
Originator.Memento m1 = originator. new Memento("test");
// The state variable is final, you cannot edit it
m1.state = "arbitrary state";
```

- The caretaker (Client2.java) is very similar to the one in demonstration 1 except this time you need to use Originator. Memento instead of Memento.

- In demonstration 1, you declare the variables `originator` and `savedMementos` outside of the `main()` method. This time you declare and use them inside the `main()` method. (You can follow either approach.)

Let's go through demonstration 2 now.

Class Diagram

Figure 20-3 shows the modified class diagram.

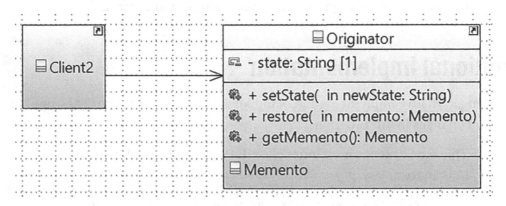

Figure 20-3. *Class diagram for demonstration 2*

Package Explorer View

Figure 20-4 shows the modified high-level structure of the program.

```
v  ⊞ memento
   >  ⊞ implementation_1
   v  ⊞ implementation_2
      v  🗋 Client2.java
         v  🄲 Client2
            ⚙ main(String[]) : void
            ⚙ saveSnapShot(Originator, String, List<Memento>) : void
      v  🗋 Originator.java
         v  🄲 Originator
            >  🄲 Memento
               ▫ state
            ● getMemento() : Memento
            ● restore(Memento) : void
            ● setState(String) : void
```

Figure 20-4. *Package Explorer view for demonstration 2*

450

Demonstration 2

Here's the modified implementation:

// Originator.java

```java
package jdp3e.memento.implementation_2;

class Originator {
    private String state;

    // Setting a new internal state
    public void setState(String newState) {
        this.state = newState;
        System.out.print("The current state is " + state);
    }

    // Back to an old state (Restore)
    public void restore(Memento memento) {
        this.state = memento.state;
        System.out.println("Restored to state: " + state);
    }

    public Memento getMemento() {

        Memento currentMemento = new Memento(state);
        return currentMemento;
    }

     class Memento {
        final String state;
        private Memento(String state) {
            this.state = state;
        }
    }
}
```

// Client2.java

```java
package jdp3e.memento.implementation_2;

import java.util.ArrayList;
```

```java
import java.util.List;

class Client2 {

    public static void main(String[] args) {
        System.out.println("***Memento Pattern Demonstration-2.***\n");

        Originator originator = new Originator();

        // This list stores the checkpoints
        List<Originator.Memento> savedMementos = new
                        ArrayList<Originator.Memento>();
        // Snapshot #0
        saveSnapShot(originator, "Snapshot #0", savedMementos);
        // Snapshot #1
        saveSnapShot(originator, "Snapshot #1", savedMementos);
        // Snapshot #2
        saveSnapShot(originator, "Snapshot #2", savedMementos);
        // Snapshot #3
        saveSnapShot(originator, "Snapshot #3", savedMementos);
        // Snapshot #4. Taking a snapshot,
        // but not adding as a restore point.
        originator.setState("Snapshot #4");

        // Undo's
        // Roll back everything...
        System.out.println("\n\nStarted restoring process...");
        for (int i = savedMementos.size(); i > 0; i--) {
            // Get a restore point
            originator.restore(savedMementos.get(i - 1));
            // Update the list if required.
        }

        // Redo's
        System.out.println("\nPerforming redo's now.");

        // Restore starts from "Snapshot #1" now.
        for (int i = 2; i <= savedMementos.size(); i++) {
```

```
            // Get a restore point
            originator.restore(savedMementos.get(i - 1));
            // Update the list if required.
        }

        // Restoring to any specified checkpoint
        System.out.println("\nRestoring to Snapshot #1.");
        originator.restore(savedMementos.get(1));

    }

    private static void saveSnapShot(Originator originator,
            String checkPoint, List<Originator.Memento>
                                    savedMementos) {
        // Setting a new state
        originator.setState(checkPoint);
        // Get the current state from the
        // originator through a memento
        Originator.Memento memento =
                                originator.getMemento();
        System.out.println(". Saving this checkpoint.");
        savedMementos.add(memento);
    }
}
```

Output

Here is the output. You can see that apart from the initial console message, the output of demonstration 1 and demonstration 2 is the same, but programmatically there are more constraints in this example.

```
***Memento Pattern Demonstration-2.***

The current state is Snapshot #0. Saving this checkpoint.
The current state is Snapshot #1. Saving this checkpoint.
The current state is Snapshot #2. Saving this checkpoint.
The current state is Snapshot #3. Saving this checkpoint.
The current state is: Snapshot #4
```

```
Started restoring process...
Restored to state: Snapshot #3
Restored to state: Snapshot #2
Restored to state: Snapshot #1
Restored to state: Snapshot #0

Performing redo's now.
Restored to state: Snapshot #1
Restored to state: Snapshot #2
Restored to state: Snapshot #3

Restoring to Snapshot #1.
Restored to state: Snapshot #1
```

Analysis

I hope that you have a clear idea about the Memento design pattern from these examples. I just want you to note a point: you may notice that once you revert to an old state, you do not removed the state from the saved list. This is because you use this list when you perform redo operations. So, depending on the need, you may need to implement complex undo and redo operations.

CHAPTER 21

Strategy Pattern

This chapter covers the Strategy pattern. It is also known as the Policy pattern.

GoF Definition

It defines a family of algorithms, encapsulates each one, and makes them interchangeable. The Strategy pattern lets the algorithm vary independently from the clients that use it.

Concept

A client can select an algorithm from a set of algorithms dynamically at runtime. This pattern also provides a simple way to use the selected algorithm.

You know that an object can have states and behaviors. And some of these behaviors may vary among the objects of a class. This pattern focuses on the changing behaviors that can be associated with an object at a specific time.

In this example, you will see a `Vehicle` class. Once a `Vehicle` instance is created, you can add and set behaviors to this object. Inside the client code, you can replace the current behavior with a new behavior, too. Most interestingly, you will see that since the behaviors can be changed, the vehicle class does NOT define the behavior; it simply delegates the task to a particular object referenced by a vehicle. The complete implementation can make the concept clearer to you.

© Vaskaran Sarcar 2022
V. Sarcar, *Java Design Patterns*, https://doi.org/10.1007/978-1-4842-7971-7_21

Real-Life Example

Consider a common scenario in a soccer match. Suppose team A has a 1–0 lead over team B toward the end of the game. In a situation like this, instead of attacking, team A becomes defensive in order to maintain the lead. At the same time, team B goes for an all-out attack to score the equalizer.

Computer World Example

Suppose you have a backup memory slot. If your primary memory is full but you need to store more data, you can use a backup memory slot. If you do not have this backup memory slot and you try to store the additional data into your primary memory, that data will be discarded (when the primary memory is full). In this case, you may receive an exception or you may encounter some peculiar behavior (based on the design of the program). So, a runtime check is necessary before you store the data. Here is another example for you:

- You can consider the interface `java.util.Comparator` in this context. You can implement this interface and provide different algorithms to do various comparisons using the `compare()` method. This comparison result can be further used in various sorting techniques. The `Comparator` interface plays the role of the strategy interface in this context.

Implementation

This demonstration focuses on different vehicle behaviors (or capabilities). You start with a simple class called `Vehicle`. To instantiate this class, you need to pass a `String` argument to indicate the type of vehicle. Here is the definition of the `Vehicle` class:

```
class Vehicle {
    String vehicleType;

    public Vehicle(String vehicleType) {
        this.vehicleType = vehicleType;
    }
```

```
    public String getVehicle() {
        return vehicleType;
    }
}
```

In this implementation, you focus on the changing behaviors of a vehicle only. This is why you see that once a vehicle object is created, it is associated with an InitialBehavior that simply tells you that in this state, the vehicle cannot do anything special. But once you set a FlyBehavior, the vehicle can fly. When you set the FloatBehavior, it can float. Since a vehicle can show a particular behavior at a time and this behavior can vary, all these changing behaviors are maintained in a separate hierarchy as follows:

```
// Abstract Behavior
interface VehicleBehavior {
    void showDetail(Vehicle vehicle);
}

// Capability to float
class FloatBehavior implements VehicleBehavior {
    @Override
    public void showDetail(Vehicle vehicle) {
        System.out.println("The " + vehicle.getVehicle() +
                            " can float now.\n");
    }
}

// Capability to fly
class FlyBehavior implements VehicleBehavior {
    @Override
    public void showDetail(Vehicle vehicle) {
        System.out.println("The " + vehicle.getVehicle() +
                            " can fly now.\n");
    }
}
```

```
/**
 * This class used to show the initial
 * behavior of a vehicle. It cannot do
 * anything special.
 */

class InitialBehavior implements VehicleBehavior {
    @Override
    public void showDetail(Vehicle vehicle) {

        System.out.println("The " + vehicle.getVehicle() +
                            " is in born state.");
        System.out.println("It cannot do anything special.\n");
    }
}
```

Now comes the most important class, which is often termed as a **context** class. VehicleSupervisor is the context class in this demonstration. This class adds/sets the capability of a vehicle.

```
class VehicleSupervisor {
  VehicleBehavior behavior;

  public VehicleSupervisor(VehicleBehavior behavior) {
      this.behavior = behavior;
  }

  /**
   * You can use this method when you want to change
   * the "vehicle behavior" on the fly.
   */
  public void setVehicleBehavior(VehicleBehavior behavior){
      this.behavior = behavior;
  }

  /**
   * Delegates the behavior to the object referenced by
   * a vehicle.
   */
```

```
    public void displayDetail(Vehicle vehicle) {
        behavior.showDetail(vehicle);
    }
}
```

Inside the client code, you start with an initial behavior that is altered later using the setVehicleBehavior(...) method. The displayDetail(...) delegates the task to the particular object. This code demonstrate these activities. The important lines are shown in bold.

```
Vehicle vehicle = new Vehicle("airplane");
VehicleSupervisor supervisor = new VehicleSupervisor(new InitialBehavior());
supervisor.displayDetail(vehicle);

System.out.println("Setting flying capability to it.");
supervisor.setVehicleBehavior(new FlyBehavior());
supervisor.displayDetail(vehicle);
```

Note   You can use either a constructor or a setter method or both to set a vehicle behavior.

Class Diagram

Figure 21-1 shows the important parts of the class diagram.

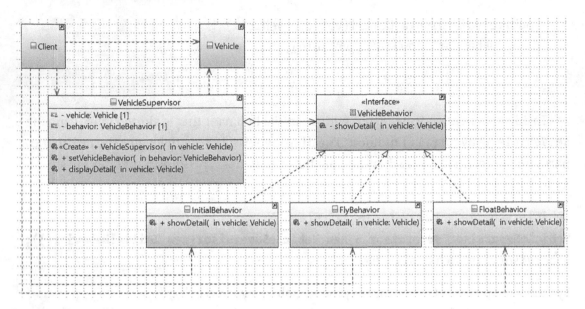

Figure 21-1. *Class diagram*

Package Explorer View

Figure 21-2 shows the high-level structure of the program.

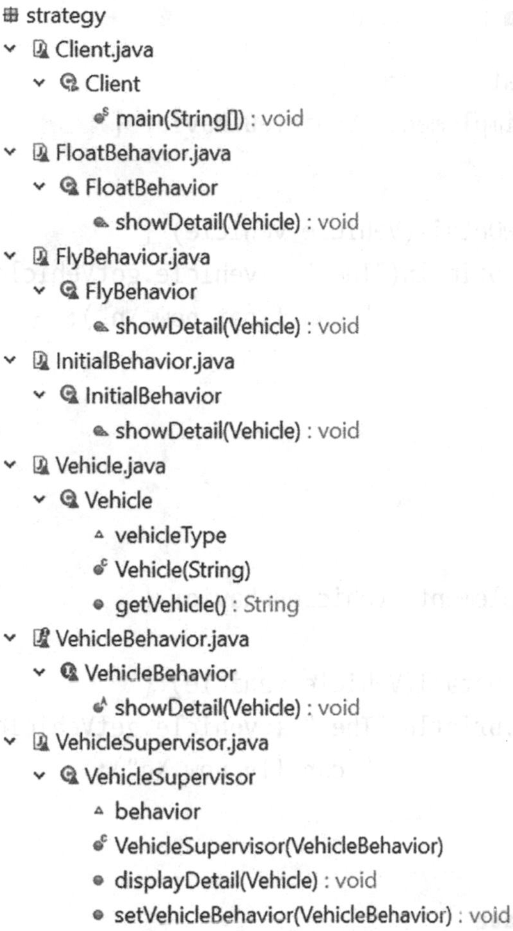

```
⊞ strategy
∨  🗎 Client.java
   ∨  🄌 Client
         ⬧ main(String[]) : void
∨  🗎 FloatBehavior.java
   ∨  🄌 FloatBehavior
         ● showDetail(Vehicle) : void
∨  🗎 FlyBehavior.java
   ∨  🄌 FlyBehavior
         ● showDetail(Vehicle) : void
∨  🗎 InitialBehavior.java
   ∨  🄌 InitialBehavior
         ● showDetail(Vehicle) : void
∨  🗎 Vehicle.java
   ∨  🄌 Vehicle
         ▵ vehicleType
         ⬧ Vehicle(String)
         ● getVehicle() : String
∨  🗎 VehicleBehavior.java
   ∨  🄌 VehicleBehavior
         ⬧ showDetail(Vehicle) : void
∨  🗎 VehicleSupervisor.java
   ∨  🄌 VehicleSupervisor
         ▵ behavior
         ⬧ VehicleSupervisor(VehicleBehavior)
         ● displayDetail(Vehicle) : void
         ● setVehicleBehavior(VehicleBehavior) : void
```

Figure 21-2. *Package Explorer view*

Demonstration

Here's the implementation. All parts of the program are stored inside the package jdp3e.
strategy.

// VehicleBehavior.java

```
// Abstract Behavior
interface VehicleBehavior {
    void showDetail(Vehicle vehicle);
}
```

461

// FloatBehavior.java

```java
// Capability to float
class FloatBehavior implements VehicleBehavior {

    @Override
    public void showDetail(Vehicle vehicle) {
        System.out.println("The " + vehicle.getVehicle() +
                            " can float now.\n");

    }
}
```

// FlyBehavior.java

```java
// Capability to fly
class FlyBehavior implements VehicleBehavior {
    @Override
    public void showDetail(Vehicle vehicle) {
        System.out.println("The " + vehicle.getVehicle() +
                            " can fly now.\n");
    }
}
```

// InitialBehavior.java

```java
/**
 * This class used to show the initial
 * behavior of a vehicle. It cannot do
 * anything special.
 */

class InitialBehavior implements VehicleBehavior {
    @Override
    public void showDetail(Vehicle vehicle) {

        System.out.println("The " + vehicle.getVehicle() +
                            " is in born state.");
```

```
        System.out.println("It cannot do anything special.\n");
    }
}
```

// Vehicle.java

```java
class Vehicle {

    String vehicleType;

    public Vehicle(String vehicleType) {
        this.vehicleType = vehicleType;
    }

    public String getVehicle() {
        return vehicleType;
    }
}
```

// VehicleSupervisor.java

```java
/**
 * The VehicleSupervisor class represents the
 * context class in this example.
 */

class VehicleSupervisor {

    VehicleBehavior behavior;

    public VehicleSupervisor(VehicleBehavior behavior) {
        this.behavior = behavior;
    }

    /**
     * You can use this method when you want to change
     * the "vehicle behavior" on the fly.
     */
```

```java
    public void setVehicleBehavior(VehicleBehavior behavior){
        this.behavior = behavior;
    }

    /**
     * Delegates the behavior to the object referenced by
     * a vehicle.
     */
    public void displayDetail(Vehicle vehicle) {
        behavior.showDetail(vehicle);
    }
}
```

```java
// Client.java
class Client {

    public static void main(String[] args) {

        System.out.println("***Strategy Pattern Demo.***\n");
        Vehicle vehicle = new Vehicle("airplane");
        VehicleSupervisor supervisor=new
                    VehicleSupervisor(new InitialBehavior());
        supervisor.displayDetail(vehicle);

        System.out.println("Setting flying capability to it.");
        supervisor.setVehicleBehavior(new FlyBehavior());
        supervisor.displayDetail(vehicle);

        System.out.println("Changing the vehicle behavior again.");
        supervisor.setVehicleBehavior(new FloatBehavior());
        supervisor.displayDetail(vehicle);

    }
}
```

Strategy Pattern Demo.

The airplane is in born state.
It cannot do anything special.

Setting flying capability to it.
The airplane can fly now.

Changing the vehicle behavior again.
The airplane can float now.

Q&A Session

21.1 It appears to me that you are complicating everything by focusing on changing behaviors. Also, I do not understand why you need the context class at all. You could simply use the inheritance mechanism and proceed. Can you please address these concerns?

If a particular behavior is common for all subtypes, it's okay to use inheritance. For example, you can make an abstract class and put the common behavior into it, so that all child classes get the common behavior. But the real power of the strategy comes into the picture when the behaviors can vary across the objects and maintaining them using inheritance is difficult.

For example, let's say, you start with different behaviors and you place them in an abstract class as follows:

```
public abstract class Vehicle
{
    public abstract void aboutMe();
    public abstract void floatBehavior();
    public abstract void flyBehavior();
```

```
    public virtual void defaultJob()
    {
        System.out.println("By default, I float.");
    }
}
```

Now let's say `Boat` and `Car` are two concrete classes that inherit from it. You understand that a `Boat` object should not fly, so inside the `Boat` class, you can simply override `flyBehavior` as follows:

```
public override void flyBehavior() throws Exception
{
    throw new Exception("Invalid vehicle feature.");
}
```

Similarly, a `Car` object should not float in water, so inside the `Car` class, you override the floating capability as follows:

```
public override void floatBehavior()throws Exception
{
  throw new Exception("Invalid vehicle feature.");
}
```

Now consider the case when you have lots of changing behaviors across objects like these. This kind of maintenance can be overhead for you.

Apart from this, let's consider a vehicle that has specialized features. If you simply put those special features in the abstract class, all other vehicle objects will inherit those features and need to implement them. But it is not over yet. Further, assume that there is a constraint on the `Boat` class that simply says that it cannot have any special behavior. Now you encounter a deadlock situation. If you implement this special method, you are violating the constraint, and if you do not implement it, the system architecture will be broken because as per the language construct, you need to implement the behavior. (Or you need to mark the class with the `abstract` keyword, but at the same time, remember that you cannot create an instance from an abstract class.)

To overcome this, you may say that you'll create a separate inheritance hierarchy where you'll make an interface to hold all the specialized features, and your classes can implement the interface if needed. This may solve the problem partially. This is because typically an interface contains abstract methods only (default methods in the Java interface were allowed from Java 8). So, there is no code reuse. Apart from this point, you may also note that an interface may contain multiple methods, but your class may need to implement only one of them. In a case like this, you need to consider the Interface Segregation Principle that you learned in Chapter 1. In the end, in either case, the overall maintenance becomes tough. Apart from this, a specific behavior may also change in the near future and if so, you will need to track down all the classes that implement these behaviors.

In a situation like this, a context class acts as a savior for you. For example, the clients know that they should NOT set the fly behavior for a Boat class object. They also know that they should NOT set the set float behavior for a Car object. In short, they know which behavior is expected from the particular vehicle. If you want, you can guard the situation when a client by mistake sets an incorrect behavior to a vehicle, too.

To simplify this, the context class holds a reference variable for the changing behaviors of an object. At any particular moment, it can set the desired behavior and delegate the task to the appropriate behavior class.

So, a "has-a" relationship fits better than an "is-a" relationship in a similar situation. This is one of the primary reasons why most design patterns encourage you to prefer composition over inheritance.

21.2 What are the key advantages of using a Strategy design pattern?

Here are some key advantages:

- This design pattern makes your classes independent of algorithms. Here a class delegates the algorithms to the strategy object (that encapsulates the algorithm) dynamically at runtime. So, the choice of algorithms is not bound at compile time.

- It's easier to maintain your codebase.

- It's easily extendable.

You can refer to the answer to Q&A 21.1 in this context.

21.3 What are the key challenges associated with a Strategy design pattern?

The disadvantages can be summarized as follows:

- The addition of context classes causes more objects to exist in your application.

- Users of the application must be aware of different strategies; otherwise, the outputs may surprise them.

21.4 How does this pattern differ from the Template Method pattern?

You have asked a good question. These patterns have similarities. In the Strategy pattern, you can vary the entire algorithm using delegation. The Template Method pattern suggests you vary certain steps in an algorithm using inheritance but the overall flow of the algorithm is unchanged.

CHAPTER 22

State Pattern

This chapter covers the State pattern.

GoF Definition

It allows an object to alter its behavior when its internal state changes. The object will appear to change its class.

Concept

The GoF definition is easy to understand. It states that an object can change what it does and this depends on its current state.

Suppose you are dealing with a large-scale application where the codebase is rapidly growing. As a result, the situation becomes complex and you may need to introduce lots of if-else blocks/switch statements to guard the various conditions. The State pattern fits in such a context. It allows your objects to behave differently based on their current states and you can define state-specific behaviors with different classes.

In this pattern, start thinking in terms of possible states of your application and segregate the code accordingly. Ideally, each state is independent of the other states. You keep track of these states, and your code responds as per the behavior of the current state. For example, suppose you are watching a program on your television (TV). If you press the Mute button on the TV's control panel, you will notice a state change in your TV. But you won't notice any change if the TV is already in the switched-off mode.

The basic idea is if your code can track the current state of the application, you can centralize the task, segregate your code, and respond accordingly. This is why in this chapter you'll see state-specific behaviors in separate classes. In short, this is the key concept in the State pattern.

© Vaskaran Sarcar 2022
V. Sarcar, *Java Design Patterns*, https://doi.org/10.1007/978-1-4842-7971-7_22

Real-Life Example

The functionalities of a traffic signal or television can be considered as examples of the State pattern. For example, you can change the channel if the TV is already in the switched-on mode. It will not respond to the channel change request if it is in the switched-off mode.

Computer World Example

Here are some examples for you:

- Consider the scenario of a network connection, say a TCP connection. An object can be in various states. For example, a connection might already be established, a connection might be closed, or the object has already started listening through the connection. When this connection receives a request from other objects, it responds according to its present state.

- Consider another example. Suppose you have a job processing system that can process a certain number of jobs at a time. When a new job appears, either the system processes the job or it signals that it is busy with the maximum number of jobs that it can process at that time. This busy signal simply indicates that its total number of job-processing capabilities has been reached and the new job request cannot be fulfilled immediately.

Implementation

This example models the functionalities related to a television, which has a control panel to support on, off, and mute operations. For simplicity, assume that at any given point in time the TV can be in either of these three states: On, Off, or Muted. So, there is an interface called IPossibleStates as follows:

```
interface PossibleState {
    // Users can press any of these buttons-On, Off or Mute
    void pressOnButton(Television tvContext);
```

```
    void pressOffButton(Television tvContext);
    void pressMuteButton(Television tvContext);
}
```

Three concrete classes called OnState, OffState, and MuteState implement this interface. The basic functionality can be described as follows. Initially, the TV is in the Off state. So, when you press the On button on the control panel, the TV moves to the On state. Then if you press the Mute button, it will go into the Mute state.

Assume that if you press the Off button when the TV is already in the Off state, if you press the On button when the TV is already in the On state, or if you press the Mute button when the TV is already in Mute mode, there will be no state change for the TV. The TV can go into the Off state from the On state or the Mute state (when you press the Off button). To help you understand this easily, Figure 22-1 describes this situation. (It is from my other book, *Design Patterns in C#* (Second Edition) which is published by the same publisher).

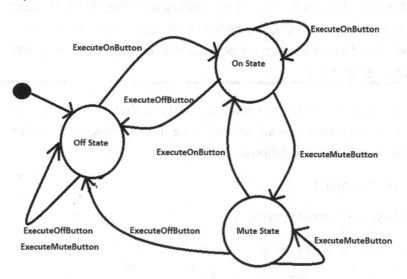

Figure 22-1. *Different states of a TV*

POINTS TO REMEMBER

- In this diagram, I have not marked any state as the final state, although in this illustration, in the end, I switch off the TV.

- To make the design simple, assume that if you press the Off (or Mute) button when the TV is already in the Off state or if you press the On button when the TV is already in the On state, or if you press the Mute button when the TV is already in the Mute mode, there will be no state change for the TV. But in the real world, a control panel may work differently. For example, if the TV is currently in the On state and you press the Mute button, the TV can go into Mute mode, and then if you press the Mute button again, the TV may come back to the On state. So, you may need to update your program logic accordingly.

- In Figure 22-1, the method names start with capital letters. But in the upcoming demonstration, following Java's method naming convention, I make the first letter of each method lowercase, such as `executeOffButton()` and `executeOnButton`.

There is a class called TV in this example. I told you that the TV has a control panel to support on, off, and mute operations. So, inside the TV class, you see three different methods, which are defined as follows:

```
class Television {

PossibleState currentState;

// Some code skipped here

public void executeOffButton() {
    System.out.println("You pressed the Off button.");
    // Delegating the state behavior
    currentState.pressOffButton(this);
}
```

```
    public void executeOnButton() {
        System.out.println("You pressed the On button.");
        // Delegating the state behavior
        currentState.pressOnButton(this);
    }

    public void executeMuteButton() {
        System.out.println("You pressed the Mute button.");
        // Delegating the state behavior
        currentState.pressMuteButton(this);
    }
}
```

Notice that these methods invoke or "delegate to" the current state object's method. For example, when you press executeMuteButton(), the control will invoke pressMuteButton(...) based on the current state of the television.

When you assign a new value to the currentState variable, the program appears to change its class because different code will be invoked from the same method call based on whichever PossibleState object is current.

Let's follow the class diagram now.

Class Diagram

Figure 22-2 shows the key participants in the upcoming example.

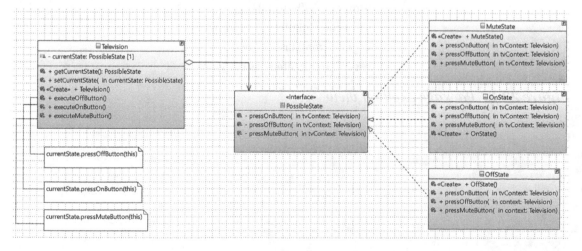

Figure 22-2. *Class diagram*

Package Explorer View

Figure 22-3 shows the high-level structure of the program. To make the diagram short and concise, I just expand one of the three possible states.

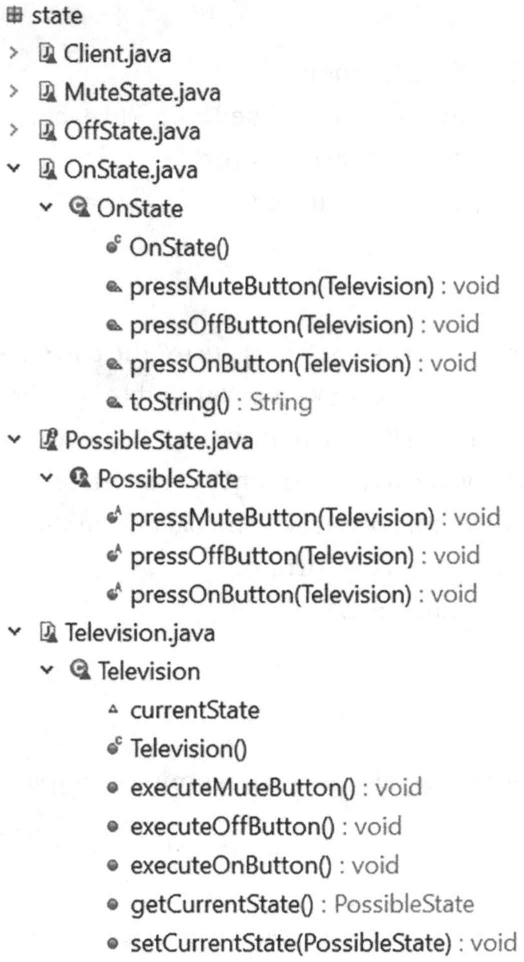

⊞ state
> 🗎 Client.java
> 🗎 MuteState.java
> 🗎 OffState.java
∨ 🗎 OnState.java
　∨ ◎ OnState
　　⚬ OnState()
　　◉ pressMuteButton(Television) : void
　　◉ pressOffButton(Television) : void
　　◉ pressOnButton(Television) : void
　　◉ toString() : String
∨ 🗎 PossibleState.java
　∨ ◎ PossibleState
　　◆ pressMuteButton(Television) : void
　　◆ pressOffButton(Television) : void
　　◆ pressOnButton(Television) : void
∨ 🗎 Television.java
　∨ ◎ Television
　　△ currentState
　　⚬ Television()
　　⚬ executeMuteButton() : void
　　⚬ executeOffButton() : void
　　⚬ executeOnButton() : void
　　⚬ getCurrentState() : PossibleState
　　⚬ setCurrentState(PossibleState) : void

Figure 22-3. *Package Explorer view*

Demonstration

All parts of the program are stored inside the package jdp3e.state. Here's the complete implementation:

// PossibleState.java

```
interface PossibleState {
    // Users can press any of these buttons-On, Off or Mute
    void pressOnButton(Television tvContext);

    void pressOffButton(Television tvContext);

    void pressMuteButton(Television tvContext);
}
```

// OffState.java

```
// Subclasses do not contain any local state.
// Only one unique instance of IPossibleStates is required.
// This class describes the off state behavior

class OffState implements PossibleState {
    public OffState() {
        System.out.println("The TV is Off now.\n");
    }

    // TV was off. The user presses the On button now.
    @Override
    public void pressOnButton(Television tvContext) {
        System.out.println("The TV was Off. Going from Off to On state.");
        tvContext.setCurrentState(new OnState());
    }

    // TV was off. The user presses the Off button now.
    @Override
    public void pressOffButton(Television tvContext) {
        System.out.print("The TV was already in Off state.");
        System.out.println(" So, ignoring this operation.");
    }
```

```java
    // TV was off. The user presses the mute button now.
    @Override
    public void pressMuteButton(Television tvContext) {
        System.out.print("The TV was already off.");
        System.out.println(" So, ignoring this operation.");
    }

    @Override
    public String toString() {
        return " Switched off.";
    }

}
```

// OnState.java

```java
// This class describes the on state behavior

class OnState implements PossibleState {
    public OnState() {
        System.out.println("The TV is On now.\n");
    }

    // TV is already On. The user presses the On button now.
    @Override
    public void pressOnButton(Television tvContext) {
        System.out.print("The TV was already on.");
        System.out.println(" Ignoring repeated on button press operation.");
    }

    // TV is already On. The user presses the off button now.
    @Override
    public void pressOffButton(Television tvContext) {
        System.out.println("The TV was on. So,switching off the TV.");
        tvContext.setCurrentState(new OffState());
    }
```

```java
// TV is already On. The user presses the mute button now.
@Override
public void pressMuteButton(Television tvContext) {
    System.out.println("The TV was on. So,moving to the silent mode.");
    tvContext.setCurrentState(new MuteState());
}
@Override
public String toString(){
    return " Switched on.";
}
}
```

// MuteState.java

```java
class MuteState implements PossibleState {

    public MuteState() {
        System.out.println("The TV is in Mute mode now.\n");
    }

    // TV is muted, but the user presses the Off button

    @Override
    public void pressOnButton(Television tvContext) {
        System.out.print("The TV was in mute mode.");
        System.out.println(" So, moving to the normal state.");
        tvContext.setCurrentState(new OnState());
    }

    // TV is muted, but the user presses the Off button

    @Override
    public void pressOffButton(Television tvContext) {
        System.out.print(" The TV was in mute mode.");
        System.out.println(" So, switching off the TV.");
        tvContext.setCurrentState(new OffState());
    }
```

```
    // TV is muted, but the user press the mute button again

    @Override
    public void pressMuteButton(Television tvContext) {
        System.out.print("The TV was already in Mute mode.");
        System.out.println("So, ignoring this operation.");

    }
    @Override
    public String toString(){
        return "Mute mode.";
    }
}
```

// Television.java

```
// Television is the context class

class Television {

    PossibleState currentState;

    public PossibleState getCurrentState() {
        return currentState;
    }

    public void setCurrentState(PossibleState currentState) {
        this.currentState = currentState;
    }

    public Television() {
        // Starting with Off state
        this.currentState = new OffState();
    }

    public void executeOffButton() {
        System.out.println("You pressed the Off button.");
        // Delegating the state behavior
        currentState.pressOffButton(this);
    }
```

```
    public void executeOnButton() {
        System.out.println("You pressed the On button.");
        // Delegating the state behavior
        currentState.pressOnButton(this);
    }

    public void executeMuteButton() {
        System.out.println("You pressed the Mute button.");
        // Delegating the state behavior
        currentState.pressMuteButton(this);
    }
}
```

// Client. Java

```
package jdp3e.state;

class Client {

    public static void main(String[] args) {
        System.out.println("***State Pattern Demonstration.***\n");
        // TV is initialized with Off state.
        Television tv = new Television ();
        System.out.println("User is pressing buttons in the
                           following sequence:");
        System.out.println("Off->Mute->On->On->Mute->Mute->On->Off\n");
        // TV is off. Pressing the off button again.
        tv.executeOffButton();
        // Pressing the mute button when the TV is off
        tv.executeMuteButton();

        //Checking the current state
        System.out.println("Current state:"+ tv.getCurrentState());

        // Switching on the television.
        tv.executeOnButton();

        //Checking the current state
        System.out.println("Current state:"+ tv.getCurrentState());
```

```
        // Pressing the On button again when the TV is On
        tv.executeOnButton();
        // Putting the TV in the mute mode.
        tv.executeMuteButton();
        // TV is already muted. Pressing Mute button again
        tv.executeMuteButton();

        // Checking the current state
        System.out.println("Current state:"+ tv.getCurrentState());

        // TV is silent now. Pressing the On Button now.
        tv.executeOnButton();
        // Switching off the TV now.
        tv.executeOffButton();

        System.out.println("Current state:"+ tv.getCurrentState());

    }
}
```

Output

Notice the state changes in the following output. I marked them in bold.

```
***State Pattern Demonstration.***
```

The TV is Off now.

```
User is pressing buttons in the following sequence:
```
Off->Mute->On->On->Mute->Mute->On->Off

```
You pressed the Off button.
The TV was already in Off state. So, ignoring this operation.
You pressed the Mute button.
The TV was already off. So, ignoring this operation.
Current state: Switched off.
You pressed the On button.
The TV was Off. Going from Off to On state.
```
The TV is On now.

```
Current state: Switched on.
You pressed the On button.
The TV was already on. Ignoring repeated on button press operation.
You pressed the Mute button.
The TV was on. So, moving to the silent mode.
```
The TV is in Mute mode now.

```
You pressed the Mute button.
The TV was already in Mute mode. So, ignoring this operation.
Current state: Mute mode.
You pressed the On button.
The TV was in mute mode. So, moving to the normal state.
```
The TV is On now.

```
You pressed the Off button.
The TV was on. So, switching off the TV.
```
The TV is Off now.

```
Current state: Switched off.
```

Analysis

The GoF mentions four important points about this pattern. Let's look at them:

- Context delegates state-specific requests to the current ConcreteState object.

- A context may pass itself as an argument to the State object handling the request. This lets the State object access the context if necessary.

- Context is the primary interface for clients. Clients can configure a context with State objects. Once a context is configured, its clients don't have to deal with the State objects directly.

- Either the Context or the ConcreteState subclass can decide which state succeeds another and under what circumstances.

Now notice your context class `Television`, any subset of `PossibleStates` such as `OffState,` and the client code. You can see that the example shown in the demonstration meets these criteria, such as

- You also delegate the task.

- You also use the context as an argument.

- The client interacts with the television objects only.

- When the client initializes the `Television` object, a state object is also initialized inside the `Television`'s constructor.

- The context object is used to set different states under different circumstances.

Q&A Session

22.1 Can you elaborate on how this pattern works in a real-world scenario?

Psychologists have repeatedly documented the fact that human beings perform their best when they are in a relaxed mood but in the reverse scenario, when their minds are filled with tension, they cannot produce great results. That is why they always suggest you work in a relaxed mood. So, the same work can be enjoyable or boring depending on your current mood.

Think about the demonstration example again. Suppose you want to watch the live telecast of the winning moments of your favorite team. To watch and enjoy the moment, you need to power on the TV first. If the TV is not functioning properly at that moment and cannot be in the On state, you cannot enjoy the moment. So, if you want to enjoy the moment through your TV, the first criterion is that the TV should change its state from Off to On. The State pattern is helpful if you want to design a similar kind of behavior change in an object when its internal state changes.

22.2 In this example, you considered only three states of a TV: On, Off, and Mute. There can be many other states; for example, there may be a state that deals with connection issues or different display conditions. Why have you ignored those issues?

The straightforward answer I ignored those states in order to keep the example simple. If the number of states increases significantly in the system, then it becomes difficult to maintain the system (and this is one of the key challenges associated with this design pattern). But if you understand this implementation, you can easily add any states you want.

22.3 I noticed that the GoF represent a similar structure for both the State pattern and the Strategy pattern in their famous book. I am confused by that.

Yes, the structures are similar, but you need to remember that their intents are different. The GoF clearly states that a strategy object encapsulates an algorithm, but a state object encapsulates a state-specific behavior. Let's analyze further.

When you use the Strategy pattern, you get a better alternative to subclassing. In the State design pattern, different types of behaviors can be encapsulated in a state object, and the context is delegated to any of these states. When a context's internal state changes, its behavior also changes. So, the State pattern can be thought of as a dynamic version of the Strategy pattern.

Consider a true case study. Once I lost my debit card on my way home. So, I needed to block the card immediately. In a situation like this, my bank provides various facilities, such as if you are a priority customer, you can block the card using your personal phone-banking pin. But for a normal customer, you need to connect with the customer care department and raise a request to block the card. Notice the end goal: I needed to block the card. So, I could opt for any of the available options to fulfill my need. The Strategy pattern helps you in a similar case because you can develop different algorithms to fulfill needs. Now think deeply: prior to using these facilities you must have a network connection, otherwise they are of no use. In other words, a customer can use the facility from a place where the network connection is active. This situation mimics the need for the State design pattern. So, it is quite possible that you need to use both patterns in an application.

You may note another interesting point: in the case of the Strategy pattern, the different algorithms are not dependent on each other. But, in the case of a State design pattern, one state can trigger a state transition to reach a different state. In such a case, one state may need to know about the other state.

Lastly, the State patterns can also help you avoid lots of if conditions in particular contexts. For example, consider the example once again. If the TV is in the Off state, it cannot go into the Mute state. From this state, it can move to the On state only. So, if you do not like the State design pattern, you may need to write code like this:

```
class TV {
//Some code before
 public void executeOnButton(){
if(currentState==Off ){
  System.out.println("You pressed On button. Going from Off to OnState");
  //Some code after
 }

 if(currentState==On ){
   System.out.println("You pressed On button. TV is already
                 in On state. So, ignoring this operation.");
    //Some code after
 }
  else {
    System.out.println("TV was in mute mode.So, moving to the normal state.");
}

 public void executeOffButton() {
  //Repeat the state check and proceed accordingly
 }

 public void executeMuteButton(){
  // Repeat the state check and proceed accordingly
 }

 //Some code after if any
```

Notice that you need to repeat these checks for different kinds of button presses (for example, for the executeOffButton() and executeMuteButton() methods, you need to repeat these checks). So, if you do not think in terms of states, over a period of time, handling different conditions with lots of if-else statements is very challenging and it can be difficult when the codebase continually grows.

22.4 I understand that the control panel of the television supports three operations: on, off, and mute. But when I add a new state, I do not need to change this class. Is this correct?

Yes. Notice that each of these television states is closed for modification, but you can add a new state to this application. When you add a new state, you do not need to change the number of buttons on the control panel. Instead, you need to focus on the transition of states. This is why a context class (`Television` in this example) does not implement a state-specific behavior directly. It simply delegates the state-specific behavior to the correct class (`states` in this example).

22.5 What are the common characteristics between the Strategy pattern and the State pattern?

The State pattern can be seen as a dynamic Strategy pattern. Both patterns promote encapsulation and delegation. But as said before, a strategy object encapsulates an algorithm, but a state object encapsulates a state-specific behavior.

22.6 It appears to me that these state objects are acting like singletons. Is this correct?

Yes, it's a nice observation. The concrete subclasses of `PossibleStates` do not contain any local state in this example and as a result, in this application, only one state instance is working. Most of the time, this pattern acts in a similar way.

22.7 Why are you using the context as a method parameter? Can you avoid them in statements like the following:

```
void pressOnButton(Television tvContext);
```

Using the context, I'm using/saving states. Also, notice that the concrete subclasses of `PossibleState` do not contain any local state. So, in this application, only one state instance is working. This construct helps you to evaluate whether you need to change a current state.

You may see many applications that don't do the same. They may initialize the value inside the constructor of a state.

22.8 What are the pros and cons of the State design pattern?

The advantages are as follows:

- You have already seen that you can add new states and extend a state's behavior easily. Also, state behavior can be extended without any hassle. Notice that in this example, you can add a new state and new behavior for a `Television` class without changing this class.

- It reduces the use of `if-else` statements. In other words, the conditional complexity is reduced. (Refer to the answer to question 22.3 earlier.)

Here is a downside of using this pattern:

- The State pattern is also known as "Objects for States." So, you can assume that more states need more code and the obvious side effect is difficult maintenance for you.

- More states mean more classes for you. It tells you to put more effort into testing the code.

- The state transitions are not always straightforward. If there are various possibilities, overall implementation can be complex, too.

- It is not always easy to predict all possible states at the beginning.

22.9 In these implementations, `Television` is a concrete class. Why are you not programming to interface in this case?

I assume that the `Television` class is not going to change. So, I ignore that part to reduce the code size of the program. But yes, you can always start from an interface, in which you can define the necessary contracts.

22.10 In your example, I see that inside the client code when you execute the On, Off, or Mute buttons on the television's control panel, the states of the television change. Does it mean that a client needs to trigger these state transitions?

A state transition can be triggered in various ways. For example, you can use a method parameter to change a state, or you can use the context class to perform the same. Consider a banking transaction in this context: after a withdrawal, if you do not maintain the minimum balance, some of the features can be disabled, or you need to pay some penalty, which is not the case if you maintain a minimum balance. So, it is important to note that the "withdrawal amount" in the withdrawal method decides the next state of the account. So, a client can pass this value inside a withdrawal method.

In this example, when I initialize the Television class, I trigger the Off state, so I use the context class to trigger a state transition. This state changes when you press the On button.

22.11 You are initializing a Television object with an Off state. So can I say that both states and the context class can trigger the state transitions?

Yes.

22.12 Does the Thread class in Java follow the State design pattern?

I do not think so. The Thread class has several states such as NEW, RUNNABLE, BLOCKED, etc. These states are defined inside an enum. I do not see any substituting class based on these states so far.

CHAPTER 23

Mediator Pattern

This chapter covers the Mediator pattern.

GoF Definition

It defines an object that encapsulates how a set of objects interact. The Mediator pattern promotes loose coupling by keeping objects from referring to each other explicitly, and it lets you vary their interaction independently.

Concept

A mediator is an intermediary through whom different objects talk to each other. It takes responsibility for controlling and coordinating the interactions of a specific group of objects that cannot refer to each other explicitly. As a result, you can reduce the number of direct interconnections and promote loose coupling among them in your application.

Real-Life Example

When an airplane needs to take off, a series of verifications take place. These kinds of verifications confirm that all components and parts (which are dependent on each other) are in perfect condition.

You can also consider the case when the pilots of different airplanes (that are approaching or departing the terminal area) communicate with the airport towers. They do not explicitly communicate with other pilots in different airlines. They send their status to the controlling tower. These towers send signals to confirm who can take off (or land). These towers do not control the whole flight. They enforce constraints only in the terminal areas.

© Vaskaran Sarcar 2022
V. Sarcar, *Java Design Patterns*, https://doi.org/10.1007/978-1-4842-7971-7_23

Computer World Example

When a client processes a business application, you may need to implement some constraints. For example, suppose you have a form where clients need to supply their user IDs and passwords to access the accounts. In the same form, you may include other mandatory fields such as e-mail ID, communication address, age, and so on. Let's assume you are applying the constraints as follows.

Initially, you check whether the user ID supplied by a user is a valid one. If it is a valid ID, then only the password field are enabled. After supplying these two fields, you may need to check whether the e-mail ID is provided by the user. Let's assume further that after providing all this information (a valid user ID, a password, a correctly formatted e-mail ID, and so on), the Submit button is enabled. In other words, the Submit button is enabled only if the user supplies a valid user ID, password, valid email ID, and other mandatory details. You can also ensure that the user ID is an integer, so if a user by mistake provides any character in that field, the Submit button will stay in disabled mode. The Mediator pattern becomes handy in such a scenario.

When a program consists of many classes and the logic is distributed among them, the code becomes harder to read and maintain. In these scenarios, if you want to bring changes into the system's behavior, it can be difficult unless you use the Mediator pattern. Here are a few more examples:

- The `execute()` method inside the `java.util.concurrent.Executor` interface follows this pattern.

- The `javax.swing.ButtonGroup` class is another example that supports this pattern. This class has a method named `setSelected()` which ensures that a user can provide a new selection.

- The different overloaded versions of various `schedule()` methods of the `java.util.Timer` class also can be considered as following this pattern.

Implementation

Wikipedia describes the Mediator pattern as shown in Figure 23-1 (which is basically adopted from the GoF).

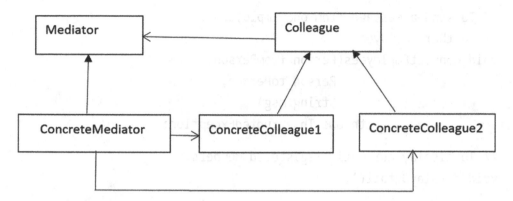

Figure 23-1. *Mediator pattern example*

The participants are described as follows:

- Mediator: It defines the interface that provides communication among Colleague objects.

- ConcreteMediator: It knows and maintains the list of Colleague objects. It implements the Mediator interface and coordinates the communication among the Colleague objects.

- Colleague: It defines the interface for communication with other colleagues.

- ConcreteColleague(s): A concrete colleague must implement the Colleague interface. These objects communicate with each other through the mediator.

In demonstration 1, I replaced Colleague with Person and ConcreteColleague(s) with Employee and Outsider. The reason is simple: I want to show how a mediator can control an outsider in an organization's chat server.

In this example, there are three different participants named amit, sohel, and joseph who can communicate with each other through a chat server. This chat server plays the role of a concrete mediator in this scenario.

In the upcoming example, Mediator is a Java interface. Refer to the comments for your easy understanding. It is defined as follows:

```
interface Mediator {
    // To register an employee
    void register(Person person);
```

```
       // To send a message from one employee to
       // another employee
       void connectEmployees(Person fromPerson,
                             Person toPerson,
                             String msg)
                      throws InterruptedException;

       // To display currently registered members.
       void displayDetail();

}
```

The ChatServer class implements this interface. It maintains the list of registered participants. So, inside this class, you see the following line of code:

```
List<Person> participants = new ArrayList<Person>();
```

Apart from this, the mediator allows only registered users to communicate with each other and post messages successfully. So, the connectEmployees(...) method in ConcreteMediator checks whether both the sender and receiver are registered users or not. The method is defined as follows:

```
@Override
public void connectEmployees(Person fromPerson, Person toPerson, String
msg) throws InterruptedException {

 // If the sender is a registered user
 if (participants.contains(fromPerson)) {
 // If the receiver is a registered user
 if (participants.contains(toPerson)) {
    System.out.println(fromPerson.getName() + " posts: " +
     Msg + " at:" + LocalDateTime.now());
    Thread.sleep(1000);
    // Target receiver receives this message.
    toPerson.receiveMessage(fromPerson, msg);
    } else {
     System.out.print(fromPerson.getName() + ", you cannot
             send message to " + toPerson.getName() + ".");
     System.out.println("He/she is NOT a registered user.");
```

```
        }
    }
    // The message sender is not a registered user.
    else {
        System.out.print("\n****ALERT: Everyone.***");
        System.out.println("An " + fromPerson.personType() + ": "
                    + fromPerson.getName()+ " is trying to send
                    some messages.");
    }
}
```

In this example, there is another inheritance hierarchy, in which you use `Person` as an abstract class so that you cannot directly instantiate it. Instead, you can instantiate objects from the concrete classes `Employee` or `Outsider`, which inherit from `Person`. This inheritance hierarchy is as follows:

```
// The abstract class-Person
abstract class Person {

    protected Mediator mediator;
    protected String name;

    public String getName() {
        return name;
    }

    // Constructor
    public Person(Mediator mediator) {
        this.mediator = mediator;
    }

    public void sendMessage(Person toEmp, String msg)
                        throws InterruptedException {
        mediator.connectEmployees(this, toEmp, msg);
    }

    public abstract String personType();

    public void receiveMessage(Person fromEmp, String msg) {
```

```java
            System.out.println(this.name + " has read " +
                        fromEmp.getName() + "'s message.");
    }

}


// Employee
class Employee extends Person {
    public Employee(Mediator mediator, String name) {
        super(mediator);
        this.name = name;
    }

    @Override
    public String personType() {
        return "Employee";
    }

}


// Unknown participant-an outsider.
class Outsider extends Person {
    // Constructor
    public Outsider(Mediator mediator, String name) {
        super(mediator);
        this.name = name;
    }

    @Override
    public String personType() {
        return "Outsider";
    }

}
```

> **Note**   Following the core architecture of a basic Mediator pattern, I use two different concrete classes to demonstrate the following fact: you should NOT assume that the communicating objects should appear from the same class only.

Inside the client code, there are different participants. Here are some examples:

```
Person amit = new Employee(mediator, "Amit");
Person sohel = new Employee(mediator, "Sohel");
Person joseph = new Outsider(mediator, "Joseph");
```

These people can communicate among themselves through a chat server. So, before passing the messages, they first register themselves to the chat server as follows:

```
// Registering participants
mediator.register(amit);
mediator.register(sohel);
mediator.register(joseph);
```

At the end of the program, you introduced two more people named todd and jack; todd is an Employee class object and jack is an Outsider class object. But neither of them registered themselves with the mediator object, so the mediator does not allow them to post any message to the target recipient.

Obviously, the Outsider instance of jack will be able to send the message properly if he registers himself to the mediator before sending the message as follows:

```
mediator.register(jack); // Not shown in Demonstration1
jack.sendMessage(joseph, "Hello Joseph...");
```

And the same comment applies to todd.

Class Diagram

Figure 23-2 shows the important parts of the class diagram.

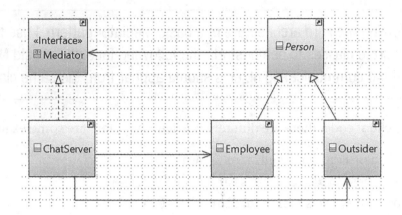

Figure 23-2. *Class diagram*

Package Explorer View

Figure 23-3 shows the high-level structure of the program.

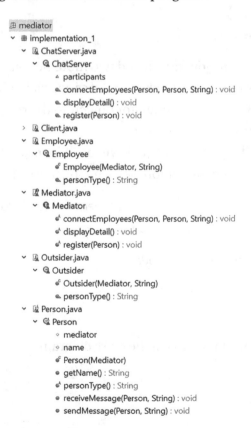

Figure 23-3. *Package Explorer view*

Demonstration 1

Here's the complete demonstration. All parts are stored inside the package jdp3e.
mediator.implementation_1.

// Mediator.java

```java
interface Mediator {

    // To register an employee
    void register(Person person);

    // To send a message from one employee to
    // another employee
    void connectEmployees(Person fromPerson, Person toPerson,
                    String msg) throws InterruptedException;

    // To display currently registered members.
    void displayDetail();

}
```

// ChatServer.java

```java
import java.time.LocalDateTime;
import java.util.ArrayList;
import java.util.List;

// ConcreteMediator
class ChatServer implements Mediator {

    List<Person> participants = new ArrayList<Person>();

    @Override
    public void register(Person employee) {
        participants.add(employee);
    }

    @Override
    public void displayDetail() {
        System.out.println("At present, the registered employees are:");
        for (Person person : participants) {
```

```java
            System.out.println(person.getName());
        }
    }

    @Override
    public void connectEmployees(Person fromPerson,
                        Person toPerson,
                        String msg)
            throws InterruptedException {
        // If the sender is a registered user
        if (participants.contains(fromPerson)) {
            // If the receiver is a registered user
            if (participants.contains(toPerson)) {
                System.out.println(fromPerson.getName()
                    + " posts: " + msg + " at:" +
                    LocalDateTime.now());
                Thread.sleep(1000);
                // Target receiver receives
                  // this message.
                toPerson.receiveMessage(fromPerson, msg);
            } else {
                System.out.print(fromPerson.getName() +
                    ", you cannot send the message to " +
                    toPerson.getName() + ".");
                System.out.println("He/she is NOT a
                    registered user.");
            }
        }
        // The message sender is not a registered user.
        else {
            System.out.print("\n****ALERT: Everyone.***");
            System.out.println("An " +
                fromPerson.personType() + ": " +
                    fromPerson.getName()     + " is trying to
```

```
                           send some messages.");
        }
    }
}
```

// Person.java

```java
// The abstract class-Person
abstract class Person {

    protected Mediator mediator;
    protected String name;

    public String getName() {
        return name;
    }

    // Constructor
    public Person(Mediator mediator) {
        this.mediator = mediator;
    }

    public void sendMessage(Person toEmp, String msg) throws
                          InterruptedException {
        mediator.connectEmployees(this, toEmp, msg);
    }

    public abstract String personType();

    public void receiveMessage(Person fromEmp, String msg) {
        System.out.println(this.name + " has read " +
                          fromEmp.getName() + "'s message.");
    }
}
```

// Employee.java

```java
class Employee extends Person {
    public Employee(Mediator mediator, String name) {
        super(mediator);
        this.name = name;
    }

    @Override
    public String personType() {
        return "Employee";
    }

}
```

// Outsider.java

```java
// Unknown participant-an outsider.
class Outsider extends Person {
    // Constructor
    public Outsider(Mediator mediator, String name) {
        super(mediator);
        this.name = name;
    }

    @Override
    public String personType() {
        return "Outsider";
    }

}
```

// Client.java

```java
class Client {

    public static void main(String[] args) throws
                            InterruptedException {

        System.out.println("***Mediator Pattern Demonstration-1.***\n");

        ChatServer mediator = new ChatServer();
```

```
Person amit = new Employee(mediator, "Amit");
Person sohel = new Employee(mediator, "Sohel");
Person joseph = new Outsider(mediator, "Joseph");

// Registering participants
mediator.register(amit);
mediator.register(sohel);
mediator.register(joseph);
// Displaying the participant's list
mediator.displayDetail();

System.out.println("Communication starts among participants...");
amit.sendMessage(sohel, "Hi Sohel, can we discuss the mediator
                 pattern?");
amit.sendMessage(joseph, "Hi Joseph, how do you do?");
sohel.sendMessage(amit, "Hi Amit. Yup, we can discuss now.");
joseph.sendMessage(amit, "Hello, friend.");

// Another employee-Todd. He does not register
// to the mediator.
Person todd = new Employee(mediator, "Todd");

// Todd is an employee, but not a registered user.
// So, he cannot send a message to a registered
// user. For the same reason, he cannot receive any
// message from a registered user.

todd.sendMessage(joseph, "Hello Joseph...");
amit.sendMessage(todd, "Hello Todd...");

// An outsider person tries to participate
Person jack = new Outsider(mediator, "Jack");

// This message also cannot reach Joseph,
 // because Jack is not the registered user.
jack.sendMessage(joseph, "Hello Joseph...");

    }
}
```

```
***Mediator Pattern Demonstration-1.***

At present, the registered employees are:
Amit
Sohel
Joseph
Communication starts among participants...
Amit posts: Hi Sohel, can we discuss the mediator pattern?
at:2021-10-05T13:11:43.860266
Sohel has read Amit's message.
Amit posts: Hi Joseph, how do you do? at:2021-10-05T13:11:44.870799500
Joseph has read Amit's message.
Sohel posts: Hi Amit. Yup, we can discuss now. at:2021-10-0
5T13:11:45.880435500
Amit has read Sohel's message.
Joseph posts: Hello, friend. at:2021-10-05T13:11:46.891890900
Amit has read Joseph's message.
```

****ALERT: Everyone.***An Employee: Todd is trying to send some messages.
Amit, you cannot send the message to Todd.He/she is NOT a registered user.

****ALERT: Everyone.***An Outsider: Jack is trying to send some messages.

Analysis

Note that only registered users can communicate with each other and post messages successfully. The mediator does not allow others into the system. (Notice the last few lines of the output).

POINT TO REMEMBER

You should not assume that there should be always one-to-one communication. This is because the GoF book says that a mediator replaces many-to-many interaction with one-to-many interaction. But in this chapter, I assume that these are private messages and thus should not be broadcasted to everyone, so I show you an example where the mediator sends the messages to an intended receiver only. The mediator broadcasts the messages to warn others only when an outsider (or an unregistered person) tries to post messages on this chat server.

Additional Implementation

Here's another implementation in which I add the following constraint: once a participant reads a message, the text color changes. In the second edition of the book, I showed you a modified application that could check the online status of the target receiver before a sender sends a message to a receiver. I changed the constraint because of the following reasons:

- You already get the idea that you can add the additional validation inside the mediator (more specifically inside the connectEmployees(...) method). So, I leave this exercise to you.

- This time I want to mimic another real-world scenario: WhatsApp users know that once you read a message, the text color changes. I want to demonstrate a similar application.

- I want to show an alternative design. In demonstration 1, I create and register users/participants inside the client code. In the upcoming example, I change the approach. Now a participant self-registers back to the mediator inside the constructor (see the code in bold):

```
// Constructor
    public Employee(ChatServer chatServer, String name) {
        this.chatServer = chatServer;
        this.name = name;
        chatServer.registerEmployee(this);
    }
```

To make this implementation short and simple, this time I do not use an interface/ abstract class. The four participants, ChatServer, Employee, Text, and Client, are concrete classes. You can easily guess that ChatServer plays the role of the mediator. Since the overall intent is similar to demonstration 1, you can directly jump into the code.

Demonstration 2

All classes are inside the package jdp3e.mediator.implementation_2. Here is the implementation:

```java
import java.time.LocalDateTime;
import java.util.ArrayList;
import java.util.List;

// Mediator
// ChatServer.java
class ChatServer {
    Text text;
    List<Employee> employees;

    public ChatServer() {
        employees = new ArrayList<Employee>();
    }

    public void registerEmployee(Employee employee) {
        employees.add(employee);
    }

    public void registerText(Text text) {
        this.text = text;

    }

    public void displayEmployees() {
        System.out.println("At present, the registered employees are:");
        for (Employee emp : employees) {
            System.out.println(emp.getName());
        }
    }
```

```java
public void postMessage(Employee fromEmp, Employee toEmp,
                String msg) throws InterruptedException {
    // Include some validation logic-if necessary

    // Posting the message
    System.out.println(fromEmp.getName() + " posts: " +
                    msg + " at:" + LocalDateTime.now());
    text.makeDefaultColor();
    toEmp.receiveMessage(fromEmp, msg);

     // Some logic (skipped) to ensure that
     // the message is received and read.

    text.makeBlueText();
    }

}
```

// Employee.java

```java
class Employee {

    private ChatServer chatServer;
    protected String name;

    public String getName() {
        return name;
    }

    // Constructor
    public Employee(ChatServer chatServer, String name) {
        this.chatServer = chatServer;
        this.name = name;
        chatServer.registerEmployee(this);
    }

     public void sendMessage(Employee toEmp, String msg)
     throws InterruptedException {
        chatServer.postMessage(this, toEmp, msg);
    }
```

```java
    public void receiveMessage(Employee fromEmp, String msg){
        System.out.println(this.name + " has read " +
                    fromEmp.getName() + "'s message now.");
    }

}
```

// Text.java

```java
class Text {
    private ChatServer chatServer;
    String color;

    public Text(ChatServer chatServer, String color) {
        this.chatServer = chatServer;
        this.color=color;
        // self-registering back to the
        // mediator(chatServer)
        chatServer.registerText(this);

    }

    public void makeDefaultColor() {
        System.out.println("Message text has a default
                        color: "+ color);
    }

    public void makeBlueText() {
        System.out.println("***Message text becomes blue.***\n");
    }
}

class Client {

    public static void main(String[] args) throws
                        InterruptedException {

        System.out.println("***Mediator Pattern Demonstration-2.***\n");

        ChatServer mediator = new ChatServer();

        Employee amit = new Employee(mediator, "Amit");
```

```
Employee sohel = new Employee(mediator, "Sohel");
Employee kate = new Employee(mediator, "Kate");
Text text = new Text(mediator, "black");

// Displaying the participant's list
mediator.displayEmployees();

System.out.println("\nCommunication starts among participants...");
amit.sendMessage(sohel, "Hi Sohel, can we discuss the mediator
                    pattern?");
sohel.sendMessage(amit, "Hi Amit. Yup, we can discuss now.");
amit.sendMessage(kate, "Hi Kate!");

    }
}
```

Output

Here's the new output:

```
***Mediator Pattern Demonstration-2.***

At present, the registered employees are:
Amit
Sohel
Kate

Communication starts among participants...
Amit posts: Hi Sohel, can we discuss the mediator pattern? at:2021-10-0
4T14:44:16.036158800
```
Message text has a default color: black
```
Sohel has read Amit's message now.
```
Message text becomes blue.
```
Sohel posts: Hi Amit. Yup, we can discuss now. at:2021-10-0
4T14:44:16.037156100
```
Message text has a default color: black
```
Amit has read Sohel's message now.
```
Message text becomes blue.

```
Amit posts: Hi Kate! at:2021-10-04T14:44:16.037156100
Message text has a default color: black
Kate has read Amit's message now.
***Message text becomes blue.***
```

Note   A few lines of the previous output are bold. They are used to demonstrate the impact of the modified program (demonstration 2).

Analysis

You can see that once a participant reads the message, the text color changes to blue. Applications such as WhatsApp follow a similar principle.

Q&A Session

23.1 Why are you complicating things? In demonstration 1, each of the participants could talk to each other directly, and you could bypass the use of a mediator. Is this correct?

In this example, you have only three *registered* participants and the mediator allows them only to communicate with each other. So, it may appear that since the participants are only three, they could communicate with each other directly. But you know that an organization can have many more employees in general.

In demonstration 1, you see that before sending a message to a target receiver, the mediator checks whether they are a registered user or not. In addition, it also checks whether the sender belongs to the same organization or is an outsider. So, you understand that a mediator can perform this kind of validation. Let's assume that you want an additional constraint:

- A participant can send a message to a target participant if and only if the target participant stays in online mode only (which is the common scenario for a chat server).

If you do not use a Mediator pattern, it is not sufficient to check whether the participant is a valid user or not; in addition to this, you need to check the target recipient's online status before you post a message. And if the number of participants keeps growing, can you imagine the complexity of the system? A mediator can rescue you from such a scenario because you can put the validation criteria inside the mediator. Figures 23-4 and 23-5 depict the scenario better.

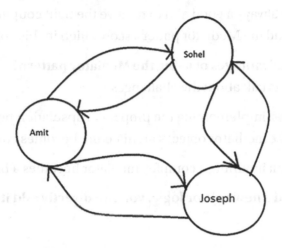

Figure 23-4. *Case 1: Without using a mediator*

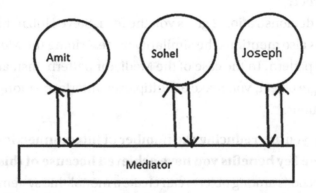

Figure 23-5. *Case 2: With a mediator*

23.2 What are the advantages of using the Mediator pattern?

Here are some advantages:

- You can reduce the complexity of objects communicating in a system.

- The pattern promotes loose coupling so objects can be reused.

- The pattern reduces the number of subclasses in the system.

- You replace a many-to-many relationship with a one-to-many relationship, so the code is much easier to read and understand. And as an obvious effect of this, maintenance becomes easier.

- You can provide a centralized control with this pattern.

- In short, it is always a good aim to remove the tight coupling from your code, and the Mediator pattern scores high in this context.

23.3 What are the disadvantages of using the Mediator pattern?

The following points talk about the challenges:

- In some cases, implementing the proper encapsulation becomes tricky, and the mediator object's architecture becomes complex.

- Sometimes maintaining a complex mediator becomes a big concern.

23.4 If you need to add a new rule or logic, you can directly add it to the mediator. Is this correct?

Yes.

23.5 I am finding some similarities between the Facade pattern and the Mediator pattern. Is this correct?

Yes. I know that demonstration 2 gives you the idea. Steve Holzner in his book *Design Pattern for Dummies* also mentions the similarity by describing the Mediator pattern as a multiplexed Facade pattern. In the case of the Mediator pattern, instead of working with an interface of a single object, you make a multiplexed interface among multiple objects to do smooth transitions.

23.6 In this pattern, you are reducing the number of interconnections among various objects. What are the key benefits you have achieved because of this reduction?

More interconnections among objects can create a monolithic system that becomes difficult to change (because the behaviors are distributed among many objects). As a side effect, you may need to create many subclasses to bring those changes into the system.

23.7 In demonstration 1, you used `Thread.sleep(1000)`. What is the reason behind this code?

Good catch. It is not necessary so you can ignore it. I use it to mimic a real-life scenario. I assume that participants are posting the messages after reading them properly, and this activity takes a minimum of 1 second.

23.8 Can I conclude the following: if a class calls methods from multiple objects, it is a mediator?

Not at all. You must note the key purpose of a mediator is to simplify the complex communications among objects in a system. Always keep in mind the GoF definition and the corresponding concepts.

23.9 In demonstration 1, the send methods for mediator and persons (i.e., employees/outsiders) are different. One is `connectEmployees(...)` and the other is `sendMessage(...)`. Do I need to follow any specific naming convention?

Both methods can have the same name, but I want you to note that it is not mandatory.

23.10 I understand that both the Mediator pattern and the Observer pattern promote one-to-many communications. How should I distinguish between these two?

Remember that the mediator encapsulates the complex communication between objects. So, once it sends a notification to the registered objects, those objects also talk about their state changes to the mediator and the mediator can act accordingly. But in the case of the Observer pattern, once a subject sends a notification to multiple objects, it does not care about their state changes.

CHAPTER 24

Visitor Pattern

This chapter covers the Visitor pattern.

GoF Definition

It represents an operation to be performed on the elements of an object structure. The Visitor pattern lets you define a new operation without changing the classes of the elements on which it operates.

Concept

This pattern can be used in many different scenarios. Using this pattern, you often add new operations to an object without modifying its class definition. To achieve this, you separate an algorithm from the object structure. This may sound surprising to you, but it is one of the key usages of this pattern. This pattern also promotes the Open/Closed Principle.

Note This is another design pattern that may seem difficult to understand at the beginning. I'll make it simple for you by excluding the "object structure" in demonstration 1. But once you understand this implementation, it will be easier for you to understand demonstration 2 where you can experience the true power of this design pattern. In demonstration 2, I combine it with the Composite pattern. Q&A 24.8 discusses the concept of the object structure in brief.

You can think of an object structure as a container. It can be helpful to think of it like a tree structure where different objects (nodes) are arranged together to form the tree. A visitor object traverses each node in the tree and captures its state. Once the visitor

© Vaskaran Sarcar 2022
V. Sarcar, *Java Design Patterns*, https://doi.org/10.1007/978-1-4842-7971-7_24

captures the state, you call the visitor-specific method. You'll learn this in detail through the different implementations in this chapter. But note a simple fact: if you deal with only one element, there is no need to create an object structure. This is why I made demonstration 1 for you.

To understand this pattern, let's consider a simple scenario. Suppose you have a tree structure where each node in the tree has methods that work differently. But your customer wants you to add more methods or update these methods (e.g., the top management of an organization changes the "promotion criteria" or the "appraisal process" frequently). You can accept this customer request as a one-off, but if your client passes a similar request multiple times and very often, will it be possible for you to introduce methods like this in each possible case, particularly when the overall code structure is very big and complex? Also, in a tree structure, if it is a branch node, can you imagine the impact of these changes across other nodes?

So, you may think of some way to handle your fickle-minded customers. The Visitor pattern can help you in a situation like this. You'll see such an implementation in demonstration 1.

Real-Life Example

Think of a taxi-booking scenario. When the taxi arrives at your door and you enter the vehicle, the taxi takes control of the transportation. It can take you to your destination through a new route that you are not familiar with, and in the worst case, it can alter the destination (which is a case generated due to improper use of the Visitor pattern).

Computer World Example

This pattern is useful when public APIs need to support *plug-in* operations. Clients can then perform their intended operations on a class (with the visiting class) without modifying the source. Here is another example for you:

- When you use the interface `javax.lang.model.element.ElementVisitor<R, P>` (where R is the return type of the visitor's method and P is the type of the additional parameter to the visitor's method), you follow this pattern. The JDK documentation says the following about it:

"A visitor of program elements, in the style of the visitor design pattern. Classes implementing this interface are used to operate on an element when the kind of element is unknown at compile time. When a visitor is passed to an element's accept method, the visitXyz *method most applicable to that element is invoked. ..."*

Implementation

I told you that you will see different implementations of the Visitor pattern in this chapter. Let's start with an example that follows the core theory of this pattern. In the next example, I enhance the example to demonstrate the real power of this pattern.

In common implementations of the Visitor pattern, you see the presence of an "object structure with multiple nodes." In such cases, remember the key steps, which are summarized as follows:

- There are two inheritance hierarchies: one is used for the existing objects hierarchy and the other one is used for the visitor hierarchy.

- A visitor visits each object one by one in this object structure

- When the visitor visits an object, that object invokes a specific method defined in the visitor.

- During this invocation, the object passes itself as an argument.

- In each object, there is an accept method. This method accepts the visitor as an argument. It helps an object invoke the particular method of the visitor. Here is a general format for this (the important portions are in bold):

```
public void acceptMethod(Visitor visitor){
        visitor.specificVisitorMethod(this);
    }
```

- When you need a new operation/functionality, you introduce another implementor of the visitor interface and implement the operation as per your need.

In demonstration 1, the concrete class `IntegerProcessor` implements the interface `NumberProcessor`. Inside the `IntegerProcessor` class is an integer called `number`. When you create an instance of this class, it is initialized with a value, say 5.

Now suppose you want to update this initialized value and display it. You can do it in different ways. For example, you can add a setter method inside `IntegerProcessor` to perform your job, or you can use the Visitor pattern, which I am about to explain.

Let's assume you opt for a setter method that may look something like the following:

```
public void setNumber(int newValue){
        number=newValue;
    }
```

But this approach will not work if you tag the `final` keyword with the number. We often use the `final` keyword to promote immutability. So, if you need to update a fixed number and use it as a variable, you need to write some intelligent code. *In a case like this, you may want to use the Visitor pattern where you do not alter the actual number, but modify the associated value based on your need.* To demonstrate a simple case study, in the following implementation, you increase the number by adding 10 to it using the Visitor design pattern.

The first and foremost thing for you to notice is the presence of the following method inside the `IntegerProcessor` class:

```
public void acceptVisitor(Visitor visitor){
        visitor.visitNumber(this);
    }
```

It gives you a clue that this method allows a `Visitor` type to do some intended work. It also indicates that there must be a method named `visitNumber(…)` inside the `Visitor` type. Let's see the `Visitor` hierarchy now:

```
interface Visitor {
    // The method to visit the IntegerProcessor.
    void visitNumber(IntegerProcessor myInt);
}
```

```java
class IncrementorVisitor implements Visitor {
    @Override
    public void visitNumber(IntegerProcessor myInt)      {

        System.out.println("The flag value is:"+ myInt.getNumber());
        System.out.println("Incrementing it by 10.");
        int temp=myInt.getNumber()+10;
        System.out.println("The new value is:"+ temp);
        // Remaining code, if any
    }
}
```

Notice that the visitNumber(…) method accepts an IntegerProcessor argument and does some work to fulfil its need. Here you increase the number by 10. This is why this code snippet in the client code

```java
NumberProcessor targetInteger = new IntegerProcessor();
Visitor visitor = new IncrementorVisitor();
targetInteger.acceptVisitor(visitor);
```

can produce the following output:

```
The flag value is:5
Incrementing it by 10.
The new value is:15
```

What is the benefit of using this approach? You'll understand it better once you cover all of the demonstrations in this chapter. For now, the first thing to notice is in the current situation, if you need one more different operation that can double the number, you may use another visitor, say DoubleMakerVisitor, and you can write something like the following:

```java
class DoubleMakerVisitor implements Visitor {
    @Override
    public void visitNumber(IntegerProcessor myInt)      {
        System.out.println("The flag value is:"+ myInt.getNumber());
        System.out.println("Multiplying it by 2.");
        int temp=myInt.getNumber() *2;
```

```
        System.out.println("The new value is:"+ temp);
        // Remaining code, if any
    }
}
```

And once you append the following two more lines (shown in bold) in the client code as follows

```
NumberProcessor targetInteger = new IntegerProcessor();
Visitor visitor = new IncrementorVisitor();
targetInteger.acceptVisitor(visitor);
visitor = new DoubleMakerVisitor();
targetInteger.acceptVisitor(visitor);
```

you get the following output:

```
The flag value is:5
Incrementing it by 10.
The new value is:15
The flag value is:5
Multiplying it by 2.
The new value is:10
```

Now you can see an advantage: when you include the operation to double the number, you do not add the behavior inside the NumberProcessor hierarchy. Notice that in the first case, you add 10 to a number and later, you make a double of the number. But inside the IntegerProcessor class, you did not add an additional method when you added the new behavior.

Similarly, if you need any more operations, you can add the intended operation in the Visitor hierarchy instead of adding it to the NumberProcessor hierarchy. As a result, you get a greater benefit: you do not need to alter existing code (the NumberProcessor hierarchy in this example) and thus you can avoid retesting it.

Now look at the complete demonstration before we further discuss the pros and cons of this approach.

Class Diagram

Figure 24-1 shows the important parts of the class diagram.

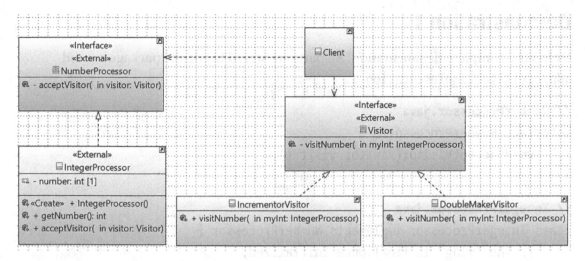

Figure 24-1. *Class diagram*

Package Explorer View

Figure 24-2 shows the high-level structure of the program.

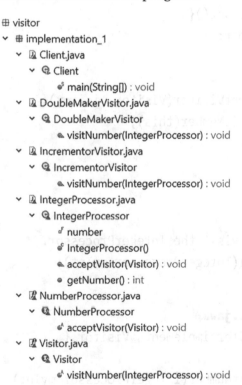

Figure 24-2. *Package Explorer view*

Demonstration 1

Here's the complete demonstration. All parts are stored inside the package named jdp3e.visitor.implementation_1.

```java
// NumberProcessor.java
interface NumberProcessor {
    void acceptVisitor(Visitor visitor);
}
```

```java
// IntegerProcessor.java
class IntegerProcessor implements NumberProcessor {
    // The "flag" is final.Once initialized,
    // it should not be changed.
    private final int number;
    public IntegerProcessor(){
        number=5;//Initial or default value
    }
    public int getNumber(){
        return number;
    }
    @Override
    public void acceptVisitor(Visitor visitor){
        visitor.visitNumber(this);
    }
}
```

```java
// Visitor.java
interface Visitor {
    //The method to visit the IntegerProcessor.
    void visitNumber(IntegerProcessor myInt);
}
```

```java
// IncrementorVisitor.java
class IncrementorVisitor implements Visitor {
    @Override
    public void visitNumber(IntegerProcessor myInt)      {
```

```
        System.out.println("The flag value is:"+
                                myInt.getNumber());
        System.out.println("Incrementing it by 10.");
        int temp=myInt.getNumber()+10;
        System.out.println("The new value is:"+ temp);
        // Remaining code, if any
    }
}
```

```
// DoubleMakerVisitor.java
class DoubleMakerVisitor implements Visitor {
    @Override
    public void visitNumber(IntegerProcessor myInt)     {
        System.out.println("The flag value is:"+ myInt.getNumber());
        System.out.println("Multiplying it by 2.");
        int temp=myInt.getNumber() *2;
        System.out.println("The new value is:"+ temp);
        // Remaining code, if any
    }
}
```

```
// Client.java
class Client {
    public static void main(String[] args) {
        System.out.println("***Visitor Pattern Demonstration-1***\n");
        NumberProcessor targetInteger = new
                                IntegerProcessor();
        System.out.println("Testing the IncrementorVisitor now.");
        Visitor visitor = new IncrementorVisitor();
        targetInteger.acceptVisitor(visitor);

        System.out.println("\nTesting the DoubleMakerVisitor now.");
        visitor = new DoubleMakerVisitor();
        targetInteger.acceptVisitor(visitor);
    }
}
```

521

```
***Visitor Pattern Demonstration-1***

Testing the IncrementorVisitor now.
The flag value is:5
Incrementing it by 10.
The new value is:15

Testing the DoubleMakerVisitor now.
The flag value is:5
Multiplying it by 2.
The new value is:10
```

Analysis

Notice that to achieve the goal, in the previous example, you separate the functionality implementations (i.e., algorithms) from the original class hierarchy. This approach helps you add the new functionality without altering the existing code (the NumberProcessor hierarchy) and thus avoid retesting it.

Using Visitor Pattern and Composite Pattern Together

In Demonstration 1, you saw a simple example of the Visitor design. Next is another implementation, but this time it's combined with the Composite pattern.

Let's consider the example of the Composite design pattern from Chapter 13. In that example, there is a college with two different departments. Each department has one head of department (HOD) and multiple teachers/lecturers. All of these HODs report to the principal of the college. I won't explain the college structure in detail again, because it is the same as described in Chapter 13.

- The Mathematics teachers are M.Jacob and M.Rustom. The Computer Science and Engineering (CSE) teachers are C.Kate, C.Jones, and C.Proctor. These lecturers do not supervise anyone, so they are treated as leaf nodes in the following tree diagrams.

- S.Som is the Principal of the college, and he holds the highest position. Two HODs named S.Das (the HOD of Mathematics) and V.Sarcar (the HOD of CSE) report to the Principal. The HODs and the Principal are non-leaf nodes.

Figure 24-3 shows the sample tree diagram for your immediate reference.

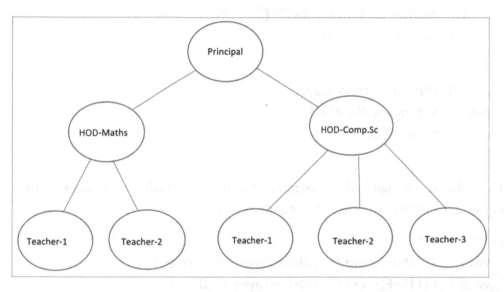

Figure 24-3. *Tree structure taken from Chapter 13 (Figure 13-1)*

Now suppose, as per the recommendation of higher management, the principal of the college wants to promote some employees. Let's say that teaching experience is the only criteria to promote someone, but the criteria vary among senior teachers (branch nodes) and junior teachers (leaf nodes) as follows: for a junior teacher, the minimum criterion for promotion is 5 years, and for senior teachers, it is 15 years.

You understand that the promotion criterion may change in the future and there may be more requirements from the higher authorities. So, the Visitor pattern is a perfect fit to fulfill the current requirement. This is why in the upcoming example, you add a new attribute and a new method in the abstract class Employee as follows:

```
// New field for this example.
// It is tagged with "final", so a visitor cannot modify it.
protected final double experience;

// Newly added for this example
public abstract void acceptVisitor(Visitor visitor);
```

You understand that the concrete implementors of the Employee class (SeniorEmployee and JuniorEmployee) need to override this method as per this requirement.

In addition, the getter methods are also present in the Employee class:

```
// Gets the years of experience
public double getExperience() {
    return experience;
}

// Get the name of employee
public String getName() {
    return name;
}
```

Following the design in demonstration 1, you call the visitor interface Visitor. This interface has two overloaded methods as follows:

```
interface Visitor {
    void visitTheElement(SeniorEmployee employees);
    void visitTheElement(JuniorEmployee employee);
}
```

The promotion criteria for a senior employee and a junior employee are different. So, you see the following code (refer to the comments for easy understanding):

```
class PromotionCheckerVisitor implements Visitor {
    @Override
    public void visitTheElement(SeniorEmployee employee) {
      // We'll promote them if experience is
      // greater than 15 years
        boolean eligibleForPromotion =
          employee.getExperience() > 15 ? true : false;
        System.out.println("\t\t" + employee.getName() +
                        " is eligible for promotion? " +
                            eligibleForPromotion);
    }
```

```
@Override
public void visitTheElement(JuniorEmployee employee) {
// We'll promote them if experience is
// greater than 5 years
      boolean eligibleForPromotion =
        employee.getExperience() > 5 ? true : false;
      System.out.println("\t\t" + employee.getName() + "
                         is eligible for promotion? " +
                         eligibleForPromotion);
   }
}
```

Demonstration 2 has a container (a List data structure called participants) in the
client code. When a visitor gathers the necessary details from this college structure,
it can show the eligible candidates for promotion. This is the reason to include the
following code segment:

```
private static void checkPromotionEligibilty(List<Employee> container) {
        Visitor visitor = new PromotionCheckerVisitor();
        // Principal holds the highest position.
        // He does not need a promotion.
        System.out.println("\nChecking the eligible
                         candidates for a promotion.");
        for (Employee emp : container) {
            emp.acceptVisitor(visitor);
        }
    }
```

Notice that the visitor collects the data one by one from the original college structure
without making any modifications to it. It analyzes the data before presenting the final
result. To understand this visually, you can follow the arrows in the upcoming figures.
*The principal is at the top of the organization; so, assume that at present no promotion is
required for him. (Do not worry! In demonstration 3, we'll promote him too).*

Step 1

Figure 24-4 shows step 1.

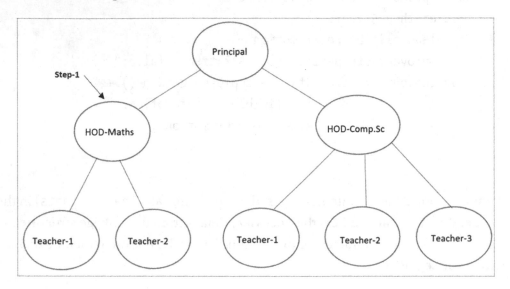

Figure 24-4. *Step 1*

Step 2

Figure 24-5 shows step 2.

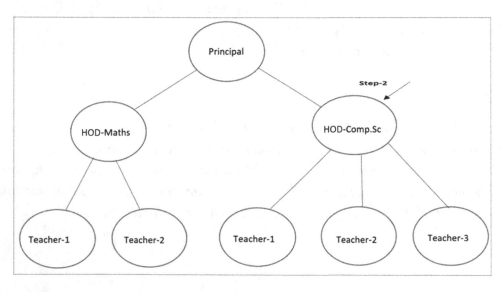

Figure 24-5. *Step 2*

Step 3

Figure 24-6 shows step 3.

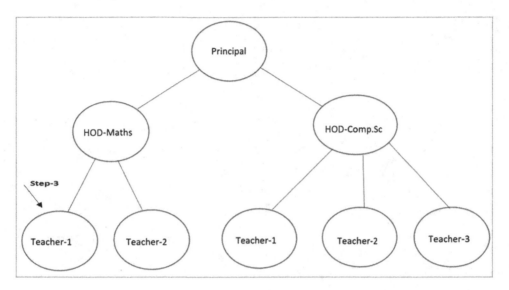

Figure 24-6. *Step 3*

Step 4

Figure 24-7 shows step 4.

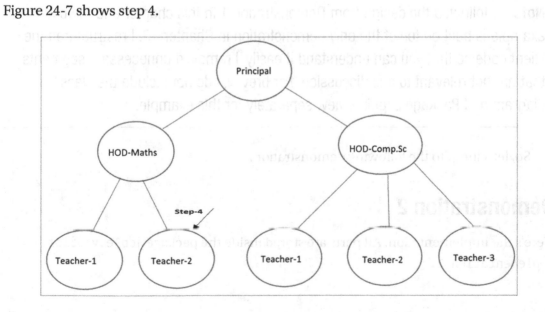

Figure 24-7. *Step 4*

Step 5

Figure 24-8 shows step 5.

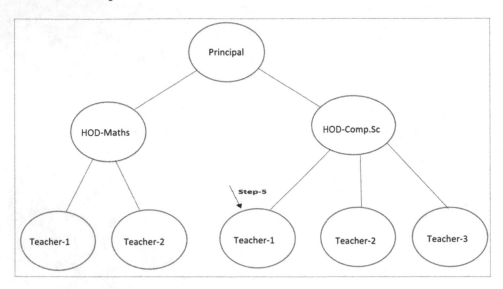

Figure 24-8. *Step 5*

And so on...

Note   I followed the design from Demonstration 1 in this chapter and the code example is built on top of the only demonstration in Chapter 13. I restructured the client code so that you can understand it easily. I removed unnecessary segments that are not relevant to this discussion. For brevity, I do not include the class diagram and Package Explorer view separately for this example.

So, let's jump to the following demonstration.

Demonstration 2

Here's the implementation. All parts are stored inside the package `jdp3e.visitor.implementation_2`.

```
import java.util.ArrayList;
import java.util.List;
```

// Employee.java
```
import java.util.ArrayList;
import java.util.List;
abstract class Employee {
    protected String name;
    protected String designation;
    protected int subordinatesCount;
    protected List<Employee> subordinates;
    // New field for this example.
    // It is tagged with "final", so a visitor
    // cannot modify it.
    protected final double experience;

    // Constructor
    public Employee(String name, String designation, double experience) {
        this.name = name;
        this.designation = designation;
        this.subordinatesCount = 0;
        this.experience = experience;
        subordinates = new ArrayList<Employee>();
    }

    protected abstract void printStructures();

    protected abstract int getSubordinatesCount();

    protected abstract void addEmployee(Employee e);

    protected abstract void removeEmployee(Employee e);

    // Gets the years of experience
    public double getExperience() {
        return experience;
    }
}
```

```java
    // Get the name of employee
    public String getName() {
        return name;
    }

    public abstract void acceptVisitor(Visitor visitor);
}
```

// SeniorEmployee.java

```java
// It is a non-leaf node
class SeniorEmployee extends Employee {
    public SeniorEmployee(String name, String designation,
                          double experience) {
        super(name, designation, experience);
    }

    @Override
    protected void printStructures() {
        System.out.println("\t" + this.name + " is a " +
                    this.designation + ". Experience:" +
                    this.experience);
        for (Employee e : subordinates) {
            e.printStructures();
        }
    }

    @Override
    protected int getSubordinatesCount() {
        subordinatesCount = subordinates.size();
        for (Employee e : subordinates) {
            subordinatesCount += e.getSubordinatesCount();
        }
        return subordinatesCount;
    }

    @Override
    protected void addEmployee(Employee e) {
```

```java
        subordinates.add(e);
    }

    @Override
    protected void removeEmployee(Employee e) {
        subordinates.remove(e);
    }

    @Override
    public void acceptVisitor(Visitor visitor) {
        visitor.visitTheElement(this);
    }
}

// JuniorEmployee.java
class JuniorEmployee extends Employee {
    public JuniorEmployee(String name, String designation,
                          double experience) {
        super(name, designation, experience);
    }

    @Override
    protected void printStructures() {
        System.out.println("\t\t" + this.name + " is a " +
                    this.designation + ". Experience: " +
                this.experience);
    }

    @Override
    protected int getSubordinatesCount() {
        return subordinatesCount;// Always 0
    }

    @Override
    protected void addEmployee(Employee e) {
        // Empty method
    }
```

```java
    @Override
    protected void removeEmployee(Employee e) {
        // Empty method
    }

    @Override
    public void acceptVisitor(Visitor visitor) {
        visitor.visitTheElement(this);
    }
}
```

// Visitor.java

```java
interface Visitor {
    void visitTheElement(SeniorEmployee employees);

    void visitTheElement(JuniorEmployee employee);
    //void visitTheElement(Employee employee);
}
```

// PromotionCheckerVisitor.java

```java
class PromotionCheckerVisitor implements Visitor {
    @Override
    public void visitTheElement(SeniorEmployee employee) {
        // We'll promote them if experience is
         // greater than 15 years
        boolean eligibleForPromotion =
            employee.getExperience() > 15 ? true : false;
        System.out.println("\t\t" + employee.getName() + "
                        is eligible for promotion? " +
                        eligibleForPromotion);
    }

    @Override
    public void visitTheElement(JuniorEmployee employee) {
        // We'll promote them if experience is
         // greater than 5 years
        boolean eligibleForPromotion =
```

```
                employee.getExperience() > 5 ? true : false;
            System.out.println("\t\t" + employee.getName() + "
                            is eligible for promotion? " +
                            eligibleForPromotion);
        }

}
```

// Client.java

```
import java.util.ArrayList;
import java.util.List;

class Client {
    public static void main(String[] args) {
        System.out.println("***Composite Pattern and
                        Visitor Pattern Demonstration.***");

        Employee hodMath = formMathDept();
        Employee hodCompSc = formComputerScDept();
        Employee principal = formPrincipal(hodMath, hodCompSc);
        printCollegeStructure(principal);

        List<Employee> participants =
            createContainer(principal, hodMath, hodCompSc);
        checkPromotionEligibilty(participants);
    }

    private static void printCollegeStructure(Employee principal) {
        // Printing the leaf-nodes and branches
        // in the same way i.e. in each case, we
        // are calling printStructures() method.

        System.out.println("The details of the Principal object:");
        // Prints the complete college structure
        principal.printStructures();

    }
```

```
    private static Employee formComputerScDept() {
        // Three lecturers other than HOD work
        // in the Computer Science Department.

        Employee cseTeacher1 = new JuniorEmployee(
                            "C.Kate","Lecturer", 8.2);
        Employee cseTeacher2 = new JuniorEmployee(
                            "C.Jones", "Lecturer", 4.5);
        Employee cseTeacher3 = new JuniorEmployee(
                            "C.Proctor", "Lecturer", 6);
        Employee hodCompSc = new SeniorEmployee(
                        "Mr. V.Sarcar", "HOD(CSE)", 15.5);

        // Teachers of Computer Science
        // directly reports to HOD-CSE
        hodCompSc.addEmployee(cseTeacher1);
        hodCompSc.addEmployee(cseTeacher2);
        hodCompSc.addEmployee(cseTeacher3);
        return hodCompSc;
    }

    private static Employee formMathDept() {
        // Two lecturers other than HOD work
        // in the Mathematics department.

        Employee mathTeacher1 = new JuniorEmployee(
                        "M.Jacob", "Lecturer", 7.5);
        Employee mathTeacher2 = new JuniorEmployee(
                        "M.Rustom", "Lecturer", 3);
        Employee hodMath = new SeniorEmployee(
                        "Mrs.S.Das", "HOD(Math)", 12.5);
        // Teachers of Mathematics directly
        // reports to HOD-Mathematics
        hodMath.addEmployee(mathTeacher1);
        hodMath.addEmployee(mathTeacher2);
        return hodMath;
    }
```

```
private static Employee formPrincipal(Employee hodMath,
                                Employee hodCompSc) {
    // Principal of the college
    Employee principal = new SeniorEmployee(
                        "Dr.S.Som", "Principal", 21);
    // The Principal is on top of the college.
    // The HOD(Mathematics) and HOD(Computer Sc.)
    // directly report to him.
    principal.addEmployee(hodMath);
    principal.addEmployee(hodCompSc);
    return principal;
}

private static List<Employee> createContainer(Employee
    principal, Employee hodMath, Employee hodCompSc) {
    List<Employee> employeeContainer = new
                            ArrayList<Employee>();
    // For employees who directly reports to Principal
    for (Employee e : principal.subordinates) {
        employeeContainer.add(e);
    }
    // For employees who directly reports to HOD(Math)
    for (Employee e : hodMath.subordinates) {
        employeeContainer.add(e);
    }
    // For employees who directly reports to
     // HOD(Comp.Sc)
    for (Employee e : hodCompSc.subordinates) {
        employeeContainer.add(e);
    }
    return employeeContainer;
}

private static void checkPromotionEligibilty(
                    List<Employee> container) {
    Visitor visitor = new PromotionCheckerVisitor();
    // Principal holds the highest position.
```

```
            // He does not need a promotion.
            System.out.println("\nChecking the eligible
                                candidates for a promotion.");
            for (Employee emp : container) {
                emp.acceptVisitor(visitor);
            }
        }

}
```

Output

Here's the output. Some portions are in bold to show you that the visitor was able to complete the job successfully.

```
***Composite Pattern and Visitor Pattern Demonstration.***
The details of the Principal object:
    Dr.S.Som is a Principal. Experience:21.0
    Mrs.S.Das is a HOD(Math). Experience:12.5
        M.Jacob is a Lecturer. Experience: 7.5
        M.Rustom is a Lecturer. Experience: 3.0
    Mr. V.Sarcar is a HOD(CSE). Experience:15.5
        C.Kate is a Lecturer. Experience: 8.2
        C.Jones is a Lecturer. Experience: 4.5
        C.Proctor is a Lecturer. Experience: 6.0
```

Checking the eligible candidates for a promotion.
       Mrs.S.Das is eligible for promotion? false
       Mr. V.Sarcar is eligible for promotion? true
       M.Jacob is eligible for promotion? true
       M.Rustom is eligible for promotion? false
       C.Kate is eligible for promotion? true
       C.Jones is eligible for promotion? false
       C.Proctor is eligible for promotion? True

Analysis

In order to avoid modifying the original data, in the Employee class you see the getter methods only. It's a better practice in an example like this. But you must remember that this is optional for you.

Demonstration 3

The point of Demonstration 2 is to help you understand the usage of the Composite pattern and the Visitor pattern together. Since I made this demonstration on top of the demonstration from Chapter 13, I did not make big changes.

I hope you have the idea now! So, it's time to refactor the code. Notice that in demonstration 2, you made a container before you traversed it using a visitor. But if you know that you can promote the principal too (say you want him to be included on the board of directors) and you'll visit all nodes of the tree, you do not need to create such a container separately. In addition, notice that this time, instead of showing subordinate counts, the focus is to investigate the potential candidates who are eligible for promotions. So, you drop the getSubordinatesCount() method and introduce a new method called getSubordinates(). By default, this method returns an empty list.

A junior employee (leaf node) does not supervise anyone. So, the JuniorEmployee class does not need to override the default implementation. But a composite node will override this method and return the list of subordinates. So, in the modified implementation, inside the SeniorEmployee class, you see the following code segment:

```
@Override
public Collection<Employee> getSubordinates(){
    return subordinates;
}
```

In demonstration 2, the visitor traverses the nodes as per the node arrangements in the container. In this demonstration, during the traversal process, once the visitor sees a composite node, it traverses all nodes associated with him. The associated output will confirm this.

There is no change in the visitor hierarchy. So, the remaining code is easy to understand. Here is the complete demonstration (the key changes are in bold). All parts are stored inside the package jdp3e.visitor.implementation_3.

// Employee.java

```java
import java.util.ArrayList;
import java.util.Collection;
import java.util.Collections;
import java.util.List;

abstract class Employee {
    protected String name;
    protected String designation;

    protected List<Employee> subordinates;
    // New field for this example.
    // It is tagged with "final", so a visitor cannot
    //   modify it.
    protected final double experience;

    // Constructor
    public Employee(String name, String designation, double experience) {
        this.name = name;
        this.designation = designation;

        this.experience = experience;
        subordinates = new ArrayList<Employee>();
    }

    protected abstract void printStructures();

    protected abstract void addEmployee(Employee e);

    protected abstract void removeEmployee(Employee e);

    // Gets the years of experience
    public double getExperience() {
        return experience;
    }
```

```java
    // Get the name of employee
    public String getName() {
        return name;
    }
    public Collection<Employee> getSubordinates(){
        return Collections.emptyList();
    }

    public abstract void acceptVisitor(Visitor visitor);
}
```

// SeniorEmployee.java

```java
// It is a non-leaf node
class SeniorEmployee extends Employee {
    public SeniorEmployee(String name, String designation,
                          double experience) {
        super(name, designation, experience);
    }

    @Override
    protected void printStructures() {
        System.out.println("\t" + this.name + " is a " +
                    this.designation + ". Experience:" +
                    this.experience);
        for (Employee e : subordinates) {
            e.printStructures();
        }
    }

    @Override
    public Collection<Employee> getSubordinates(){
        return subordinates;
    }

    @Override
    protected void addEmployee(Employee e) {
        subordinates.add(e);
    }
```

```java
    @Override
    protected void removeEmployee(Employee e) {
        subordinates.remove(e);
    }

    @Override
    public void acceptVisitor(Visitor visitor) {
        visitor.visitTheElement(this);
    }
}

// JuniorEmployee.java
class JuniorEmployee extends Employee {
    public JuniorEmployee(String name, String designation,
                          double experience) {
        super(name, designation, experience);
    }

    @Override
    protected void printStructures() {
        System.out.println("\t\t" + this.name + " is a " +
                    this.designation + ". Experience: " +
                    this.experience);
    }

    @Override
    protected void addEmployee(Employee e) {
        // Empty method
    }

    @Override
    protected void removeEmployee(Employee e) {
        // Empty method
    }

    @Override
    public void acceptVisitor(Visitor visitor) {
```

```
        visitor.visitTheElement(this);
    }

}
```

// Visitor.java

```java
interface Visitor {
    void visitTheElement(SeniorEmployee employees);
    void visitTheElement(JuniorEmployee employee);
}
```

// PromotionCheckerVisitor.java

```java
class PromotionCheckerVisitor implements Visitor {
    @Override
    public void visitTheElement(SeniorEmployee employee) {
        // We'll promote them if experience is greater
        // than 15 years
        boolean eligibleForPromotion =
            employee.getExperience() > 15 ? true : false;
        System.out.println("\t\t" + employee.getName() + "
                        is eligible for promotion? " +
                        eligibleForPromotion);
    }

    @Override
    public void visitTheElement(JuniorEmployee employee) {
        // We'll promote them if experience is greater
        // than 5 years
        boolean eligibleForPromotion =
            employee.getExperience() > 5 ? true : false;
        System.out.println("\t\t" + employee.getName() + "
                        is eligible for promotion? " +
                        eligibleForPromotion);
    }
}
```

```java
// Client.java
class Client {
    public static void main(String[] args) {
        System.out.println("***Composite Pattern and
                Visitor Pattern Modified Demonstration.***");

        Employee hodMath = formMathDept();
        Employee hodCompSc = formComputerScDept();
        Employee principal = formPrincipal(hodMath, hodCompSc);
        printCollegeStructure(principal);
        Visitor visitor = new PromotionCheckerVisitor();
        System.out.println("\nChecking potential candidates
                            for the promotion:");
         visitCandidates(principal,visitor);
    }

    private static void visitCandidates(Employee emp, Visitor visitor) {
        emp.acceptVisitor(visitor);
        emp.getSubordinates().forEach(
                        e->visitCandidates(e,visitor));
    }

    private static void printCollegeStructure(Employee principal) {
        // Printing the leaf-nodes and branches
         // in the same way
        // i.e. in each case, we
        // are calling printStructures() method.

        System.out.println("The details of the Principal object:");
        // Prints the complete college structure
        principal.printStructures();
    }

    private static Employee formComputerScDept() {
        // Three lecturers other than HOD work
        // in the Computer Science Department.

        Employee cseTeacher1 = new JuniorEmployee("C.Kate",
                                        "Lecturer", 8.2);
```

```
        Employee cseTeacher2 = new
                JuniorEmployee("C.Jones", "Lecturer", 4.5);
        Employee cseTeacher3 = new
                JuniorEmployee("C.Proctor", "Lecturer", 6);
        Employee hodCompSc = new SeniorEmployee(
                        "Mr. V.Sarcar", "HOD(CSE)", 15.5);

        // Teachers of Computer Science
        // directly reports to HOD-CSE
        hodCompSc.addEmployee(cseTeacher1);
        hodCompSc.addEmployee(cseTeacher2);
        hodCompSc.addEmployee(cseTeacher3);
        return hodCompSc;
    }

    private static Employee formMathDept() {
        // Two lecturers other than HOD work
        // in the Mathematics department.

        Employee mathTeacher1 = new JuniorEmployee(
                        "M.Jacob", "Lecturer", 7.5);
        Employee mathTeacher2 = new JuniorEmployee(
                        "M.Rustom", "Lecturer", 3);
        Employee hodMaths = new SeniorEmployee(
                        "Mrs.S.Das", "HOD(Math)", 12.5);
        // Teachers of Mathematics directly
        // reports to HOD-Mathematics
        hodMaths.addEmployee(mathTeacher1);
        hodMaths.addEmployee(mathTeacher2);
        return hodMaths;
    }

    private static Employee formPrincipal(Employee hod_Math,
                                Employee hod_CompSc) {
        // Principal of the college
        Employee principal = new SeniorEmployee("Dr.S.Som", "Principal", 21);
```

```
        // The Principal is on top of the college.
        // The HOD(Mathematics) and HOD(Computer Sc.)
        // directly report to him.

        principal.addEmployee(hod_Math);
        principal.addEmployee(hod_CompSc);
        return principal;
    }
}
```

Output

Here's the new output. It shows that you visited the nodes in a different order and this time the principal is also eligible for promotion.

```
***Composite Pattern and Visitor Pattern Modified Demonstration.***
The details of the Principal object:
    Dr.S.Som is a Principal. Experience:21.0
    Mrs.S.Das is a HOD(Math). Experience:12.5
        M.Jacob is a Lecturer. Experience: 7.5
        M.Rustom is a Lecturer. Experience: 3.0
    Mr. V.Sarcar is a HOD(CSE). Experience:15.5
        C.Kate is a Lecturer. Experience: 8.2
        C.Jones is a Lecturer. Experience: 4.5
        C.Proctor is a Lecturer. Experience: 6.0

Checking potential candidates for the promotion:
        Dr.S.Som is eligible for promotion? true
        Mrs.S.Das is eligible for promotion? false
        M.Jacob is eligible for promotion? true
        M.Rustom is eligible for promotion? false
        Mr. V.Sarcar is eligible for promotion? true
        C.Kate is eligible for promotion? true
        C.Jones is eligible for promotion? false
        C.Proctor is eligible for promotion? true
```

Q&A Session

24.1 When should you consider implementing the Visitor design pattern?

Here are some use cases to consider:

- You need to add new operations to a set of objects without changing their corresponding classes. This is the primary aim when implementing a Visitor pattern. When the operations change very often, this approach can be your savior.

- If you need to change the logic of various operations, you can simply do it through a visitor implementation.

24.2 Are there any drawbacks associated with this pattern?

Here are some drawbacks associated with this pattern:

- You can break the power of encapsulation using visitors.

- If you need to add new concrete classes to an existing architecture frequently, the visitor hierarchy becomes difficult to maintain. Suppose in demonstration 1, you want to add another concrete class in the `NumberProcessor` hierarchy now. In this case, you need to modify the visitor class hierarchy when you want to visit the newly added element.

24.3 Why are you saying that a visitor class can violate the encapsulation?

Often your visitor needs to access an object's state. To support this, you provide the getter/setter methods. Now if an object has lots of states and you expose all of them through these getters/setters, you weaken the encapsulation, because not only visitors, but other classes can use them as well.

Also, in many cases, you may see that the visitor needs to move around a composite structure to gather information and then it can modify the information. (Although in demonstration 1, I do not allow this modification). So, when you provide this kind of support, you surely violate the core aim of encapsulation.

24.4 Why does this pattern compromise encapsulation?

Here you perform some operations on a set of objects that can be heterogeneous also. And most often, your constraint is that you cannot change their corresponding classes. So, your visitor needs a way to access the members of these objects. To fulfill this requirement, you are exposing the information to the visitor.

24.5 In demonstration 2, I am seeing that in visitor interfaces, you are using the concept of method overloading. For example, you have written interface methods as follows:

```
void visitTheElement(SeniorEmployee employees);
void visitTheElement(JuniorEmployee employee);
```

It appears to me that following the GoF book, you could use something like the following:

```
void visitSeniorEmployee(SeniorEmployee employees);
void visitJuniorEmployee(JuniorEmployee employee);
```

Is this understanding correct?

Nice catch. Yes, you can do that if you do not like to use method overloading. For a beginner, it is often helpful, too.

But this example is simple, and I assume that you know the concept of method overloading. So, I do not see any harm in using this concept. You can simply remember that these interface methods should target the specific classes such as `SeniorEmployee` or `JuniorEmployee`.

24.6 Suppose in demonstration 1, I have added another concrete subclass of `NumberProcessor` **called** `RealNumberProcessor`. **How should I proceed now? Should I have another specific method in the visitor interface?**

Exactly. You need to define a new method that will be specific to this new class. So, your interface may look like the following (let's say you use method overloading here):

```
interface Visitor {
    // The method to visit the IntegerProcessor.
    void visitNumber(IntegerProcessor myInt);
    // The method to visit the RealNumberProcessor.
    void visitNumber(RealNumberProcessor myReal);
}
```

And later you need to implement this new method in the concrete visitor classes. (I know what you are thinking! Yes, following the ISP principle, you should not make a fat interface.)

24.7 Suppose I need to support new operations in the existing architecture. How should I proceed with the Visitor pattern?

For each new operation, create a new concrete implementor (or subclass) of `Visitor` and implement the operation in it. Then visit your existing structure as shown in the preceding examples. I summarize the key steps when I discuss the implementation at the beginning of this chapter.

24.8 Is creating an object structure mandatory for me?

What is an object structure? It is like a container that helps a client to visit smoothly in one shot. So, if you deal with only one element, there is no need to create an object structure. This is why I made demonstration 1 for you.

But, consider demonstration 2, where all nodes together form a tree structure. In cases like this, you can use the Visitor pattern, too. Actually, it is a versatile pattern that can be used in different situations.

CHAPTER 25

Interpreter Pattern

This chapter covers the Interpreter pattern.

GoF Definition

Given a language, it defines a representation for its grammar along with an interpreter that uses the representation to interpret sentences in the language.

Concept

This pattern plays the role of a translator, and it is often used to *evaluate sentences in a language*. So, you first need to define grammar to represent the language. Then the interpreter deals with that grammar. ***This pattern works best if the grammar is simple.***

POINTS TO NOTE

To understand this pattern, it's helpful if you are familiar with some key terms like words (or sentences), grammar, and languages in Automata, which is a big topic. A detailed discussion of this is beyond the scope of this book. For now, you simply need to know that in the formal language, an alphabet may contain an infinite number of elements, a word can be a finite sequence of letters (simply strings), and a set of all strings generated by a grammar G is called the language generated the grammar G. Normally a grammar is represented by a tuple (V, T, S, P) where V is a set of non-terminal symbols, T is a set of terminal symbols, S is the start symbol, and P is the production rules.

Consider an example. Suppose you have a grammar G=(V,T,S,P) where

V={S},

549

© Vaskaran Sarcar 2022
V. Sarcar, *Java Design Patterns*, https://doi.org/10.1007/978-1-4842-7971-7_25

T={a,b},

P={S->aSbS,S->bSaS,S->ε },

S={S};

The ε in this grammar denotes an empty string. The production rules tell you that you can substitute an S with any of aSbS, bSaS, or an empty string (ε).

On further investigation, you understand that this grammar can generate an equal number of a's and b's like ab, ba, abab, baab, and so forth. But how? The following steps show a derivation process of getting abba from this grammar. Notice that each time you substitute the leftmost variable in this example:

S

aSbS [since S->aSbS]

abS [since S->ε]

ab**bSaS** [since S->bSaS]

abbaS [since S->ε]

abba [since S->ε]

In the same way, you can generate baab from this grammar. Here are the derivation steps for another quick reference:

S

bSaS [since S->bSaS]

baS [since S->ε]

baa**SbS** [since S->aSbS]

baabS [since S->ε]

baab [since S->ε]

Each class in this pattern represents a rule in that language and it should have a method to interpret an expression. So, to handle a greater number of rules, you create a greater number of classes, and this is why the Interpreter pattern is seldom used to handle very complex grammar.

A typical structure of this pattern is often described with a diagram similar to Figure 25-1.

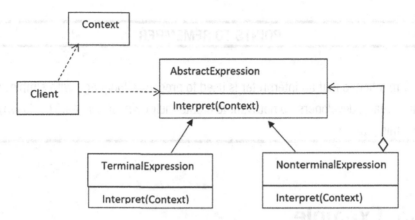

Figure 25-1. *Structure of a typical Interpreter pattern*

The terms are described as follows:

- `AbstractExpression`: Typically an interface with an `interpret` method. You need to pass a context object to this method.

- `TerminalExpression`: It is used for terminal expressions. A terminal expression does not need other expressions to interpret. They are basically leaf nodes (i.e., they do not have child nodes) in the data structure.

- `NonterminalExpression`: It is used for non-terminal expressions. It's also termed as `AlternationExpression`, `RepititionExpression`, or `SequenceExpression`. They are like composites that can contain both terminal and nonterminal expressions. When you call the `interpret` method on this, you basically call `interpret` on all of its children. To make this clear in your mind, consider a simple arithmetic expression such as `5-3`. This is a non-terminal expression where 5 and 3 are the terminal expressions with values 5 and 3, respectively. The minus (-) operator with the operands (the terminal expressions) form a non-terminal expression.

- **Context**: It holds the global information that the interpreter needs.

- **Client**: It calls the `interpret()` method. It can optionally build the syntax tree based on the rules of the language.

POINTS TO REMEMBER

It is already mentioned that an interpreter is used to process a language with simple rules or grammar. Ideally, developers do not want to create their own languages. This is why they seldom use this pattern.

Real-Life Example

Think of a translator who translates a foreign language. You can also consider music notes as grammar, where musicians play the role of interpreters.

Computer World Example

The Java compiler interprets the Java source code into bytecode that is understandable by the Java Virtual Machine. In C#, the source code is converted to Microsoft Intermediate Language (MSIL) code, which is interpreted by the Common Language Runtime. Upon execution, this MSIL is converted to native code (binary executable code) by the Just-In-Time compiler. Here is another example for you:

- If you notice the `java.util.Format` class, you will learn that this abstract class is used for formatting locale-sensitive information such as dates, messages, and numbers. So, any subclass of it can be considered to use this pattern.

Implementation

In demonstration 1, you see an example to interpret a Boolean expression. In other words, the Interpreter pattern is being used as a rule validator.

To implement this, start by defining simple grammar. The constants `true` and `false` are the terminals in this grammar and they are used to get the final value of an output.

Nonterminal symbols are the expressions that contain the following operators: and, not, and or. A client may want to know the result of a simple expression such as emp1 or they may be interested to know the value of a complex expression such as emp1 and emp2 or emp3 or emp4. So, IndividualEmployee evaluates a variable in a context and assigns a value (true or false) to each variable (emp1,emp2,emp3 or emp4). Here is the grammar for you:

```
Employee ::= IndividualEmployee| Constant | OrExp | AndExp | NotExp
AndExp ::= Employee 'and' Employee
OrExp ::= Employee 'or' Employee
NotExp ::= 'not' Employee
Constant ::= 'true' | 'false'
IndividualEmployee ::= 'emp1' | 'emp2' | 'emp3' | 'emp4'
```

The following steps show a derivation process of getting emp1 or emp2 from this grammar (the transitions are in bold and a different font):

Employee
OrExp [since Employee->OrExp]
Employee 'or' Employee [since OrExp-> Employee 'or' Employee]
IndividualEmployee 'or' Employee [since Employee-> IndividualEmployee]
IndividualEmployee 'or' **IndividualEmployee** [since Employee->
                                                    IndividualEmployee]
emp1 or IndividualEmployee [since IndividualEmployee ->emp1]
emp1 or **emp2** [since IndividualEmployee ->emp2]

Similarly, you can derive emp2 and emp4 from this grammar as follows:

Employee
AndExp [since Employee->AndExp]
Employee 'and' Employee [since AndExp-> Employee 'and' Employee]
IndividualEmployee 'and' Employee [since Employee-> IndividualEmployee]
IndividualEmployee 'and' IndividualEmployee [since Employee->
IndividualEmployee]
emp2 and IndividualEmployee [since Employee ->emp2]
emp2 and **emp4** [since IndividualEmployee ->emp4]

A client may want to know the final value of such an expression. So, in this application, you will evaluate that.

Now let's build the application. There are some important steps (which are followed in this example) to consider before you implement this pattern. They are as follows:

- Step 1: Define the rules of the language for which you want to build an interpreter.

- Step 2: Define an abstract class or an interface to represent an expression. It should contain a method to interpret an expression.

  - Step 2A: Identify terminal, non-terminal expressions, and variables. For example, in the upcoming example, the constants `true` and `false` are the terminal symbols, which are Boolean variables.

  - Step2B: Create non-terminal expression classes. Each of them calls the `interpret(...)` method on their children. For example, in the upcoming example, the `OrExpression` and `AndExpression` classes are non-terminal expression classes. In demonstration 1, you'll see that these classes implement the interface `Employee`, which has the `interpret(...)` method

  - Step2C: `IndividualEmployee` is used to evaluate a variable based on the current context. So, this class also implements the `Employee` interface and provides an implementation for the interface method.

- Step 3: Build the abstract syntax tree using these classes. You can do this inside the client code or you can create a separate class to accomplish the task.

- Step 4: The client now uses this tree to interpret a sentence.

- Step 5: Pass the context to the interpreter. It typically will have the sentences that are to be interpreted. An interpreter can also perform additional tasks using this context.

Here you instantiate different employees with their "year of experience" and current grades. For simplicity, there are four employees with four different grades: G1, G2, G3, and G4. Notice the following lines:

```
Employee emp1 = new IndividualEmployee(5,"G1");
Employee emp2 = new IndividualEmployee(10,"G2");
Employee emp3 = new IndividualEmployee(15,"G3");
Employee emp4 = new IndividualEmployee(20,"G4");
```

In this example, you want to validate some conditions against the context that says to get a promotion, an employee should have a minimum of 10 years of experience and they should be either from G2 grade or G3 grade. Once these expressions are interpreted, you will see the output in terms of a Boolean value. This is why you see the following code snippet:

```
// Minimum Criteria for promotion is:
// The year of experience is a minimum of 10 yrs. and
// Employee grade should be either G2 or G3
Context context=new Context(10,"G2","G3");
```

You have just seen that minimum experience in years and the allowed grades (for promotion) are passed to the Context class constructor. So, the following segment of code in the Context class should make sense to you:

```
private int yearofExperience;
private List<String> permissibleGrades;

public Context(int experience, String... allowedGrades) {
    this.yearofExperience = experience;
    this.permissibleGrades = new ArrayList<>();
    for (String grade : allowedGrades) {
    permissibleGrades.add(grade);
 }
}
```

In the upcoming example, you validate three different types of expressions:

- Case 1: Whether an employee is eligible for the promotion. You may need to evaluate a simple expression like emp1. In the client code, you use the method validateSingleEmployee() for this purpose.

- Case 2: Whether a combination such as emp1 or emp2, emp1 and emp2, or ! emp3 is eligible for the promotion. This is why you see the validateExpression(...) method inside the ExpressionBuilder class. In the client code, you use the method validateSimpleRules() for this purpose.

- Case 3: Finding the value of a complex expression like
  `emp1 and (emp2 or (emp3 or emp4))`. This is why you see
  the `validateComplexExpression(...)` method inside the
  `ExpressionBuilder` class. In the client code, you use the method
  `validateComplexRules()` for this purpose.

You understand that evaluating case 1 is straightforward. Evaluating case 2 is also not tough. Notice that in all these cases, the value of an expression changes if the context changes. For example, the expression `emp1 or emp3` results in `true` now. But, to get a promotion, if you change the minimum experience requirement from 10 to 16 years, then neither `emp1` nor `emp3` meets the criteria. As a result, the value of the expression-`emp1 or emp3` will become `false`.

Evaluating case 3 is not very easy. You cannot predict the value instantly. You use an optional utility class called `ExpressionBuilder`, which has two utility methods, `validateExpression` and `validateComplexExpression`. The first one is used to evaluate the expressions from case 2 and the other one is used to evaluate an expression from case 3. You follow a step-by-step approach to get the final value of the expression. Refer to the associated comments for your easy understanding. You can apply the same technique to evaluate other complex expressions. When I evaluate a complex expression, I name different `Employee` variables as `firstPhase`, `secondPhase`, and so on to help you understand the step-by-step approach of the method. Here is a sample code:

```
// Validating the rule: emp1 and (emp2 or (emp3 or emp4))

public Employee validateComplexExpression(Employee emp1, Employee emp2,
Employee emp3, Employee emp4) {
 // (emp3 or emp4)
 Employee firstPhase = new OrExpression(emp3, emp4);
 // emp2 or (emp3 or emp4)
 Employee secondPhase = new OrExpression(emp2, firstPhase);
 // emp1 and (emp2 or (emp3 or emp4))
 Employee finalPhase = new AndExpression(emp1, secondPhase);
 return finalPhase;
}
```

```
┌─────────────────────────────────────────────────────────┐
│                      POINT TO NOTE                        │
└─────────────────────────────────────────────────────────┘
```

One important point to note is that this design pattern does not instruct you on how to build the syntax tree or how to parse the sentences. It gives you the freedom of choose how to proceed. So, to present a simple scenario and keep things easy, I use class EmployeeBuilder with two methods to accomplish the task. For me, it makes sense to put these methods in a common place. But I acknowledge the fact that I violate the SRP principle here because I include methods for validating simple rules as well as complex rules. So, if you have a concern for the SRP, you can refactor the code. I leave the task for you.

Now let's see other parts of the program. The Employee is an interface with the interpret(...) method as follows:

```
interface Employee {
    public boolean interpret(Context context);
}
```

The IndividualEmployee class has the following constructor:

```
public IndividualEmployee(int experience, String grade) {
    this.experience = experience;
    this.grade = grade;
}
```

I already mentioned that to get a promotion, an employee should have minimum of 10 years of experience and they should be either from G2 grade or G3 grade. You pass this information inside the Context object. So, this class implements Employee interface method as follows:

```
    @Override
public boolean interpret(Context context) {
 if (experience >= context.getYearofExperience() &&
            context.getPermissibleGrades().contains(grade)) {
        return true;
    }
    return false;
}
```

The OrExpression is a non-terminal class and it implements Employee interface method as follows:

```
@Override
public boolean interpret(Context context) {
 return emp1.interpret(context) || emp2.interpret(context);
}
```

Similarly, AndExpression implements the Employee interface method as follows:

```
@Override
public boolean interpret(Context context) {
 return emp1.interpret(context) && emp2.interpret(context);
}
```

The NotExpression is another non-terminal class that implements the Employee interface method as follows:

```
@Override
public boolean interpret(Context context) {
   return !emp.interpret(context);
}
```

Lastly, there is an InvalidExpression class. It's used for the sake of completeness only. The interpret() method of this class always returns false. The remaining code is easy to understand, so continue reading.

Class Diagram

Figure 25-2 shows the class diagram. To make the diagram short, I show the attributes of the Context class only. You can see the other methods and fields from the Package Explorer view and the complete demonstration code.

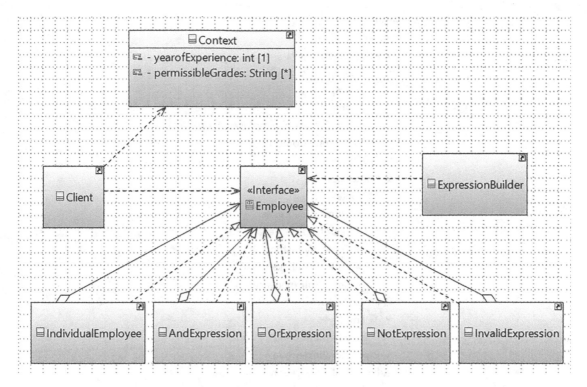

Figure 25-2. *Class diagram*

Package Explorer View

Figure 25-3 shows the high-level structure of the program. It is a big snapshot and there are many parts to this program. To display the important parts of the program, I expand some selected portions for your reference.

```
⊞ interpreter
  ⌄ ⊞ implementation_1
    ⌄ ▨ AndExpression.java
      ⌄ ⊛ AndExpression
          ▫ emp1
          ▫ emp2
          ⚿ AndExpression(Employee, Employee)
          ⚈ interpret(Context) : boolean
    › ▨ Client.java
    ⌄ ▨ Context.java
      ⌄ ⊛ Context
          ▫ permissibleGrades
          ▫ yearofExperience
          ⚿ Context(int, String...)
          ● getPermissibleGrades() : List<String>
          ● getYearofExperience() : int
    ⌄ ▨ Employee.java
      ⌄ ⊛ Employee
          ⚿ interpret(Context) : boolean
    › ▨ ExpressionBuilder.java
    ⌄ ▨ IndividualEmployee.java
      ⌄ ⊛ IndividualEmployee
          ▫ experience
          ▫ grade
          ⚿ IndividualEmployee(int, String)
          ⚈ interpret(Context) : boolean
          ⚈ toString() : String
    › ▨ InvalidExpression.java
    › ▨ NotExpression.java
    › ▨ OrExpression.java
```

Figure 25-3. *Package Explorer view*

Demonstration 1

Here's the complete demonstration. All parts of the program are inside the package `jdp3e.interpreter.implementation_1`.

// Employee.java

```java
interface Employee {
    public boolean interpret(Context context);
}
```

// IndividualEmployee.java

```java
class IndividualEmployee implements Employee {
    private int experience;
    private String grade;

    public IndividualEmployee(int experience, String grade) {
        this.experience = experience;
        this.grade = grade;
    }

    @Override
    public boolean interpret(Context context) {
        if (experience >= context.getYearofExperience() &&
            context.getPermissibleGrades().contains(grade)){
                return true;
            }
         return false;
    }

    @Override
    public String toString() {
        return "Experience: " + experience + ", grade: " +
                grade;
    }
}
```

// OrExpression.java

```java
class OrExpression implements Employee {

    private Employee emp1;
    private Employee emp2;

    public OrExpression(Employee emp1, Employee emp2) {
        this.emp1 = emp1;
        this.emp2 = emp2;
    }
```

```java
    @Override
    public boolean interpret(Context context) {
        return emp1.interpret(context) ||
                emp2.interpret(context);
    }
}
```

// **AndExpression.java**

```java
class AndExpression implements Employee {

    private Employee emp1;
    private Employee emp2;

    public AndExpression(Employee emp1, Employee emp2) {
        this.emp1 = emp1;
        this.emp2 = emp2;
    }

    @Override
    public boolean interpret(Context context) {
        return emp1.interpret(context) &&
                emp2.interpret(context);
    }
}
```

// **NotExpression.java**

```java
class NotExpression implements Employee {
    private Employee emp;

    public NotExpression(Employee expr) {
        this.emp = expr;
    }

    @Override
    public boolean interpret(Context context) {
        return !emp.interpret(context);
    }
}
```

// InvalidExpression.java

```java
class InvalidExpression implements Employee {

    @Override
    public boolean interpret(Context context) {
        return false; // result is always false
    }
}
```

// Context.java

```java
import java.util.ArrayList;
import java.util.List;
class Context {
    private int yearofExperience;
    private List<String> permissibleGrades;

    public Context(int experience, String... allowedGrades) {
        this.yearofExperience = experience;
        this.permissibleGrades = new ArrayList<>();
        for (String grade : allowedGrades) {
            permissibleGrades.add(grade);
        }
    }

    public int getYearofExperience() {
        return yearofExperience;
    }

    public List<String> getPermissibleGrades() {
        return permissibleGrades;
    }
}
```

// ExpressionBuilder.java

```java
class ExpressionBuilder {

    public Employee validateExpression(Employee emp1, String
                                    operator, Employee emp2) {
```

```java
        // Converting the input into the lower case
        switch (operator.toLowerCase()) {

        case "or":
            return new OrExpression(emp1, emp2);
        case "and":
            return new AndExpression(emp1, emp2);
        case "not":
            return new NotExpression(emp1);
        default:
            System.out.println("You have used an invalid
                operator:" + operator);
            System.out.println("(The result is always
                false for this expression)");
            return new InvalidExpression();

        }
    }

    // Validating the rule: emp1 and (emp2 or (emp3 or emp4))
      public Employee validateComplexExpression(
                                Employee emp1,
                                Employee emp2,
                                Employee emp3,
                                Employee emp4
                                ) {

  // (emp3 or emp4)
  Employee firstPhase = new OrExpression(emp3, emp4);
  // emp2 or (emp3 or emp4)
  Employee secondPhase = new OrExpression(emp2, firstPhase);
  // emp1 and (emp2 or (emp3 or emp4))
  Employee finalPhase = new AndExpression(emp1, secondPhase);
  return finalPhase;
 }
}
```

// Client.java

```java
class Client {

    static Employee emp1, emp2, emp3, emp4;
    static Employee employee;
    static boolean result;
    static ExpressionBuilder builder = new
                                    ExpressionBuilder();
    // Minimum Criteria for promotion is:
    // The year of experience is minimum 10 years and
    // Employee grade should be either G2 or G3
    static Context context = new Context(10, "G2", "G3");

    public static void main(String[] args) {
        System.out.println("***Interpreter Pattern Demo***\n");
        initializeEmployees();
        validateSingleEmployee();
        validateSimpleRules();
        validateComplexRules();
    }

    private static void initializeEmployees() {
        emp1 = new IndividualEmployee(5, "G1");
        emp2 = new IndividualEmployee(10, "G2");
        emp3 = new IndividualEmployee(15, "G3");
        emp4 = new IndividualEmployee(20, "G4");

        System.out.println("Employee details are as follows:\n");
        System.out.println(emp1);
        System.out.println(emp2);
        System.out.println(emp3);
        System.out.println(emp4);
        System.out.println("---------");
    }
```

```java
    private static void validateSingleEmployee() {
        System.out.println("Is emp1 eligible for promotion?
                            " + emp1.interpret(context));
        System.out.println("Is emp2 eligible for promotion?
                            " + emp2.interpret(context));
        System.out.println("Is emp3 eligible for promotion?
                            " + emp3.interpret(context));
        System.out.println("Is emp4 eligible for promotion?
                            " + emp4.interpret(context));
        System.out.println("---------");
    }

    private static void validateSimpleRules() {
        System.out.println("\nIs either emp1 or emp3
                            eligible for promotion?");
        employee = builder.validateExpression(emp1, "Or", emp3);
        result = employee.interpret(context);
        System.out.println(result);

        System.out.println("\nAre both emp2 and emp4
                            eligible for promotion?");
        employee = builder.validateExpression(emp2, "And", emp4);
        result = employee.interpret(context);
        System.out.println(result);

        System.out.println("\nIs the statement- 'emp3 is
                    NOT eligible for promotion' correct?");
        employee = builder.validateExpression(emp3, "Not", null);
        result = employee.interpret(context);
        System.out.println(result);
        System.out.println("---------");

    }
```

```
    private static void validateComplexRules() {
        // Validating the complex rule
        System.out.println("Are emp1 and any of emp2, emp3,
                    emp4 is eligible for promotion?");

        employee = builder.validateComplexExpression(
                            emp1, emp2, emp3, emp4);
        result = employee.interpret(context);
        System.out.println(result);

        // Validating the complex rule
        System.out.println("Are emp2 and any of emp1, emp3,
                    emp4 is eligible for promotion?");

        employee = builder.validateComplexExpression(
                            emp2, emp1, emp3, emp4);
        result = employee.interpret(context);
        System.out.println(result);
        System.out.println("---------");

    }

}
```

Output

Here's the output:

```
***Interpreter Pattern Demo***

Employee details are as follows:

Experience: 5, grade: G1
Experience: 10, grade: G2
Experience: 15, grade: G3
Experience: 20, grade: G4
---------
Is emp1 eligible for promotion? false
Is emp2 eligible for promotion? true
```

```
Is emp3 eligible for promotion? true
Is emp4 eligible for promotion? false
---------

Is either emp1 or emp3 eligible for promotion?
true

Are both emp2 and emp4 eligible for promotion?
false

Is the statement- 'emp3 is NOT eligible for promotion' correct?
false
---------
Are emp1 and any of emp2, emp3, emp4 is eligible for promotion?
false
Are emp2 and any of emp1, emp3, emp4 is eligible for promotion?
true
---------
```

Analysis

In this implementation, I evaluate many different expressions. For your easy understanding, I categorize them in different methods where each of them is used to evaluate similar kinds of expressions.

Q&A Session

25.1 When should you use this pattern?

In daily programming life, to be honest, it is not needed much. However, in some rare situations, you may need to work with your own programming language where it could come in handy. But before you proceed, you must ask yourself, what is the Return on Investment (ROI)?

25.2 What are the advantages of using the Interpreter design pattern?

You can have the following advantages:

- You are very much involved in the process of how to define grammar for your language and how to represent and interpret those sentences. You can change and extend the grammar also.

- You have full freedom over how to interpret these expressions.

25.3 What are the challenges associated with using the Interpreter design pattern?

I believe that the amount of work is the biggest concern. Also, maintaining complex grammar becomes tricky because you need to create (and maintain) separate classes to deal with different rules.

25.4 In demonstration 1, when you evaluated a complex expression, you passed four arguments inside the method `validateComplexExpression(…)`. How should I proceed if I need to parse a variable number of arguments?

It's a sample demonstration to give you an idea about the Interpreter design pattern. Let's consider an alternative implementation, which is as follows.

Alternative Implementation

Here I present an alternative demonstration. If you know how to evaluate postfix notations, it will be very easy for you to understand this implementation; otherwise, let's have a quick discussion on this.

You may have seen three different notations for a mathematical expression, which are as follows:

- **Infix** notation is the common arithmetic and logical formula notation in which operators are written between the operands such as 5+2.

- **Postfix** (a.k.a. Reverse Polish notation) is a mathematical notation in which every operator follows all of its operands such as 52+.

- **Prefix** (Polish notation) operators appear to the left of their operands such as +52.

The infix notation is common in mathematical expressions. The other two notations can be used for interpreters of programming languages.

Demonstration 2

In the upcoming implementation, I changed `ExpressionBuilder.java`. This means I had to rewrite the client code accordingly. There is no change in the remaining parts of demonstration 1. All parts of the program are inside the package `jdp3e.interpreter.implementation_2`.

Let's have a look at this new `EmployeeBuilder.java`. Here are the key characteristics:

- All the valid employees are initialized inside the constructor.

- There is a `parse(…)` method inside this class. When it sees the string `emp1` in input, it pushes the `emp1` instance inside a stack. It works similarly for `emp2`, `emp3`, or `emp4`. Otherwise, it assumes that it gets an operator.

- When it sees a binary operator (the and operator and or operator), it pops up the top two elements from the stack, evaluates the complex expression, and pushes back the result on the stack. You understand that for a unary operator such as not, you need to pop only the top element from the stack and proceed.

- If the operator is other than or, and, or not, it throws an exception.

- You use the `toLowercase()` method to convert these words into lowercase before you evaluate a complex expression. As a result, a client need not worry about the case sensitivity of the following words: 'and', 'or', and 'not'.

Here is the `EmployeeBuilder` class:

```java
// This class can parse the input

class EmployeeBuilder {

    Employee emp1, emp2, emp3, emp4;
    Employee tempEmp;// Used as a temporary variable

    public EmployeeBuilder() {
        // Initialize valid Employees
        emp1 = new IndividualEmployee(5, "G1");
        emp2 = new IndividualEmployee(10, "G2");
```

```java
        emp3 = new IndividualEmployee(15, "G3");
        emp4 = new IndividualEmployee(20, "G4");
}

Stack<Employee> currentStack = new Stack<>();

public void parse(String input) {
    String[] tokens = input.split(" ");
    for (String token : tokens) {
        if (token.equals("emp1"))
            currentStack.push(emp1);
        else if (token.equals("emp2"))
            currentStack.push(emp2);
        else if (token.equals("emp3"))
            currentStack.push(emp3);
        else if (token.equals("emp4"))
            currentStack.push(emp4);
        // Got an operator

        else {
            Employee emp1, emp2 = null;
            emp1 = currentStack.pop();
            // Expression 2 is not needed for a
            // 'not' operator
            if (token.equals("and")||
                    token.equals("or") ) {
                emp2 = currentStack.pop();
            }
            tempEmp = evaluate(token, emp1, emp2);
            currentStack.push(tempEmp);
        }
    }
}
```

```
        private Employee evaluate(String operator, Employee emp1,
                                  Employee emp2) {

            switch (operator.toLowerCase()) {
            case "and":
                tempEmp = new AndExpression(emp1, emp2);
                break;
            case "or":
                tempEmp = new OrExpression(emp1, emp2);
                break;
            case "not":
                tempEmp = new NotExpression(emp1);
                break;
            default:
                throw new IllegalArgumentException("Invalid
                                    operator: " + operator);
            }
            return tempEmp;
        }

}
```

Now let's look into the client class. Notice that this time the input follows the postfix notations. Additional expressions (that are commented out now) are supplied for your reference so that you can uncomment and verify the final value of these expressions.

```
class Client {

    public static void main(String[] args) {
        System.out.println("***Modified Interpreter Pattern
                            Demonstration-2***\n");

        // Minimum Criteria for promotion is:
        // The year of experience is a minimum of 10 yrs.
         // and Employee grade should be
         // either G2 or G3
        Context context = new Context(10, "G2", "G3");
         // String input="emp1";//false
         // String input="emp1 not";//true
```

```
// String input="emp2 not";//false
// String input="emp4 emp2 not and";//false
// String input="emp3 emp4 emp2 not and or";//true
String input = "emp2 emp3 emp4 emp2 not and or
                  or";// true

EmployeeBuilder builder = new EmployeeBuilder();
builder.parse(input);
Employee finalExpression =
                builder.currentStack.pop();
Boolean result =
                finalExpression.interpret(context);
System.out.print(input + ":" + result);

 // Removing additional elements(if any)
builder.currentStack.clear();

    }

}
```

Output

When you run this modified program, you'll see the following output:

```
***Modified Interpreter Pattern Demonstration-2***

emp2 emp3 emp4 emp2 not and or or:true
```

That's the end of part II of the book. I hope you enjoyed the detailed implementations of the GoF patterns. Now you can move to the next part of the book, which covers a few more interesting patterns.

PART III

Additional Design Patterns

In Part I, you saw the Simple Factory pattern that does not directly fall into the GoF design pattern category. In Part III, you'll see two more non-GoF patterns:

- Chapter 26 covers the Null Object pattern.

- Chapter 27 covers the Model-View-Controller(MVC) pattern.

The MVC, a very common pattern, is used when you divide your program logic into interconnected modules/elements. The Null Object pattern deals with the null object in object-oriented programming. Learning about these additional patterns raises your confidence to the next level.

Null Object Pattern

This chapter covers the Null Object pattern.

Definition

It's not a GoF design pattern. Here's the definition from Wikipedia:

> *"In object-oriented computer programming, a null object is an object with no referenced value or with defined neutral ('null') behavior. The null object design pattern describes the uses of such objects and their behavior (or lack thereof). It was first published in the Pattern Languages of Program Design book series."*

Concept

The pattern can implement a "do-nothing" relationship, or it can provide a default behavior when an application encounters a null object instead of a real object. Using this pattern, our core aim is to make a better solution by avoiding a "null objects check" or a "null collaborations check" through `if` blocks. Normally, you encapsulate the absence of an object by providing a default behavior that does nothing. The basic structure of this pattern is shown in Figure 26-1.

© Vaskaran Sarcar 2022
V. Sarcar, *Java Design Patterns*, https://doi.org/10.1007/978-1-4842-7971-7_26

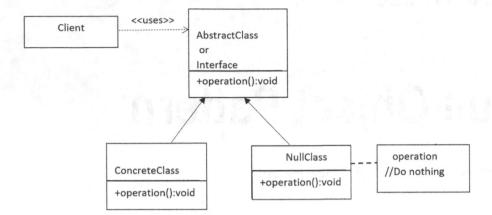

Figure 26-1. *The basic structure of a Null Object pattern*

In this chapter, I begin with a program that seems to be ok, but it has a serious potential bug. When you analyze the bug with a potential solution, the need for the Null Object Pattern will become clear. So, let's jump to the next section.

A Faulty Program

Let's assume that you have two different types of vehicles, Bus and Train, and a client can pass in different inputs. These clients can type b to create a Bus object, t to create a Train object, or exit to quit the application. The following program demonstrates this. This program runs smoothly when the inputs are valid, but the potential bug will be revealed when they supply an invalid input. Here's the faulty program:

```
package jdp3e.null_object;

import java.util.Scanner;

interface Vehicle {
    void travel();
}

class Bus implements Vehicle {
    public static int busCount = 0;

    public Bus() {
        busCount++;
    }
```

```java
    @Override
    public void travel() {
        System.out.println("Let us travel on a bus.");
    }
}

class Train implements Vehicle {
    public static int trainCount = 0;

    public Train() {
        trainCount++;
    }

    @Override
    public void travel() {
        System.out.println("Let us travel on a train.");
    }
}

class NeedForNullObjectPattern {

    public static void main(String[] args) {
        System.out.println("***This program demonstrates
                the need for a Null Object pattern.***\n");
        String input = null;
        Vehicle vehicle = null;
        Boolean flag = true;
        int totalObjects = 0;
        Scanner scanner = new Scanner(System.in);
        try {
            while (flag) {
                System.out.println("Enter your choice(
                    Type 'b' for Bus, 't' for Train ) ");
                input = scanner.next();
                switch (input.toLowerCase()) {
                case "b":
                    vehicle = new Bus();
```

```
                    vehicle.travel();
                    break;
            case "t":
                    vehicle = new Train();
                    vehicle.travel();
                    break;
            case "exit":
                    flag = false;
                    System.out.println("Closing the application.");
                    break;
            default:
                    System.out.println("Invalid input.");
                    System.out.println("Using the vehicle that was
                                    created earlier.");
                    vehicle.travel();
            }
            totalObjects = Bus.busCount +
                            Train.trainCount;
            System.out.println("Number of objects
                            created:" + totalObjects);
        }
    } finally {
        scanner.close();
    }
  }
}
```

Output

Let's focus on the potential bug. Here is the output with some valid and invalid inputs:

```
***This program demonstrates the need for a Null Object pattern.***

Enter your choice( Type 'b' for Bus, 't' for Train )
b
Let us travel on a bus.
Number of objects created:1
```

```
Enter your choice( Type 'b' for Bus, 't' for Train )
e
Invalid input.
Using the vehicle that was created earlier.
Let us travel on a bus.
Number of objects created:1
Enter your choice( Type 'b' for Bus, 't' for Train )
t
Let us travel on a train.
Number of objects created:2
Enter your choice( Type 'b' for Bus, 't' for Train )
e
Invalid input.
Using the vehicle that was created earlier.
Let us travel on a train.
Number of objects created:2
Enter your choice( Type 'b' for Bus, 't' for Train )
b
Let us travel on a bus.
Number of objects created:3
Enter your choice( Type 'b' for Bus, 't' for Train )
exit
Closing the application.
Number of objects created:3
```

An Unwanted Input

Let's assume that by mistake, a user supplied an invalid input, say e as the first input, as shown here:

```
***This program demonstrates the need for a Null Object pattern.***

Enter your choice( Type 'b' for Bus, 't' for Train )
e
```

You receive the following runtime exception:

```
Invalid input.
Exception in thread "main" java.lang.NullPointerException: Cannot invoke
"jdp3e.null_object.Vehicle.travel()" because "vehicle" is null
    at jdp3e.null_object.NeedForNullObjectPattern.
    main(NeedForNullObjectPattern.java:64)
Using the vehicle that was created earlier.
```

The Potential Fix

The immediate remedy that may come to mind is to do a null check before invoking the operation, as shown here:

```
if (vehicle != null){
  vehicle.travel();
}
```

Analysis

The prior solution will work in this case. But think of an enterprise application. When you do null checks like this and put if conditions like this in each possible place, you make your code dirty. This kind of code is difficult to maintain. The concept of the Null Object pattern is useful in similar cases.

POINT TO NOTE

A particular language can have special support in a similar context. For example, C# programmers can avoid the null check using the null conditional operator like the following: vehicle?.Travel();

This operator is available in C# 6 and later versions only. Still, it can be beneficial to look into the implementation details of the Null Object pattern. For example, when you use the Null Object pattern, instead of doing nothing, you can supply a default behavior (that suits your application best) for those null objects.

Another point: in a similar program in C#, following the naming convention, the method name should start with a capital letter, so I use the method Travel() instead of travel().

Real-Life Example

A washing machine can wash properly if there is a smooth water supply without any internal leakage. But suppose, on one occasion, you forget to supply the water before you start washing the clothes, but you pressed the button that initiates washing the clothes. The washing machine should not damage itself in such a situation so it may beep an alarm to get your attention and indicate that there is no water supply at the moment.

Computer World Example

Assume that in a client-server architecture, the server does a calculation based on client input. The server needs to be intelligent enough so that it will not initiate any calculation unnecessarily. Prior to processing the input, it may want to do a cross-verification to ensure whether it needs to start the calculation at all or just ignore invalid input. You may notice the use of the Command pattern with the Null Object pattern in such a case.

In Java, you may have seen the use of various adapter classes in the `java.awt.` `event` package. These classes can be considered as closer examples to the Null Object pattern. For example, consider the `MouseMotionAdapter` class. It is an abstract class but it contains methods with empty bodies like `mouseDragged(MouseEvent e){}` and `mouseMoved(MouseEvent e){}`. However, since the adapter class is tagged with the `abstract` keyword, you cannot directly create objects of the class.

Basically, in an enterprise application, you can avoid a big number of **null checks and if/else blocks** using this design pattern. The following implementation will give you a quick overview of this pattern.

Implementation

Let's modify the faulty program we discussed before. You handle the invalid input through a `NullVehicle` object this time. So, if by mistake the user supplies any invalid data (in other words, any input other than *a, b,* or *exit* in this case), the application will do nothing. It will ignore those invalid inputs through a `NullVehicle` object, which actually does nothing. The class is defined as follows:

```java
class NullVehicle implements Vehicle {
    // Early initialization
    private static NullVehicle instance = new NullVehicle();
    public static int nullVehicleCount;
    // The constructor is private to prevent the use of "new"
    private NullVehicle() {
        nullVehicleCount++;
        System.out.print("A null vehicle object created.");
    }
    // Global point of access.
    public static NullVehicle getInstance(){
        return instance;
    }
    @Override
    public void travel(){
        // Do nothing
    }
}
```

You apply the concept of the Singleton design pattern when you create a NullVehicle object. Because there can be an infinite number of invalid inputs, in the following example you do not want to create the NullVehicle object repeatedly. Once you have a NullVehicle object, you want to reuse that object.

POINTS TO REMEMBER

For a null object method, you need to return whatever seems sensible as a default. In this example, you cannot travel in a vehicle that does not exist. So, it makes sense that for NullVehicle class, the travel() method does nothing.

Class Diagram

Figure 26-2 shows the class diagram.

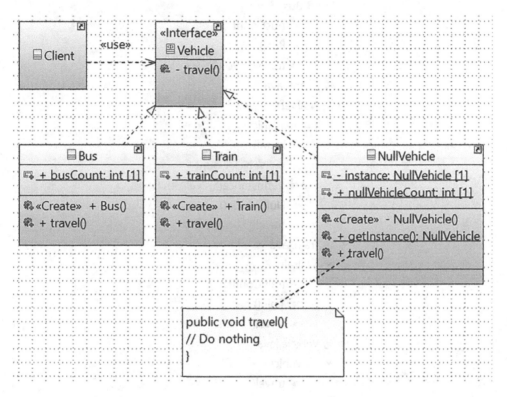

Figure 26-2. *Class diagram*

Package Explorer View

Figure 26-3 shows the high-level structure of the program.

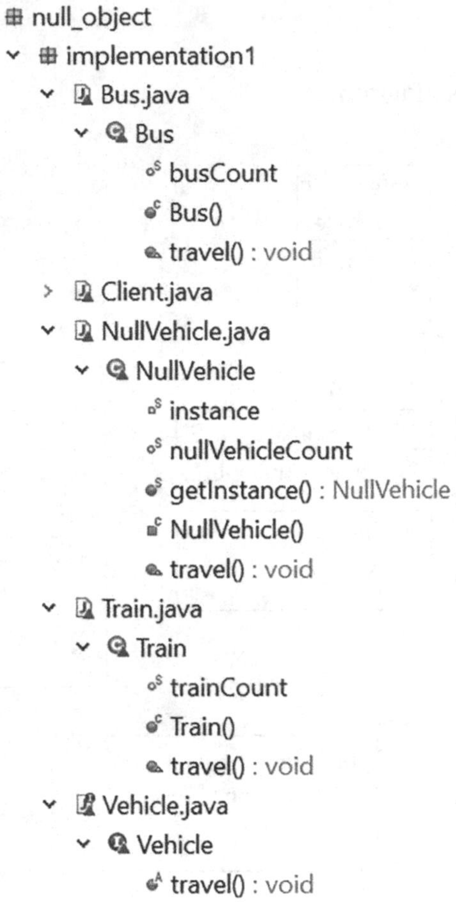

```
⊞ null_object
∨ ⊞ implementation1
  ∨ 🗋 Bus.java
    ∨ ⓠ Bus
         ◦ˢ busCount
         ⸱ᶜ Bus()
         ⸱ travel() : void
    > 🗋 Client.java
    ∨ 🗋 NullVehicle.java
      ∨ ⓠ NullVehicle
           ◦ˢ instance
           ◦ˢ nullVehicleCount
           ⸱ᶜ getInstance() : NullVehicle
           ⸱ᶜ NullVehicle()
           ⸱ travel() : void
    ∨ 🗋 Train.java
      ∨ ⓠ Train
           ◦ˢ trainCount
           ⸱ᶜ Train()
           ⸱ travel() : void
    ∨ 🗋 Vehicle.java
      ∨ ⓠ Vehicle
           ⸱ᴬ travel() : void
```

Figure 26-3. *Package Explorer view*

Demonstration

All parts of the program are stored inside the package `jdp3e.null_object.`
`implementation1`. Here's the complete implementation:

// Vehicle.java

```
interface Vehicle {
    void travel();
}
```

// Bus.java

```java
class Bus implements Vehicle {
    public static int busCount = 0;

    public Bus() {
        busCount++;
    }

    @Override
    public void travel() {
        System.out.println("Let us travel on a bus.");
    }
}
```

// Train.java

```java
class Train implements Vehicle {
    public static int trainCount = 0;

    public Train() {
        trainCount++;
    }

    @Override
    public void travel() {
        System.out.println("Let us travel on a train.");
    }
}
```

// NullVehicle.java

```java
class NullVehicle implements Vehicle {
    // Early initialization
    private static NullVehicle instance = new NullVehicle();
    public static int nullVehicleCount;
    // The constructor is private to prevent the use of "new"
    private NullVehicle() {
     nullVehicleCount++;
```

```java
        System.out.print("A null vehicle object is created.");
    }
    // Global point of access.
    public static NullVehicle getInstance(){
        return instance;
    }
    @Override
    public void travel(){
        // Do nothing
    }
}
```

// Client.java

```java
import java.util.Scanner;

class Client {

    public static void main(String[] args) {
        System.out.println("***The Null Object pattern demonstration.***\n");
        String input = null;
        Vehicle vehicle = null;
        Boolean flag = true;
        int totalObjects = 0;
        Scanner scanner = new Scanner(System.in);
        try {
            while (flag) {
                System.out.println("Enter your choice(
                    Type 'b' for Bus, 't' for Train ) ");
                input = scanner.next();
                switch (input.toLowerCase()) {
                case "b":
                    vehicle = new Bus();
                    break;
                case "t":
                    vehicle = new Train();
                    break;
```

```
                        case "exit":
                            flag = false;
                            System.out.println("Closing the application.");
                            break;
                        default:
                            System.out.println("Invalid input.");
                            vehicle=NullVehicle.getInstance();
                    }
                    // There is no need to do a null check now.
                    vehicle.travel();
                    totalObjects =
                            Bus.busCount +
                            Train.trainCount +
                            NullVehicle.nullVehicleCount;
                    System.out.println("Number of objects
                            created:" + totalObjects);
                }
            } finally {
                scanner.close();
            }
        }
    }
}
```

Output

Here's the output:

```
***The Null Object pattern demonstration.***

Enter your choice( Type 'b' for Bus, 't' for Train )
a
Invalid input.
A null vehicle object is created.
Number of objects created:1
Enter your choice( Type 'b' for Bus, 't' for Train )
b
```

```
Let us travel on a bus.
Number of objects created:2
Enter your choice( Type 'b' for Bus, 't' for Train )
t
Let us travel on a train.
Number of objects created:3
Enter your choice( Type 'b' for Bus, 't' for Train )
```
xyz
Invalid input.
Number of objects created:3
```
Enter your choice( Type 'b' for Bus, 't' for Train )
exit
Closing the application.
Number of objects created:3
```

Analysis

I draw your attention to the following points:

- Invalid inputs and their effects are shown in bold.

- There is only one null vehicle object. This count does not increase due to invalid input.

- You did not perform a null check. Still, the program execution is not interrupted because of invalid user input.

- Following the DRY principle, there is a single occurrence of `vehicle.travel();` but in the faulty program (which was shown earlier), this line appears multiple times inside the `switch` block.

Q&A Session

26.1 At the beginning of the implementation, I see an additional object is created. Is this intentional?

To save computer memory/storage, I follow a Singleton design pattern that supports early initialization when I construct the `NullVehicle` class. This is why you see this additional object. You do not want to create a `NullVehicle` object for each invalid input because your application may receive a large number of invalid inputs. If you do not guard against this situation, a huge number of NullVehicle objects may reside in the system (which is basically useless), and they can occupy a big amount of computer memory, which in turn can cause some unwanted side effects. (For example, the system may become slow, the application's response time may increase, etc.)

26.2 When should you use this pattern?

This pattern can be useful in the following cases:

- You do not want to encounter a NullPointerException (for example, if by mistake you try to invoke a method from a null object).

- You like to ignore lots of null checks in your code.

- You want to make your code cleaner and easily maintainable.

- Finally, I want to draw your attention to another interesting point. The Null Object pattern can be useful in another context. Consider the following segment of code:

```
System.out.println("Doing an additional test");
System.out.println("We'll iterate over the list of vehicles.");
List<Vehicle> vehicleList = new ArrayList<Vehicle>();
vehicleList.add(new Bus());
vehicleList.add(new Train());
vehicleList.add(null);
```

When you use this code segment, you'll receive java.lang.NullPointerException again. But if you replace

```
vehicleList.add(null);
```

with

```
vehicleList.add(NullVehicle.getInstance());
```

there is no runtime exception so you can loop through easily. This is another important usage of this pattern.

26.3 What are the challenges associated with the Null Object pattern?

You need to be aware of the following scenarios:

- Most often, you may want to find and fix the root cause of a failure. So, if you throw a `NullPointerException`, that can work better for you. You can always handle those exceptions in a `try-catch` block or in a `try-catch-finally` block and update the log information accordingly.

- The Null Object pattern basically helps you implement a default behavior when you unconsciously want to deal with an object that is not present at all. But trying to supply such a default behavior may not always be appropriate.

- Incorrect implementations of the Null Object pattern can suppress the true bug that may appear as normal in your program execution.

26.4 Looks like null objects are working like proxies. Is this understanding correct?

No. In general, proxies act on real objects at some point in time and they can be used to provide a special behavior. But a null object should not do any such thing.

26.5 The Null Object Pattern is always associated with `NullPointerException`. Is this understanding correct?

The concept is the same, but the exception name can be different or language specific. For example, in Java, you use this pattern to guard against `java.lang.NullPointerException` but in C#, you use it to guard against `System.NullReferenceException`.

CHAPTER 27

MVC Pattern

This chapter covers the MVC pattern.

Definition

Trygve Mikkjel Heyerdahl Reenskaug, a Norwegian computer scientist, introduced the concept of the model–view–controller (MVC) pattern for graphical user interface (GUI) software design. He formulated this during his visit to the Xerox Palo Alto Research Center (PARC) in 1979. The Wikipedia link at `https://en.wikipedia.org/wiki/Trygve_Reenskaug` includes his quote:

> *"MVC was conceived as a general solution to the problem of users controlling a large and complex data set. The hardest part was to hit upon good names for the different architectural components. Model-View-Editor was the first set. After long discussions, particularly with Adele Goldberg, we ended with the terms Model-View-Controller."*

Throughout this book, I started with the definitions of the respective patterns. For this pattern, here is Wikipedia's simple definition (see `https://en.wikipedia.org/wiki/Model-view-controller`):

> *"Model–view–controller (MVC) is a software design pattern commonly used for developing user interfaces that divide the related program logic into three interconnected elements. This is done to separate internal representations of information from the ways information is presented to and accepted from the user."*

© Vaskaran Sarcar 2022
V. Sarcar, *Java Design Patterns*, https://doi.org/10.1007/978-1-4842-7971-7_27

My favorite description of MVC comes from Connelly Barnes (`http://wiki.c2.com/?ModelViewController`). He says,

> *"An easy way to understand MVC: the model is the data, the view is the window on the screen, and the controller is the glue between the two."*

Note that instead of calling it the MVC Pattern, some developers prefer to call it MVC Architecture.

Concept

Using this pattern, you separate the user interface logic from the business logic and decouple the major components in such a way that they can be reused efficiently. This approach promotes parallel development.

From the definition, it is apparent that the pattern consists of these major components: model, view, and controller. The controller is placed between the view and model in such way that they can communicate to each other only through the controller. This model separates the mechanism of how the data is displayed from the mechanism of how the data will be manipulated. Figure 27-1 shows a typical MVC pattern.

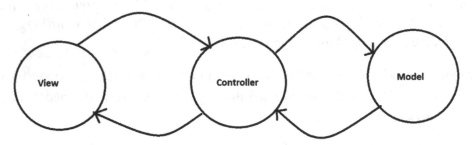

Figure 27-1. *A typical MVC architecture*

Key Points to Remember

Here are brief descriptions of the key components in this pattern:

- The view layer is used to represent the final output. It can also be used to accept user input. It is a presentation layer, and you can think of it as a GUI. You can design it with various technologies. For example, in a .NET application, you can use HTML, CSS,

594

WPF, etc., and for a Java application, you can use AWT, Swing, JSF, JavaFX, etc. (You may know that AWT is platform-dependent and an older technology. Swing comes after it and it is suitable for desktop applications. JavaFX is newer than Swing and AWT, but it is separate from JDK 11. JavaFX can work in both desktop and mobile applications.)

- The model acts as the actual brain of your application. It manages the data and business logic. It knows how to store, manage, or manipulate the data and handle the requests that come from the controller. But this component is separate from the view component. A typical example is a database, a file system, or a similar kind of storage. It can be designed with Oracle, SQL Server, DB2, Hadoop, MySQL, and so on.

- The controller is the intermediary. It accepts a user's input from the view component and passes the request to the model. When it gets a response from the model, it passes the data to the view. It can be designed with C#, .NET, ASP.NET, VB.NET, Core Java, JSP, Servlets, PHP, Ruby, Python, and so on.

You may notice varying implementations in different applications. Here are some examples:

- You can have multiple views.

- Views can pass runtime values (for example, using JavaScript) to controllers.

- Your controller can validate the user's input.

- Your controller can receive input in various ways. For example, it can get input from a web request via a URL or input can be passed by clicking a Submit button on a form.

- In some applications, you may also notice that the model can update the view component.

Figures 27-2, 27-3, and 27-4 show known variations of the MVC architecture.

Variation 1

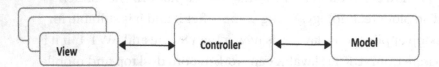

Figure 27-2. *An MVC framework with multiple views*

Variation 2

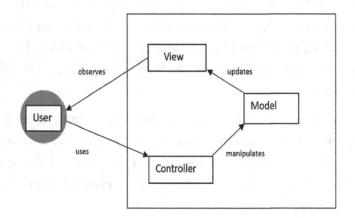

Figure 27-3. *A typical MVC framework with a variation*

Variation 3

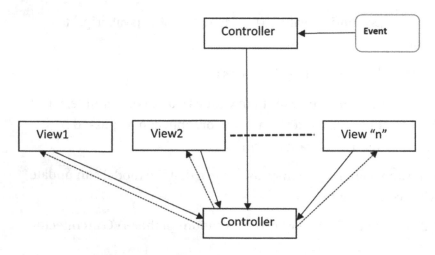

Figure 27-4. *An MVC pattern implemented with an Observer pattern/event-based mechanism*

In short, you use this pattern to support your own needs.

Real-Life Example

Consider the Template Method pattern's real-life example. But this time let's interpret it differently. I said that in a restaurant, based on customer input, a chef will vary the taste and make final products. But you know that the customer does not place their order directly with the chef. The customer looks at a menu card and may consult with the server and then place their order. The server passes the order slip to the chef, who gathers the required materials from the restaurant's kitchen (similar to storehouses or computer databases). Once prepared, the server carries the plate to the customer's table. So, you can consider the role of a server as the controller, the menu card as the view, and chefs with their kitchen as the model (and the food preparation materials as data).

Computer World Example

Many web programming frameworks use the concept of the MVC framework. Typical examples include Django, Ruby on Rails, and ASP.NET. In the Java world, in an MVC architecture, the Java servlets can act as controllers and JavaBeans as models whereas JSPs can be used to create different views. In fact, Java's Swing components follow a variation of MVC architecture. If interested, you can go to `www.oracle.com/technical-resources/articles/javase/mvc.html` to understand how to design MVC using Java SE and the Swing libraries.

Since in this section we discuss computer-world examples, here's a non-Java example, too. Consider a typical ASP.NET MVC project's Solution Explorer screenshot, which is shown in Figure 27-5. Notice the pointed arrows in this figure: they represent the views, models, and controllers separately.

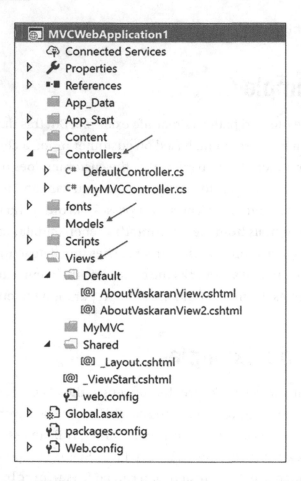

Figure 27-5. Solution Explorer View of a typical ASP.NET MVC project

---

POINTS TO NOTE

Different technologies can follow different structures and so you don't need to get a folder structure with the strict naming convention shown in Figure 27-5.

Implementation

One of the best descriptions for MVC comes from wiki.c2.com (http://wiki.c2.com/?ModelViewController) where it says the following: "*We need SMART Models, THIN Controllers, and DUMB Views.*" In the upcoming example, we'll try to implement this suggestion.

Once you examine the Package Explorer view in Figure 27-7, you will understand that the separate folders are created to accomplish the respective tasks. For simplicity and to match the core concept, I also divided the upcoming implementation into three major parts: model, view, and controller. Here are some important points before you read further:

- `Model`, `View`, and `Controller` are three abstract classes that are extended by the concrete classes `EmployeeModel`, `ConsoleView`, and `EmployeeController`, respectively. Seeing these names, you can assume that they are representatives of the Model, View, and Controller layers of the MVC architecture.

- In this application, the requirement is very simple. There are some employees who need to register themselves in an application. Initially the application will register three employees: Amit, Jon, and Sam. Each employee has a name and an ID. Thus the following constructor:

```
public EmployeeModel() {
// Adding 3 employees at the beginning.
    enrolledEmployees = new ArrayList<Employee>();
    enrolledEmployees.add(new Employee("Amit", "E1"));
    enrolledEmployees.add(new Employee("John", "E2"));
    enrolledEmployees.add(new Employee("Sam", "E3"));
}
```

- At any point in time you should be able to see the enrolled employees in the system. In the client code, you can invoke `displayEnrolledEmployees()` on a `Controller` object as follows:

```
controller.displayEnrolledEmployees();
```

- Then the controller retrieves the data from the model and forwards the call to the view layer as follows:

```
// Get the data from the model layer
List<Employee> enrolledEmployees = model.
                          getEnrolledEmployeeDetailsFromModel();
```

```
// Connect to the view layer
view.showEnrolledEmployees(enrolledEmployees);
```

- And you'll see that a concrete implementor of the View interface (ConsoleView.java) describes the method as follows:

```
System.out.println("\n ***This is a console view of
                currently enrolled employees.*** ");
 for(Employee employee : enrolledEmployees)
 {
    System.out.println(employee);
 }
System.out.println("---------------------");
```

- You can add a new employee or delete an employee from the registered employees list. To do this, you call addEmployeee(...) and removeEmployee(...) on a Controller object. These methods, in turn, invoke the addEmployeeToModel(Employee employee) and removeEmployeeFromModel(String employeeIdToRemove) methods. Seeing the method signature of removeEmployeeFromModel(...), you can guess that to delete an employee, you need to supply the ID of an employee (which is a String in this example).

- When a client invokes a delete request, if the employee ID is not found, the application will ignore this delete request.

- Before you add an employee to the application or remove an employee from the application, you perform a simple validation. For example, before you add an employee to an EmployeeModel instance, you ensure that you do not add an employee with the same ID repeatedly in the application. So, you see the following code snippet:

```
System.out.println("\nTrying to add an employee with the
                name: "+ emp.getEmpName()+" and
                ID: "+emp.getEmpId());
```

```
Employee search_emp =
                    findEmployeeWithId(emp.getEmpId());
if (search_emp != null) {
 System.out.print("FAILED! Duplicate ID.");
 System.out.println(emp.getEmpId() + " is already
                    added to the system.");
} else {
 enrolledEmployees.add(emp);
 System.out.println(emp + " [is added now.]");
}
```

The remaining code is easy to understand, and you can go through the complete demonstration now. Yes, it's big but when you analyze it part by part with the help of the previous bullet points and the supporting diagrams, you should not face any difficulties in understanding the code. You can also consider the associated comments for your immediate reference.

POINTS TO NOTE

Most of the time, you may want to use the concept of MVC with technologies that can give you some built-in support and perform lots of groundwork for you. For example, a .NET programmer often uses ASP.NET (or similar technology) to implement the MVC pattern because it offers a lot of built-in support. Still, you must agree that in these cases, you need to learn the new terminology.

Throughout this book, I use console applications for different design pattern implementations. So, let's continue to use the same for the upcoming implementations because our focus is on MVC architecture only, not on new technologies.

Class Diagram

Figure 27-6 shows the class diagram.

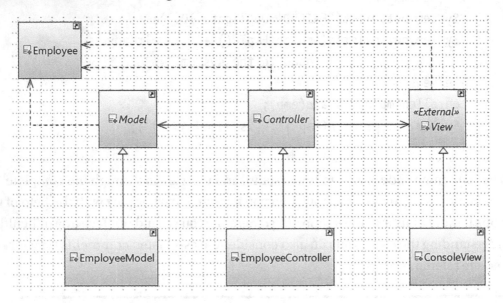

Figure 27-6. *Class diagram*

Package Explorer View

Figure 27-7 shows the high-level structure of the program. There are many parts to this diagram. To accommodate the size in a single page, I expand some important portions only.

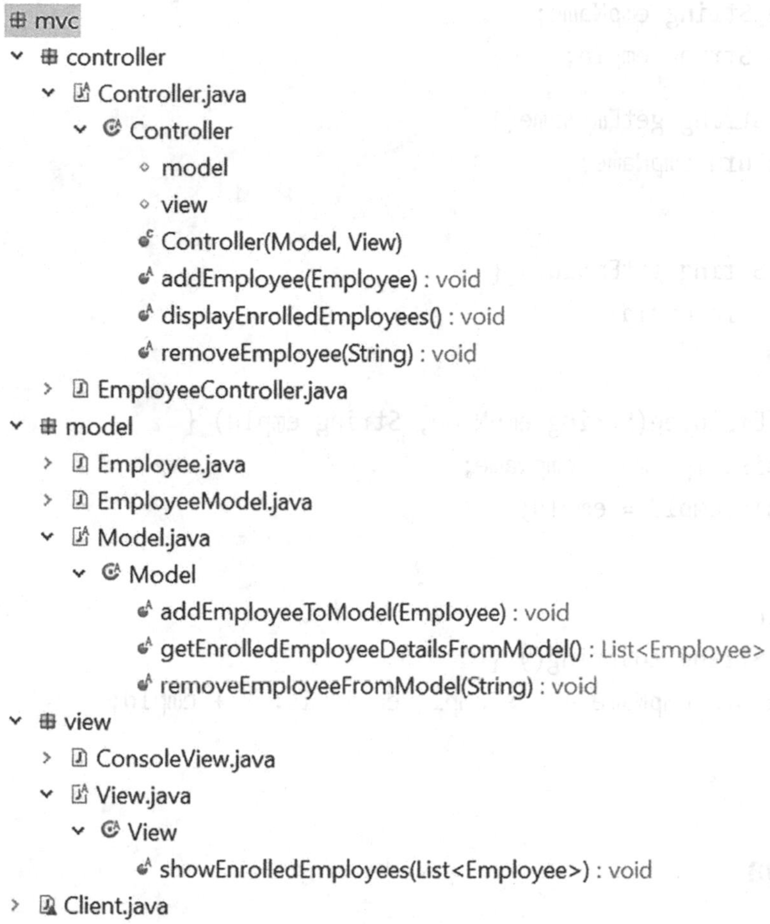

```
⊞ mvc
  ∨ ⊞ controller
      ∨ ☖ Controller.java
          ∨ © Controller
              ○ model
              ○ view
              ☌ Controller(Model, View)
              ☌ addEmployee(Employee) : void
              ☌ displayEnrolledEmployees() : void
              ☌ removeEmployee(String) : void
      > ▯ EmployeeController.java
  ∨ ⊞ model
      > ▯ Employee.java
      > ▯ EmployeeModel.java
      ∨ ☖ Model.java
          ∨ © Model
              ☌ addEmployeeToModel(Employee) : void
              ☌ getEnrolledEmployeeDetailsFromModel() : List<Employee>
              ☌ removeEmployeeFromModel(String) : void
  ∨ ⊞ view
      > ▯ ConsoleView.java
      ∨ ☖ View.java
          ∨ © View
              ☌ showEnrolledEmployees(List<Employee>) : void
  > ▯ Client.java
```

Figure 27-7. Package Explorer view

Demonstration

Here's the complete demonstration.

Contents in Model Folder

// Employee.java

```
package jdp3e.mvc.model;

// The key "data" in this application
public class Employee {
```

```java
    private String empName;
    private String empId;

    public String getEmpName() {
        return empName;
    }

    public String getEmpId() {
        return empId;
    }

    public Employee(String empName, String empId) {
        this.empName = empName;
        this.empId = empId;
    }

    @Override
    public String toString() {
        return empName + "'s employee id is: " + empId;
    }
}
```

// Model.java

```java
package jdp3e.mvc.model;

import java.util.List;

public abstract class Model {

    public abstract List<Employee>
                getEnrolledEmployeeDetailsFromModel();
    public abstract void addEmployeeToModel(
                                Employee employeee);
    public abstract void removeEmployeeFromModel(
                                String employeeId);
}
```

// EmployeeModel.java

```java
package jdp3e.mvc.model;

import java.util.ArrayList;
import java.util.List;

public class EmployeeModel extends Model {
    private List<Employee> enrolledEmployees;

    public EmployeeModel() {
        // Adding 3 employees at the beginning.
        enrolledEmployees = new ArrayList<Employee>();
        enrolledEmployees.add(new Employee("Amit", "E1"));
        enrolledEmployees.add(new Employee("John", "E2"));
        enrolledEmployees.add(new Employee("Sam", "E3"));
    }

    @Override
    public List<Employee>
                  getEnrolledEmployeeDetailsFromModel() {
        return enrolledEmployees;
    }

    // Adding an employee to the model
    @Override
    public void addEmployeeToModel(Employee emp) {
        System.out.println("\nTrying to add an employee
                with the name: "+ emp.getEmpName()+" and ID:
                "+emp.getEmpId());
        Employee search_emp =
                  findEmployeeWithId(emp.getEmpId());
        if (search_emp != null) {
            System.out.print("FAILED! Duplicate ID.");
            System.out.println(emp.getEmpId() + " is
                        already added to the system.");
```

```java
        } else {
            enrolledEmployees.add(emp);
            System.out.println(emp + " [is added now.]");
        }
    }
    // Removing an employee from model
    @Override
    public void removeEmployeeFromModel(String employeeIdToRemove) {
        System.out.println("\nTrying to remove the employee
                            with id: " + employeeIdToRemove);
        Employee emp =
                    findEmployeeWithId(employeeIdToRemove);
        if (emp != null) {
            System.out.println("Removing this employee.");
            enrolledEmployees.remove(emp);
        } else {
            System.out.println("At present, there is no
                employee with id: " + employeeIdToRemove);
            System.out.println("So, this request is ignored.");
        }
    }

    Employee findEmployeeWithId(String employeeId) {
        Employee searchEmp = null;
        for (Employee emp : enrolledEmployees) {
            if (emp.getEmpId().equals(employeeId)) {
                System.out.println(" Employee Found. " +
                            emp.getEmpName() + " has id: " +
                            employeeId);
                searchEmp = emp;
            }
        }
        return searchEmp;
    }
}
```

Contents in View Folder

// View.java

```java
package jdp3e.mvc.view;

import java.util.List;
import jdp3e.mvc.model.Employee;

public abstract class View {
    public abstract void showEnrolledEmployees(
                        List<Employee> enrolledEmployees);
}
```

// ConsoleView.java

```java
package jdp3e.mvc.view;

import java.util.List;

import jdp3e.mvc.model.Employee;

public class ConsoleView extends View {
    @Override
    public void showEnrolledEmployees(List<Employee>enrolledEmployees){
        System.out.println("\n ***This is a console view of
                        currently enrolled employees.*** ");
        for( Employee employee : enrolledEmployees){
            System.out.println(employee);
        }
        System.out.println("--------------------");
    }
}
```

Contents in Controller Folder

// Controller.java

```
package jdp3e.mvc.controller;
import jdp3e.mvc.model.Employee;
import jdp3e.mvc.model.Model;
import jdp3e.mvc.view.View;

public abstract class  Controller {
    protected Model model;
    protected View view;

    public Controller(Model model, View view){
        this.model = model;
        this.view = view;
    }
    public abstract void displayEnrolledEmployees();
    public abstract void addEmployee(Employee employee);
    public abstract void removeEmployee(String employeeId);
}
```

// EmployeeController.java

```
package jdp3e.mvc.controller;

import java.util.List;
import jdp3e.mvc.model.*;
import jdp3e.mvc.view.*;

public class EmployeeController extends Controller {

    public EmployeeController(Model model, View view){
        super(model,view);
    }
    @Override
    public void displayEnrolledEmployees() {
        // Get the data from the model layer
        List<Employee> enrolledEmployees =
         model.getEnrolledEmployeeDetailsFromModel();
```

CHAPTER 27   MVC PATTERN

```
        // Connect to the view layer
        view.showEnrolledEmployees(enrolledEmployees);
    }

    // Sending a request to model to add an
    // employee to the list.
    @Override
    public void addEmployee(Employee employee){
        model.addEmployeeToModel(employee);
    }
    // Sending a request to model to remove
    // an employee from the list.
    @Override
    public void removeEmployee(String employeeId){
        model.removeEmployeeFromModel(employeeId);
    }
}
```

Client Code

// Client.java

```
package jdp3e.mvc;

import jdp3e.mvc.model.*;
import jdp3e.mvc.view.*;
import jdp3e.mvc.controller.*;

class Client {
    public static void main(String[] args) {
      System.out.println("***MVC architecture Demo***");
        // Model
        Model model = new EmployeeModel();

        // View
        View view = new ConsoleView();
```

```
        // Controller
        Controller controller = new
                    EmployeeController(model, view);
        controller.displayEnrolledEmployees();

        // Add an employee
        Employee kevin=new Employee("Kevin", "E4");
        controller.addEmployee(kevin);
        controller.displayEnrolledEmployees();

        // Remove an existing employee using
        // the employee id.
        controller.removeEmployee("E2");
        controller.displayEnrolledEmployees();

        // Cannot remove an employee who does not
        // belong to the registered list.
        controller.removeEmployee("E5");
        controller.displayEnrolledEmployees();

        // Avoiding duplicate entries.
        controller.addEmployee(kevin);
        controller.addEmployee(new Employee("Kate", "E4"));
    }
}
```

Output

When you run this program, you see the following output:

```
***MVC architecture Demo***

 ***This is a console view of currently enrolled employees.***
Amit's employee id is: E1
John's employee id is: E2
Sam's employee id is: E3
--------------------
```

Trying to add an employee with the name: Kevin and ID: E4
Kevin's employee id is: E4 [is added now.]

 This is a console view of currently enrolled employees.
Amit's employee id is: E1
John's employee id is: E2
Sam's employee id is: E3
Kevin's employee id is: E4

Trying to remove the employee with id: E2
  Employee Found. John has id: E2
Removing this employee.

  This is a console view of currently enrolled employees.
Amit's employee id is: E1
Sam's employee id is: E3
Kevin's employee id is: E4

Trying to remove the employee with id: E5
At present, there is no employee with id: E5
So, this request is ignored.

  This is a console view of currently enrolled employees.
Amit's employee id is: E1
Sam's employee id is: E3
Kevin's employee id is: E4

Trying to add an employee with the name: Kevin and ID: E4
  Employee Found. Kevin has id: E4
FAILED! Duplicate ID.E4 is already added to the system.

Trying to add an employee with the name: Kate and ID: E4
  Employee Found. Kevin has id: E4
FAILED! Duplicate ID.E4 is already added to the system.

Q&A Session

27.1 Suppose you have a programmer, a DBA, and a graphic designer. Can you predict their roles in an MVC architecture?

The graphic designer will design the view layer, the DBA will make the model, and the programmer will work to make an intelligent controller. Obviously, if needed, a programmer can work in multiple places.

27.2 What are the key advantages of using the MVC design pattern?

Some important advantages are as follows:

- High cohesion and low coupling are the benefits of MVC. You have probably noticed that tight coupling between the model and the view is easily removed in this pattern. So, the application can be easily extendable and reusable.

- The pattern supports parallel development.

- You can also accommodate multiple runtime views.

27.3 What are the challenges associated with the MVC pattern?

Here are some challenges:

- It requires highly skilled personnel.

- For a tiny application, it may not be suitable.

- Developers may need to be familiar with multiple languages, platforms, and technologies.

- Multi-artifact consistency is a big concern because you are separating the overall project into three major parts.

27.4 Can you provide multiple views in this implementation?

Sure. Let's add a new shorter view called `MobileDeviceView` in the application. Let's add the following code snippet inside the `View` folder as follows:

```
package jdp3e.mvc.view;

import java.util.List;
import jdp3e.mvc.model.Employee;
```

```java
public class MobileDeviceView extends View {
    @Override
    public void showEnrolledEmployees(List<Employee>enrolledEmployees){
        System.out.println("\n ***This is a mobile view of
                        currently enrolled employees.*** ");
        System.out.println("Employee Id"+ "\t"+ " Employee Name");
        System.out.println("_____");
        for( Employee employee : enrolledEmployees){
            System.out.println(employee.getEmpId() + "\t"+
                            employee.getEmpName());
        }
        System.out.println("++++++++++++++++++++");
    }
}
```

Once you add this class, your modified Package Explorer view should be similar to Figure 27-8.

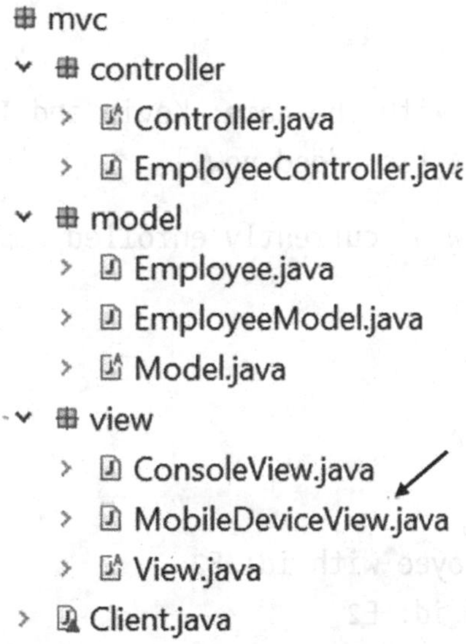

```
# mvc
  ∨ # controller
      >  Controller.java
      >  EmployeeController.java
  ∨ # model
      >  Employee.java
      >  EmployeeModel.java
      >  Model.java
  ∨ # view
      >  ConsoleView.java
      >  MobileDeviceView.java
      >  View.java
  >  Client.java
```

Figure 27-8. *New Package Explorer view after the addition of MobileDeviceView.java*

Now add the following segment of code at the end of your client code (see the comment for reference):

```
// Added for Q&A Session
view = new MobileDeviceView();
controller = new EmployeeController(model, view);
controller.displayEnrolledEmployees();
```

Modified Output

Notice the last part of this new output to see the effect of your new changes. These changes are shown in bold.

```
***MVC architecture Demo***

 ***This is a console view of currently enrolled employees.***
Amit's employee id is: E1
John's employee id is: E2
Sam's employee id is: E3
---------------------

Trying to add an employee with the name: Kevin and ID: E4
Kevin's employee id is: E4 [is added now.]

 ***This is a console view of currently enrolled employees.***
Amit's employee id is: E1
John's employee id is: E2
Sam's employee id is: E3
Kevin's employee id is: E4
---------------------

Trying to remove the employee with id: E2
 Employee Found. John has id: E2
Removing this employee.

 ***This is a console view of currently enrolled employees.***
Amit's employee id is: E1
Sam's employee id is: E3
Kevin's employee id is: E4
---------------------
```

```
Trying to remove the employee with id: E5
At present, there is no employee with id: E5
So, this request is ignored.

 ***This is a console view of currently enrolled employees.***
Amit's employee id is: E1
Sam's employee id is: E3
Kevin's employee id is: E4
---------------------

Trying to add an employee with the name: Kevin and ID: E4
 Employee Found. Kevin has id: E4
FAILED! Duplicate ID.E4 is already added to the system.

Trying to add an employee with the name: Kate and ID: E4
 Employee Found. Kevin has id: E4
FAILED! Duplicate ID.E4 is already added to the system.
```

This is a mobile view of currently enrolled employees.
Employee Id   Employee Name

E1   Amit
E3   Sam
E4   Kevin
+++++++++++++++++++++

Analysis

This modified example shows how to use a new view. Similarly, you can add a new model too. For example, you can add a new model named SqlDataModel as follows:

```
package jdp3e.mvc.model;

import java.util.ArrayList;
import java.util.List;

public class SqlDataModel extends Model {
    List<Employee> enrolledEmployees;
```

```
    public SqlDataModel() {
    // Adding 4 employees at the beginning.
    enrolledEmployees = new ArrayList<Employee>();
    enrolledEmployees.add(new Employee("Amit", "E1"));
    enrolledEmployees.add(new Employee("John", "E2"));
    enrolledEmployees.add(new Employee("Sam", "E3"));
    enrolledEmployees.add(new Employee("Patrick", "E4"));
 }
// Remaining code skipped
```

In this case, the Package Explorer view is shown in Figure 27-9.

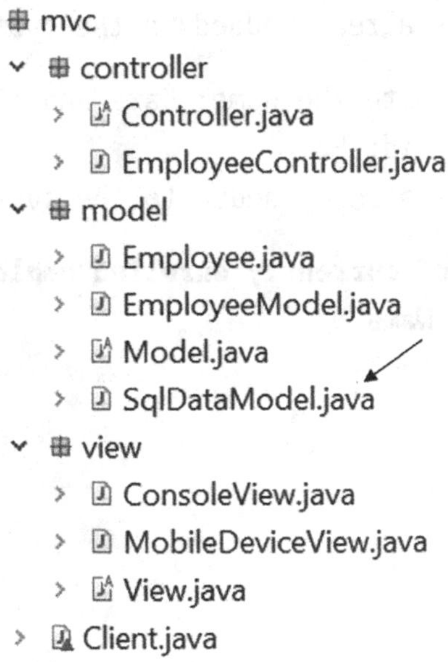

Figure 27-9. *New Package Explorer view after the addition of SqlDataModel.java*

And then you bind this model with the mobile device view (which was shown previously) as follows:

```
// Testing a new model
model = new SqlDataModel();
view = new MobileDeviceView();
controller = new EmployeeController(model, view);
controller.displayEnrolledEmployees();
```

This segment can produce the following output:

```
***This is a mobile view of currently enrolled employees.***
Employee Id       Employee Name

_____

E1      Amit
E2      John
E3      Sam
E4      Patrick
++++++++++++++++++++
```

Note that inside `SqlDataModel` you could use a different data structure, such as a `LinkedList` to serve your purpose. This is why you don't declare the `List` (`enrolledEmployees`) in the super class (`Model.java`).

I hope that you can now include a new controller too if you want. In short, you can easily add (or plug in) a model, view, or controller in this system. It is possible because each component is independent of the other and they do not have any direct knowledge about the other components.

I repeat, it is not mandatory to separate components in a similar manner. For example, if you believe that for your application you should combine the view layer and the controller layer, it's ok. To follow the core theory, I separated the layers in these examples. In this context, I like to include the following quote from Trygve Reenskaug (`https://folk.universitetetioslo.no/trygver/themes/mvc/mvc-index.html`):

> *An important aspect of the original MVC was that its Controller was responsible for creating and coordinating its subordinate views. Also, in my later MVC implementations, a view accepts and handles user input relevant to itself. The Controller accepts and handles input relevant to the Controller/ View assembly as a whole, now called the Tool.*

This is the end of this part. I hope you enjoyed learning all of the patterns in this book. It is time to look into some other aspects of design patterns, which you'll see in the following part.

PART IV

The Final Talks on Design Patterns

Part IV consists of three chapters. In this part, you'll find answers to some important questions such as

- What are criticisms associated with the design patterns?

- How can you avoid the anti-patterns?

- What are the frequently asked questions in this field?

A quick overview of these topics can help you to think and program better in the future.

CHAPTER 28

Criticisms of Design Patterns

Design patterns help you benefit from other people's experiences. This is often termed *experience reuse.* You learn how they solved challenges, how they tried to adopt new behaviors in their systems, and so on. A pattern may not perfectly fit into your work, but if you know the best practices as well as the problems of a pattern at the beginning, you are more likely to make a better application. This is why I now tell you about the criticisms of design patterns. Knowing about them can offer you some real value. If you think critically about these patterns before you design your software, you can predict the return on investment (ROI) to some degree. So, let's go through the following points, which are often raised by some developers:

- The concept of patterns came through Christopher Alexander. He was an architect, not a computer programmer. He considered a domain that did not change a lot over the years (compared to the software industry). On the contrary, the software industry is always changing so changes to software development are much faster compared to other domains. This is why critics often say that you cannot start from the domain of buildings and towns that Christopher Alexander considered.

- The way you used to write a program in the early days is not comparable to today. The way of writing codes has changed a lot. In today's world, computer languages support many built-in advanced features as well. So, the facilities that you have nowadays are much more compared to the old days of programming. So, when you extract patterns based on old practices, you show additional respect to them.

© Vaskaran Sarcar 2022
V. Sarcar, *Java Design Patterns*, https://doi.org/10.1007/978-1-4842-7971-7_28

- Many of these patterns are similar, and there are always pros and cons associated with each pattern (I discuss them in the Q&A sessions at the end of each chapter). A pitfall in one case can be a real virtue in a different case.

- The pattern that supplies satisfactory results today can be a big burden in the near future due to the continuous changes in the software industry.

- It is very unlikely that the infinite number of requirements can be well designed with these finite number of design patterns.

- Designing software is an art. And there is no definition or criteria for the best art.

- Design patterns give you the idea but not the implementation (like libraries and frameworks). You know that each human mind is unique. So, each engineer may have preferences for implementing a similar concept, and this can create chaos on a team if mindsets vary widely.

- Consider a simple example. Patterns encourage people to code to a supertype (abstract class/interface). But for a simple application where you know that there is no upcoming change in the near future, or an application created for a demo purpose only, this idea may not make much sense to you.

- Similarly, in smaller applications, you may find that enforcing the rules of design patterns increases your code size and maintenance costs.

- Erasing the old and adopting the new is not always easy. For example, when you first learned about inheritance, you were excited. You probably wanted to use it in many ways and saw only the benefits from the concept. But later when you started experimenting with design patterns, you learned that in many cases compositions are preferred over inheritance. This shifting of programming mindsets is not easy.

- Design patterns are based on key principles, and one of them is to *identify the code that may vary and then separate it from the rest of the code*. This sounds very good from a theoretical perspective. But in real-world implementations, who guarantees that your judgment is perfect? The software industry always changes, and it needs to adapt to new requirements/demands continuously.

- Many patterns are already integrated with modern-day languages. Instead of implementing the pattern from scratch, you can use the built-in support in the language constructs.

- Inappropriate use of patterns can lead to anti-patterns. For example, an inappropriate use of the Mediator Pattern can lead to the God Class anti-pattern. I provide a brief overview of anti-patterns in Chapter 29.

- Many people believe that the concepts of design patterns simply indicate that a programming language may need additional features. So, patterns will have less significance with the increasing capability of modern-day programming languages. Wikipedia says that computer scientist Peter Norvig believes that 16 out of the 23 GoF design patterns are simplified or eliminated via direct language support in Lisp or Dylan. You can see similar thoughts at `https://en.wikipedia.org/wiki/Software_design_pattern`.

- The patterns I discuss in this book are solely based on object-oriented programming. The efficiency and applicability of these patterns are questionable in other domains.

- These patterns are not interchangeable.

- In the end, design patterns help you to get benefit from the experiences of others. You are getting their thoughts, you come to know how they encountered the challenges, how they implemented new behaviors in their systems, and more. But if you dive deep down to the basic thought, you will find that they start with the assumption that a beginner or relatively less experienced person cannot solve a problem better than their seniors. On some specific occasions, though, a relatively less experienced person can have a better vision than their seniors and become more effective in the future.

Q&A Session

28.1 Is there any catalog for these patterns?

I started with GoF's 23 design patterns and then discussed more patterns in this book. The GoF catalog is considered the most fundamental pattern catalog.

But definitely, there are many other catalogs that may focus on particular domains. The Portland Patterns Repository and The Hillside Group's website are well known in this context. You can get valuable insights and thoughts from these resources. As a starting point, you can browse through the following links:

```
https://wiki.c2.com/?PortlandPatternRepository
https://hillside.net/patterns/patterns-catalog
```

From the Hillside group website, you can learn about various conferences and workshops also.

Note   At the time of writing, the links in this book worked, but these links and policies to access these links may change in the future.

28.2 Why are you silent about other patterns?

These are my personal beliefs:

- Computer science will keep growing, and you will keep getting new patterns.

- If you are not familiar with the fundamental patterns, you cannot evaluate the true needs of the remaining or upcoming patterns. For example, if you know MVC well, you can see how it is different from Model-View-Presenter (MVP) or Model-View-ViewModel (MVVM) and understand why they are needed.

- The book is already fat. A detailed discussion of each pattern would need many more pages, which would make the book too big to digest.

So, in this book, I focus on fundamental patterns that are still relevant in today's programming world.

28.3 I often see the term "force" with the description of design patterns. What does it mean?

It is the criteria on which developers justify their developments. Broadly, your target and current constraints are two important parts of your force. Therefore, when you develop your application, you can justify your development with these parts.

28.4 In various forums, I have seen that people are fighting about the pattern definition and say something like this: "A pattern is a proven solution to a problem in a context." What does this mean?

This is a simple and easy-to-remember definition of what a pattern is. But simply breaking it down into three parts (problem, context, and solution) is not enough.

As an example, suppose you are headed to an airport and you are in a hurry. Suddenly, you discover that you have left your boarding pass at home. Let's analyze the situation:

Problem: You need to reach the airport on time.

Context: You left the boarding pass at home.

The solution that may come into your mind: Turn back and rush toward home at a high speed to get the boarding pass.

This solution may work once, but can you apply the same procedure repeatedly? You know the answer. This is not an intelligent solution because it depends on how much time you currently have to collect the pass from home and go back to the airport. It also depends on the current traffic on the road and many other factors. So, even if you're successful once, you may want prepare a better solution for a similar situation in the future.

So, try to understand the meaning, intent, and context to understand a pattern clearly.

28.5 Sometimes I am confused by similar UML diagrams for two different patterns. I am further confused with the classification of the patterns in many cases. How can I overcome this?

This is perfectly natural. The more you read and analyze the implementations and the more you try to understand the intent behind these designs, the distinctions among them will be clearer to you.

Lastly and most importantly, following a pattern is not your ultimate goal. Your primary goal is to produce an efficient solution that is simple, efficient, and serves your current need.

28.6 When should I consider writing a new pattern?

Writing a new pattern is not easy. You need to study a lot and evaluate the available patterns before you make such an attempt. But if you do not find an existing pattern to serve your domain-specific need, you may need to write your own pattern. It will be very good if your solution passes the "Rule of Three" test, which simply says that to get the tag "pattern," a solution needs to be applied in a real-world solution at least three times successfully. Once you have done this, you can let others know about it, participate in discussion forums, and get feedback from others. This activity can help both you and the development community.

28.7 Can you name a few patterns outside the GoF's catalog?

Here are two that you commonly see in other patterns:

- **Utility pattern**: A utility class with static methods only. You avoid the instantiation of this class using a private constructor.

- **Lazy Instantiation pattern**: It delays the object instantiation process until it is truly required. It is useful to deal with resource-hungry/ resource-heavy objects.

CHAPTER 29

Anti-Patterns

The discussion of design patterns is not complete without discussing anti-patterns. This chapter covers a brief overview of anti-patterns. Let's start.

Overview

In real-world application development, some approaches are very attractive at the beginning, but in the long run, they create problems. Consider the case when you try to get a quick fix to meet a delivery deadline. If you are not aware of the potential pitfalls, you may pay a big penalty.

Anti-patterns alert you to common mistakes by describing how attractive approaches can make your life difficult in the future. At the same time, they suggest alternate solutions that may seem tough or ugly at the beginning but ultimately help you build a better solution. So, you must take precautionary measures to avoid those mistakes. The proverb "prevention is better than cure" very much suits this context.

POINTS TO REMEMBER

In short, anti-patterns identify problems with established practices and can map general situations to a specific class of highly productive solutions. They can also provide you with better plans to reverse bad practices and make healthy solutions. In addition, remember that the concept of anti-patterns is not limited to object-oriented programming.

© Vaskaran Sarcar 2022
V. Sarcar, *Java Design Patterns*, https://doi.org/10.1007/978-1-4842-7971-7_29

Brief History of Anti-Patterns

The original idea of design patterns came from building architect Christopher Alexander, a professor at the University of California, Berkeley. He shared his ideas for the construction of buildings within well-planned towns. Gradually these concepts entered into software development, and they started gaining popularity through leading-edge software developers like Ward Cunningham and Kent Beck. In 1994, the idea of design patterns entered into the mainstream of object-oriented software development through an industry conference called Pattern Languages of Program Design (PLoP) on design patterns. It was hosted by the Hillside Group, and Jim Coplien's paper "A Development Process Generative Pattern Language" is a famous one in this context. With the launch of the classic textbook *Design Patterns: Elements of Reusable Object–Oriented Software* by the GoF, the idea of design patterns became extremely popular.

Undoubtedly, the idea of design patterns helped (and are still helping) programmers develop high-quality software. But in some cases, people started noticing the negative impacts, also. Here is an example: many developers wanted to show their expertise without a true evaluation of the consequences of these patterns in their specific domains. As an obvious side-effect, patterns were implemented in the wrong context, produced low-quality software, and ultimately caused big penalties to them or their organizations.

So, the software industry needed to focus on the negative consequences of similar mistakes and eventually the idea of anti-patterns evolved. Many experts contributed to this field, but the first well-formed model came through Michael Akroyd's presentation entitled "AntiPatterns: Vaccinations against Object Misuse." It was the antithesis of the GoF's design patterns.

The term *anti-pattern* became popular with the authors Raphael C. Malveau, William J. Brown, Hays W. "Skip" McCormick, and Thomas J. Mowbray via their famous book titled *Anti Patterns: Refactoring Software, Architectures, and Projects in Crisis* (Robert Ipsen/Wiley, 1998). They said the following:

> *"Because AntiPatterns have had so many contributors, it would be unfair to assign the original idea for AntiPatterns to a single source. Rather, AntiPatterns are a natural step in complementing the work of the design pattern movement and extending the design pattern model."*

Examples of Anti-Patterns

These are examples of anti-patterns and the concepts/mindsets behind them:

- **Overuse of Patterns**: Developers use patterns at any cost, regardless of whether they are appropriate or not.

- **God Class**: A big object that tries to control almost everything with many unrelated methods. Inappropriate use of the Mediator pattern may end up with this anti-pattern.

- **Not Invented Here**: I am a big company and I want to build everything from scratch. Although a library is available (developed by a small company), I won't use it. I make everything on my own and once it is developed, I use my brand value to announce "Hey guys, the ultimate library is launched for you."

- **Zero Means Null**: Consider a case when a developer makes an application form with some mandatory fields. In this form, if you do not enter a number, the developer treats it as a 0. There are some variations of this anti-pattern. For example, some developers like to use -1, 999, or anything like that to represent an inappropriate integer value for a context or to exit from a loop. Sometimes they treat 09/09/9999 as a null date in an application. In these cases, if the user needs to use the numbers -1 or 999 or the date 09/09/9999, they won't be able to do so.

- **Golden Hammer**: Mr. X believes that technology T is the best. When he develops a new system (which requires new learning), he tries to use T even if it is inappropriate. He thinks, "I am old enough and quite busy. I do not need to learn any more technology if I can somehow manage it with T."

- **Shoot the Messenger**: "I'm already under pressure and the program deadline is approaching. The tester, John, always finds defects, which are hard to fix. Also, John does not like me so he likes to find defects in my code. At this stage, I do not want him to validate my code; he will find more defects and I will miss my target deadline".

- **Swiss Army Knife**: Demand for a product that will serve every need of a customer, or a drug that will cure all illnesses, or software that will serve a wide range of customers with varying needs. It does not matter how complex the interface is.

- **Copy-and-Paste Programming**: You need to solve a problem, but you already have a piece of code to deal with a similar situation. So, you take a copy of the old code that is currently working, and you start modifying it if required. But when you start from an existing copy, you essentially inherit all the potential bugs associated with it. Also, if the original code needs to be modified in the future, you may need to apply the modification in multiple places. This approach also violates the Don't Repeat Yourself (DRY) principle.

- **Architects Don't Code**: Mr. X thinks, "I am an architect. My time is valuable. I only show paths or give great lectures on coding. There are enough implementers who should implement my idea." **Architects Play Golf** is a brother of this anti-pattern.

- **Hide and Hover**: Do not expose edit or delete links until a user hovers over the element.

- **If It's Working, Don't Change It**: You identify some poorly structured code that is still working. Some of your colleagues say, "Do not make any change to it because it is still working. Unless it causes big trouble, leave it."

- **Disguised Links and Ads**: A mindset that thinks that to make a profit, it is OK to fool users and earn revenue when they click on a link or an advertisement although they may not get the information.

- **Management by Numbers**: A mindset that thinks that greater numbers of commits, greater numbers of lines of code, or greater numbers of defect fixing, etc. are signs of a great developer.

In this context, I like to mention the following quote by Bill Gates (source: `www.goodreads.com/quotes/536587-measuring-programming-progress-by-lines-of-code-is-like-measuring`):

"Measuring programming progress by lines of code is like measuring aircraft building progress by weight."

Bill Gates

POINTS TO NOTE

- Nowadays you can learn about various anti-patterns from different websites/sources. For example, the following Wikipedia link talks about various anti-patterns: `https://en.wikipedia.org/wiki/Anti-pattern`.

- You can also get a detailed list of the anti-pattern catalog at `http://wiki.c2.com/?AntiPatternsCatalog` to learn more.

Types of Anti-Patterns

Anti-patterns can belong to different categories. Even a typical anti-pattern can belong to more than one category. Here are some common classifications:

- **Architectural**: The Swiss Army Knife anti-pattern is an example in this category.

- **Development:** The God Class and the Overuse of Patterns anti-patterns are examples in this category.

- **Management:** The Shoot the Messenger anti-pattern falls in this category.

- **Organizational:** Architects Don't Code and Architects Play Golf belong in this category.

- **User Interface:** Examples include disguised links/ads.

Note   Disguised links and advertisements are known as Dark Patterns.

Q&A Session

29.1 How are anti-patterns related to design patterns?

When you use design patterns, you reuse the experiences of others who came before you. When you start blindly using those concepts for the sake of use only, you fall into the trap of *reuse of recurring solutions*. This can lead you to a bad situation in the future where you identify that your return of investment (ROI) keeps decreasing but maintenance costs keep increasing. In simple words, attractive solutions (or patterns) may cause more problems for you in the future.

29.2 A design pattern may turn into an anti-pattern. Is this understanding correct?

Yes, if you apply a design pattern in the wrong context, it can cause more trouble than the problem it solves, and eventually it will turn into an anti-pattern. So, before you start, understanding the nature and context of the problem is very important. If you are not sure, follow the Keep It Simple, Stupid (KISS) principle and make your solution as simple as possible.

29.3 Antipatterns are related to software developers only. Is this understanding correct?

No. The usefulness of an anti-pattern is not limited to developers; it may apply to others also. For example, it is useful to managers and technical architects, too.

29.4 Even if you do not get much benefit from anti-patterns now, they can help you adapt new features easily with fewer maintenance costs in the future. Is this understanding correct?

Yes.

29.5 What are the probable causes of anti-patterns?

They can come from various sources/mindsets. Here are some common examples:

- "We need to deliver the product as soon as possible."

- "We have a very good relationship with the customer. So, at present, we do not need to analyze the future impact."

- "I am an expert of reuse. I know design patterns very well."

- "We use the latest technologies and features to impress our customers. We do not need to care about legacy systems."

- "More complicated code will reflect my expertise in the subject."

29.6 Can you mention some symptoms of anti-patterns?

In object-oriented programming, the most common symptom is that your system cannot adopt a new feature easily. Also, you discover that the maintenance costs are continuously increasing. You may also notice that you have lost the power of key object-oriented features like inheritance and polymorphism.

Apart from these, you may notice some (or all) of the following symptoms:

- Use of global variables

- Code duplication

- Limited/no reuse of code

- One big class (God class)

- Presence of a big number of parameterless methods

29.7 What is the remedy if you detect an anti-pattern?

You may need to refactor your code and find a better solution. For example, here are some solutions to avoid the following anti-patterns:

- **Golden Hammer**: You may try to educate Mr. X through proper training.

- **Zero Means Null**: You can use an additional Boolean variable that is more sensible for indicating a null value properly.

- **Management by Numbers**: The counting of numbers is good if you can use them wisely. You cannot judge the ability of a programmer just by the number of defects they fix per week. Quality is also important. A typical example: fixing a simple UI layout is much easier than fixing a critical memory leak in the system. Consider another example. "More tests are passing" does not indicate that your system is more stable unless these tests exercise different code paths/branches.

- **Shoot the Messenger**: Welcome tester John and involve him immediately. Don't consider him as a rival. You can properly analyze all of his findings and fix the real defects early to avoid last minute surprises.

- **Copy-and-Paste Programming**: Instead of searching for a quick solution, you can refactor your code. You can also make it commonplace to maintain the frequently used methods to avoid duplicates and easier maintenance.

- **Architects Don't Code**: Involve the architects in some parts of the implementation phase. This can help both the organization and the architects. This activity can give them a clearer picture of the true functionalities of the product. And truly, they should value your effort.

29.8 What do you mean by refactoring?

In the coding world, the term *refactoring* means improving the design of an existing code without changing the external behavior of the system/application. This process helps you get more readable code. At the same time, the code should be more adaptable to new requirements (or change requests) and more maintainable.

CHAPTER 30

FAQ

This chapter is a subset of the Q&A sessions of the chapters in this book. Many of these questions were not discussed in a previous chapter because the related patterns were not covered at that time. So, it is highly recommended that in addition to the following Q&As, you go through all the Q&A sessions in the book for a better understanding of these patterns.

30.1 Which design pattern do you like the most?

It depends on many factors such as the context, situation, demand, constraints, and so on. If you know about all of the patterns, you have more options to choose from.

30.2 Why should developers use design patterns?

They are reusable solutions for software design problems that appear repeatedly in real-world software development.

30.3 What is the difference between the Command and Memento patterns?

These two patterns can be used together, but their intents are different. Mementos store object states, but commands store the intended operations. Only the originator can store and retrieve necessary information from a memento. This memento is "opaque" to other objects. In the Command pattern, you do not see a similar kind of restriction. So, the states of the commands are often readable, but this is not true for mementos.

You store mementos for future use. On the other hand, once a command is executed, its job is done. Now it is up to you whether you want to store it. If you do not want to support the undo functionality, you may not be interested in storing such a command.

Lastly, you can simply remember that to perform an undo operation, you can opt for either of these patterns. In this context, when you use the Memento pattern, you replace a state from a cache. But if you opt for the Command pattern, you re-execute the commands in the same order to reach a particular state.

30.4 What is the difference between the Facade pattern and the Builder pattern?

The Facade pattern aims to make a specific portion of code easier to use. It abstracts details away from the developer.

V. Sarcar, *Java Design Patterns*, https://doi.org/10.1007/978-1-4842-7971-7_30

The Builder pattern separates the construction of an object from its representation. In Chapter 6, when I discuss the Builder pattern, you see that the director can call the same method (refer to the `instruct()` method in Demonstration 1) to create different types of vehicles. In other words, you can use the same construction process to create different types.

30.5 What is the difference between the Builder pattern and the Strategy pattern? They have similar UML representations.

First, you must take care of the intent. The Builder pattern falls into the category of creational patterns, and the Strategy pattern falls into the category of behavioral patterns. Their areas of focus are different. With the Builder pattern, you can use the same construction process to create different types, and with the Strategy pattern, you have the freedom to select an algorithm at runtime.

30.6 What is the difference between the Command pattern and the Interpreter pattern?

In the Command pattern, the commands are objects, but in the Interpreter pattern, the commands are sentences. In the Interpreter pattern, you can make your own rule for evaluation and build the syntax tree. If you deal with simple grammar, it is fine. But implementing the Interpreter pattern is tough when your grammar is complex. It is because the cost of building an interpreter can be a big concern for you.

30.7 What is the difference between the Chain of Responsibility pattern and the Observer pattern?

For the Observer pattern, all registered users will be notified or get requests (for the change in subject) in parallel, but for the Chain of Responsibility pattern, you may not reach the end of the chain, so all users do not need to handle the same scenario. The request can be processed much earlier by a handler object that is placed at the beginning of the chain. I suggest you refer to Q&A 17.7 to understand it clearly.

30.8 What is the difference between the Chain of Responsibility pattern and the Decorator pattern?

They are not the same at all, but you may feel that they are similar in their structures. Similar to the previous difference, at a given point in time, in the Chain of Responsibility pattern, only one class handles the request, but in the case of the Decorator pattern, all classes handle the request. You must remember that decorators are effective in the context of adding and removing responsibilities only, and if you can combine the Decorator pattern with the Single Responsibility Principle (SRP), you can add (or remove) a single responsibility at runtime.

30.9 What is the difference between the Mediator pattern and the Observer pattern?

The GoF says this: "These are competing patterns. The difference between them is that the Observer distributes communication by introducing observer and subject objects, whereas a mediator object encapsulates the communication between other objects."

Normally you see the use of observers for one-to-many communications. So, this type of communication is simple to understand and often used as a Publisher-Subscriber (Pub-Sub) model.

On the other hand, mediators are common for many-to-many communications. If any of the participants change, all other participants are notified. So, compared to the Observer pattern, this kind of communication is harder to implement.

The GoF also found that you may face fewer challenges when making reusable observers and subjects than when making reusable mediators, but regarding the flow of communication, the Mediator pattern scores higher than the Observer pattern.

30.10 Which one do you prefer: a singleton class or a static class?

In Chapter 2 (Q&A 2.4), I told you that at the time of this writing a top-level static class is not possible in Java. Although it is possible in a different programming language such as C#, you need to obey the language-specific restrictions for using this construct.

So, the general answer is, it depends on many factors. But the key takeaway is you can create objects of a singleton class, which is not possible with a static class. So, the concepts of inheritance and polymorphism can be implemented with a singleton class. Also, you can pass a singleton instance as a method parameter.

30.11 How can you distinguish between proxies and adapters?

Proxies work on similar interfaces as their subjects. Adapters work on different interfaces (to the objects they adapt).

30.12 How are proxies different from decorators?

There are different types of proxies, and they vary as per their implementations. So, some of these implementations may be close to decorators. For example, a protection proxy might be implemented like a decorator. But you must remember that decorators focus on adding responsibilities, while proxies focus on controlling the access to an object.

30.13 How are mediators different from facades?

In general, both simplify a complex system. In the case of a Mediator pattern, a two-way connection exists between a mediator and the internal subsystems, whereas in the case of a Facade pattern, in general, you provide a one-way connection (the subsystems do not know about facades).

30.14 Is there any relation between the Flyweight pattern and the State pattern?

The GoF says that the Flyweight pattern can help you to decide when and how to share the state objects.

30.15 What are the similarities among the Simple Factory, Factory Method, and Abstract Factory design patterns?

All of them encapsulate object creation. They suggest that you try to code to the abstraction (interface) but not to the concrete classes. In simple words, each of these factories promotes loose coupling by reducing the dependencies on concrete classes.

30.16 What are the differences among the Simple Factory, Factory Method, and Abstract Factory design patterns?

This is an important question that you may face in various job interviews. So, first, I refer you to Q&A 3.6 in Chapter 3 and Q&A 4.3 in Chapter 4. If needed, you can go through all the Q&A sessions in Chapter 3 and Chapter 4.

30.17 How can you distinguish the Singleton pattern from the Factory Method pattern?

The Singleton pattern ensures you get a unique instance each time. It also restricts the creation of additional instances.

But the Factory Method pattern does not say that you will get a unique instance only. Most often this pattern is used to create as many instances as you want, and the instances are not necessarily unique. These newly typed instances may implement a common parent class. (Just remember that the Factory method lets a class defer instantiation to subclasses, per the GoF definition.)

30.18 How does the Template Method pattern differ from the Strategy pattern?

In the Strategy pattern, you can vary the entire algorithm using delegation. On the other hand, using the Template Method pattern you vary only certain step(s) in an algorithm using inheritance, but the overall flow of the algorithm is unchanged.

30.19 How can you distinguish the Visitor pattern from the Strategy pattern?

In the Strategy pattern, each subclass uses a different algorithm to solve a common problem. But in the case of the Visitor design pattern, each visitor subclass may provide different functionalities.

30.20 How are null objects different from proxies?

In general, proxies act on real objects at some point in time and they may also provide some behavior. But, in general, a null object does not do any such operation.

30.21 How can you distinguish the Interpreter pattern from the Visitor pattern?

In the Interpreter pattern, you represent a simple grammar as an object structure, but in the case of the Visitor pattern, you define some specific operations that you want to use on an object structure. In addition to this, an interpreter has direct access to the behaviors that are needed but in the case of the Visitor pattern, you need special functionalities (similar to an observer) to access them.

30.22 How can you distinguish the Flyweight pattern from the Object Pool pattern?

In the case of the Flyweight pattern, flyweights can have intrinsic and extrinsic states. So, you can say that if a flyweight has both states, its states are divided and the client needs to pass part of the state to it. Also, in general, the client does not change the intrinsic state because it is shared.

I did not discuss the Object Pool pattern in this book. But if you know this pattern already, you will notice that the Object Pool pattern does not store any part of the state outside; all state information is stored/encapsulated inside the pooled object. Also, clients can change the state of a pooled object.

30.23 How are libraries (or frameworks) similar (or different) from design patterns?

They are not considered design patterns. They provide the implementations that you can use directly in your application. But they can use the concept of the patterns in those implementations.

30.24 How can you compare decorators and adapters?

The common theme between object adapters and decorators is that they both promote object composition, but there are many differences.

You use decorators to enhance an object's behavior. You do not alter the original interface, so you can decorate an object with a decorator, and then you can again decorate this decorated object with another decorator. This kind of recursive decoration/composition is easy in the Decorator pattern.

But adapters are useful for incompatible interfaces. There you adapt the original behavior, but do not impose any change in this behavior. In this pattern, it is not easy to implement a recursive composition.

30.25 How can you distinguish the Prototype pattern from the Singleton pattern?

In the case of the Singleton pattern, you always work on the same instance. But in the case of the Prototype pattern, you work on a copied/cloned instance. The state(s) between two copied instances may vary, but it is not possible when you work with the Singleton pattern because every time you work on the exact same instance.

30.26 How can you distinguish between a Chain of Responsibility pattern and a Command pattern?

In the Chain of Responsibility pattern, handlers pass requests one after another, but there is no guarantee that they will be fully processed by any of them.

In the case of the Command pattern, you do not see similar kinds of passing requests. But you can track commands to provide undo operations, which is not seen with the Chain of Responsibility pattern.

APPENDIX A

A Brief Overview of GoF Design Patterns

We all have unique thought processes. So, in the early days of software development, engineers faced a common problem. There was no standard to instruct them on how to design their applications. Each team followed its own style, and when a new member joined an existing team, understanding the architecture was a gigantic task. Senior or experienced members of the team had to explain to the new joiner about the advantages of the existing architecture and why alternative designs were not considered.

The experienced developer also knew how to reduce future efforts by simply reusing the concepts already in place. Design patterns address this issue and provide a common platform for all developers. You can think of them as the recorded experience of experts in the field. These patterns were intended to be applied in object-oriented designs with the intention of reuse.

In 1994, Erich Gamma, Richard Helm, Ralph Johnson, and John Vlissides published the book *Design Patterns: Elements of Reusable Object-Oriented Software* (Addison-Wesley, 1994). In this book, they introduced the concept of design patterns in software development. *These authors became known as the Gang of Four. I refer to them as the **GoF** throughout this book.* The GoF described 23 patterns that were developed by the common experiences of software developers over a while. Nowadays, when new members join a development team, they are expected to know about the design patterns and then they learn about the existing architecture. This approach allows them to actively participate in the development process within a short period.

© Vaskaran Sarcar 2022
V. Sarcar, *Java Design Patterns*, https://doi.org/10.1007/978-1-4842-7971-7

The first concept of a real-life design pattern came from the building architect Christopher Alexander. During his lifetime, he discovered that many of the problems he faced were similar in nature. So, he tried to address those issues with similar types of solutions.

> *Each pattern describes a problem, which occurs over and over again in our environment, and then describes the core of the solution to that problem, in such a way that you can use this solution a million times over, without ever doing it the same way twice.*

> Christopher Alexander

The software engineering community started believing that although these patterns were described for buildings and towns, the same concepts could be applied to patterns in object-oriented design. So, they substituted the original concepts of walls and doors with objects and interfaces. The common thing in both fields is that, at their cores, patterns are solutions to common problems.

Lastly, it is important to note that the GoF discussed the original concepts of design patterns in the context of C++. But Sun Microsystem released its first public implementation of Java 1.0 in 1995 and then it went through various changes. So, in 1995, Java was totally new to the programming world. But it grew rapidly and secured its rank in the world's top programming languages within a short period of time. In today's market, it is always in high demand. On the other hand, the concepts of design patterns are universal. So, when you exercise these fundamental concepts of design patterns with Java, you will be a better programmer and you'll remake yourself in the programming community. Here are some important points to remember:

- A design pattern describes a general reusable solution to software design problems. While developing software, you may encounter these problems frequently. The basic idea is that you can solve similar kinds of problems with similar kinds of solutions. And these solutions have been tested over a long period.

- These patterns provide you with a template of how to solve a problem and can be used in many different situations. At the same time, they help you to get the best possible design much faster.

- These patterns are descriptions of how to create objects and classes and then customize them to solve a general design problem in a particular context.

The GoF discussed 23 design patterns. Each of these patterns focuses on a particular object-oriented design. Each pattern can also describe the consequences and tradeoffs of use. The GoF categorized these 23 patterns based on their purposes, as shown here:

A. Creational patterns: These patterns abstract the instantiation process. You make the systems independent from how their objects are composed, created, and represented. In these patterns, you should have a basic concern: "Where should I place the 'new' keyword in my application?" This decision can determine the degree of coupling of your classes. The following five patterns belong to this category:

- Singleton pattern

- Prototype pattern

- Factory Method pattern

- Builder pattern

- Abstract Factory pattern

B. Structural patterns: Here you focus on how classes and objects can be composed to form a relatively large structure. They generally use inheritance or composition to group different interfaces or implementations. Your choice of composition over inheritance (and vice versa) can affect the flexibility of your software. The following seven patterns fall into this category:

- Proxy pattern

- Flyweight pattern

- Composite pattern

- Bridge pattern

- Facade pattern

- Decorator pattern

- Adapter pattern

C. Behavioral patterns: Here you concentrate on algorithms and the assignment of responsibilities among objects. You also need to focus on the communication between them and how the objects are interconnected. The following eleven patterns fall into this category:

- Observer pattern

- Strategy pattern

- Template Method pattern

- Command pattern

- Iterator pattern

- Memento pattern

- State pattern

- Mediator pattern

- Chain of Responsibility pattern

- Visitor pattern

- Interpreter pattern

The GoF made another classification based on scope. It examines whether the pattern primarily focuses on the classes or its objects. Class patterns deal with classes and subclasses. They use inheritance mechanisms, so they are static and fixed at compile time. Object patterns deal with objects that can change at run time. So, object patterns are dynamic.

For a quick reference, you can refer to Table A-1, which was introduced by the GoF.

Table A-1. *Classification of the GoF Design Patterns*

		Purpose		
		Creational	**Structural**	**Behavioral**
Scope	**Class**	1. Factory Method	1.1. Adapter(class)	1. Interpreter 2. Template Method
	Object	2. Singleton 3. Prototype 4. Builder 5. Abstract Factory	1.2. Adapter(object) 2. Proxy 3. Flyweight 4. Composite 5. Bridge 6. Facade 7. Decorator	3. Observer 4. Strategy 5. Command 6. Iterator 7. Memento 8. State 9. Mediator 10. Visitor 11. Chain of Responsibility

Q&A Session

A1.1 What are the differences between class patterns and object patterns?

In general, class patterns focus on static relationships, but object patterns can focus on dynamic relationships. As the names suggest, class patterns focus on classes and their subclasses, and object patterns focus on the object's relationships.

Table A-2 shows the summarized content that was discussed in the GoF's famous book.

Table A-2. *Needs Caption*

	Class patterns	**Object patterns**
Creational	Can defer object creation to subclasses	Can defer object creation to another object
Structural	They focus on the composition of classes (primarily using the concept of inheritance).	They focus on the different ways to assemble objects.
Behavioral	Describes the algorithms and execution flows. They also use the inheritance mechanism.	Describes how different objects can work together and complete a task.

A1.2 Can I combine two or more patterns in an application?

Yes. In real-world scenarios, this type of activity is common.

A1.3 Are these patterns dependent on a particular programming language?

Programming languages can play an important role. But the basic ideas are the same. Patterns are just like templates and they will give you some idea in advance of how you can solve a particular problem. In this book, I primarily focus on object-oriented programming with the concept of reuse. But instead of a object-oriented programming language, suppose you have chosen some other language like C. In that case, you may need to think about the core object-oriented principles such as inheritance, polymorphism, encapsulation, abstraction, and so on, and how to implement them. So, the choice of a particular language is always important because it may have some specialized features that can make your programming life easier.

A1.4 Should I consider common data structures like arrays and linked lists as different design patterns?

The GoF excludes these, saying that *they are not complex, domain-specific designs for an entire application or subsystem*. They can be encoded in classes and reused as-is. So, they are not your concern in this book.

A1.5 If no particular pattern is 100% suitable for my problem, how should I proceed?

An infinite number of problems cannot be solved with a finite number of patterns for sure. But if you know these common patterns and their trade-offs, you can pick a close match. Lastly, no one prevents you from using a pattern that serves your need. But you have to tackle the risk and you need to think about your return on investment.

A1.6 Any general advice before I jump into the topics?

I prefer to follow in the footsteps of my seniors and teachers who are experts in this field. And here are some general suggestions from them:

- Program to a supertype (abstract class/interface), not an implementation.

- Prefer composition over inheritance in most cases.

- Try to make a loosely coupled system.

- Segregate code that is likely to vary from the rest of your code.

- Encapsulate what varies.

A1.7 How can I use this book effectively?

This book focuses on commonly used design patterns. Most likely, you will face them very often in your everyday life. But the world is always changing, so known patterns keep evolving and many new patterns are created. To understand the necessity of a new pattern, you may also need to understand why an old/existing pattern is not enough to fulfill the requirement. You may consider this book as an attempt to make a solid foundation with design patterns, so that you can code smoothly in your professional life and you can adapt to upcoming changes easily.

The Road Ahead

Congratulations! You have reached the end of the journey. Anyone can start a journey, but only a few can complete it with care. So, you are among the minority who possess the extraordinary capability to cover the distance successfully. I believe that you have enjoyed your learning experience, which can help you to learn and experiment further in this category. I said earlier that if you repeatedly think about the discussions, examples, implementations, and the Q&A Sessions in the book, you will have more clarity about them, you will feel more confident about them, and you will remake yourself in the programming world.

Truly, a detailed discussion of any particular design pattern in depth would need many more pages and then the size of the book would be too gigantic to digest. In addition, although you have seen the GoF design patterns and a few more patterns, you can surely guess that there are many more pattern catalogs including domain-specific patterns such as enterprise patterns, concurrent system patterns, etc. So, what's next? You should not forget the basic principle that *learning is a continuous process*. So, this book was an attempt to encourage you to learn the fundamental patterns in depth so that you can enjoy your future learning in this field.

However, learning and thinking by yourself will not be enough. You can participate in open forums and join discussion groups to get more clarity on this subject. This is why searching in Google, Stack Overflow, Quora, or similar places can help you a lot. The only caution is that you must be careful when processing that information. How will the clarity come? Keep analyzing and see whether you are satisfied with the answer. This process will not only help you; it will help others also.

© Vaskaran Sarcar 2022
V. Sarcar, *Java Design Patterns*, https://doi.org/10.1007/978-1-4842-7971-7

A Personal Appeal to You

Over the years, I have seen a general trend for my books. When you like the book, you send me messages, write nice emails, and motivate me with your kind words and suggestions. But many of them do not reach review platforms like Amazon and others. But when the opposite happens, I see all the criticisms on those pages.

Please know that these criticisms help me to write better. But it's also helpful to know what you liked about a book. These constructive suggestions help me to keep that information in an updated edition of the book.

So, I have a request for you: You can always point out the improvement areas of this work but at the same time, please let me know about the areas you liked. In general, it is always easy to criticize, but an artistic view and open mind are required to discover the true efforts that are associated with any kind of work. Thank you and happy coding!

APPENDIX C

Recommended Reading

This appendix lists some useful resources. I have learned from them. I believe that you'll benefit from these great books (or the updated editions):

- *Design Patterns: Elements of Reusable Object-Oriented Software* by Erich Gamma et al. (Addison-Wesley, 1995).

- *Head First Design Patterns* by Eric Freeman and Elisabeth Robson (O'Reilly, 2004).

- *Design Patterns for Dummies* by Steve Holzner

    (Wiley Publishing, Inc, 2006).

- *Java Design Pattern Essentials* by Tony Bevis (Ability First Limited, 2012).

In today's world, online platforms are very powerful. In Appendix B, I told you that you can also learn from online platforms such as Google, Stack Overflow, Quora, YouTube, Udemy, etc. You can use the power of these online platforms to learn not only design patterns but almost anything you want. But you must validate that information before you process it. Here I include some helpful online resources/websites for your immediate reference:

- http://sourcemaking.com/design_patterns

- https://en.wikipedia.org/wiki/Software_design_pattern

- www.codeproject.com/

- https://dzone.com/

- www.tutorialspoint.com/

© Vaskaran Sarcar 2022
V. Sarcar, *Java Design Patterns*, https://doi.org/10.1007/978-1-4842-7971-7

- www.udemy.com/courses/search/?src=ukw&q=design+patterns
- https://en.wikipedia.org/wiki/Design_pattern
- http://wiki.c2.com/?AntiPatternsCatalog
- http://hillside.net

Index

A

Abstract Factory pattern, 98, 116
  analysis, 110
  class diagram, 102
  client code variations, 110, 112
  demonstration, 104, 106, 109
  implementation, 99, 100
  output, 109
  package explorer view, 103
  Q&A, 113
Abstract Window Toolkit (AWT), 284
Adapter pattern, 227–229
  analysis, 244
  demonstration, 240–242
  implementation, 229–232
    analysis, 238, 239
    class diagram, 233
    demonstration, 235, 238
    output, 238
    package explorer view, 234
  output, 243
Adapters and decorators, 639
AlternationExpression,
    RepititionExpression/
    SequenceExpression, 551
animal.displayBehavior()
    analysis, 91
AnimalFactory class, 88
Anti-patterns
  code, 633, 634
  definition, 627
  examples, 629, 630, 632

real-world application
    development, 627
refactoring, 634
symptoms, 633
types, 631

B

Bridge pattern
  adapter design, 323
  advantages, 323
  connection, 303
  Driver, 302
  GUI frameworks, 302
  implementation
    class, 305
    class diagram, 306, 316
    design, 303
    flexibility, 312
    implementors, 313, 314, 316
    interface, 308, 310–312
    modified program, 317–321
    output, 312, 322
    package, 307
    package explorer view, 307
    structure, 304
  interface, 301
  real-life example, 301
Builder pattern, 340, 636
  computer world example, 151
  definition, 149
  immutable object, 174
  implementation

W

X, Y, Z

Printed in the United States
by Baker & Taylor Publisher Services

Printed in the United States
by Baker & Taylor Publisher Services